T3-BOE-108

Concepts of Person in Religion and Thought

Religion and Reason 37

Method and Theory
in the Study and Interpretation of Religion

Mouton de Gruyter
Berlin · New York

Concepts of Person in Religion and Thought

Edited by

Hans G. Kippenberg
Yme B. Kuiper
Andy F. Sanders

Mouton de Gruyter
Berlin · New York 1990

Mouton de Gruyter (formerly Mouton, The Hague)
is a Division of Walter de Gruyter & Co., Berlin.

Library of Congress Cataloging-in-Publication Data

Concepts of person in religion and thought / edited by Hans G. Kippenberg, Yme B. Kuiper, and Andy F. Sanders.
p. cm. — (Religion and reason ; 37)
Includes bibliographical references.
ISBN 0-89925-600-7 (alk. paper)
1. Self. 2. Man. 3. Self (Philosophy) 4. Man (Theology)
I. Kippenberg, Hans G. (Hans Gerhard) II. Kuiper, Yme B.
III. Sanders, Andy F. IV. Series
BL65.S38C65 1990
291.2'2—dc20 89-48472
CIP

Deutsche Bibliothek Cataloging-in-Publication Data

Concepts of person in religion and thought / ed. by Hans G. Kippenberg ... — Berlin ; New York : Mouton de Gruyter, 1990
(Religion and reason ; 37)
ISBN 3-11-012159-X
NE: Kippenberg, Hans G. [Hrsg.]; GT

∞ Printed on acid free paper.

Printing: Ratzlow-Druck, Berlin. —
Binding: Lüderitz & Bauer, Berlin. Printed in Germany.

PREFACE

The present volume is the third joint publication of the Groningen Working Group for the Study of Religious Symbols. This multidisciplinary group (founded in 1983) consists of scholars in the Faculties of Theology, Philosophy, Arts, and Social Sciences. Apart from setting up a number of Ph.D. programmes, our group has extended its contacts with scholars abroad. We are grateful to Professor Ulrich Berner (Bayreuth), Professor Michel Meslin (Paris), and to Professor Armin Geertz and Dr. Jeppe Jensen (Aarhus) for their cooperation and their stimulating and friendly criticisms.

We also wish to thank Professor Herman te Velde and Dr. Hans A. Witte for their editorial advice, and the staff-members of the Institute of Religious Iconography (University of Groningen) who loyally assisted us by type-setting the texts and by compiling the indices: Margreet Hagelstein-Mandersloot, Anneke Knoppert, Pieter Huiser and David J. Bos. Most articles have been translated by Mrs. M. de Rooij.

We wish to dedicate this volume to the memory of our most esteemed colleague and friend, Professor Hubertus G. Hubbeling. His untimely death on October 7th 1986 was, and still is felt by us as a heavy loss. From 1968 onwards, Huib Hubbeling has played an important role in our present Working Group and in its precursor. We greatly benefitted from his knowledge of the history of philosophy, of modern philosophy of science and methodology, and particularly from the way in which he sought to relate the philosophy of religion to the science of religion. One of his last papers is published in this volume.

Groningen, April 1989

Hans G. Kippenberg
Yme B. Kuiper
Andy F. Sanders

CONTENTS

PART III
NON-WESTERN CONCEPTS OF PERSON

PART IV
SPECIAL ISSUES

STUDYING CONCEPTS OF PERSON

General Introduction

Can one think of any past or present culture whose members lack any idea of themselves as persons? According to the anthropologist Clifford Geertz, the answer to this question should be negative:

> Peoples everywhere have developed symbolic structures in terms of which persons are perceived not baldly as such, as mere unadorned members of the human race, but as representatives of certain distinct categories of persons, specific sorts of individuals (Geertz: 1973b, 363).

Though this implies that the concept of person is a cultural universal, it is clear that conceptions of the person as they are, or were, actually used in various cultures may differ greatly. But how, and in what respects? Assuming with Geertz that the concept of person is a universal, in what forms and symbols does it become manifest? How and where do we have to look for it in a particular culture?

In 1938 the French sociologist Marcel Mauss (1892-1950) published an inspiring essay on what he considered to be a fundamental category of the human mind: the concept of person (Mauss: 1985). Mauss made use of the latin notion 'persona', that has had a history of its own. Its original meaning is 'mask' (ancestral mask, mask used in the theatre), but it also referred to the role an individual played in the public life of Roman society (Fuhrmann: 1979). The idea of role slowly became deemphasized, though it can still be detected in the well known theological formula of Tertullian 'una substantia, tres personae'. The Latin meaning of 'persona' illustrates Mauss's main concern: that all definitions and conceptions concerning the human self are part of a cultural and historical context. The notion of person in the various modern European languages lost its implicit judicial meaning only gradually. From the 18th century onwards a different meaning came into use, expressing the specific individuality of a human being: the notion 'personality', 'Persönlichkeit', 'personnage'. Since it is hardly possible to deal exhaustively with this subject here, we confine ourselves to referring to the relevant literature mentioned in the bibliography at the end of this volume.

On the basis of the psychological and linguistic insights of his days,

Mauss stipulated that 'person' and 'self' are embedded in every language and culture. The degree to which they are made explicit or reflected upon, however, may vary considerably. To illustrate this variety, Mauss pointed out some remarkable contrasts between the meaning of 'person' and 'self' in our Western culture and the meaning of these notions in both tribal and more complex alien cultures, past and present. Being aware of the tentative character of his essay, Mauss made a plea for a broad and coordinated inquiry into the social history of the notions of person and self. Such an inquiry was to address itself to the problem of how they developed, how, and in what ostensible ways, they became entrenched in various cultural systems of law, morality, common sense and ideology.

Since the publication of Mauss's essay few attempts have been made to carry out the multi-disciplinary research he advocated. Apart from two recent volumes in English, surprisingly few studies of the intercultural aspects of the concept of person can be found (cf. Shweder - LeVine: 1984; Carrithers - Collins - Lukes: 1985). In the conclusion of the collection of essays mentioned, S. Lukes has given an elegant description of several possibilities of research which, in our view, can clarify a number of problems. Referring to the work of Durkheim, Mauss, G.H. Mead and the British philosopher P. Strawson, Lukes points out that many scholars advocate the idea that the concept of person stands for a structure of beliefs: 'a certain structure of thinking concerning the person or self is to be held fundamental, universal and necessary, but to take different forms in different contexts'. In his view, this statement can be interpreted as a hermeneutic injunction 'to read and interpret the explicit and implicit ideas of different cultures as versions, or perversions, of some such core notion or deep structure' (Carrithers - Collins - Lukes: 284, 289).

According to Lukes, two broad fields of investigation can be distinguished: first, research on the more explicit and sophisticated concepts of person used by intellectuals, religious specialists, philosophers, and the like, within more complex cultures. These concepts can be found not only in the Western world, in Antiquity, in Christianity and in current secularized ideologies, but also in many other non-Western 'great traditions', e.g., classical Chinese philosophy, Hinduism and Buddhism.

Second, many other cultures, illiterate and tribal ones, as well as the more peripheral parts of complex societies, did not, and do not have intellectual systems containing explicit ideas on person or self. Embedded in more collective traditions these notions are implicitly used in everyday life, in specific social roles and in rituals. In these cases, it is the task of the ethnographer or the historian to reconstruct native mental categories from field-work data or historical sources.

Both research strategies show that our Western concept of person is by no means a 'natural' or 'unchangeable' datum. Therefore we should avoid using the Western conception of person as an absolute, universal standard. In intercultural studies, however, we do need some point of reference, some particular dimensions or aspects of the universal 'deep structure' of the concept of person. Without such a 'bridgehead', and the subsequent specification of relevant contrasts, it is impossible to arrive at an adequate interpretation of concepts of person in various cultures (cf. Schweder - Bourne: 1984).

A fundamental challenge to this kind of research is to develop strategies, methods and hypotheses for finding the implicit notions of personhood in non-Western societies, and for explicating both their resemblances to and differences from the Western concept of person.

The present volume is the result of the combined efforts of historians, philosophers, anthropologists and sociologists of religion associated with the Groningen Working Group for the Study of Religious Symbols. Its members share the conviction that analysis of religion should start with the symbolic forms that express it. This shared interest in symbolic representations also underlay an earlier publication of the Groningen Working Group (Hubbeling - Kippenberg: 1986).

In respect to this particular volume we would like to make explicit a further important common assumption of our research on concepts of person. From G.H. Mead we adopted the view that the human self may be conceived both as a more private, subjective, reflexive instance (the 'I') and a more socially determined, objective instance (the 'Me'). Every individual obtains self-awareness only by being an object to others: the individual both internalizes the attitudes of other people towards him as social relations and presents himself to others through means provided by the culture to which he belongs. This distinction between social role, and the culturally determined symbolic presentation of the self, is an important starting-point for research on concepts of person.

In line with this distinction we discern three fundamental issues in our project: 1) a philosophical and theoretical analysis of the terms 'individual' and 'person'; 2) a historical account of the dissociation of social roles and the 'self' in ancient history which is fundamental to the present Western concept of person; 3) comparative studies of the collective, implicit notions of person(hood) in non-Western cultures and especially the analyses of symbolic forms which express these notions. Accordingly, the various contributions to this volume were brought under three general headings: 'Theoretical Contributions', 'Ancient Mediterranean Concepts of Person' and 'Non-Western Concepts of Person', each of which is introduced separately. A supplementary part has been reserved for the somewhat unorthodox contributions of B.P. Hofstede and W.B. Drees.

PART ONE
THEORETICAL CONTRIBUTIONS

INTRODUCTION

The first part of this volume contains articles that deal with general theoretical and methodological aspects of research on the concept of person. The article by H.G. Hubbeling provides a brief historical outline of philosophical accounts of the concept of person within our Western tradition. It shows that our modern, rather sophisticated understanding of personhood should be conceived as the *terminus ad quem* of a long development to which classical moral philosophy, Roman law and Christian theology have made important contributions. As an item of philosophical reflection and legislation, the concept of person became to a certain extent explicit. In earlier days of Western history, and in non-Western cultures, however, it remained largely implicit and disparate.

Beside his reflections on personal identity and the personhood of God, Hubbeling develops a general methodology for analyzing conceptions of the person irrespective of the culture in which they have their meaning and function. Using our Western concept of person as an illustration, his aim is to explore some relevant logical relations between its defining characteristics. Though Hubbeling claims that a particular being must have these properties in order to count as a person, they are not 'eternal essences'.

Inspired by Wittgenstein's *Philosophical Investigations,* Oosten tries to supplement Hubbeling's logical analysis by drawing attention to the link between our ordinary use of concepts of 'person' and generally accepted, but morally defective, Western ideologies. According to Oosten, the concept of person is often used in an implicitly ideological way, which is a far cry from the moral criteria for personhood formulated in the Universal Declaration of Human Rights. Oosten also warns against the danger of ethnocentrism in studying 'person' in other cultures: one has to beware of easy and cheap judgements that are based on our own implicit understanding of the term.

The articles by Y.B. Kuiper and A.F. Sanders deal with the theoretical and methodological problems of tracing and comparing notions of the person. Kuiper is an anthropologist and Sanders a philosopher and their articles complement each other.

In his contribution Kuiper reconstructs the research-programme of the American cultural anthropologist Clifford Geertz. Apart from a reconstruction of the historical background of this programme, Kuiper draws attention to Geertz's fundamental notion of culture as a system of meanings embodied in (religious) symbols. According to Geertz, a concept of person functions in every society as a necessary means of orientation for the human individual. From the more detached view of cultural anthropology such a concept can be seen as a cultural characterization of the individual.

In his ethnographical studies Geertz emphasizes the different ways in which concepts of the person are constructed in specific cultures. His approach implies that the Western concept of the person has no privileged intellectual status. Being sceptical of 'grand theory' and of the usefulness of cultural universals, Geertz's work on concepts of the person is, nevertheless, an important plea for comparative research, because in these concepts a culture reveals its specific character.

Following a different line of reasoning, Sanders affirms that 'to find the concept of person is to find the type of culture in which it is advocated'. Taking Kuiper's contribution as his starting-point, Sanders deals with the question of how and where to find the concept of the person in a given society. He shows that this is not an easy thing to do, even in our own culture. He discusses some ordinary uses of the term person in order to determine its range of application, and indicates that an exhaustive specification of the intension of the concept would be extremely complicated, if not impossible.

In his article Sanders introduces the notion of ideal personhood that gives form, order and direction to the lives of the individuals within a given cultural system. This ideal is manifested in the overt and recognizable form of social behaviour. However, the best, if more difficult, way to gain access to the concept of the person, is to study the shared beliefs, intentions and emotions and the attitudes which underlie them. Drawing on Searle's theory of intentionality, Sanders suggests that we have to look for the more covert uses of the term, as manifested in speech acts and social action, in what Searle calls the intentional network and its background.

The final contribution to this part, by M. Meslin, stems from a continental, phenomenological tradition and is markedly different from Hubbeling's analytical approach. Meslin argues that one can only become a true person by affiliating oneself to a cultural tradition, because it is only in this way that the full meaning of one's existence can be known and felt in real life. According to him, full participation in a live tradition comes about most adequately in religious ceremonies.

SOME REMARKS ON THE CONCEPT OF PERSON IN WESTERN PHILOSOPHY

Hubertus G. Hubbeling

In this article I shall give a short survey of the various interpretations and problems with respect to the concept of person in Western philosophy. This survey is far from complete and many problems can only be indicated.

The article will be built up as follows: first I shall give a very short survey of the development of the concept of person in history and at the same time I shall give a provisional specification of its various characteristics. Obviously there could be endless discussions as to the interpretations of the scholars dealt with in the historical survey, but we cannot of course, do this here. Next, I shall give an equally brief systematic survey of the various characteristics of the person and I shall at the same time indicate the various possible logical relations between them. Then I shall consider some problems involved in determining personal identity. This matter is connected but not identical with what has been discussed before. Finally, I shall consider the problem of God as a person.

A short historical survey

The term 'person' stems from the Latin word *persona*, meaning *mask*. Its etymology has often been disputed. In antiquity, *persona* was derived from *personare* (to ring through). Modern investigators seek its origin rather in the Etruscan word for mask, *phersu*. Its second meaning 'face', however, is also already an old one. *Persona* has also come to mean 'person'. This meaning occurs more often. In Hebrew the word *panim* also has the meaning of face or of person. In Greek we find the word *prosôpon* for 'person', its first meaning also being 'face'. Already in the writings of the philologist Aristarchus of Samothrace (c. 150 B.C.), this word serves to indicate the conjugation of the verb. By then the meaning 'person' had developed. Ever since ancient times the concept 'person' has acquired all kinds of connotations. In his well-known book, *De Persoon*,

A. de Wilde remarks that a sentence such as 'latro personam regis agressus est' includes more indignation than 'latro regem agressus est' and from this he concludes that there must be an element of *dignity* in the concept of *persona*.

In Greek antiquity a grand ideal of humanity was developed in which man was seen as the bearer of irreplaceable values. Biblical Christianity took over Old Testament thought by emphasizing the idea of man's standing in relation to God. Here man is not primarily seen as a bearer of values; the reason for his existence lies in the I - Thou relation to God and he finds his liberation and redemption in the personal bond with his Saviour, Jesus Christ. Already at an early stage, however, Greek and Roman ideas were taken over as well. The term 'persons' for the three modes of existence in God (the Trinity) stems from Tertullian. In the wording of the Synod of Rome: 'Si quis tres personas non dixerit veras Patris et Filii et Spiritus Sancti aequales, semper vivantes... anathema sit'(If someone denies that the three true persons of the Father, the Son and the Holy Spirit are equal, live forever... cursed be he). The famous 'classical' definition of person stems from Boethius: 'Persona est naturae rationalis individua substantia' (A person is an individual substance with a rational nature). In this line of thought a substance is a being that can be thought of as a relatively independent whole in contradistinction to properties which can only be defined as existing in something else. In the concept of an individual Boethius refers to something that excludes all divisibility. In logic an individual cannot replace a predicate.

In the Middle Ages the concept of a person was not elaborated further. However, God plainly acquired personal aspects. As for man, there was a discussion as to what constituted his individuality. Following Aristotle, Thomas Aquinas said that the body (matter) constituted individuality, whereas Duns Scotus was of the opinion that a special individuality (*haecceitas*) was the foundation of each soul.

For the rest, people in the Middle Ages were more interested in God than in the dignity of man. Man received his dignity in relation to God. 'Alle creâture sint ein lûter niht' (All creatures are a pure nothing) (Meister Eckhart).

In the Renaissance, man became the centre of interest. The ideal of the *huomo universale* (universal man) emerged, a being rich in capacities and interests. He is the bearer not only of moral, but also of aesthetic values. Human creativity and freedom were emphasized. A great problem for many scholars was how to reconcile freedom with God's omnipotence. In the Reformation stress was laid on man's dependence on God. Luther, for instance, defended the predestined human will against Erasmus.

Descartes emphasized human consciousness. For him this was the foundation and starting point of his philosophy and of scientific knowledge in general. For a long time philosophers continued to concentrate on human consciousness ('Cogito, ergo sum'), although one of Descartes's great 'disciples', Spinoza, was an exception. According to Descartes, man is primarily subject (self-consciousness + the consciousness of being an *ego*). Because of this he had great difficulty establishing man's relation to and contact with things and persons outside his consciousness. In this he only succeeded by introducing God, who guarantees that man's observations are not deceptive. Spinoza put less emphasis on the personhood of man, because he did not teach man's free will as Descartes did. The common interpretation that Spinoza knew only an impersonal conception of God must, however, be rejected. In Spinoza's work God definitely has self-consciousness and the same applies to man. I shall come back to this later. Leibniz emphasized individual man in his doctrine of the monads. Nonetheless, he too needed God in order to bring these monads into connection with the outside world (the doctrine of the *harmonia praestabilita*).

As is well known, the English empiricists and the rationalists of the Continent were diametrically opposed to each other. Empiricism was in conflict with thinking. But both groups started from the data of the human consciousness. The rationalists proceeded from human thinking, the empiricists from the 'sense data' and both groups had difficulties in accounting for man's relation with the external world (i.e., the world outside human consciousness). Of course, this difficulty existed only in their philosophical theories and not in the actual practice of their lives! As we have seen, it is possible to produce this contact with the outer world with the help of God, who guarantees that our senses do not deceive us. The concept of analogy can be used to explain this. We have a certain body and a certain consciousness, we hear our fellow men say that they have a consciousness and we see that they have a body. Now by analogy we may conclude that the relation between body and consciousness in our fellow men is the same as it is in us, i.e.,, that they indeed have consciousness.

In German Idealism the personhood of man was again strongly

emphasized. Like Descartes, German Idealism started with man as a conscious being, but in contradistinction to Descartes man was seen primarily, not as a subject, but as a moral and aesthetic personality. Kant laid the foundation for this idea by stating that the noumenal human being is man as a person, i.e.,, the bearer of moral practical reason. Therefore he is purpose in himself (*Zweck an sich*) and he has dignity (*Würde*), i.e.,, an absolute inner value. Moral man is the final purpose (*Endzweck*) of nature. He is purpose in himself and may therefore not be reduced to a mere means to an end. Thus Kant arrived at the famous categorical imperative: 'Handle so, dass du die Menschheit sowohl in deiner Person, als in der Person eines jeden Andern, jederzeit zugleich als Zweck, niemals bloss als Mittel brauchst' (Act in such a way that humanity both in your own person and in the person of anybody else is at the same time the purpose of your actions and is never merely needed as a means). This does not imply that the concrete human being is always dignified: 'Der Mensch ist zwar unheilig genug, aber die Menschheit in seiner Person muss ihm heilig sein' (Although man is rather unholy, humanity in his personhood ought to be sacred to him). He who acts in accordance with the categorical imperative, acts autonomously. Here freedom as a positive value emerges as the property of the human will to act in accordance with the moral law that is present in man's inner life and has been completely accepted by him (freedom as a negative value is man's freedom from the constraints of nature!).

Goethe, in particular, spoke about the concept of the human personality. For him it was the concept of an ideal. Goethe revived the ideal of the *huomo universale* of the Renaissance, in which, not only moral and religious, but also aesthetical values play an important part.

A description of man as a person from the point of view of German Idealism is beyond the scope of this article. Suffice it to say that the person in German Idealism is more than merely a thinking and volitional subject; he is the bearer of moral, religious and aesthetic values.

In his protest against Hegel, Kierkegaard emphasized the old Christian I - Thou relation, which later on can again be found in the Christian existentialism of, among others, Marcel, Brunner, and Buber. These personal aspects were also brought forward by philosophers who were no longer Christians, but who were certainly influenced by Christian doctrine: Feuerbach, Dühring, and others. In the 20th century personalism has become an important trend in philosophy. To mention a few names:

Brightman, Stern, Mounier and, in the Netherlands, Kohnstamm. These personalists hold considerably different views. A comparative study of the various personalists would therefore certainly be worth while. Obviously, for reasons of space such a study cannot be undertaken here.[1]

A *short systematic survey*

The aim of this section is to specify the main characteristics of the concept of person and to elucidate the logical relations that exist between them.

1) According to most philosophers, including myself, the basic element that constitutes a person is the fact that man has self-consciousness. According to the standard theories, animals lack self-consciousness, although they have consciousness in contrast to plants:

(i) Plants have no consciousness; animals have consciousness, but no self-consciousness; only man has self-consciousness.

Thesis (i) can be criticized on two points. Panpsychists, for example, maintain that plants do have consciousness, if only in a weak form. One can bring forward many empirical arguments in order to support this idea, but it must be admitted that panpsychism strongly contradicts common sense ideas. It is not necessary to discuss this problem here, because this article is concerned, not with consciousness in general, but with self-consciousness, which is not ascribed to plants.

The thesis that animals have no self-consciousness can be criticized

---

[1] I would like to restrict myself to indicating two things. First, the coming into existence of the Dutch Labour Party (*Partij van de Arbeid*) through the activities of W. Banning occurred on the basis of a personal socialism. The present basis of the *Partij van de Arbeid* is an explicitly different one. New Left emphasizes structural rather than personal relations. Second, the Declaration of Human Rights has a personalistic foundation, as has been pointed out by many jurists.

too. Many scholars maintain that animals lack a consciousness of distance and that therefore it is impossible for them to have self-consciousness. However, Köhler's famous experiments have demonstrated that some monkeys certainly deliberate before they act. Nevertheless, it took rather a long time before Köhler could draw this conclusion, for at first the results of his investigations pointed in another direction. Furthermore, it would be wrong to assert that all monkeys engage in deliberation and thus show a kind of self-consciousness.

In order to prove that man has a special human self-consciousness in contrast to monkeys it has been emphasized that man possesses a language and monkeys do not. Only a being that has a language can say 'I' and thus develop an ego-consciousness. Therefore only man can have an ego-consciousness. This fact has not always been interpreted positively. For example, E. Brunner asserts that the moment that man learns to say 'I' is the moment of his Fall. However, I do not want to go into this aspect of the problem. It may be clear that when a being has an ego-consciousness, he must also have self-consciousness, but the reverse need not be true. This is expressed by the following formula:

(ii) $\text{person}_{a'} \rightarrow \text{person}_a$

(In this formula 'person_a' stands for the concept of person characterized by self-consciousness and '$\text{person}_{a'}$' stands for the concept of person characterized by an ego-consciousness.) This does not mean that self-consciousness automatically implies ego-consciousness:

(ii)' $\text{person}_a \rightarrow \text{person}_{a'}$

As a characteristic criterion which distinguishing man from animals, however, it is insufficient, for it appears to be possible to teach a language to both chimpanzees and gorillas. They are not capable of *speaking* a human language, but they certainly speak with each other. Besides, it is not necessary to speak in order to have self-consciousness or an ego-consciousness. Are we then to conclude that person_a and $\text{person}_{a'}$ cannot by themselves constitute a person? Yet what is wrong in stating that those monkeys that have learned a language and are able to communicate with man in a more or less human way do have the status of personhood (in a weak sense)? One can have a relationship with such an animal that differs markedly from the relationship one can have with, say, a fish!

We have seen above that especially figures like Descartes emphasized self-consciousness as constituting man as a person. Whether or not one finds this criterion sufficient depends on the view one has of man. The characteristics of personhood described below are no doubt more thorough, but it is impossible to decide whether or not they are necessary in order to determine whether a being is a person without further investigation, i.e., without developing a whole philosophical system.

2) Another characteristic of the concept of person is the human *will.* According to some philosophers, the ability to take voluntary decisions is the essential feature of a person. The idea of the human will as one of the characteristics of a person can also be found in the work of Descartes and his followers. Obviously nobody can take decisions by means of his will without at the same time reflecting upon himself and being self-conscious. The reverse probably need not be true. One can imagine that a being may have self-consciousness without taking decisions. In Spinoza's completely deterministic system, for instance, man is denied freedom of will; will and intellect coincide. The will is nothing else than confirmation or denial of what the intellect teaches. If we symbolize a person that is characterized by voluntary decisions by means of the symbol 'person_b' the following thesis is valid:

(iii) $\text{person}_b \rightarrow \text{person}_{a+}$ $(\text{person}_{a+} = \text{person}_a$ and/or $\text{person}_{a'})$

But the reverse is not valid, at least not universally:

(iv) $\text{person}_{a+} \rightarrow \text{person}_b$

Yet there are philosophical systems in which (iv) is valid and in which thinking is seen as a mode of decisions of the will. Here we may think of the various forms of existentialism, but also of forms of French spiritualism as represented by Blondel, Duméry, Thévénaz, Teilhard de Chardin, and others. This French trend has a rather long tradition and can be traced back to Maine de Biran. From Maine de Biran it runs via Renouvier, Leclier, Lachelier, Hamelin and others to the thinkers mentioned above. French spiritualism has always had its own particular character, which has not always been recognized in Germany and the Netherlands. I cannot go further into this interesting line of thought, since I intend to elucidate the concept of person and not the material aspects of the various philosophical systems. It is obvious that the question as to whether (iv) is valid or not cannot be decided by an analysis of the concept of person alone or by reference to generally accepted truths. Deeper philosophical and empirical considerations are necessary for this.

3) So far we have considered the person as such without taking his relation to God and to his fellow men into consideration. Nor did we consider the person as bearer of aesthetic and moral values. This was done by German Idealism, as we have seen above. The term 'personality' has very often been introduced for man as bearer of moral, aesthetic and religious values. A person who is subsumed under moral categories is responsible for his deeds. It is characteristic of moral categories that they are universally valid, or at least that they are claimed to be so. In this respect moral categories differ from customs and manners. When I went to the United States in 1960 I saw to my surprise that many visitors to the university library were sitting comfortably with their legs on a table. When I visited a professor he did the same and he invited me to do likewise. Chairs are also built for this purpose. I can assure everyone that I did not find it difficult to adopt this pleasant custom. However, moral categories, such as respect for other people's life and property, etc., are valid in the USA in the same way as they are valid in Europe or anywhere else.

If one is responsible for one's deeds this implies that one ought to be free ('ought' implies 'can'; 'Sollen setzt Können voraus'). The person as a bearer of moral values is thus characterized as being responsible and at the same time as being free and able to perform the deeds he ought to do. He ought to have knowledge of certain moral norms and also of certain facts. The latter is certainly necessary, for although one cannot deduce moral norms from pure facts ('is' does not imply 'ought'; 'Aus einem Sein lässt sich kein Sollen ableiten'), in moral reasonings facts nevertheless play an important role as I have shown elsewhere (Hubbeling: 1985). Moreover, this is a generally accepted view. Of course, there are purely moral reasonings:

(I) $O(p \rightarrow q)$
Op

Oq

As is well known the sign 'O' is the deontic functor: 'Op' means that p (a proposition that refers to a state of affairs) must be realized. But most of the time we do not have to deal with purely moral reasonings, i.e., with premises that contain only deontic functors. One has to deal with facts. For moral reasonings to be valid these facts must have an imperative character. Here I must refer to the relevant literature (e.g., Hubbeling: 1985). Of the following deductions (III) is valid, but (II) is not ('L' is the necessity functor):

(II) Op
$p \rightarrow q$

Oq

(III) Op
$L(p \rightarrow q)$

Oq

When we compare the concept of a person characterized by moral categories with the preceding ones, it is obvious that they imply a will as well as self-consciousness. Thus the following theses are valid:

(v) $person_c \rightarrow person_b$

(Here we follow our usual reference system: $person_c$ refers to a person characterized by moral categories). Of course, the following thesis is also valid:

(vi) $\text{person}_c \rightarrow \text{person}_{a+}$

(vi) is self-evident, but it can also be deduced from (iii) and (v) by means of the logical law of syllogism.

The reverse, however, need not be true. Spinoza, for instance, does not ascribe freedom of will to man and in certain interpretations he does not attribute responsibility to human beings. In addition, in Cartesianism man is not primarily seen as bearer of moral values.[2]

Although it is not generally accepted, there are schools (existentialism, French spiritualism, most German idealists, etc.) that subscribe to the following thesis:

(vii) $\text{person}_{a+} \rightarrow \text{person}_c$

The aesthetic characteristics form a special case. Sometimes man is also seen as bearer of aesthetic values. We have seen above that especially in German Idealism this is a generally accepted view. We shall indicate this whole of aesthetic characteristics by c'. $\text{Person}_{c'}$ is a person characterized by aesthetic values, whereas person_c is a person characterized by moral values. Should we say now that

(viii) $\text{person}_c \Leftrightarrow \text{person}_{c'}$

that is, are person_c and $\text{person}_{c'}$ equivalent, do they imply each other? Of course, here we are dealing with the difficult problem of the relation between aesthetics and ethics or between art and morals. As far as this is concerned, there are various points of view which we cannot deal with here. The common view is that neither of the two implications is universally valid, that is, neither (ix) nor (x) is universally valid:

(ix) $\text{person}_c \rightarrow \text{person}_{c'}$

---

[2] Of course, we could say many interesting things concerning this area, e.g., about Geulincx's ideas ('Where you are not able to perform something, you ought not to want to do it'), ethics that result in humility and humbleness towards God.

(x) $\text{person}_{c'} \rightarrow \text{person}_c$

Yet there are people who defend either (ix) or (x), or both. The people who defend both implications are therefore adherents of thesis (viii), which, of course is the Greek ideal of *kalokagathos*. I shall not deny that it has a limited validity, i.e., that for part of the human personality the ideal of (viii) is valid, but most of the time moral deeds are not aesthetic and vice versa.

4) Now I would like to consider man in his relation to his fellow men and to God. In philosophy the question whether a being's relations belong to his essence or not is always problematic. It is obvious that not all relations can be ascribed to the essence of a certain being. At this moment I am sitting behind my typewriter. This relation to my typewriter (sitting behind it) does not belong to my essence. Nor does 'being in front of Hubbeling' belong to the essence of the typewriter. That means that not all relations are essential relations without which a certain being cannot exist or be thought of. But the I - Thou relation is very often numbered among the essential relations of a person. A man knows his mother before he knows himself. On the other hand it can be said that not before a child knows itself, i.e., knows some kind of self-reflexion and can say 'I', does it stand in an 'I - Thou' relation. That does not remove the fact that it is plausible to say that a man cannot exist without at least some essential relations (to God and/or his fellow men) and that these relations belong to his essence. This 'Thou' can be interpreted in a threefold way:

d = an individual Thou
d' = a collective Thou of a group (a political party, tribe, people, etc.)
d" = God

Those who adhere to person_d are sometimes not inclined to insist that this implies $\text{person}_{d'}$ while defenders of $\text{person}_{d'}$ are not inclined to state that it implies person_d. In other words both (xi) and (xii) are sometimes denied:

(xi) $\text{person}_d \rightarrow \text{person}_{d'}$

(xii) $\text{person}_{d'} \rightarrow \text{person}_{d}$

(xiii) and (xiv), on the other hand, are not denied:

(xiii) $\text{person}_{d} \rightarrow \text{person}_{a+}$

(xiv) $\text{person}_{d'} \rightarrow \text{person}_{a+}$

The relation to person_c is more difficult to define, but in general (xv) and (xvi) are considered to be true, especially by adherents of the I-Thou philosophy.

(xv) $\text{person}_{d} \Leftrightarrow \text{person}_{c}$

(xvi) $\text{person}_{d'} \Leftrightarrow \text{person}_{c}$

It is different with $\text{person}_{d''}$. Kierkegaard, for instance, indicated that religious categories transcended moral ones. The autonomy of morals is also defended. This means that both (xvii) and (xviii) are denied, although proponents of these theses can also be found, viz., those scholars who defend a close connection between religions and morals.

(xvii) $\text{person}_{d''} \rightarrow \text{person}_{c}$

(xviii) $\text{person}_{c} \rightarrow \text{person}_{d''}$

It is, of course, not my task to solve all these problems here. The main aim of this section has been to give a conceptual apparatus by means of which one can further define one's concept of person (or that of the philosopher or thinker one is dealing with). It is clear that this conceptual apparatus is a logical system, so that the meaning of a word or concept depends also on its implications or consequences. One has to indicate the rules of implication that go with a certain characteristic of the concept of person. Some of them are generally accepted, but others are not. The kind of concept of person one is dealing with depends on the rules of implication that are used.

Personal identity

The problem of how to determine somebody's identity does not coincide with the problems dealt with so far. However, it is connected with these problems, in that it shows what the main characteristic of being a person is. Generally speaking, the following views can be distinguished:

a) One sees the identity of a person in the body's remaining the same, that is, in corporeal continuity. Whether or not we are dealing with the same person depends on whether or not we are dealing with the same body. However, a number of objections can be raised to this view. In science fiction bodies can change while the 'I' remains the same. It is evident that criterion a) is then insufficient. Besides, it is possible that man (his soul) continues to live after death, which is excluded beforehand by criterion a). In addition, a considerable corporeal change can take place without change of identity, e.g., when a surgeon gives a patient a totally new face, the patient's personal identity still remains the same.

b) Sometimes it is said that someone's identity depends on retaining the same brain. Suppose, however, that in the future a skilful surgeon is able - and at least this is logically possible - to replace someone's left half of the brain with that of someone else. Does his body then contain two persons? Or none?

c) A better criterion seems to be the continuity of memory. But this too can lead to difficulties. Someone who suffers from loss of memory has not become another person.

d) Another possibility is to seek the criterion in the continuity of the ego. This is the characteristic of person_{a+} as discussed above. We see that the various criteria emerge again.

e) Another possibility is to seek personal identity in being addressed by someone else and in communicating with him. In this case we have arrived at person_{d}, etc.

All these problems also play their role in the doctrine of human immortality. How can one determine whether the person who survives death is the same person he was on earth?

Therefore some philosophers, such as Spinoza, bluntly deny that one remains the same person when one suffers from loss of memory. Spinoza also asserts that the child is another person than the adult, etc. One probably has to use a combination of the criteria mentioned above and one cannot restrict oneself to one criterion only.

God as a person

So far we have dealt exclusively with man as a person. When we want to deal with God as a person we have to state first that all properties can only be ascribed to God *analogice*. This is a theory with a long tradition, but it can be given a modern logical mathematical reformulation (cf. Bochenski: 1965, 156ff; Hubbeling: 1987, 198ff). I cannot go deeply into this matter, but I presuppose that it is possible to ascribe *analogice* human properties to God. As for the logical relations between the various concepts of person, they are the same when applied to God (Hubbeling: 1981, 173ff). Various scholars have ascribed different concepts of person to God. One can map this discussion very well by means of the concep-tual system given above, e.g., Spinoza ascribes the concept of $person_a$ to God. One may perhaps maintain that he also ascribes the concept of a $person_c$ to God, *viz.,* if we read 'highest perfection of being' instead of 'morally good'. In any case he refuses *expressis verbis* to ascribe the concept of $person_b$ to God (and man) or, better formulated: in Spinoza's view $person_b$ and $person_a$ coincide. He also denies that $person_{d+}$ can be ascribed to God. ($Person_{d+}$ is understood to mean: $persond_d$ + $person_{d'}$ + $person_{d''}$). In the case of God we must think of an I - Thou relation to an individual person, an I - Thou relation to a group respectively, whereas $person_{d''}$ is an I - Thou relation of God to Himself as it is expressed in the doctrine of the Trinity. Before one criticizes Spinoza I would like to state that some strong philosophical arguments can be put forward to support his position. In the first place we may refer to the problem of God's relation to logical and mathematical laws. Are they created by God? This is Descartes's doctrine. In that case the world as a whole is completely contingent. God could have created a mountain without a valley (this is the common example in Cartesianism!). But the Cartesian position poses a problem. If God can produce what is logically contradictory (and this is included in the view that God can eliminate and replace any logical law) then it is not possible to answer the question of where evil comes from. All possible answers presuppose that there are facts that even God cannot change. But if on the other hand we assert with Leibniz that the logical laws are valid independently of God we submit God to logic, which also incurs a number of difficulties. The most profound doctrine is Spinoza's idea that the logical laws are an expression of God himself. God cannot transgress them, but at the same time he is not subjected to something that is alien to him.

Spinoza takes approximately the same position with respect to the question as to God's relation to the good. Is something good because God wants it (that is Duns Scotus's position which runs parallel to that of Descartes) or does God want something, because it is good (Thomas Aquinas's answer which thus runs parallel to that of Leibniz)? Spinoza does not speak about the concept of good with respect to God. He restricts this concept to human society. With respect to God he speaks of *perfection*· (= complete realization of being). According to Spinoza, perfection is an expression of God himself.

To a certain extent his doctrine is plausible also with respect to God's will. If we *analogice* ascribe a human will to God we run into difficulties, for man first considers all kinds of possibilities and after having examined them carefully he makes a decision. It is absurd to think that God makes his decisions in an analogous way, given the traditional definitions of God's omnipotence, omniscience, etc. In accordance with these definitions God knows at the same time (or rather from eternity) what the state of affairs is and what decisions he has to take. These decisions come from God, because in him $person_a$ and $person_b$ coincide. If one rejects this and if one wants to ascribe also $person_{d+}$ to God one has to introduce a doctrine like that of process philosophy (or process theology) which says that the relations in God belong to his essence and that God considered in himself is not the same God as God considered in his relations to man and the world. According to process philosophy, God has changed by entering into a relation with the world and God will become another God if this relation is improved, i.e.,, if man acts better than he is doing now, God will become more God, as it were! According to process philosophy, God is no longer omniscient in the traditional way. Man is free in taking his moral decisions and God does not know them in advance.

In traditional theology there was an apparent contradiction in the attribution of the natures of *aseitas* and $person_{d+}$ to God. This problem was solved by means of the doctrine of the Trinity in which God stands in relation to himself (Father - Son - Holy Spirit). The relation God-man is then a derivation from these relations within the Trinity.

Final remarks

It has not been my intention to advance a doctrine of my own with respect to God's and man's personhood. In my *Einführung in die Religionsphilosophie* and *Principles of the Philosophy of Religion* I have put forward some arguments in order to defend the concept of God as a person. Within a strict rational system it can be justifable to ascribe person_a and person_b to God. The attribution of person_{d+} to God requires reference to religious experience, and the attribution of person_c to God requires at least a reference to moral and/or aesthetic experience.

It may, of course, be possible to give more characteristics of the concept of person especially if other cultures are taken into consideration. In that case it is necessary to indicate the logical relations between these other characteristics and the ones given above. I wish to emphasize once more that the meaning of the various concepts of person also depends on the inferences that can be drawn from them, i.e., on what they do or do not imply. Being a person_a that implies being a person_c is different from being a person_a that does not imply being a person_c, although the other properties may be entirely the same.

Bibliography

Bochenski, J.M.
1965 *The Logic of Religion*, New York U.P., New York

Hubbeling, H.G.
1981 *Einführung in die Religionsphilosophie*, Vandenhoeck & Ruprecht, Göttingen.
1985 'Logische analyse en waardenleer'. In: H.G. Hubbeling en R. Veldhuis (eds.), *Ethiek in meervoud*, Van Gorcum, Assen.
1987 *Principles of the Philosophy of Religion*, Van Gorcum, Assen/Wolfeboro.

Wilde, A. de
1951 *De Persoon. Historisch-systematisch onderzoek naar de betekenis van het persoonssymbool*, Van Gorcum, Assen.

A FEW CRITICAL REMARKS ON THE CONCEPT OF PERSON

Jasper J. Oosten

A great number of articles concerning the concept 'person' have been gathered in the present publication, which deals with different aspects of this concept and the way in which it manifests itself in various cultures. To arrange this somewhat systematically a philosophical treatment is desirable. This can be found in Hubbeling's survey of the various interpretations and problems concerning the concept of person in Western philosophy. In his article Hubbeling deals with the contents and the logical structure of the philosophical concept of person.

It is my intention to supplement this approach by drawing attention to the way in which the concept 'person' is used in practice. I will try to show that the concept of person is closely linked with generally accepted Western ideologies, so that it cannot simply be applied to non-Western cultures. To make this clear, I have made a detailed study of the relation between 'person' and 'personality'.

The concept of person

The concept 'person' plays an important part in our culture. We can find it in, for instance, the Universal Declaration of Human Rights as set forth by the General Assembly of the United Nations in 1948. In article 3 it says: 'Everyone has the right to life, liberty and security of person' and in article 6: 'Everyone has the right to recognition everywhere as a person before the law'. The concept 'person' is used to indicate the human individual to whom certain rights can be assigned and who may be held responsible for his actions.

This use of the term 'person' rests upon a long tradition laid down in philosophy. Hubbeling's contribution shows how the concept of person has developed since antiquity. After the definition provided by Boethius *(persona est naturae rationalis individua substantia)* had been current for centuries, modern thinking regarding the person was especially influenced by the formulations of Immanuel Kant who, among other things, described 'person' as 'that subject who can be held responsible for his actions'.

While reviewing present-day usage of words in philosophy, Hubbeling distinguishes the following characteristics as constituting personal being: consciousness of self, a will of one's own, a sense of responsibility, a certain measure of freedom of action and some knowledge of facts and norms. Having relationships with others and the continuity of a personal identity (in whatever way one wishes to specify this) can also be counted as belonging to the characteristics of the person according to Hubbeling.

It is evident from this that the concept 'person' belongs in the first place to an ethical or juridical context, where the stress falls on the one hand upon the unique and irreplaceable value of the person and on the other hand upon the responsibility the person has for his actions and its consequences. The concept of person is of a strongly formal nature, as is clearly revealed by Hubbeling's enumeration of characteristics of 'being a person'. What counts is the presence of these characteristics, not their strength.

Owing to this formal character the concept 'person' is rather empty in everyday usage where it means about the same as the term 'individual', a term which is also almost exclusively applied to human beings. The meaning of a concept lies in its usage and this usage is influenced by the availability of other concepts that are related to it but have a slightly different meaning. Related to the concept 'person' is the concept 'personality', which is less formal and consequently appeals more to the imagination than 'person'.

The concept of personality

Everyone is a person, but we do not call everyone a personality. The concept of personality represents an ideal that is deeply rooted in our society. It was already formulated by Aristotle in his description, in book four of the *Nicomachean Ethics*, of 'he great-souled man' who, according to A. MacIntyre, 'is very nearly an English gentleman' (MacIntyre: 1971, 79). The German Romantic Period, in particular, was concerned with the ideal personality as is shown by Hubbeling. In the following, however, I, will concentrate on the everyday usage of the concept of person.

If one wants to become a real personality, if one wants to leave one's mark on one's contemporaries and perhaps also even on posterity, then one must develop all one's hidden talents as best one can. Aristotle described this as converting potentiality into actuality. Nowadays we speak of fully developing the personality, but we are, in fact, referring to the same thing.

The ruling practical ideal in our society is to become a real personality. It offers a prospect of various kinds of reward. To attain this one must make use of one's talents, but these are very unequally distributed. Thus everyone will have to make the most of his possibilities. The best way to attain the goal is to arrange one's own life in such a way as to make optimal use of one's own specific possibilities. An excellent means of doing this is a suitable choice of profession. This is why each group consisting of people who are at a disadvantage in our society tries to bring this means within its reach.

If one wants to demonstrate what one is worth, one must do this by means of the situations in which one finds oneself. These situations, however, are socially determined and the number of roles one can choose from is only limited. Each role is determined by a great number of rules one must observe and each role makes specific demands one must comply with to be able to fill that role. Many women very reluctantly play the part of a housewife, and many men strive for a successful career by undertaking increasingly difficult roles. The acceptance of a new role implies a further development of the personality, and it begins with an initiation. It is true that in our culture this initiation usually entails very few rites and ceremonies, but all the same it is important for the development of the individual. By developing into a personality, one forms an identity of one's own in close connection with the group one belongs to and the role one plays in this group. Members of a group can often be recognized by specific behaviourisms.

Our society is engaged in a process of increasing differentiation and individualization. Owing to this increasing differentiation, people are more and more compelled to associate in daily life with persons with whom they are only superficially acquainted and whom they only meet in a specific role. The role someone plays determines his behaviour in many respects, because the role provides a series of directions as regards behaviour towards other people. Some of these directions are very strict. Other directions are very flexible and leave much room for private initiative.

Personal responsibility

An important consequence of this is that the person has every possibility of hiding behind the mask provided by his role, thus negating personal responsibility for his actions. The soldier cannot be held accountable for the commands of his superior officer, nor the official for the rules he must observe, nor the judge for the ruling legislation, etc. It is questionable whether a person can be held responsible for his conduct as long as he strictly follows the rules of his socially accepted role.

In our society a soldier has hardly any possibility of disobeying the much-hated *Befehl-ist-Befehl* rule in forces in the army. Ministers and generals and other persons with important positions who misbehave are often able to show that their conduct is a direct consequence of their great devotion to duty, so that instead of laying it to their personal charge it must be attributed to their role. If indeed they did something wrong, this happened, not to benefit themselves, but with an eye to the common good, which they claim always to have put first, as befits someone in their position.

A socially precisely circumscribed role relieves the individual to a very great extent of his personal responsibility for each decision that has to be taken and for the resulting actions. In so far as these decisions and these actions can be directly derived from a conscientious carrying-out of the role concerned, it is not so much the person who decides and acts that is responsible as the structure he represents, which is usually the outcome of a historical process. Consequently no one can really be held accountable. This problem was highlighted when after the Second World War the allies felt the need to condemn individual Germans and Japanese for their war-time conduct, while the latter pointed out that they had simply been doing their duty.

Every hierarchically or bureaucratically organized structure greatly complicates the question as to the individual responsibility of the persons belonging to this structure. A personality is someone who can manage quite well in a hierarchic or bureaucratic system also. He plays his parts with ease and, when necessary, switches easily from one to the other without mixing them up. He quickly distinguishes between situations in which persons must be held accountable and situations in which the responsibility for what happens must be attributed to the system. If he shows that he can play more difficult parts as well, he will undoubtedly make a career for himself.

As a rule the question of the individual responsibility of persons does not arise until something goes wrong. Then a scapegoat must be found to save the system. It is often not clear who should be pointed out as the guilty person. Everyone tries to save his bacon and to minimize his personal share in the matter. Thus a common trial of strength arises, the outcome of which determines who is to be held responsible for what went wrong. This procedure takes place everywhere in our society and at all levels: in the government, in business, in the family, etc.

In this struggle for power a strong personality will be better able to maintain his position than a weak personality. He will have more success in presenting his case in a clear and convincing manner, so that others are impressed by his good intentions and minimal liability. Someone who is not so good at defending himself is more often blamed for something, and consequently he is more often held personally responsible for undesired events. No wonder everyone in our society would like to become a real personality.

In our society there is a never-ending rivalry among individuals who are trying to develop themselves by means of the best jobs, i.e. the most attractive roles. This rivalry is mitigated by a number of rules which people are supposed to observe, just as, according to Hobbes, the war of all against all is avoided by means of a social contract. These rules are in part explicit (e.g., existing legislation) and in part implicit (e.g., social manners).

The ideological function of the concept of person

In order to be able to justify the rules of our society, it is usual to have recourse to the concept of person. The Universal Declaration of Human Rights is a clear example of this. The justification of these rules, however, also entails the legitimation of the actual practice covered by them. Thus the concept of person is used to legitimize a reality which is mainly directed to the development of individual personalities.

When a philosopher tries to explain what 'person' really is, he at the same time uncovers something of the ideological foundations of our society. Since the Renaissance these foundations have developed in a humanistic and individualistic direction. As this development goes on, a continual re-evaluation of the concept of person is necessary, for when it serves to justify a changing reality, the contents of the concept change. A historical review of the development of the concept 'person' in relation to the society in which it functions would give us a better understanding of the ideological function of the concept, i.e. the ways in which it was and is used to legitimize existing social practices.

Philosophers all too often make the mistake of taking insufficient account of the ideological function in society of their assertions. From bitter political experience, from the writings of Orwell as well as from the dialectical philosophy of Hegel and Marx, we have learned that in daily life all kinds of statements and concepts can come to mean something that is quite different from what well-meaning persons originally intended them to mean. In our culture the concept of person is theoretically central, but everyday reality hinges on personalities. In our theories we speak of Human Rights (i.e. the rights of the person), but in practice we chiefly attend to the right of freedom of opinion and hardly at all to the right to work, which has also been laid down in the Universal Declaration of Human Rights. Not our theory, but actual practice betrays the ideological function of the concept of person in our society. If one wishes to fathom the meaning and the contents of the concept of person this must not be disregarded.

Penetrating the meaning of concepts has occupied Western philosophy since Socrates. It is indeed an open question whether the modern analytically schooled philosophers are any more adept at this than their illustrious Athenian predecessors. In any case it has become clear that there is a great difference between being able to use and being able to explicate most concepts. In the introduction to his book 'The Concept of Mind' the English philosopher G. Ryle writes about this:

> It is, however, one thing to know how to apply such concepts, quite another to know how to correlate them with one another and with concepts of other sorts. Many people can talk sense with concepts but cannot talk sense about them; they know by practice how to operate with concepts, anyhow inside familiar fields, but they cannot state the logical regulations governing their use. (Ryle: 1966, 9).

This can also be applied to the concept of person. Moreover, even if we succeeded in making the rules for the use of the concept of person completely explicit, philosophers and students of the social sciences could not be satisfied with this, because they would also have to make a study of the ideological function of these rules in society.

The opacity of the concept of person

A full understanding of the concept of person also requires a good command of the relations between this concept and other concepts. In the course of time interesting changes appear to have taken place in these relations. Thus we can observe that familiar concepts such as 'soul' and 'honour' which not so long ago seemed to be essential to a sensible discussion about the human person and his destination, are less and less often mentioned in various Western countries. They no longer seem to fit in with our modern society and they are disappearing from our world. They vanish from the language that we are using and in which we have come to formulate everything that is related to the person by means of other words, e.g., personality, liberty, right, responsibility, etc. The disappearance of concepts such as 'soul' and 'honour' from ordinary usage is not without significance. It shows that we are no longer concerned about our honour or the fate of our immortal souls. This is a considerable change in the attitude of Western man towards himself, and it is accompanied by an unobtrusive shift in the contents of his concept of person, which can no longer be brought into connection with 'soul' and 'honour'.

If one wishes to examine all aspects of the concept of person, such matters will have to be considered as well. One can of course try to give the concept of person a definite place in a scientific language-game by means of a stipulative definition. Hubbeling's approach goes in that direction and there is certainly nothing wrong with that, as long as one realizes that in this way the many shades of meaning of the concept in ordinary usage are by no means fully fathomed. His approach bears the mark of the Western philosophical tradition, so that it is imbued with the ideology of enlightened Christian humanism, liberalism and individualism which is expressed in the terminology he uses. It is therefore a moot question to what extent this approach is suitable for a better understanding of foreign cultures that view themselves on the basis of quite a different tradition and intellectual concepts of quite a different structure.

Other cultures

The problem pointed out by Ryle applies to the same extent to other cultures. For the Indian *karma* is, and for the ancient Egyptian *ka* was, just as complicated a concept as the concept of person is for us. In the case of each of these concepts it is not possible to elucidate all its aspects so as to arrive at a complete understanding of all the shades of meaning covered by the concept. All the same, one can gain some insight by examining the rules for the use of the word in the language in which it occurs.

By studying the language of a non-Western culture one can obtain knowledge about the way in which members of this culture interpret themselves, the world and the relations between the two. In doing this, one does not come across the concept of person, for this belongs to one's own culture and not to the subject of research. If one uses the concept of person, this means that one is applying a Western concept to a non-Western culture. This standard implies the set of characteristics that are mentioned by Hubbeling and which pertain to the concept of person, e.g., consciousness of self, a will of one's own and a sense of responsibility. These notions are not merely characteristics of a philosophical concept, but represent important Western values. Thus, in applying the concept of person to another culture, one also applies these Western values to that culture. One has then exchanged the old theological standard for a newer humanistic one, and consequently one has again a considerable chance of undervaluing the specific character of the foreign culture (and particularly its own values).

One can of course suggest that this is a progressive development because this standard is becoming more and more universal since the non-Western cultures are giving up their own character and are adapting themselves to our own so praiseworthy 'American way of life', but then one has to admit that one is not really interested in other cultures, and by no means everyone will be ready to do this.

Bibliography

MacIntyre, A.
1971 *A Short History of Ethics*, Routledge and Kegan Paul, London.

Ryle, G.
1966 *The Concept of Mind*, Penguin Books, Harmondsworth.

THE CONCEPT OF PERSON IN AMERICAN ANTHROPOLOGY

The Cultural Perspective of Clifford Geertz

Yme B. Kuiper

About twenty years ago Clifford Geertz published his famous essay 'Religion as a Cultural System' (Geertz: 1973b). Inspired by the German sociologist Max Weber, Geertz characterised the anthropological study of religion as a two-stage operation: in the first place, an analysis of the system of meanings embodied in the symbols which make up religion, and, in the second place, the relating of these systems to social-structural and psychological processes. According to 'meanings-and-symbols anthropologists' like Geertz, the importance of religion consists in its capacity to serve, for the individual as well as for the group, as a source of general, yet distinctive conceptions of the world, the self, and the relations between them. Religion provides its believers with a world view. At the same time, Geertz argues, this model of reality indicates how people have to behave in certain situations. Geertz calls this programme for action an ethos. The term 'ethos' also refers to the tone, character, and quality of people's life.[1]

However, Geertz ended his essay in a rather sceptical tone: "My dissatisfaction with so much of anthropological work in religion is not that it concerns itself with the second stage - social-structural and psychological analysis of religion - but that it neglects the first" - ; in my words: the cultural analysis of significant symbols and meanings in various religions; an analysis that also avoids the pitfalls of a complete

---

1 See Geertz: 1973c, 126-127: "In recent anthropological discussion, the moral (and aesthetic) aspects of a given culture, the evaluative elements, have commonly been summed up in the term 'ethos', while the cognitive, existential aspects have been designated by the term 'world view'. A people's ethos is the tone, character, and quality of their life, its moral and aesthetic style and mood: it is the underlying attitude towards themselves and their world that life reflects. Their world view is their picture of the way things in their sheer actuality are, their concept of nature, of self, of society. It contains their most comprehensive ideas of order."

reduction of culture (or religion) to social structure, political ideology, economic systems and the like. According to Geertz, anthropology (and especially the anthropology of religion) needs models for analysing symbolic action.

Today, twenty years later, Geertz's reflections seem to have been prophetic. In my view, his plea for a symbolic, interpretive approach in the anthropology of religion, has turned out to be self-fulfilling (Ortner: 1984; Boon: 1982). There are few students of present-day anthropology who are not acquainted with the essay, 'Religion as a Cultural System'. No doubt most specialists in the anthropology of religion are likely also to have read also some of Geertz's monographs and articles on religious phenomena in Morocco and Indonesia (see among others, Geertz: 1960; 1968; 1973d-g; 1979; 1980; 1983a). Over the past few years Geertz seems to have become a kind of ambassador for cultural anthropology: his works are discussed by many non-anthropologists as well. Among his public one can find historians - including historians of religion - scientists of religion, sociologists, psychologists, philosophers, linguists, and theologians (Morgan: 1977; Walters: 1980; Hofstee: 1986). Geertz's work shows a remarkable integration of theoretical, methodological analysis and empirical data (see Bakker: 1988, 92-98). Geertz does not pretend to construct grand, all-encompassing theories. Nor does he deliberately collect exotic facts - 'the stranger the better' - to destroy universal theories of sociologists and the like. In fact Geertz detests the so-called 'Bongo-Bongo attitude' of many of his colleagues: "what you assert may be true, but it does not apply to my tribe of the Bongo-Bongo." Geertz's kind of anthropology rather consists of specific research (e.g., on public, religious ritual) in a specific context (e.g., a village in Bali, a small town in Morocco) in order to gain an insight into *a* culture or *a* religion (the Balinese, Moroccan, etc.). Many of Geertz's case-studies also offer a general understanding of culture or religion, or, to put it in Geertz's words: "All ethnography is part philosophy" (Geertz: 1967).

In this article I will analyse the Geertzian programme for research on the concept of person. To characterise Geertz's ideas more adequately I will also sketch his intellectual background and his notion of culture as a system of meanings, embodied in symbols. Using a certain conception of the idea of person in concrete ethnographic research always implies, as Geertz's work shows, specific views on analytical and methodological problems. The main thesis of my analysis is that, notwithstanding some possible, relevant criticism of his approach to culture(s) and religion(s), Geertz developed a fruitful, *cultural*-anthropological research programme for empirical-theoretical analyses of concepts of person.[2]

Backgrounds of Geertz's kind of anthropology

Geertz's approach to the subject of this book is partly a result of and partly a deviation from a certain tradition within classical American anthropology. What I am aiming at is the so-called 'Culture and Personality' approach of anthropologists like, among others, Ruth Benedict, Margaret Mead, Abraham Kardiner, Cora Dubois, Clyde Kluckhohn and Ralph Linton. This tradition was especially popular in the thirties and forties of this century (see de Waal Malefijt: 1974). These American anthropologists gave the concept of culture a meaning that differed from more traditional interpretations. In 1934, Ruth Benedict wrote in her famous study 'Patterns of Culture': "... a culture, like an invidual, is a more or less consistent pattern of thought and action". The comparison she made between culture and individual, was certainly not accidental. Benedict, as well as some of her colleagues, presumed that the typical features of a culture as a whole are expressed by the personality of each individual representative of that culture. Within the 'culture and

---

2 According to Sherry B. Ortner, Geertz's cultural approach can also be seen as part of an important shift in the anthropology of the eighties to a new theoretical orientation which she labelled "practice" (or "action")- anthropology: "For the past several years, there has been growing interest in analysis focused through one or another of a bundle of interrelated terms: practice, praxis, action, interaction, activity, experience, performance. A second, and closely related, bundle of terms focuses on the doer of all that doing: agent, actor, *person*, *self*, individual, subject." [my italics, YBK] A crucial point is that "the study of practice is not an antagonistic alternative to the study of systems or structures [for instance: "society" or "culture"; YBK], but a necessary complement to it." Besides, Ortner remarks, this theoretical movement appears much broader than the field of anthropology alone; recent linguistics, sociology, history and literary studies have also been influenced by this new trend. In anthropology there is "a growing body of literature which explores the variable construction of self, person, emotion, and motive in cross-cultural perspective"; Ortner: 1984, 127, 144-147 and 151.

personality' approach the idea of personality was conceived in different ways.

On the whole, three main variants of classical anthropological research on personality can be distinguished: 1. psychological and individualistic research on 'personality traits'; 2. more interactionist research on interpersonal dispositions; and 3. research on the ways in which an individual's experience and behaviour are integrated - the cultural context then serves explicitly as the framework of research (Bock: 1980, chapter 3). The work of Geertz represents the third variant; in several articles Geertz criticised the first variant.

With their field-work data, collected among American Indians, in the Far East and in Oceania, the 'culture and personality' anthropologists attempted to trace the relation between culture and personality within relatively simple societies. During the Second World War this programme was extended to encompass very complex societies like Japan, Germany and the Soviet Union, and research was focused on the concept of national character.

Once again, these American anthropologists considered culture as an important factor in the development of personality and they held individuals to be the ultimate locus of culture. Given these presuppositions and their affinity with psychoanalysis one can understand the emphasis they put on processes of socialization and enculturation.

I have already stipulated that the work of Clifford Geertz can be understood in connection with the third tradition of the 'culture and personality' approach. I would like to illustrate this assertion by referring to a study by the couple Gregory Bateson and Margaret Mead, called 'Balinese Character', published in 1942. It is remarkable that this elegant, rich study with hundreds of photographs, contains a lot of concepts and ideas also present in Geertz's kind of anthropology and in his ethnographic studies on Balinese culture, thought and action. Just as Geertz was to do later, Bateson and Mead focused their research on the ethos-aspect of Balinese culture, that is, they tried to describe the way the emotional life of the Balinese was organized in culturally standarised forms. Just like Geertz they were quite aware of the fact that in doing research an anthropologist needs his own concepts and abstractions, or, as Bateson and Mead put it in their introduction to 'Balinese Character':

> This is not a book about Balinese custom, but about the Balinese - about the way in which they, as living persons, moving, standing, eating, sleeping, dancing, and going into trance, embody that abstraction which (after we have abstracted it) we technically call culture (Bateson, Mead: 1942, xii).

I already pointed out that Geertz does not like ethnographers of the Bongo-Bongo type. His kind of anthropology has been profoundly influenced by two important guides of twentieth century sociology: Max Weber and Talcott Parsons. The latter introduced the work of Weber in the United States and became Geertz's teacher (Peacock: 1981).

In his so-called 'action-theory' Parsons approached culture as one of the three interdependent systems which regulate human behaviour; the other two are society and the individual. Parsons tried to develop a model that could integrate the perspectives of Durkheim, Weber and Freud. Geertz, however, does not use Parsons's model altogether. What he adopts is Parsons's conception of culture within that model of systems (Geertz: "I tried to develop it from where he had left it"; Geertz: 1979). Geertz combines this notion of cultural system with Weber's insight that the behaviour of individuals always consists in 'meaningful action'. One may summarise Geertz's synthesis of Weber and Parsons as follows: a major task of the anthropologist is, in the first place, to understand behaviour in terms of the meanings that participants ascribe to it. As I already pointed out, the next step is to relate that behaviour to a configuration of the ideals, values and attitudes it reflects.

Geertz's view on culture

Given the background I have sketched just now, the question arises what the typical trait of the Geertzian view on culture might be. According to Geertz, culture has a rather objective and autonomous character. As culture is a complex of systems of symbols it should be conceived not in a mentalistic or psychological, but rather in a pragmatic way. Symbols should be looked for not in the heads of people, but in their public and collective actions. To put it differently: meaning is a public fact. Geertz considers, e.g., the behaviour of people in visible, complex rituals as a kind of busy traffic of symbols. These symbols then he calls 'vehicles of meanings'. Geertz borrowed the metaphor of traffic and vehicles from Wittgenstein's and Ryle's 'ordinary language philosophy'

- a kind of philosophy he appreciates very much.[3]

An analogy cherished by Geertz is the characterisation of the anthropological analysis of e.g., crucial religious rituals as the reading of a text containing various messages. In the cremation of a Balinese prince he identifies the following messages: a certain consciousness of the divine, the invocation of a sacred atmosphere, societal prestige and the public imposition of a feeling of togetherness.

I have just mentioned Geertz's sympathy for a specific variant of British philosophy. Most British anthropologists however - calling themselves, *nomen est omen*, 'social anthropologists' - do not appreciate Geertz's work. They think Geertz is much too little of a sociologist. Moreover, they think that Geertz depicts the cultures he studied (Java, Bali, Morocco) in a much too homogeneous way, as if they were simple, 'primitive' cultures. To illustrate this point I will quote a comment by Sir Edmund Leach on Geertz's ethnographic studies of Bali:

> Geertz makes the categorical, but quite unverifiable assertion that "all Balinese share the same general beliefs, the same broad ideas of how their society is or should be arranged". Geertz is here writing about Balinese 'culture' as the counterpart of Balinese 'society'. This style of argument makes axiomatic that every 'society' ('social group') is culturally homogeneous. But from a sociological point of view this is totally misleading. Almost all empirical societies are socially stratified and each stratum in the system is marked by its own distinctive cultural attributes - linguistic usages, manners, styles of dress, food, housing etc (Leach: 1982, 43).[4]

---

[3] Cf. also Geertz's use of Ryle's notion "thick description"; Geertz: 1973h. With respect to the philosophical analysis of symbols and meanings Geertz has also been influenced by the works of the American philosopher, logician and art critic Susanne Langer; cf. Jeunhomme: 1986.

[4] This dualism also occupies a key position in the anthropology of religion of the Dutch scholar Jan van Baal; cf. Kuiper: 1986.
Some recent results of this more *social* anthropological research programme can be found in: Carrithers - Collins - Lukes (eds.): 1985. The book is dedicated to the memory of Marcel Mauss. None of the twelve authors refer to the work of Geertz.
In the conclusion of this book S. Lukes states: "What preoccupies Mauss, and the

In a certain sense Sir Edmund is right, but what his criticism demonstrates on a more general level is a difference in theoretical point of view. So, criticism of Geertz's work is concerned not only with details but also with fundamental theoretical problems that cannot be analysed in detail here.[5]

---

contributors to this volume, is ... 'the notion or concept that different men in different ages have formed' of the person in the narrow sense - more particularly 'according to their systems of law, religion, customs, social structures and morality'. What is this wider 'notion or concept' or structure of thinking concerning the person that is held to be fundamental, universal and necessary? ... Mauss, and most contributors (see) the category of the person ... as a *structure of beliefs*"; op. cit., p.285. Notwithstanding a certain general resemblance between Lukes's formulation and Geertz's approach, there still remains a significant difference: Geertz puts more stress on the autonomy of the person as a cultural concept, whereas in Lukes's statement one misses the notion of culture.

5 One of these problems has been discussed with respect to Geertz's approach to religion 'as a cultural system'. His work has been criticised for being too culturological and too a-historical; some critics state that Geertz's approach does not leave enough room for specific research into the social and political conditions and forces that generate and change cultural systems like religion; cf. Bax: 1987.
In his 'Anthropological Studies of Religion', however, Brian Morris gives a fine evaluation of this criticism: "Given his stress on religion as a symbol system and his tendency to see religion as an inner state - a 'faith' - Geertz never *fully* explored the social forces that produced the religious beliefs and practices. Geertz's whole outlook remained close to the German idealist tradition ... But in attempting to understand religion within a *specific* sociopolitical context, Geertz certainly provides a more dynamic approach to religion than that evinced by anthropologists who have not been influenced by Weberian sociology - Douglas and Turner, for example. His studies of the religious systems of Java and Bali, in fact, indicate the pervasive influence of Weber, and though Geertz accepts the notion that his own approach is one of cultural hermeneutics, these studies go beyond that of simply interpreting the religious symbolism. As with Durkheim and Weber, there is a discrepancy in Geertz between his theoretical intent, specified in general programmatic statements, and his substantive analyses." [my italics, YBK]; Morris: 1987, 316, 318.

In a way, social anthropology has its own research programme for the concept of person. Its starting point was Marcel Mauss's essay "Une catégorie de l'esprit Humain: La Notion de Personne, Celle de moi" (A Category of the Humain Mind: the Notion of Person, the Notion of Self), published in 1938, in the *Journal of the Royal Anthropolopgical Insitute*. According to Mauss, our seemingly natural and self-evident conceptions of the self and the person are in fact outcomes of a long and very complex social history of Western civilization. Other societies have held very different notions of the self, and each society's notion is connected with its form of social organisation. Mauss's basic view on *the* individual was dualistic: the individual has a double existence. the one purely individual, subjective, the other social and nothing but an extension of society. In every age and in every society man has been intensely aware of this duality. The beliefs, and particularly the religious beliefs and the concept of person, of all societies (including our own) can be seen as interpretations, in more or less explicit form, of this permanent duality of society and individual and the tension between them.

Concepts of person: Java, Bali and Morrocco

According to Geertz, the task of a cultural anthropologist is to map out systems of symbols. In doing this a difficult problem arises: how are the most important systems of symbols of a given society to be selected? This task is somewhat simplified by the fact that some systems are universal - systems that embody a means of orientation that is indispensable to human beings, or, as he nicely puts it: "the problems, being existential, are universal; their solutions, being human, are diverse" (Geertz: 1973h, 363).

One of these means of orientation is the concept of person: the cultural characterisation of individual human beings (or the cultural part of the self). Every society has the disposal of systems of symbols in terms of which persons are conceived as representatives of certain distinct categories of the person, specific sorts of individuals. Geertz makes a sharp distinction between the individual and the person. An individual is a living, biological being that is born, grows to maturity, grows old and dies; the person is a vehicle of meaning, a representation of a kind of individual.

In one of his essays Geertz sketches a plurality of symbol systems which can define concrete classes of determinate persons:

> And the symbol systems which define these classes are not given in the nature of things - they are historically constructed, socially maintained, and individually applied ... Some, for example, kinship terminologies, are ego-centered; that is, they define the status of an individual in terms of his relationship to a specific, social actor. Others are centered on one or another subsystem or aspect of society and are invariant with respect to the perspectives of individual actors: noble ranks, age-group statuses, occupational categories. Some - personal names and sobriquets - are informal and particularizing; others- bureaucratic titles and caste designations - are informal and standardizing (Geertz: 1973h, 363-364).

Even though the starting point of Geertz's view on 'concept of person' is a very general one, he is above all other things interested in a. the intracultural concept of person in a specific society, and b. differences between actual conceptions of the person in various societies. Within the range of the world's cultures the Western concept of person is a rather peculiar idea. The Western person is 'a bounded, unique, more or less integrated motivational and cognitive universe'. A Western person is a dynamic centre of awareness, emotion, judgment, and action. It would be a categorical mistake to place the experience of person of others within this Western framework. Understanding other people demands setting aside this Western conception and interpreting their experiences within the framework of their own idea of what selfhood is.[6] Besides, Geertz's own analyses demonstrate that the Javanese, Balinese and Moroccan concepts of person differ markedly, that is, not only from a Western conception but, not less clearly, from one another.

Characteristic of the Javanese concept of person is the sharp separation between inward feelings and outward actions. These two sets of phenomena are not regarded as functions of one another but as independent realms of being to be put in proper order independently. In both realms a Javanese individual tries to be, or to act, or to think 'pure', 'refined', 'polished', 'subtle' and 'civilised' - to use our terms. In

---

[6] Geertz: 1983b, 59. My summaries of Geertz's analyses of Javanese, Balinese, and Moroccan concepts of person were also derived from this essay.

the inner world this is to be achieved mostly through mystical, religious discipline. In the outer world, it is to be achieved through etiquette, even if its rules are not extremely elaborate. The result is then an inner world of stilled emotion and an outer world of shaped behaviour. To illustrate this, Geertz tells the touching story of a young informant whose wife had died suddenly. The reaction of the informant was, to approach his neighbours with a smile on his face, laboriously apologising for the absence of his wife.

The Balinese concept of person is quite different. What is philosophy in Java, is theatre in Bali. Balinese society and culture, Geertz argues, are an enactment of hierarchy, a theatre of status. The Balinese see their life as a play. Not the actors, but the parts they play will last. This play is about status and hierarchy. The staging of hierarchy is a recurrent aspect of Balinese culture. In his book *Negara* Geertz analyses the Balinese theatre-state in the nineteenth century. In those days mass-rituals (e.g., cremation of kings, princes or lords, pilgrimages, temple dedications) did not serve to legitimise the Balinese state, it was precisely the other way round: the state existed to make mass-rituals possible. Ceremony was not form but substance, or, to quote a well-known passage from one of Geertz's articles: "Power served pomp, not pomp power" (Geertz: 1973f, 335)

Present-day Balinese culture is, to a certain degree, still characterised by the principles of status and hierarchy. Given this situation, one specific emotion is very central to Balinese life. The Balinese term for this emotion is *lek*. Geertz points out that this term is often mistranslated by our term 'shame'. According to Geertz, 'stage fright' would be a much better translation. The core of this emotion is the fear that, for want of skill or self-control, or perhaps by accident, the illusion will not be maintained - the fear that the actor will show through his part. When this happens a Balinese person feels naked. Consequently, the behaviour of the Balinese aims at preventing this.

Characteristic of the Moroccans, Geertz wrote, is their hyper-individualistic behaviour in public relationships. The so-called mosaic system of organization in Morocco has two important implications: a. the behaviour of individuals is constantly contextualised, and b. in public behaviour participants are continuously searching for information about one another. This does not mean, however, that the specifically Moroccan concept of person will always change essentially in accordance with the context of behaviour. Central to the Moroccan idea of self is the confidence that one can be rather pragmatic, adaptive, and opportunistic in one's relations with others, or, as Geertz puts it, "a fox among foxes, a crocodile among crocodiles". Interaction with others then is usually no threat to the person or the self.

Some concluding remarks

Exactly what kind of light can my sketch of Geertzian anthropology shed on research on concepts of person, on ideas of self? In the first place, Geertz's research on concepts of person is closely connected with his views on culture. Anthropologists should map out the relevant systems of symbols of specific cultures. They have to do that step by step, using the method of induction: from "directly observable modes of thought" to theoretical statements, and, next, using the latter to improve the original interpretations of empirical data:

> The analysis of culture comes down therefore not to an heroic 'holistic' assault upon the 'basic configurations of the culture', an overarching 'order of orders' from which more limited configurations can be seen as mere deductions, but a searching out of significant symbols, clusters of significant symbols, and clusters of clusters of significant symbols ... and the statement of the underlying regularities of human experience implicit in their formation (Geertz: 1973h).

By comparing these cultures one can also trace the characteristic aspects of certain systems of symbols. A Geertzian comparison of Indian and Balinese systems of name giving does not aim at constructing a general theory , but rather at showing differences and resemblances. The contrasts between them give an insight into the character of both cultures. Diversity is Geertz's real concern, universality is mostly used merely as a strategic starting point. This research strategy, however, does not imply that Geertzian ethnography would fall back into a sort of 'descriptivism'. As another American anthropologist, James L. Peacock, recently put it:

> Ethnography generalizes ... in some respects more akin to literature than to science. Ethnography reveals the general through the particular, the abstract

> through the concrete ... Ethnography is unlike literature and like science in that it endeavors to describe real people systematically and accurately, but it resembles literature in that it weaves facts into a form that highlights patterns and principles. As in good literature, so in good ethnography the message comes not through explicit statement of generalities but as concrete portrayal (Peacock: 1986, 83; see also Geertz: 1988, Ch. I).

In the second place, it is remarkable that in spite of Geertz's assertion that concepts of person are expressed in actual, visible behaviour, these conceptions are not easy to pick up. An anthropologist is not a vacuum-cleaner. He has to make elementary - methodological and theoretical - decisions (cf. Shweder - LeVine: 1984, 1-24).

In the third place, globally speaking, Geertz regards concepts of person as relatively stable, durable products of culture. Culture, Geertz once wrote, moves like an octopus. But, of course, concepts of person have a historical dimension. To what degree can the genesis of concepts of person be described and interpreted in terms of continuity and durability? Although Geertz's kind of anthropology and his interpretation of religion have - unjustly, I think - been labelled as an a-historical perspective, Geertz's approach is not per se hostile to historical questions.[7] For instance, Geertz's research on the process of religious modernisation in Bali shows his talent as a cultural historian (Geertz: 1973e).

Finally, the work of Geertz is an excellent starting-point for a debate on relativism. Geertz himself is certainly not an *extreme* relativist. He explicitly rejects the idea that our scientific, anthropological models should never be applied to the analysis of other cultures. He once called this sort of relativism an 'academic neurosis'. 'Relativist' is not an adequate term to characterise - the implicit philosophy in - Geertz's work. In my opinion, 'pluralist' is a more appropriate term. Geertz values the differences between peoples, cultures, and societies. In his research

---

7 According to Asad, Geertz's definition of religion "omits the crucial dimension of power, ignores the varying social conditions for the production of knowledge, and its initial plausibility derives from the fact that it resembles the privatised forms of religion so characteristic of modern (Christian) society, in which power and knowledge are no longer significantly generated by religious institutions"; Asad: 1983, 237.

on concepts of person Geertz tries not so much to find an answer to our (or his) deepest questions but rather to gain access to answers provided by other peoples.

This short article does not pretend to be more than an exploration of a problem and a concept. What is more, its main purpose is to show that the real challenge to anthropological research on concept of person is "not to define it, but to find it".

Bibliography

Asad, T.
1983 'Anthropological Conceptions of Religion: Reflections on Geertz', in: *Man* 18, 237-259.

Bakker, J.W.
1988 *Enough Profundities Already. A Reconstruction of Geertz's Interpretive Anthropology*, Utrecht.

Bateson, G. - M. Mead
1942 *Balinese Character. A Photographic Analysis*, New York.

Bax, M.
1987 'Religious Regimes and State Formation: Towards a Research Perspective', in: *Anthropological Quarterly* 60, 1-11.

Bock, Ph.K.
1980 *Continuities in Psychological Anthropology. A Historical Introduction*, San Francisco.

Boon, J.A.
1982 *Other Tribes, Other Scribes. Symbolic Anthropology in the Comparative Study of Cultures, Histories, Religions, and Texts*, Cambridge.

Carrithers, M. - S. Collins - S. Lukes (eds.)
1985 *The category of the person. Anthropology, philosophy, history*, Cambridge.

Geertz, C.
1960 *The Religion of Java*, Glencoe, Ill.
1967 'The Cerebral Savage', in: *Encounter* 4, 25-32.
1968 *Islam Observed. Religious Development in Morocco and Indonesia*, Chicago.
1973a *The Interpretation of Cultures*, New York.

1973b 'Religion as a Cultural System'. In: Geertz: 1973, 87-125 (orig. in: M. Banton (ed.), *Anthropological Approaches to the Study of Religion*, London 1966, 1-46).

1973c 'Ethos, World View, and the Analysis of Sacred Symbols'. In Geertz: 1973, 126-127.

1973d 'Ritual and Social Change: a Javanese Example'. In: Geertz: 1973, 142-169 (orig. 1959).

1973e "Internal Conversion' in Contemporary Bali'. In: Geertz: 1973, 171-189 (orig. 1964).

1973f 'Politics Past, Politics Present: Some Notes on the Uses of Anthropology in Understanding the New States'. In: Geertz: 1973, 327-341 (orig. 1967).

1973g 'Deep Play; Notes on the Balinese Cockfight'. In: Geertz: 1973, 412-453 (orig. 1972).

1973h 'Thick Description: Toward an Interpretive Theory of Culture'. In: Geertz: 1973, 3-30.

1973i 'Person, Time and Conduct in Bali'. In: Geertz: 1973, 342-411 (orig. 1966).

1980 *Negara. The Theatre State in Nineteenth-Century Bali*, Princeton.

1983a 'Centers, Kings, and Charisma: Reflections on the Symbolics of Power'. In: *Local Knowledge. Further Essays in Interpretive Anthropology*, 121-146 (orig. 1977).

1983b "From the Native's Point of View': On the Nature of Anthropological Understanding'. In: *Local Knowledge. Further Essays in Interpretive Anthropology*, 55-70 (orig. 1974).

1988 *Works and Lives. The Anthropologist as an Author*, Stanford.

Geertz, C. - H. Geertz - L. Rosen

1979 *Meaning and Order in Moroccan Society. Three Essays in Cultural Analysis*, Cambridge.

Hofstee, W.

1986 'The Interpretation of Religion. Some Remarks on the Work of Clifford Geertz'. In: H.G Hubbeling - H.G. Kippenberg (eds.), *On Symbolic Representation*, Berlin/New York, 70-83.

Jeunhomme, J.M.P.

1986 'The Symbolic Philosophy of Susanne K. Langer'. In: H.G.

Hubbeling - H.G. Kippenberg (eds.), *On Symbolic Representation*, Berlin/New York, 84-101.

Kuiper, Y.B.
1986 'Religion, Symbols, and the Human Condition. An Analysis of the Basic Ideas of Jan van Baal'. In: H.G. Hubbeling-H.G. Kippenberg (eds.), *On Symbolic Representation*. Berlin/New York, 57-69.

Leach, E.
1982 *Social Anthropology*, Glasgow.

Morgan, J.
1977 'Religion and culture as meanings systems: A dialogue between Geertz and Tillich', in: *J. Relig.* 57.

Morris, B.
1987 *Anthropological Studies of Religion*, Cambridge.

Ortner, S.
1984 'Theory in anthropology since the sixties', in: *Comparative Studies in Society and History* 26, 126-166.

Peacock, J.L.
1981 'The Third Stream: Weber, Parsons, Geertz'. in: *Journal of the Anthropological Society of Oxford* 12, 122-129.
1986 *The Anthropological Lens: Harsh Light, Soft Focus*, Cambridge.

Pinxten, R.
1979 'Clifford Geertz'. In: R. Pinxten, *On Going beyond Kinship, Sex and the Tribe. Interviews on Contemporary Anthropology, Its Philosophical Stands and Its Applicability in the USA*, Gent.

Schweder, R.A. - R. A. LeVine (eds.)
1984 *Culture Theory. Essays on Mind, Self, and Emotion*, Cambridge.

Waal Malefijt, A. de
1974 *Images of Man. A History of Anthropological Thought*, New York.

Walters, R.G.
1980 'Signs of the Times: Clifford Geertz and the historians', In: *Social Research* 47, 537-556.

THE CONCEPT OF PERSON: SOME HEURISTICAL NOTES

Andy F. Sanders

1. *Looking for a problem*

What to expect from a philosophical contribution to a multi-disciplinary enquiry into something so utterly basic as the concept of person? As with other basic things, we feel that this concept is highly complex and therefore difficult to analyse. Arthur Danto points out at least one reason for this: 'Neither in common usage nor in philosophy has there been a univocal concept of "person"' (cf. Danto: 1967, 110). A further, and strongly argued for, reason is given by P. Strawson, who maintains that it is logically primitive: 'The concept of person is logically prior to that of an individual consciousness' (cf. Strawson: 1959, 103). Indeed, philosophical traditions from past and present, non-Western and Western, offer a staggering number of more or less rival theories, ideas and insights which implicitly or explicitly deal with that concept. Before singling out a problem for further discussion, let us briefly consider a number of possible questions one might wish to raise.

For example, 'What are the truly essential characteristics of a person?' is quite different from, say, 'What are the necessary conditions for any ascription of states of consciousness to anything?' or 'Why are one's states of consciousness ascribed to the very same thing as certain corporeal characteristics?' (Strawson: 1959, 90, 106). A question like 'What is a person?' may be interpreted in quite distinct ways. For instance, we may understand it as a rather ambiguous request for an answer to 'What is the meaning of "person"?'. The latter question can be concerned either with the reference or with the sense of the term 'person'. 'What kind of entities are referred to by the word "person"?', however, is again quite distinct from the question 'What are the main characteristics of the term "person"?', which concerns its sense, or senses. One might even go further with, say, 'What determines the true significance of being a person?' or 'What does it mean to be or to become a person?', which lead to even deeper questions concerning the value or purpose of being a person. Finally, 'What is a person?' may be also be construed as a problem concerning the factual characteristics of entities which count as persons. Perhaps we may also classify problems concerning the actual linguistic and social function of the term 'person' under this heading. Of course, the concern is not with the facts 'as such' (if there are any), but rather with what they signify. In any case, asking for the use or function of a concept inevitably brings in the conceptual scheme (framework or 'form of life') within which it has its proper place.

It is obvious that the problems are multiplied as soon as we go on asking questions concerning the reference, sense and significance of concept of person in other cultures. Let *P* be the nearest equivalent of the English word 'person' in some alien culture *C*. Then, say, 'How is *P* used in culture *C* at time *t*?' is a question that cannot be tackled by common analytical means alone. The more specific the problems are, the more relevant factual information (linguistic, psychological, sociological, historical) about the behaviour of people of different cultures and epochs becomes. As soon as the questions become purely empirical or historical, the anthropologist or historian will have to take over. Not merely because of the sound principle of the division of labour, but because on at least one rather common understanding of his practice, the philosopher takes himself to be primarily concerned with conceptual analysis and not, or at least not directly, with questions of historical, sociological, psychological, etc., fact. This is neither to say that facts are not relevant to philosophical inquiry, nor that conceptual analysis is irrelevant to historical or anthropological research. After all, historians and anthropologists not only implicitly make all kinds of philosophical assumptions, they are in their research directly concerned with the problem of understanding the meaning of concepts used by people from other cultures.

The field of common interest may even be enlarged by invoking problems of method. 'How to analyse the concept of person?' would be a case in point. More specifically, this problem could be given the following form: 'What symbols, rituals, etc., should we select for study in order to find an answer to the question of how the concept of person is used in culture *C* at time *t*?'. If I take him correctly, Y. Kuiper regards this meta-problem as even the main challenge. According to him, the anthropological issue is not primarily to define 'person' in terms of, or relative to, the conceptual scheme embedded in the language of particular culture, but rather 'to find it' (cf. Kuiper: 1989, 42). Though it is not quite clear what the difficulty is, I assume that it is a problem of heuristics, and what is interesting about it is not so much the possibility of a some general solution, but rather why it is a problem in the first place.

Taking Kuiper's problem of heuristics as my main concern, I shall now proceed as follows. In section 2 I shall briefly consider some aspects of the problem of defining the concept of person. Before starting to look for its meaning and use in alien cultures, it seems useful to inquire after our own employment of it, if only because it is against the background of our own knowledge and understanding of what counts as a person that we have to approach other uses and conceptions of it. Philosophical analysis is useful here because it gives us at least some clues to the problem of how and where to find the concept of person in our own culture. If this already proves to be a highly complex and intricate affair, we have little reason to suspect that its function in other cultures will be much easier to analyse, let alone to understand. Next, I shall extend the analysis in section 3 by briefly considering the use of 'person' in what I take to be its more overt, cultural and social dimensions, namely in the sense of 'personality'. In order to provide at least some clues to the heuristic problem I shall introduce in section 4 the notions of intentional network and background, as recently developed by J.R. Searle.

2. *The problem of defining 'person'*

A common way to define some concept *X*, is to define the intension (sense, connotation, *Sinn*) of *X*. The extension (reference, denotation, *Bedeutung*) of *X* is simply the class of things or entities which have the properties as specified by its intension. Notice that as far as intension and extension are concerned, the distinction as such between them is neutral with respect to the culture, language or conceptual framework within which *X* may have its proper setting. Thus, the criteria for personhood (intension) and, hence, also the things to which it refers, may to a certain extent vary as between different cultures, their practices, languages and the conceptual schemes embedded in them. Apart from the fact that there is nothing here which suggests that intension and extension are essentially or uniquely determined, also notice that the individual entities which are proper members of the extension of *X*, need not really exist. For example, 'Kierkegaard's wife' has a perfectly good sense but, for all we know, no reference. Equally good sense is made by, say, 'UFO', 'extra-terrestrial life', 'witch', 'ghost', 'photon', etc., but whether they refer to real entities still is a matter of considerable dispute.

Trying to specify the extension and intension of the concept of person is, of course, by no means easy. This already becomes clear as soon as we consider the various ways in which it is used in our own ordinary language. For instance, in *The Shorter Oxford English Dictionary* we find the following list of lexical meanings of 'person':

> (I) A part played in a drama, or in life; hence, function, office, capacity; guise, semblance; character in a play or story.
> (II) An individual human being; a man, woman or child.
> (III)(1) The living body of a human being; either (a) the actual body, as distinct from clothing, etc., or from the mind or soul, or (b) the body with its clothing, etc.
> (2) The actual self of a man or woman, individual personality.
> (IV) *Law.* A human being (*natural p.*) or ... corporation (*artificial p.*) having rights or duties recognized by law.
> (V) *Theological.* (a) Applied to the three modes of the divine being in the Godhead ... which together constitute the Trinity. (b) The personality of Christ, esp. as uniting the two natures, divine and human.
> (VI) *Grammatical.* Each of the three classes of pronouns, and corresponding distinctions in verbs.
> (VII) *Zoological.* Each individual of a compound or colonial organism.

A few remarks on this list of various, but intricately connected, uses of the term 'person' seem in order. Except for the specialised zoological use (VII) of 'person', each of these lexical meanings had occurred already (in English) before 1600. Setting aside the grammatical (VI) and zoological uses, (II) and (III) are probably the ordinary everyday use: a person is an individual human being, conceived either as a tangible bodily form or as a less tangible 'self' or individual personality, or both. Note, however, that if (III.1) and (III.2) is not an exclusive disjunction, a person does not have to have a (human) body. Moreover, there seems to be a conceptual connection with the original theatrical sense (I). An individual may speak or act as himself ('in person') or as an actor. He or she may also act in a certain capacity, function, or office. According to Danto, the latter leads in the legalistic direction because rights, and, we may add, duties go with offices (cf. Danto: 1967, 111). On the other hand, the legal sense (IV) is clearly parasitic on (II). As Teichman points out, individual human beings are the first, and most basic, subjects of legal and moral rights; artificial persons have legal rights ascribed to them only by analogy (cf. Teichman: 1985, 179).

The legal, and the connected moral, sense is no doubt a very important one. Notice, however, that these uses entitle us to say that the extension of the concept of person includes both individual human beings and, at least within legal contexts, corporate beings (corporations, trade unions, universities, etc.). If the theological use (V) may be broadened into a more general religious one, we have to include still another category of things which fall under the concept: divine persons, disembodied spirits and 'super-human' beings. And again, if (III) is not to be understood as an exclusive disjunction, creatures from outer space with a consciousness like ours, also have to count as (non-human) persons. Again, whether gods, angels, spirits or extra-terrestrials really do exist, is a matter of dispute, but if they exist, they too are persons.

What about the intension? One can easily agree with Teichman's conclusion that 'the term "person" has several interconnected senses' (Teichman: 1985, 184). But it is quite obvious that we are not even remotely near a specification of the intension of our concept. A full blown analysis of but one of its senses would vastly exceed the limits and scope of this paper. The notions of individual, self-consciousness, personality, legal and moral rights and the ones we normally employ in explaining them (e.g., animal, consciousness, substance, mind, body, identity, God, etc.) are about as complex as the concept of person itself.

Still, at least two general points can be made. Since different senses of 'person' determine different classes of beings, it follows that we have to beware of stipulative definitions. For the question as to what entities count as persons is not merely a classificatory one, but one that is of considerable social and moral significance. If an individual human being lacks, or has in an insufficient degree one or more of the defining characteristics of the concept of person, it follows that he or she is not, or is less of, a person and need not be treated as such.

For example, if a person is an individual human being that is aware of itself as existing over time, a human foetus does not count as a person. As De Beaufort has shown, some moral philosophers have wrongly argued on the basis of this definition that killing a foetus or a baby of less than, say, one month old, is morally equally permissible (cf. De Beaufort: 1985, 156f). Similar examples concerning medical practice can be easily multiplied. Another example may be taken from daily social life. If within some society the criteria for personhood were to become progressively interchangeable, or even identified with, superficial and secondary characteristics of what popularly counts as a 'personality', it is only to be expected that individual human beings who seem to be lacking in social standing, wealth, looks etc., would be held in less esteem and treated with less respect than those who do possess these things. Though standards of what counts as a person are explicitly stated in law, the question as to what are the correct standards for determining the degree of respect in which human beings *qua* persons should, at least *prima facie*, be held, is undoubtedly a moral and a normative one.

The second point concerns the interpretation of the philosophical sense of 'person' which the *Oxford English Dictionary* defines as 'a self-conscious or rational being'(cf. Teichman: 1985, 178). Teichman points out that this definition is capable of more than one interpretation. It might mean that each individual human being must be rational or self-conscious or both, or else, that (s)he 'must belong to a species typified by rationality or self-consciousness or both' (Teichman: 1985, 181). The first reading implies that people who display no signs of self-consciousness or rationality are not persons, and is likely to give rise to the view that only white Anglo-Saxon (Dutch, South African, etc.) Protestants really matter. Somewhat similar seems the Javanese view, reported by Geertz, that 'to be human is to be Javanese' (cf. Geertz: 1965, 116). On the second reading, however, this consequence does not follow. If a human being is not in fact rational, he or she still counts as a person in virtue of his or her belonging to a rational kind. Because it is not only in accordance with the ordinary and juridical senses of 'person', but also with our moral intuitions, the second interpretation, I suggest, is to be preferred.

If, as I said, at least some defining characteristics of 'person' allow of degrees, this implies that personhood may come in degrees. To see the point of distinguishing between degrees of personhood, I suggest we briefly consider the relation between the notions of person and personality.

3. *Person and personality*

Let me state at the outset that introducing the notion of degrees of personhood is not to deny the moral ideal, acknowledged in the Universal Declaration of Human Rights, that each human individual is to be treated with due respect in virtue of his or her inherent dignity. My point concerns personhood in the sense of 'individual personality'. Obviously, 'person' and 'personality' are not equivalent in meaning. For instance, persons, but not personalities, are said to have inalienable rights. One and the same person can be said to have multiple personalities, but it is rather odd to speak of one and the same personality having more persons. How should we distinguish between them?

Mackie takes 'personality' as a term belonging to psychological theory and distinguishes between three senses it has within that context, namely: referential, dispositional and descriptive. It may be used to denote a supposed psychic structure or organization underlying a person's dispositions, as a general term for these dispositions (to have a personality is to have a set of dispositions), or merely to describe a person's behaviour (cf. Mackie: 1985, 5f). In 4 I shall come back to what Mackie calls the referential use of the term. My present concern is with the uses that concern publicly recognizable and socially conditioned patterns of human behaviour.

According to De Wilde, one ,should distinguish between (*i*) the intrinsic value (dignity, *Würde*) of a person and (*ii*) the relative value (*Preis*) of a personality (cf. De Wilde: 1951, 135). The point of this distinction is, of course, a moral one. Interestingly, De Wilde then goes on to define 'personality' as 'the developed and developing person'. Thus, it is personhood *qua* individual personality that allows of degrees and requires a cultural or social context within which this developing can take place. However, the notion of development not only carries a connotation of process, but also allows of degrees. Consequently, without denying that persons are equal in the sense of having an intrinsic value, personhood in the sense of personality comes in degrees, and this raises the question as to the function of 'full' or 'ideal' persons. In an admittedly rather pedestrian way, I would like to point out the following.

First, a disclaimer. Introducing the notion of ideal personhood is by no means to suggest that we should strive exclusively for the ideal of general theoretical understanding. Geertz may well be right in warning us that the result of a quest for this ideal is that living detail is drowned in dead stereotype which precludes us from taking seriously the relevant differences between individuals and groups of individuals. To look for ideal personhood in a culture neither implies a search for some 'underlying, unchanging, normative type', nor is it to construct some image of man as an archetype, 'with respect to which actual men .. are but reflections, distortions, approximations' (cf. Geertz: 1965, 114f). Rather, I wish to venture the hypothesis that, embedded in the specific cultural patterns which guide human life, paradigm cases of ideal personhood might play an important role. The life, deeds and sayings of 'ideal' persons as transmitted by, and embedded in, the historically created systems of meaning do have this role precisely because they give form, order, point, and direction to our lives. The ways in which they led their lives function as the paradigm examples or, to borrow Kuhn's term, the exemplary past achievements of a cultural tradition, and it is partly in terms of these examples that the meaning of what it is to be a person in a given culture is, and should be, understood. There are overwhelming quantities of historical fact about the matter, but if only for reasons of space, the question as to what constitutes ideal personhood for any particular culture cannot be considered here. Instead, I shall briefly develop my hypothesis by pointing out a few general consequences of the hypothesis.

First, though paradigm persons may embody ideal personhood to a very high, perhaps even to the highest degree, I suggest that their being exemplary paradigms itself functions as a never quite attainable limit to which 'normal' persons may strive in organizing and conducting their lives in a meaningful way. This seems to imply, next, that at any given period of time the actual manifestations of personhood can only partly be explained by reference to, or in terms of, the prevailing aesthetic, moral and/or religious standards. It is no doubt possible to specify some of them. But, as Polanyi has pointed out, in actual life and practice they function to a certain extent at a tacit or subsidiary level. That is to say, on account of their embeddedness in cultural frameworks, conceptual schemes, forms of life, practical and intellectual skills, these standards serve as maxims in the ongoing quest for the true ideal. Moreover, though the ideals are often said to remain the same, the way in which they are formulated often changes. Third, it seems clear that ideal personhood, in order to serve as a paradigm example for a given society, has to pertain to, not just any, but certain specific aspects of personality, e.g., specific traits of character, social status, abilities, skills, achievements, etc.

For instance, it might be crucially important for one's social prestige to have acquired or achieved things like, say, a Ferrari, more than two wives or husbands, a large herd of cattle, good health, a successful career or whatever. The degree to which a person has acquired things like these may be a criterion for one's personality as exhibiting cunning, intelligence, wisdom, prudence, good fortune, high birth, smooth relations with the gods or simply hard work. However, a person may be known as a great scientist, artist, politician or philosopher, but at the same time lack certain traits of character which make him or her in a sense less exemplary *qua* personality. That is, a person may be held in great esteem for being a great scientist, artist, etc. and therefore count as the concrete embodiment of excellence for a particular social practice. However, to count as an exemplary person for a culture at large this is perhaps neither necessary, nor sufficient.

Limitations of space and relevance make it unprofitable to embark on a discussion of what virtues and vices one might have to possess in order to count as an 'exemplary' personality within a particular culture. What I wish to propose for consideration and further inquiry is the idea that one way to look for, and find, the uses of the concept of person within a particular culture might be to inquire after the ideal, or ideals, of personhood which happen to exist within that culture.

No doubt it is something of a truism to point out that what counts as exemplary or ideal within local culture C_1 might differ markedly from the ideal in C_2. In the light of our heuristic problem, however, this is not merely stating the obvious. If the personality of a human being may be found to be more or less defective, virtuous, superficial, developed, interesting, profound, powerful, or whatever it is not only proper, but also fruitful to raise the question 'In respect to what?', that is, to inquire after the ideal standards both from a descriptive and a normative point of view.

Let us now return to our heuristic problem. So far, the difficulty of finding the characteristics which have to be included in the intension of the concept of person only seem to confirm Kuiper's premonitions as to the unfruitfulness of aiming at instant definitions of concepts of person. This should not surprise us, for its complexity matches that of, say, the concept of culture. From a holistic point of view, at least one good reason for this seems to be that the notions can only be adequately explained in terms of each other. To find the concept of person is to find the (local) culture within which it has its function.

4. *On where to look for the concept of person*

Why, then, is it so difficult to find the ways in which the concept of person is used? The reason, already alluded to, is that even in order to understand our own use of the concept, we have to invoke what Michael Polanyi calls the 'tacit dimension' (cf. Polanyi: 1958, Pt. II; 1967, ch. 1). Since part of what Polanyi has in mind can be reconstructed and elucidated by drawing on J.R.Searle's recent account of intentionality, I shall for brevity's sake only concern myself with the latter (cf. Searle: 1983).

Normally, we are able to see, hear, feel, identify, recognize, believe, know, love, like, hate etc., etc., persons. Apart from all sorts of physical characteristics, we ascribe to other persons and to ourselves actions and states of consciousness, such as intentions, sensations, feelings, emotions, thoughts, beliefs, perceptions, memories, etc., etc. According to Searle some, but not all, of these mental states are characteristically *intentional*: e.g. emotions, beliefs and intentions. Leaving out much that is not relevant to our purpose, the bare essentials of what Searle takes to be the nature of a (mental) intentional state can be stated as follows. Intentional states represent objects and states of affairs in the same sense of 'represent' that speech acts represent objects and states of affairs. The parallel between states and acts is derived from the fundamental thesis that the performance of a speech act 'is *eo ipso* an expression of the corresponding Intentional state' (Searle: 1983, 9). Thus, just as in the speech act a propositional content is expressed with a particular illocutionary force, so in an Intentional state a representative or intentional content is contained in a particular psychological mode (Searle: 1983, 15). For example, if someone believes that it is now snowing, the intentional content of his belief is a representation of a state of affairs, namely, that it is snowing. If you assert that it is snowing, then your assertion (speech act) represents that state of affairs in the same sense. Similar examples can be given for emotions (e.g., desire, fear) and intentions to do something.

Intentional states (representations) do not function in isolation but are part of, and stand in relation to, a large complex of other psychological states. Think only of the beliefs and desires that we normally understand someone to have when he or she forms the intention, say, to light a fire, open a door, wash a car or participate in a ritual. One does not normally form the intention to open a door without the belief that there is a door within reach, that it is closed, that one gets in or out a room through it, etc. Further, we would not understand someone who intends to become a door or to write a fire. One of the reasons for this, Searle tells us, is that we do not know how to fit such intentions into the network of intentional states.

Suppose we accept the hypothesis of a holistic intentional network and, next, try to specify all the beliefs contained in it. According to Searle (1983, 141f), this would be a hopeless endeavour. First, a great number of our beliefs, let alone other states of mind are submerged in the unconscious 'and we don't quite know how to dredge them up'. Second, intentional states do not individuate: we don't know, for example, how to count beliefs. Though Searle does not mention them in this connection, no doubt beliefs which are expressed in metaphorical and analogical discourse are included in the network also. The intentional contents of, say, Bororo beliefs expressed by 'we are red macaws', or those of the Christian belief 'God loves us as like a father loves his children' cannot exhaustively be specified in terms of complete propositions. Following Sperber, we might call these contents 'semi-propositional' (Sperber: 1982, 167ff). Third, even if we tried to list all our present beliefs, at some point we would encounter states which are in a sense too fundamental to qualify as beliefs. For example, one may find oneself holding proper beliefs, say, that there has been a Theological Faculty in Groningen since 1614, or that Admiral De Ruyter was not killed near Chatham in 1667. However, they should be distinguished from such stances or attitudes as 'objects offer resistance to touch', 'people only vote when awake' and 'elections are held near the surface of the earth'. These are Searle's examples, but in the light of our present theme we may just as well add: 'other persons are in many respects like me', 'I am a person', or 'persons are not trees'.

The point of the distinction between beliefs and stances or attitudes is important for two reasons. First, stances embody a kind of knowledge both of 'how things are' and of 'how to do things'. For instance, my stance that tables offer resistance to touch manifests itself in the fact that I know how to sit at a table, that I can write on a table, put stacks of books on tables, etc. Whatever one does at, on, or with tables, one does not normally think unconsciously to oneself: 'it offers resistance to touch'. The same, I suggest, goes for persons. One's attitudes or stances ('persons are not animals', 'other persons are at least *prima facie* worthy of respect') manifest themselves in the way in which one deals with, or treats, other persons.

An even more important reason for the distinction is that stances or attitudes normally lack the representational or intentional character of intentional states proper. We could, of course, treat 'tables offer resistance to touch', or 'I am a person', as beliefs, i.e. as a representations, but that is not to say that when such 'beliefs' are functioning, they are functioning as representations (Searle: 1983, 157f). Rather, such stances are pre-intentional, and taken together they form part of a body of know-how which enables all representing to take place. The hypothesis that this body of know-how exists, is called 'the hypothesis of the Background' and a minimal geography of it includes at least both a local and a deep Background. The 'deep' Background comprises a) all of those capacities that are common to all normal human beings in virtue of their biological make-up (e.g., eating, drinking, walking, perceiving, recognizing, etc., etc.) and b) pre-intentional stances (towards the solidity of things, the independent existence of objects and other people). The 'local' Background includes the know-how (e.g., opening doors, drinking beer from bottles, etc.) and the stances (e.g., towards refrigerators, cocktail parties, money, cars, etc.) embodied in local cultural practices (Searle: 1983, 143f).

The Searlean Background, then, is to be conceived as a set of non-representational mental capacities, abilities, skills, stances, and practices, that underly the Intentionality of the mind in the sense that they enable, but do not determine, all representation. However, the metaphor of underlying should not deceive us, for, says Searle, 'the Background is not on the *periphery* of Intentionality but *permeates* the entire Network of Intentional states' (Searle: 1983, 151).

Where does this leave us in respect to our heuristic problem? First, on the assumption that Searle's hypothesis of the Background is plausible, it seems to me that we can only gain access, so to speak, to the concept of person *via* the pre-intentional stances and attitudes that people may adopt to each other *qua* persons. The interesting point is that

Searle addresses himself to the question as to how we can best study the Background. In his view it is most useful to study it in cases of breakdown, that is, 'cases where Intentional states fail to achieve their conditions of satisfaction because of some failure in the set of pre-intentional Background conditions on Intentionality' (Searle: 1983, 155; 115). A breakdown in 'how to do things' would occur, for example, if you were to attempt to swim, and find yourself suddenly unable to. Suppose you have been able to swim since early childhood. Obviously, both your belief that you are able to swim has been falsified and your intention to swim has been frustrated. However, the failure is not due to either one of these intentional states, rather, it is your capacity to swim, which is neither an intention nor a belief, that has failed you.

Second, Searle's examples seem to suggest that breakdowns in the functioning of the Background are often suprising because they concern things of which we are, to borrow Polanyi's idiom, most of the time only tacitly aware. It seems to me that a parallel can be drawn in the case of present subject. For instance, when a woman's desire to be treated as a person gets frustrated, her fundamental stance or knowledge of 'how things are', viz., that she is a person, is, in a sense, falsified. This says something, not only of that particular woman, but of the society in which she lives. In the case of alien cultures this seems to suggest that it will not suffice to look merely for the rather obvious *differentia* in the social behaviour of their members. It may well be that we can learn much from these differences compared with our own culture, particularly when they falsify, or contradict, our own stances and attitudes as regards persons. If Searle is right, however, and if we really wish to know the manner in which the members of alien cultures conceive of each other and themselves as persons, we should look for, and try to understand, breakdowns in their own Background. I am not quite sure whether this requires that we have to become members of their societies. But even if it does not, the task of understanding them as persons will not be less demanding than that of understanding ourselves.

Bibliography

Beaufort, I.D. de
1985 *Ethiek en medische experimenten met mensen*, Van Gorcum, Assen.

Danto, A.C.
1967 'Persons'. In: P. Edwards (ed.), *The Encyclopedia of Philosophy*, Macmillan/Free Press, Vol. 6, London/New York, 110-114.

Geertz, C.
1965 'The Impact of the Concept of Culture on the Concept of Man'. In: J.R. Platt (ed.), *New Views on the Nature of Man*, Univ. of Chicago Pr., Chicago/London, 93-118.

Kuiper, Y.B.
1989 'The Concept of Person in American Anthropology. The Cultural Perspective of Clifford Geertz'. In: H.G. Kippenberg and others (eds.), *Concepts of Person in Religion and Thought*, Mouton, New York/Berlin.

Mackie, J.L.
1985 *Persons and Values. Selected Papers*, (eds. J. Mackie - P. Mackie), Oxford University Press, Oxford.

Polanyi, M.
1958 *Personal Knowledge. Towards a Post-Critical Philosophy*, Routledge & Kegan Paul, London.
1967 *The Tacit Dimension*, Doubleday Inc., New York.

Searle, J.R.
1983 *Intentionality. An Essay in the Philosophy of Mind*, Cambridge University Press, Cambridge.

Sperber, D.
1982 'Apparently Irrational Beliefs'. In: M. Hollis - S. Lukes (eds.), *Rationality and Relativism*, Blackwell, Oxford, 149-180

Strawson, P.F.
1959 *Individuals. An Essay in Descriptive Metaphysiscs*, Methuen, London.

Teichman, J.
1985 'The Definition of Person', in: *Philosophy* 60, 175-185.

Wilde, A. de
1951 *De Persoon. Historisch-systematisch onderzoek naar de betekenis van het persoonssymbool*, Van Gorcum, Assen.

RELIGIOUS TRADITIONS AND THE HUMAN PERSON

Michel Meslin

The linking of the terms 'tradition' and 'person' may seem to establish a tension, a radical incompatibility even. For our Western conception of man remains more or less profoundly marked by the belief in continuous progress, in a liberating development of the individual which would be restrained, if not blocked, by the force and weight of traditions which are thought to be out of date. Has not the irresistible rise of individualism - by which modern man has been characterized until recently - definitively relegated the mere idea of tradition to the past? No human society, however, can deny the imperative need man feels to examine his past, to return to his origins. This holds as much for archaic and 'traditional' societies - where the collective memory performs an important social function by transmitting the myths that regulate the whole of social life and which, by sacralizing it, justify it - as for 'historic societies', where the historical memory is continuously and progressively relived, where the continual reference to a tradition is present and plays an active role.

On the other hand, we begin to realize that the hypersocialization and rapid materialization of our present-day world impose singular limits on the development of the human person. Do religions - still presenting themselves as a double tradition of stereotyped gestures called 'rites', and of foundation myths and sacred scriptures containing mental images and values - have a particular role to play in favour of the person? For their success seems to be the greater the more they offer a more adequate answer to man's questions, needs and desires, and the more they succeed in forming areas of contestation and protest against the outrages of a society that is felt to be alienating. But what is a person?

The concept of person is one of the most difficult concepts to define - even though it is always burdened with hopes and revendications. It is neither a simple fact, nor evident throughout human history. A large number of societies still function without this concept, which was solemnly ratified in the 1945 Charter of the United Nations - apparently as one of the essential foundations of this organization. Actually, the concept of the person is bound up with a society's adjudication of a certain amount of rights, prerogatives and knowledge to the individual.

On the face of it, then, one might think that every totalitarian society excludes the free development of the human person, and that, conversely, every liberal and democratic society would favour it. Historical reality, however, is much more complex. Yet it is true that the contemporary experience of totalitarian régimes has shown us the importance of this dialectical tension between the person and the state. Karl Jaspers, among many others, has emphasised that the transcendental value of the human person surpasses the value of political society, notwithstanding the constraints it can exert. Once the concept of the person is formulated and lived through - even by a small number of individuals - it works as a factor of modification, change, evolution and, often, progress. Indeed, as an individual who is part of a particular society every man gets in touch with the social, but as a person he can escape from the alienating constraints of the group and from the tyranny of the social. Here it is appropriate to call to mind Simone Weil's (1972, 184) striking remark: 'Il n'y a que par l'entrée dans le transcendant, le surnaturel, le spirituel authentique que l'homme devient supérieur au social'. That is exactly why religious traditions play an indispensable part in the development of the human person.

But what is a tradition? Not a collection of practices from a distinct age whose existence would be merely folkloristic, whose interest would be merely tourist - that is a plural, derived sense of the word. Tradition is a complex of attitudes and conducts that guide present actions by referring to the past. In every society the past constitutes the very sense of the present, without the slightest discontinuity in time, without the past being over and done with. Tradition is the awareness of a human group, that one and the same principle of identity links one generation with the other and that - this principle still being operative - it permits people to live and stay themselves throughout a history that is a source of change. Remember Pascal:

> De sorte que toute la suite des hommes pendant le cours de tant de siècles doit être considérée comme un même homme qui subsiste toujours et qui apprend continuellement. (Brunschvicg: 1904, 80)

But does not religion then run the risk of being nothing but a simple, conservative memory of ancient values which appear to be fundamental to the human group or, in the case of religious values, to a community of believers? Here Paul Claudel's imagery appears to be relevant. Tradition, he says, is like a man walking; the only way he can move is by keeping one foot on the ground and raising the other one. If he were to keep both his feet on the ground he would not be able to move, and if he were to lift both of them he would fall. Every tradition is at the same time continuity and progress; it is the memory of an experience acquired to enrich the present. That is what M. Blondel proved to understand so well when he spoke of

> ...cette puissance conservatrice et protectrice qui est en même temps instructrice et initiatrice. Tournée amoureusement vers le passé où est son trésor elle va vers l'avenir où est sa conquête et sa lumière. (Blondel: 1904, 145f)

Indeed, as the etymology of the Latin word *traditio* clearly demonstrates, our word tradition covers two distinct realities: the transmission to someone of a model of life, of a wisdom he did not yet have, and the content of that which is transmitted. In the case of religious traditions, the content is a complex of symbolic values that inform myths and rites, and whose meaning must be unveiled - a body of doctrines to be taught, a belief to be explained. It is appropriate, then, to distinguish carefully between the act of transmitting and that which is communicated to all the members of the community and which becomes their common property - the principle of identity and the model of action by which they can recognize one another. Consequently, it is not so hard to understand why every tradition is educative: it takes charge of the individual and teaches him a discipline of life in accordance with the rules of his community: it unveils the meaning of life to him, starting from the experience of a reality which is an everyday assumption of religious beliefs. Essentially it is a life, at the same time transmitted and received.

But how is this transmission effected? As tradition does not exist outside a social group, and as religious traditions do not exist outside a community of believers, it is evident that this tradition can only be transmitted to those who join that group or community in accordance with the precise rules of initiation. It is in this intrinsic relationship between tradition and initiation that the development of the human person is to be found. Initiation is a complex of highly symbolic rites and ethical-practical instructions that aim at acquiring a certain wisdom which is founded on initial knowledge and which results in a modification of the social or religious status of the individual. After having been initiated and having received the traditional instructions, the individual changes - but he does not become somebody else - for henceforth he will live a life that is founded on different values: values that have been revealed to him.

This holds for all rituals of initiation which ensure the passage of boys and girls from the world of childhood into the adult world, and prepare them to assume their social responsibilities. Strictly organized by the ethnic community which refers to its own tradition, those initiations aim at socializing the individual, who is cut off from the world of childhood and instinct, by revealing to him sexuality, death (symbolically), and the sacred at the same time. Indeed, these rites teach him to pass from a natural, unrestrained sexuality expressed whenever and however it is prompted by uncontrolled impulses to a sexuality which is ritualized and purified, because it is voluntarily regulated and sublimated by the community. In this sense, initiation in traditional societies consists in revealing to each individualhis or her proper male or female identity.

Unlike these rites of social aggregation, initiation into a religious community is free, open to all ages. It marks the passage from one, natural stage of life to a different, sacralized, supernatural stage which presupposes a more or less explicitly affirmed, but always subjacent, soteriological dimension. In this the role of symbols is particularly important, for they mediate the passage into Being initiation consists in, and make it significant. It is the symbol that provides the real sense of rites: the symbolism of nudity, for example, goes with the initiate's obligation to keep everything that has been revealed to him secret. 'When we are naked, we have no words', as Ogotemmêli, the wise Dogon, explained to Marcel Griaule (1966, 77). Or, to mention another example, the symbolism of kaolin paintings in African initiation, of wearing white clothes after the handing down of the Symbol of faith in the ancient Christian Church.

Consequently, that which is transmitted by tradition is always heritage. The authenticity of the wisdom conveyed and the validity of the model proposed to present action are guaranteed by the fact that he who passes them on received them from a qualified master who, in turn, owed it to a predecessor - and so on, back to the founder of the school, the sect or the religion. Ever since Greek antiquity the idea of *diadokhè*, of succession, has been fundamental to, and almost identical with, the core of all religious traditions. It makes the spiritual master the custodian of that heritage and the guarantor of spiritual continuity. In Christianity this idea is to be found in apostolic succession, from which all episcopal legitimacy originates, as in the succession of Hassidic *Tzadiks* in the 18th and 19th centuries. It is this same idea that justifies the Zen master's investiture of enlightened disciples. In the *tariqa*, the Islamic fraternities, this idea is to be found in the *silsila*, the uninterrupted chain that links the initiate to God through the mediation of his *sheikh*. From this general fact proceeds the particularity of the relationships that unite the spiritual master, who is the keeper of tradition, and his disciples. The disparity in their ages makes connotations of kinship possible.

The Father or Mother who introduces the initiate into the religious community thereby ushers those who follow their instructions into a new existence - just as parents guide the first steps of their little children. By initiation into the tradition the neophytes are new born. Such a metaphor can be found both in the *Vodoun* or Candomblé and in Hinduism - 'The Master is pregnant with the neophytes', says the *Satapatha Brahmana* (11,5,4) - as well as in the writings of Peter (1 Pe.2,2) and Paul (1 Cor.3,1-2; 2 Cor.6,13) and in those of John. On the spiritual level the initiates experience by their new birth, which symbolizes their entry into the religious tradition, a dependence that is analogous to the biological dependence on their parents.

Initiation thus functions against the stream of time the initiate experiences physically: his entry into the Tradition invites him to experience a kind of existential flash-back, a return to the original past which is sometimes ritually marked by a symbolic *regressus ad uterum*. It is by entering into a different time dimension that the entry of the individual into the tradition comes about. Indeed, it often involves anamnestic practices that enable the neophyte to discover his true identity by recalling the primordial time from which he derives his origin, and to which he is connected by the succession of the spiritual masters: the last of them has just borne him into a new life.

One of the clearest examples of this can be found among the Aranda of Australia in the rites that surround the handing over of the *tjurunga* to the newly initiated. When 'he hears the truth for the first time' the Master reveals to him that he, in turn, has become the reincarnation of the founding hero, the chief of the clan, and that, consequently, from now on he has to see to it that the clan's traditions - which were kept by his parents and which he, in turn, will have to transmit to others- will be maintained. His *tjurunga* is the tangible sign that now he has entered the *altjira*, 'the dream-time', where he will find his mythical ancestor, who is the model for all his actions. As Strehlow has justly remarked, by entering into the *altjira*, the very tradition of his people, man relives the biography of his mythical hero as a recital of his own actions from the mythical beginnings at the dawn of all life, when the world in which he is living now was given shape, onwards (Strehlow: 1957, 119-122; Berndt: 1946, 138).

The role of a memory of sacred things is essential: it permits the discovery that this world has a secret meaning that man can only know by going back, by means of the tradition, to the origins, by recalling the sacred history of his family and clan. It is this memory that makes the world real and, by sacralizing it, invests it with meaning. Man's one and only function, then, is to maintain the cohesion of this world by incessantly repeating, in each individual existence, the events of the Dream-Time. This past is always a lived-through present, for man has the duty to repeat the actions of the founding heroes and ancestors at every moment in his life. Through him they continue to build the very history of the human group. This anamnesis sets the individual in a time that is never a mere unchanging and permanent present, but rather a time of the very principles of life. The time of tradition which the *tjurunga* symbolizes is certainly a past time, but it informs every moment of the present time by making its existence possible. The scrupulous respect for tradition, then, brings back into existence a latent past that becomes present.

This is, of course, a borderline case of the most archaic societies one can observe, where the omnipotent tradition fertilizes man's time to realize, by sacralizing it, a balanced life and adjustment to his environment, thus warranting the well-being of the individual, his family and his group. But everything we know about other traditional societies proves to us that it is actually through the part he plays in religious rituals that the individual - who does not exist except in and through his clan- appears as something that is, in a way, autonomous and detached from it from the very moment he wears a mask: he really is *persona* then, the god present.

In these societies the valorization of individual trials outside rites of passage and religious initiation have contributed to a greater awareness of the person. As Ruth Benedict puts it: 'there is no antinomy between society and the individual'. Some traditional societies even know systems of initiation in which the putting into practice of ancestral traditions leads the individual to a true theomorphosis. In his study of 'the societies of Bambara initiation' D. Zahan has clearly demonstrated how much the integration into *korè* aims at achieving perfection in man's relation with his God (Zahan: 1960). Initiation forms an experience that is enriched every day because it is an uninterrupted deepening of the person, a progressive incarnation of the God in man, the latter staying in the world. The new man, reborn after initiation, then has to grow and mature, for he does not possess the totality of his being. He is called to take possession of all divine principles, by experiencing identification with God - a truly mystical experience. In black Africa, as well as in other human societies, the person is never a natural *datum*. In fact it is the product of a history that is peculiar to everyone, that is realized within the frame of tradition. It is '...l'histoire d'un *je-avec* qui est conscience de soi, de l'autre et du Tout-Autre' (Agossou: 1982, 239).

One could mention many other examples that demonstrate that tradition inserts itself into the particular history of the human being who receives it and to whose transformation it contributes. In fact, it offers him a particular way of participating in the world surrounding him, a regulation of inter-human relationships, and gives him access to the divine. It performs an educative function, by shaping his spiritual evolution. For tradition is permanence of the past in an individualized present with a particular future already turning up. It would be a mistake, then, to think that every religious tradition is nothing but the ritual and quasi-mechanical transmissian of an inert stock of lore, ossified by the past. On the contrary, it is the communication of a wisdom, a belief, by one subject to another - both living and being inserted in history. Therefore, the spiritual master who gives the instruction cannot make an abstraction of himself, as if he were a robot, nor can he who receives his instruction avoid, by incorporating it, adding quite a bit of himself to it.

The religious tradition appears to be a process that is alive in two ways: not only because it is inseparable from the particular histories of those who transmit and those who receive, but also because both of them are inserted in the history of their time, their society and culture. Tradition is the continuity of a wisdom and a faith received from the Fathers, the ancestors. But this continuity is a historical continuity: in order to remain meaningful the forms have to change, to renew and enrich themselves with the input of each generation, whereas the contents remain identical and permanent: *non nova sed nove*. In essence tradition consists as much in development as in memory. It is this continuous interaction of a past that is relived in the present which makes tradition - carried by living, historical people - something that is alive. Ignoring this living and diachronical aspect of each tradition leads to the mistake of believing, as R. Guénon did, that basically all religions and all philosophies have one primordial, esoteric and universal tradition which is more or less adapted to the cosmic religious, the transcendent divine and the natural knowledge of God, which leads to a superreligion for the initiated. In fact every religious tradition is absolutely inseparable from the culture in which it was conceived, whose concepts it has used and whose values it has adopted. It is this historical character of each religious tradition that enable us to determine its specific character and particular role.

This is clearly demonstrated in Judaism. The profound originality of Israel's religious experience consists in the certitude that its national past is the time of the Covenant with God, and that this time is interlarded with favours, the 'miracles' of Jahweh. The history of Jahweh's relationship with the people he has chosen is a truly sacred history, structured by divine interventions. Likewise, on the personal level 'the history of the soul' is the continually meditated memory of God's relationship with the faithful, the history of abandonments and returns that will succeed each other until the day of the eternal face to face.

In Christianity this is exactly the same. The Revelation of Jesus, Christ and Saviour, to the apostles constitutes the very stock of faith. It is the duty of each successive generation until the end of times to preserve that stock, while continually attempting to explicate, to reinvent permanently in order to explicate - by transmitting it - an unchanging truth, that is, the divine Word. The faith that animates the Christian people during their pilgrimage on earth - that long march of God's People from Abraham up to the *Parousia* - that faith, received from the apostles, constantly has to be brought into continuity with the life of the Christians themselves, to provide an answer to their questions, their needs, their desires. Christian Tradition is a living memory, not the nostalgia for a past that is believed to be preferable to the present. As early as 1930 J. Maritain, in his reflections on *Religion et Culture*, denounced

> ...l'erreur qui consisterait à rester attachés à des fragments du passé, à des moments de l'histoire immobilisés et comme embaumés par le souvenir et sur lesquels nous nous couchons pour dormir (Maritain: 1930).

Indeed, if there is the slightest touch of nostalgia in the Christian attitude informed by Tradition, it is nostalgia for the Eternal, and the desire to find - by and in the very heart of Tradition - the peace and quiet of the seventh day, 'the peace without night, without sleep' St. Augustine spoke of (*Confessions* XIII, 36). The Christian interpretation of existence is an interpretation of life in which God is perceived as he who comes unceasingly, he who opens an eternal future. No doubt the distinguishing mark of Christian tradition is this idea of adding something radically new to man's relationship with the divine. The youth and novelty of Christianity are themes Paul always returns to, as Clement of Alexandria (*Paedagogus*, I,20,3) explained: by its Lord the new, Christian people partake in an eternal spring that renews itself without ever growing old. For the novelty that tradition repeats incessantly is that man participates actively in his own salvation; because the Christian faith implies a renewal of his whole being, a complete *metanoia*.

Whether it is for humanity as a whole or for each individual member of it, Christianity has continuously asserted itself as an essential novelty, because the Incarnation of the divine Logos has come to set up a perfect life, in its definitive form, which the faithful will know after their terrestrial life, when they have returned into the glory of God. As St. Augustine, in very late antiquity, told the faithful in Hippo:

> [Christ] came when all things had grown old, and he has renewed you ... do not refuse to be rejuvenesced in Christ, who says to you: The world perishes, the world grows old, the world fails ... Do not fear, your youth will be renewed like the eagle's (Migne: 1978, 504f).

And, because it offers a wisdom and a way of life for present life, each religious tradition appears as the guarantee of an inner life by which man has access to the ontological dimension of a person. It does not thwart, in the name of outworn values, the development of the personality - on the contrary, it furthers it, by aiming at the unity of the human being and his God, by directing man's entire energy to a future where he will be free to meet at any moment the grace of Him who comes and in whose glory he will share; by leading him to the face to face that will never end.

Translation: David J. Bos

Bibliography

Agossou, J.M.
1982 'Anthropologie africaine et la notion de personne'. In: *L'Expérience religieuse africaine et les relations interpersonnelles*, ICAO, Abidjan.
Berndt, C.H.
1946 *The World of the First Australians*, Chicago.
Blondel, M.
1904 'Histoire et Dogme', in: *La Quinzaine* 56, 145ff.
Brunschvicg, L, (ed.)
1904-1914 *Oeuvres de Blaise Pascal*, Paris.
Griaule, M.
1966 *Dieu d'Eau. Entretiens avec Ogotemmêli*, Paris.
Maritain, J.
1930 *Religion et Culture*, Paris.
Migne, J.-P. (ed.)
1978 Aurelius Augustinus, *Sermones*. In: *Patrologia Latina* XXXVIII, Turnhout (Paris 1841).
Strehlow, J.G.H.
1957 *Aranda Traditions*, Melbourne.
Weil, S.
1972 *La Pesanteur et la Grâce*, Paris.
Zahan, D.
1960 *Le N'domo, le Korè*, Paris.

PART TWO
ANCIENT MEDITERRANEAN CONCEPTS OF PERSON

INTRODUCTION

The papers collected in this section show that the the process of explication of, and reflection upon, the traditional Mediterranean category of the person by ancient 'intellectuals'- e.g., philosophers and theologians - was closely linked to various social practices (e.g., actual behaviour, self-presentation and political legitimation). The Western concept of person therefore acquired its present logical structure and social function only very gradually. As L. Dumont (1985) has shown, Christianity made fundamental contributions to this development.

It was E.R. Dodds who came up with the bold and productive idea of analyzing the Greek concept of the person by means of an isolated case. The author of the *Iliad* and the *Odyssey* ascribed extraordinary irrational deeds to the influence of gods. The state of dazzlement in which Agamemnon stole Achilles's mistress had been inflicted upon him by the gods, who could directly influence human actions. In this way deviations from generally accepted behaviour were transferred to an external world. Non-rational impulses were excluded from man's self and attributed to non-human sources.

Dodds's treatment of this matter has been so fruitful because it enables us to understand the special nature of later philosophical and Christian-Gnostic anthropology. Characteristic of this anthropology was the notion of man as a composite being consisting of matter (*hyle*) - soul (*psyche*) - mind (*nous*). The irrational had become part of man and lived within him. The later developed conception of the person to be found in the writings of Boethius did not yet exist. This can be illustrated by a comparison made by the Gnostic philosopher Valentine. He compared man to an inn in which the soul lives on its own, or with the sinful demons or - and then salvation beckons - with the mind. What applies to the non-western cultures also applies to a great part of classical antiquity: an explicit and generally accepted concept of the person in the sense used by H.G. Hubbeling did not exist. The self was conceived as a conglomerate of conflicting elements.

The study of classical conceptions of the person therefore cannot be based on a presupposed explicit classical conception. One can attain one's end only indirectly and we have to bear in mind the fundamental fact that, no matter how different cultures and their language systems are, the individual acquires self-awareness only by becoming an object to others and by internalizing the attitude of others towards himself as social relation. This was G.H. Mead's basic insight, and it is still valid. The individual becomes an object to others by adopting social roles (the functional aspect) and by presenting his 'self' to others by cultural means. The difference between social roles (*personnage* in French) and the conception of the human self is crucial. Even when an elaborate concept of the person is missing (e.g., in Egypt) important insights into the Egyptian conception of the person can be gained from the ways in which the self is represented. H. te Velde's article deals with these means of representation, with concepts and rituals.

The concept of the person in a legal sense developed late in antiquity. It was not until the 3rd century A.D. that Greek *prosopon* acquired this meaning. When people wanted to lay down the rights and duties of a citizen they used the name of this citizen. The name was the most important means of representing the individual. This was taken for granted by Christian theologians, as has been pointed out by J. Daniélou (1973). In the first three centuries A.D. a unified concept of the person did not exist. When people referred to the Revelation of the infinite (*aperigraptos*) and ineffable (*arretos*) God they used the notion that the Word (*logos*) had defined itself, had named itself and had thus become the Son. Valentinian Gnostics expressed this as follows: 'The name of the Father is the Son'. Here a person's name had the same function the concept of the person would have in later times. H.G. Kippenberg's article deals with what (apart from the image) was the most important means of representing a human being: the name.

U. Berner demonstrates how, in the philosophy and religion of the 3rd century A.D., philosophers, by adopting an ascetic way of life, discarded their social identity in order to bring their life into harmony with reason as well as with faith. Social roles and cultural conceptions of the self began to diverge.

H.J.W. Drijvers describes this process in his article on saints' lives. These biographies reveal the concepts of the person current in late antiquity, which can be interpreted as models for human action. The classical dichotomy between matter and mind is a metaphor for the individual's relation to society. In this respect Drijvers's position comes close to Mead's idea of self-consciousness as awareness of being an object to others.

N. Elias, finally, draws attention to the relationship between the process of conscience-formation and the rise of certain forms of individualism in Ancient civilizations. In his essay Elias traces this development by focussing on the sociogenesis of attitudes towards death. This investigation leads to a critique of modern Western culture, especially its ideology of individualism.

SOME REMARKS ON THE CONCEPT 'PERSON' IN THE ANCIENT EGYPTIAN CULTURE

Herman te Velde

In his article on the concept of person in Western philosophy Hubbeling several times drew attention to the I-Thou relation of man to God as the starting-point or terminal point for an understanding of the concept 'person'. This I-Thou relation, which has a central place in the modern monotheistic religions, is also found in primitive and ancient near eastern religions. This has sometimes been greatly exaggerated, because it was thought that primitive and ancient eastern man had personal relations with all kinds of things in nature. Thus Wilson writes (1949, 49):

> The Egyptians might - and did - personify almost anything: the head, the belly, the tongue, perception, taste, truth, a tree, a mountain, the sea, a city, darkness, and death. But few of these were personified with regularity or with awe; that is, few of them reached the stature of demi-gods. They were forces with which man had the 'Thou' relation. And it is a little difficult to think of anything in the phenomenal world with which he might not have that relation as indicated in scenes and texts. The answer is that he might have the 'Thou' relation with anything in the phenomenal world.

However, closer examination of the available Egyptian textual and visual material often shows, at least as regards the Egyptian material referred to above (cf. Baines: 1985, 10) that the personifications are little more than metaphors - certainly with regard to the first three examples mentioned above - or speculative figures. When poets of Egyptian love songs let trees speak in their poems, this really does not mean that people, even when in love, have an I-Thou relation with trees. Egyptian gods and goddesses could indeed reveal themselves in trees, but one cannot deduce from this that Egyptians had an I-Thou relationship with trees as such.

Even if the personal relation of man with his god is not so central in the primitive and antique religions as in the modern monotheistic religions, it is not so surprising that the I-Thou relationship is found, not only in the Hebrew psalms and elsewhere in the Old Testament, but also in Egypt. This relationship is found in many religions, also in the Egyptian which, besides its differences, bears many resemblances to the Israelite religion. In Egypt this I - Thou relationship is found especially in the material concerning what is usually called personal piety. Especially from the second half of the history of the ancient Egyptian religion that comprises more than thirty centuries, i.e., which from the period after Akhenaten, we know many impressive documents of personal piety. We cannot treat these systematically here, and will only quote some parts of a text dating from the 13th century B.C., which was found a few decades ago in a tomb near Luxor (Abdul-Quader Muhammed: 1966, Pl. 58ff.; cf. Assmann: 1975, no. 173; Vernus: 1978, 144f.):

There was a man of Southern Heliopolis
a true scribe in Thebes,
whose name of his mother was Si-Mut (= son of Mut) and
who was called Kiki.
Now his god took notice of him
and instructed him in his wisdom.
He set him upon the way of life
to protect his body (also).
God knew him as a child
and assigned to him plenty and prosperity.

Then he took counsel with himself
to find a divine patron for himself
and he found that Mut is the best of the gods.
Talent and development lie in her hand
duration of life and breath of life lie under her command.
All that takes place is at her command.
He said: Behold, I give her my possessions and acquisitions
for I know that she is benevolent in my eyes
that she alone is trustworthy
that for me she causes fear to disappear
that she protects me in time of evil
that she comes with the north wind before her
when I call upon her name.
I am a pauper in her city
a needy pilgrim in her temple precinct.

...
I rejoice at thy strength
for thou art greater than any god whatever.
My heart is filled with my mistress.
I fear no human being.
When I lay me down, I can sleep
for I have a protectress.
Who makes Mut his protectress,
no god can attack him.
He has the favour of the king of his time
until he has reached the venerable state
(beatitude of the hereafter).

Who makes Mut his protectress
no evil touches him.
He is well protected at all times
until he joins the city of the dead.

Who makes Mut his protectress
how fair is his lifetime.
The favour of the king penetrates to the physical existence
of him
who has placed her in his heart.

Who makes Mut his protectress
blessed did he issue from his mother's body.
Good fortune is assigned to him at birth
and he will be venerable (in death).

Who makes Mut his protectress
how blessed is he who longs for her.
No god will cast him down
because he is one who does not know death.

Kiki begins to testify to 'his god' and 'god', who at first is still nameless, but to whom afterwards he ascribes the plenty and prosperity of the years of his childhood or youth. Then the time arrives of when he has to make a choice, when he confers with himself. He chooses the goddess Mut from all the gods to be considered in Thebes. The fact that at his birth his mother had already given him the name Si-Mut (son of Mut), indicates that this religious decision was not entirely unexpected. In the part not quoted above, he writes, among other things, that he has not chosen a human protector. He thought, or if one prefers a more serious phrase, he came to realize that for him this goddess was the one under whose care he could best put himself, so that it is to her that he gives all his possessions. In the beginning it is clearly stated that 'his god' has formed or taught him and has made him sensible or learned in his teaching or wisdom. Personal piety or devotion here proves to be not a matter of faith, but of knowing about the god and even a knowledge that has issued from the god. It is a matter of divine wisdom or teaching and human experience and human choice or action but not of faith. What is remarkable is the factual information that the goddess causes his fear to disappear and that at night he can sleep peacefully in her care. The relationship between this human being and his protectress is one of close attachment. Kiki calls himself poor, so that it is clear that the goddess gives him what he needs. The relation with her is his safeguard against evil. He finds favour with the king upon earth and becomes one of the venerable dead (*imakh*).

Being in favour with the king and attaining the status of a venerable dead person, represented in the document quoted above as following from the I-Thou relation with the divinity, are well-known desiderata in Egyptian culture and of great importance for an understanding of the Egyptian concept of a person, because in Egyptian culture life was to a very great extent determined - if we are to believe the official documents preserved - by the cult of gods, the cult of the king and the cult of the dead.

It is well known that in comparison with other cultures the Egyptian culture invested an unusual amount of exertion and attention in the cult of the dead. The Egyptian cult of the dead and everything belonging to it from mummies to pyramids, from books of the dead and all the rest of the funerary literature to plastic art and grave-gifts like the treasures of Tut-ankh-amen is directed to and centres around the person of the deceased. One might call the Egyptian cult of the dead personal glorification, if nowadays such a term did not suggest a specific political meaning and thus cause misunderstanding. Morenz (1969, 44ff.) put the Egyptian cult of the dead under the heading 'Personalität'. The human person that grew naturally and developed in history is preserved in the cult of the dead and raised to the highest possible status of the king and god Osiris.

In the cult of the dead death is negated by positing and bringing it about that a human being continues to exist as an honourable dead person (*imakh*). In the document of personal piety quoted above it is stated that man attains this status through the care of the deity. In the cult of the dead we usually find not only mere references to such a personal relationship with the deity, but also a separate more or less complete synopsis of how the person wishes to live on as an honoured one, i.e., who he is and what he is like and wants to be like as a person and what, in Egyptian opinion, is essential for a human person and his eternal life. It thus becomes evident that the person is not merely a spiritual being in relation with the deity or with himself, but also a social and corporeal being.

The familiar distinction between *signifiant* and *signifié*, or, as history of religions used to put it, between symbol and reality, is not always so easy to make when examining the Egyptian material. This clearly appears from, for instance, the meaning of a person's name in Egypt. Men and gods have a personal name. But some animals, that is some favourite animals, also have a proper name corresponding to the personal name of people. We know many names of dogs, a few of horses, but not a single name of a cat or a monkey, which apart from that were mummified just like humans, buried in a sarcophagus and had the ritual of opening the mouth carried out for them. These animals, which had names of their own and with whom their masters considered themselves to have a personal relationship, may, submissive as they were, nonetheless have been credited with a certain independence and individuality. Furthermore, personifications of lifeless objects, such as a pyramid, a temple, a gateway, etc., to which were given personal status, and over which the ritual of opening the mouth was also performed, could also have a special proper name.

How close the connection between the person and the name representing him was considered to be in Egypt, is evident from the phenomenon of the *damnatio memoriae*, by which certain pharaohs and other persons in Egypt were struck long before some Roman emperors. Names were deleted, scratched out, obviously to strike down the person himself. Names of criminals were altered to bring them into agreement with their owner's criminal personality.

Gods often have many names, pharaohs have five names, which may well be changed in the course of their rule. Humans have a name that was given them at birth, and sometimes a second name, the so-called 'beautiful name', which seems to have been given later. In the late period name and *ka*, and even the way of writing them, are increasingly confused and interchanged (Derchain: 1979, 4). The essential connection which is supposed to exist between *signifiant* and *signifié* is also evident from the countless puns on proper names in religious texts from early times till late. The Egyptians themselves seem to have regarded the name as an aspect of the person.

The grave and its equipment, varying from simple pots of food, a mirror, a weapon, to the many precious treasures, determine the status of the person. They are not merely a greater or lesser accumulation of material goods and possessions, but also have a personal aspect. Grave-gifts are gifts depending upon the favour of the kind and/or of others, although the owner of the grave already cares for the matter during his lifetime. Grave-gifts may bear the name of the departed, or sometimes also that of others and then especially of members of the family, ancestors or descendants. Especially images representing men and/or women in an idealized form, placed in the grave and later sometimes also in temples, are provided with the name, titles and sometimes (auto)biography of the deceased. To provide materially for the dead person was by modern standards sometimes an almost unimaginably costly matter. A sarcophagus alone was worth as much as a house (Morenz: 1969, 58). The grave and its equipment enable the dead to continue to exist as a person. It is difficult to determine in how far the grave and material grave-gifts do indeed present the person. In the two series of nine elements that seem to present the person in the tomb of Amenemhet, which dates from the time of the 18th Dynasty, 'this tomb that is in the necropolis' is expressly mentioned as a constituent element of the person (see below). One of the four *ka*-s particularly mentioned in late times is 'beautiful funeral' (see below). A person, at least a person belonging to the elite, seems not to have been complete and finished to the Egyptian mind without a tomb. Gods also have a tomb. Precisely because here we are far removed from the modern Western concept of a person, there is a great likelihood of misinterpreting the data. Egypt is the country of pyramids and mummies and we should consider whether there a tomb may not have been as important for a person or even more important than the I - Thou relation, consciousness of self, will, etc.

It becomes even more difficult to make a clear distinction between the person on the one hand and his social and material presentation in name and effigy on the other by means of the Egyptian source material when we pay attention to the person and the body. What has sometimes been called the most typical Egyptian custom, i.e., mummification, indicates that the Egyptians could not distinguish the person from the body. The body had to be preserved to guarantee the continued existence of the person. Cremation was only known as an exceptional punishment. If the body had accidentally been lost through fire or by drowning, one had to resort to magical spells to obtain a new body. Moreover, there was the fear of being chopped into bits or burned in the hereafter (Hornung: 1968, 10-36). There was an extensive funerary literature dealing with ways to avoid such dangers. On the other hand there was also, for instance, a rescue party at work in the hereafter to pull out of the water the bodies of people who had drowned, and whose bodies had therefore not been buried in the earth but had floated away; they were now brought ashore and thus preserved, according to the books of the netherworld Amduat, tenth hour, and Book of Gates, ninth hour (cf. Hornung: 1982, 137f.).

Two Egyptian words for body *(hc ; d*t) have, besides the principal meaning of body, also the secondary meaning of self. A third word for body *(ht)* has, besides the meaning of belly, also the wider meaning of inner life, the location of thoughts, feelings and memories (Assmann: 1982, 965). The body then is not just a body, but an aspect of the person from whom it cannot be separated. The flowering of sculpture in Egypt can in part be explained from the wish, the need and the forethought to provide the departed with extra bodies as standbys in the shape of images of wood, stone or other material marked with his name and titles. Something very noticeable is the attention paid to the body, not only at the end of life in mummification, but also during life in hair-style, cosmetics and dress both for men and women in such a way that the individual person is stylized into a type. De Buck (1928) already showed the great extent to which individuality comes to be hidden behind the typical in art and literature of Egypt.

In the remarks above about the specific individuality of the person from the material and physical point of view, we have already referred to the person's social symbol, i.e., his name. In addition to the name we usually see the titles of the offices that were held by the dead person and sometimes his genealogy written upon effigies, stelae, tomb walls, etc. This may be extended into an ideal autobiography in the first, sometimes in the third, and rarely in the second person. Biography is the oldest literary genre that we know in Egyptian literature, and it existed or flourished into Roman times (Van de Walle: 1975, 815). These biographies are by no means 'personal' ego-documents, but accumulations of always the same conventional phrases, offering not an individual but a typical, ideal, moral portrait of the dead person conforming to social relationships and living in favour with the pharaoh. Here the king personifies the category of social acknowledgement that makes someone a person and a grave-owner. The king bestows upon his officials their biography and their personality not only in the sense that he allows the description to be laid down forever in stone, but also because he has let his officials play the roles in well-ordered society that, summarized in the biography, belong to the perfected person in the way the departed wishes to live on in memory. The emphasis is always on the favour *(hswt)* of the king, of parents, of fellow men and later of gods (see the text from Kiki's tomb quoted above). Thus we may read in the tomb of Harkhuf (+ 2200 B.C.) after the customary offering of formulas, name and titles and before the report of his African travels of discovery and the story of how upon the pharaoh's written order he hastily brought the Pigmy from the land of the horizon-dwellers to court to demonstrate his dancing there (Lichtheim: 1973, 24):

I have come here from my city,
I have descended from my home;
I have built a house, set up (its) doors
I have dug a pool, planted sycamores.
The king praised me,
My father made a will for me.
I was one worthy...
One beloved of his father,
Praised by his mother
Whom all his brothers loved.
I gave bread to the hungry,
Clothing to the naked,
I brought the boatless to land.

This autobiography of the explorer and ruler Harkhuf, like that of so many other Egyptian officials, is determined by the Egyptian ideal of life, which as Assmann (1980, 58) once formulated it 'nicht vom Willen zur Macht, sondern vom Willen zur Gunst bestimmt war'. This personality ideal of serving the pharaoh and thus realizing *ma-at* (truth, justice, the correct order) or being in the king's favour was particularly strong in the time of the Old Kingdom. Later on we see more and more that the personality ideal is no longer so strongly founded upon the social relation with king, family and fellow men, but also and especially in the relation with oneself, one's heart, or one's god.

The collapse of the Old Kingdom with its destructive social consequences and sometimes so touching pessimistic literature, made room for a different type of person. The self-assured or self-glorifying note of the autobiography of Ankhtifi (+ 2100 B.C.), however, remains rather exceptional in Egyptian history (Vandier: 1950, 185-190; cf. Assmann: 1982, 972):

> I am the vanguard of men and the rearguard of men
> One like me has not developed
> Neither will such a one develop
> One like me has not been born
> And will not be born.
> I have surpassed the deeds of the ancestors.
> No-one after me shall attain what I have done,
> in these millions of years.

It was in the First Intermediate Period when this local potentate Ankhtifi lived and the favour of the king was no longer important, or at any rate no longer had any real meaning, that the 'The Dispute between a Man and his *ba*' was written. A man asks (Lichtenheim: 1973, 167):

> To whom shall I speak today?
> Hearts are greedy,
> Everyone robs his comrade's goods.
>
> To whom shall I speak today?
> Kindness has perished,
> Insolence assaults everyone. ...

In spite of the question there is a dialogue. We would call it a dialogue of man with himself. It lies beyond the scope of this article to give an analysis of this text as a whole or to attempt to summarize the diverging explanations of Egyptologists. The partner in the conversation is called the *ba*.

In graphic or plastic art the *ba* was represented in the shape of a bird (jabiru stork) or as a bird with a human head, male or female according to the hairdress. Traditionally the *ba*, like the *ka* and akh, is counted among the Egyptian representations of the soul. Horapollo did indeed translate *ba* as psyche. This late explanation of the *ba* as soul may well be based upon Egyptian textual and visual material where the *ba*-bird unites itself with or settles upon the mummy. The *ba* is, however, not exclusively a spiritual-psychic being. Gods and men have a *ba*. It is known that the Apis bull is the *ba* of Ptah. The translation psyche is not really possible then: revelation or manifestation is more acceptable. The *ba* is an alter ego of humans both in a psychic and in a corporeal sense. The bird form of the *ba* indicates that the *ba* represents man's ability to move about. It unites itself with the mummy in the grave, but it also leaves the grave or the realm of the dead to behold the sun and to adore it. As a rule the *ba* of humans is not separately perceptible until after their death. A confrontation with the *ba* during one's lifetime upon earth, as in the conversation between the man who is weary of life and his *ba*, is exceptional. But a student given to drinking, is warned once that his *ba* might begin to wander about (papyrus Anastasi IV 11, 10; cf. Caminos: 1954, 182). This sounds like the conscious self contrasted with the 'unconsciousness' of intoxication. A man might go to the places he knows upon earth with his *ba*, i.e., consciousness of self, while his mummy remained in the grave. One might also, like Derchain (1979, 8), think of memory as the sum of a person's past. The *ba* of gods and men has to do with their identity. The *ba* is the alter ego or external manifestation, dealing with 'die äussere Kommunikation' (Assmann: 1979, JEA 65, 71). During life it is usually not distinguished from the person.

The akh is the human being as a glorified departed one, who resides in the grave or the realm of the dead, but can also intervene in life upon earth. In Christian-Coptic times the word lives on to indicate spirits and ghosts.

Although a human being can be said to dispose of akhu (divine, creative or magical power) during his lifetime, the human person on earth as such is not an akh. Man is not an akh, but is acknowledged as an akh when the rites of glorification have been solemnized over him (Demarée: 1983, 190ff; England: 1978, 206ff.).

Man is also a shade, whose function can often be compared with the *ba*, i.e., external manifestation. Connected with the shade are the notions of coolness, protection and speed and mobility. The human shade is depicted as a black person (George: 1970 and 1983).

The specific qualities of the person on the spiritual-psychical level are indicated by the concept 'heart' (Brunner: 1977, 1158-1168). It is written with a hieroglyph that represents an animal's heart. The hearts of gods, humans and also animals, in so far as in this latter case it is not a poetic metaphor, were regarded as a purely physical matter. The heart of man is his core. The expression 'on the heart' *(hr-ib)* functions in the language as the preposition 'in the middle'. The heart as man's centre 'speaks', i.e., beats, in his members ('Book of the Dead' 27) and directs (Sauneron: 1962, 96). The heart must remain in the body for mummification. A heart-scarab may be added to the mummy, so that the human centre can continue to function. Many texts show that the heart was regarded as the seat not only of feelings, but also of understanding and memory. The heart has left a man, so that he has no self-control, when he is emotionally upset and fearful or when he is homesick. Someone 'without a heart' however is stupid rather than unfeeling. In the judgement of the dead the human heart, which is his true core and which has renounced his sins, is weighed against the ostrich feather, the symbol of social, ethical, and cosmic order. A lonely shipwrecked sailor, cast ashore on an uninhabited island, still has his heart as a companion, that is he is a person who remains conscious of himself, even if he is lonely. The pharaoh in his loneliness as a monarch consults his heart. The heart may have been thought of here as an organ with which he can learn to know his god and the directions he gives. God reveals himself and his will in the human heart. Kiki, who has a personal relationship with his goddess (see above), also declares that his heart is filled with his mistress. In harper's songs, biographies and wisdom literature man is called upon to follow his heart. A yet unformed student may indeed be warned not to throw himself into the arms of the heart (Brunner: 1977, 1163). But a man well aware of the right path, because his heart is well formed and uninjured, can and must follow his heart. An Egyptian ideal is to have an 'attentive heart' as we see from the autobiography of Amenhotep, the son of Hapu (Urk. IV: 1817, 8). We may compare this to Solomon's prayer for a heart with the ability to listen (1 Kings 3: 9).

He whose heart is injured is in a sorry state *(hd-ib)*. His words are quicker than wind and rain (Amenemope 12, 1; cf. Brunner: 1977, 1162). He is characterized by lack of control, deceitfulness and mendacity. He is quarrelsome and a beast of prey (wolf) in the fold.

The heart of man is the *ka*, which is in his body (Book of the Dead 30 B). Ptahhotep says (186-189; cf. Lichtenheim: 1973, 66):

> Follow your heart as long as you live,
> Do no more than is required,
> Do not shorten the time of 'follow-the-heart',
> Trimming its moment offends the ka.

In one of the manuscripts line 186 is changed into: 'Follow your *ka* as long as you live' (Zaba: 1956, 30 and 79).

The *ka* is rarely depicted in such a way that we can be absolutely certain. And when it is, it is always a kind of double of the human being created with it. Usually however the innumerable funerary figures which represent the departed in an idealized form, and which are provided with name, titles and offering formulas addressed to the *ka*, are interpreted as images of the *ka*.

The hieroglyph for *ka* represents two raised arms, i.e., a stylized representation of an embrace. This gesture could mean protection (Assmann: 1979, 71) or the transfer from the father to the son of that which is symbolized by the *ka* (Kaplony: 1980, 275). It seems less probable that the *ka* hieroglyph might be a gesture of adoration and indicate man's ability to have intercourse with the deity (Morenz: 1960, 214 Anm. 89).

Maspero (1878, 7, 47, 77ff.) called the *ka* the spiritual double, and Steindorff (1911, 152-159) referred to it as the genius or protective spirit of a man. The *ka* can, also in earlier times, be written with the single-letter signs k and aleph. Jacobsohn (1939, 57) connected the *ka* with the divine sexual or creative power and pointed out that the word *ka*, written with bull or phallus, can mean 'bull'. The king's *ka* would, in modern language, be 'die Erbmasse der Dynastie'. Frankfort (1948, 62) called the *ka* the 'vital force'. J. Sainte Fare Garnot (1955, 20) in his definition of the *ka* expressly used the term person:'le *ka* est l'ensemble des forces vitales qui permettent à l'homme et à d'autres créatures raisonnables et conscientes (notamment les dieux) de subsister en tant qu'être et d'exister en tant que personnes'. In describing the *ka* Gardiner used the concepts 'spirit', 'personality', 'soul', 'individuality', 'temperament', 'fortune' and 'position' (1957, 172). Elsewhere (1950, 7 note 2) he wonders whether or not the word 'personality' really covers the various applications of the Egyptian word: 'The main point in which the Egyptian conception of personality would then differ from our own is that it assumes a separation from the owner's physical person'. If however one does not fix the identity of the person in the body remaining the same or in physical continuity and does not exclude, as the Egyptians did not, man's living on after death, then Gardiner's objection does not seem to be so decisive. For that matter, the mummification rituals clearly show to what an extent the Egyptians wrestled with the problems around physical continuity and identity of the person.

It seems clear even without entering here into a full account of the two monographs devoted to the *ka* by Greeven (1952) and Schweitzer (1956), that the concept '*ka*' is at least as complex as our concept 'person'. In text translations Egyptologists usually leave the word untranslated. In recent lexicographical research (Meeks: 1981, 393 and 1982, 306) the translation 'person' is also given for *ka*, besides other shades of meaning.

Summing up, one might call the *ka* the vital energy of men or gods or the ability to function as a person. It must be remarked here that the emphasis is not upon the person as an individual but on the person as a type, entirely in accordance with the fact that in Egyptian literature and art and other Egyptian phenomena it is not the individual but the typical which is stressed. Men and gods have a *ka*, have a personality structure that they have usually inherited or received from their ancestors. In so far as one would wish to go on ranking the *ka* among the various conceptions of the soul, the *ka* is the ancestral soul, the total of hereditary qualities that an individual human has received from the ancestors, his typical personal structure. Hence we can understand that the offerings to the dead made especially by the eldest son and members of the family are addressed to the *ka* of the departed. Children resemble their parents in the structure of their personality. That the Egyptians had observed this or hoped for it when a child was born, is evident from such personal names as Wehemkai (my *ka* repeats itself) and Kaesites (her *ka* is her father), Wetetka(i) (my begetter is my *ka*), Kairi (my *ka* is my begetter) (Schweitzer: 1956, 36). Elsewhere also *ka* and ancestor are connected with one another. A wish expressed for the departed is 'that his hand may be taken by his *ka*-s, by his fathers' (Sethe: 1933, 189, 190; cf. Schweitzer: 1956, 84). Gardiner's descriptions of the *ka* as 'fortune' and 'position' become clearer if one considers the *ka* as ancestor-soul or hereditary structure of the person.

In this connection it is interesting to note the cult of the king's *ka*. In a recent study Bell (1985, 258) has remarked: 'the royal *ka* represents the 'dignity' or office of kingship, while the individual king is viewed as a link in the chain of divine kingship which stretches back into the very dawn of Egyptian history'. In the case of each king it had to be established that he really had a royal *ka*. The *ka* is not only passed on from father to son. This is evident, for instance, from one of the female names given above, but also from the case of the female pharaoh Hatshepsut. One of her names is Weseret-kau (rich in *ka*-s). On the other hand Thutmosis III could afterwards annul the legitimacy of Hatshepsut and deny that she had a royal *ka* by destroying her *ka*-statues. Especially the element *ka* in her name Maat-ka-Re was attacked (Bell: 1985, 257 and note 20) when her names were scratched out. From the fact that dynasties replaced one another one can deduce that the *ka* is not passed on exclusively by biological inheritance. This is evident for instance from a story in the Westcar papyrus relating how the woman Reddedet, married not to a pharaoh but to a priest, becomes pregnant with three children who will afterwards become kings. This is a miraculous birth. Usually the reigning pharaoh functions as a *ka-mutef* (bull of his mother), the self-begetting god of fertility, father and son in one, who is reborn from sexual intercourse with his wife.

One god can be the *ka* of another god. The king is the *ka* of Egypt and of his officials and his subjects (Kaplony: 1980, 277), that is to say they are marked by his 'person'. The meaning of *ka* that Jacobsohn described as 'Erbmasse' comes close to the meaning of fate *(shai)*. A pharaoh can be called: Shai of Egypt, *ka* of those who are in it (Quaegebeur: 1975, 111). From the New Kingdom onwards the pharaoh is credited with 14 *ka*'s. Later on these 14 *ka*'s are specified in diverse lists. One list (papyrus Nedjemet; cf. Schweitzer: 1956, 74) gives the following enumeration: riches, prosperity, abundance, glory, prestige, acumen, lastingness, sight, hearing, wisdom, creative word, creative power, emanation and strength. Here we note the enormous attention that is paid, not only to the spiritual, but also to the social, physical and material aspects or capacities of the person concerned.

Later texts also mention the fourfold *ka* of non-royal persons. This special lot, happiness or possibility of functioning as a person that Ptah had created for meritorious humans at the creation of the world, included for instance plenty, long life, a beautiful funeral after a happy old age, and worthy descendants (Meeks: 1971, 40).

The sacrifices for the dead, as we have already remarked, were brought especially and particularly to the *ka*. But that was not always all. In the Theban tomb of Amenemhet (Davies-Cardiner: 1915, pls. 19, 20, 22, 23 and p. 99), the sacrifice to the deceased is made on the southern wall to the name and title of the dead man, his *ka*, his stela, to this tomb in the necropolis, to his fate, to his life-time, to his birth goddess, to the goddess of his upbringing, to his creation god and on the northern wall to the name and title of the dead man, to his *ka*, to his stela, [to this grave in the necropolis, to his *ba*], to his akh, to his body, to his shade, to all his forms of appearance.

We may reasonably suppose that on the damaged part of the northern wall the tomb and *ba* were written. Here the person proves to have many aspects that we see unfolded in personal relationships on the material, social, spiritual and divine level. Two series are offered, which differ from each other in part, though each series has 9 elements.

I do not know of identical series from elsewhere. It seems that a random selection was made from an available supply of concepts determining the person. It is the number that is systematic, here the number 9, as elsewhere the number 14 with regard to the *ka*-s of the pharaoh and the number 4 with regard to the *ka*-s of non-royal dead persons. One cannot assume that in these series one element implies the other. There was no academic philosopher at work here, but someone who reminds us of the famous 'bricoleur' of Levi-Strauss. Nevertheless it gives some insight into the Egyptian idea of what a person is. Apart from the first element in the two enneads consisting of the title and name of the person, all elements except the unmistakeable 'this tomb that is in the necropolis' in which the inscription itself is placed, are provided with a possessive pronoun, which in Egyptian is at the same time a personal pronoun of the third person: To the person belongs that which one essentially is. The Egyptian person manifests himself, as Assmann has expressed it in 'die Sphäre des Seinigen' (Assmann: 1969, 342). This 'sphere of that which is his' can be variously specified and formulated. In the network of personal relations various points of junction can be pointed out, some of which can sometimes be regarded as the kernel, for instance the heart or the *ka* of the person. Yet the plurality also remains essential; like God, the human person in Egypt was also conceived as a plurality with material, bodily, spiritual and divine aspects.

Bibliography

Assmann, J.
1969 *Liturgische Lieder an den Sonnengott*, Berlin.
1975 *Ägyptische Hymnen und Gebete*, Zürich-München.
1979 'Harfnerlied und Horussöhne', in: *The Journal of Egyptian Archaeology*, 65, 54-77.
1980 'Grundstrukturen der ägyptischen Gottesvorstellungen', in: *Biblische Notizen*, Bamberg, Heft 11, 46-62.
1982 'Persönlichkeitsbegriff und -bewusztsein'. In: *Lexikon der Aegyptologie*, IV, 963-978.

Baines, J.
1985 *Fecundity Figures. Egyptian Personification and the Iconology of a Genre*, Warminster.

Bell, L.
1985 'Luxor Temple and the Cult of the Royal *ka*', in: *Journal of Near Eastern Studies*, 44, 251-294.

Brunner, H.
1977 'Herz'. In: Lexikon der Aegyptologie, II, 1158-1168.

Buck, A. de
1928 *Het typische en het individuele bij de Egyptenaren*, Leiden.

Caminos, R.A.
1954 *Late Egyptian Miscellanies*, London.

Demarée, R.J.
1983 *The ikr n R^{c}-stelae*, Leiden.

Derchain, Ph.
1979 'Egypt'. In: *Dictionnaire des Mythologies*, Paris, 1-47.

Englund, G.
1978 *Akh. Une notion religieuse dans l'Égypte ancienne*, Uppsala 1978.
Frankfort, H.
1948 *Kingship and the Gods*, Chicago.
Gardiner, A.H.
1915 *The Tomb of Amenemhet*, London.
1950 'The Baptism of Pharaoh', in: *The Journal of Egyptian Archeology*, 36, 3-12.
1957 *Egyptian Grammar*, London.

Garnot, J. Sainte Fare
1955 'L'anthropologie de l'Égypte ancienne'. In: *Anthropologie religieuse (= Supplements to Numen 2)*, Leiden, 14-27.
George, B.
1970 *Zu den Altägyptischen Vorstellungen vom Schatten als Seele*, Bonn.
1983 'Gottesschatten = Götterbild in Widdergestalt', in: *Die Welt des Orients*, 14, 129-134.
Greven, L.
1952 *Der ka* in Theologie und Köningskult der Ägypter des Alten Reiches, Glückstadt.
Hornung, E.
1968 *Altägyptische Höllenvorstellungen*, Abh.Sächs.Ak.d.W. Philos.-Hist. Kl., Bd. 59, Heft 3, Berlin.
1982 *Tal der Könige*, Zürich-München.
Jacobsohn, H.
1939 *Die dogmatische Stellung des Königs in der Theologie der Alten Ägypter*, Glückstadt.
Kaplony, P.
1980 '*ka*'. In: *Lexikon der Aegyptologie*, III, 275-282.
Lichtheim, M.
1973 *Ancient Egyptian Literature I*, Berkeley-Los Angeles-London.
Maspero, G.
1878 *Études de Mythologie et d'Archéologie I*, Paris.

Meeks, D.
1971 'Génies, anges, démons en Égypte', in: *Sources Orientales* VIII, Paris, 19-84.
1981 *Année Lexicographique. Égypte Ancienne 2* (1978), Paris 1981.
1982 *Année Lexicographique. Égypte Ancienne 3* (1979), Paris 1982.
Morenz, S.
1960 *Ägyptische Religion*, Stuttgart.
1969 *Prestige-Wirtschaft im alten Ägypten*. Sitzungsberichte Bayerische Akademie der Wissenschaften. Philos.-Hist.Kl., Jhrg. 1969, Heft 4, München.

Muhammed, Abdul-Qader
1966 'Two Theban Tombs, Kyky and Bak-en-Amun', in: *Annales du Service des Antiquités de l'Égypte*, 59, 143-155.
Quaegebeur, J.
1975 *Le dieu égyptien Shai dans la religion et l'onomastique*, Leuven.
Sauneron, S.
1962 *Les fêtes religieuses d'Esna*, Cairo.
Schweitzer, U.
1956 *Das Wesen des ka* im Diesseits und Jenseits der Alten Ägypter, Glückstadt.
Sethe, K.
1933 *Urkunden des Alten Reiches*, Leipzig.
Steindorff, G.
1911 'Der *ka* und die Grabstatuen', in: *Zeitschrift für Aegyptische Sprache und Altertumskunde*, 48, 152-159.
Urk.
1958 *Urkunden des aegyptischen Altertums*. Vierte Abteilung. Urkunden der 18. Dynastie, Heft 21, bearbeitet von W. Helck.
Vandier, J.
1950 *Mo^{c}alla. La tombe d'ankhtifi et la tombe de Sebekhotep*, Cairo.

Vernus, P.
1978 'Les inscriptions de Sa-Mwt surnommé Kyky' in: *Revue d'Égyptologie,* 30, 115-150.
Walle, A. van de
1975 'Biographie'. In: *Lexikon der Aegyptologie,* I, 815-821.
Wilson, J.A.
1949 'Egypt'. In: *Before Philosophy. An Essay on Speculative Thougth in the Ancient Near East* by H. and H.A. Frankfort, J.A. Wilson and T. Jacobsen, Harmondsworth.
Zába, Z.
1956 *Les maximes de Ptahhotep*, Prague.

NAME AND PERSON IN ANCIENT JUDAISM AND CHRISTIANITY

Hans G. Kippenberg

Introduction

A closer examination of the names of a culture does not necessarily lead to a more intimate knowledge of the conceptions that people in this culture have formed of the person, for in our Western understanding a name is usually seen as an arbitrary linguistic symbol for a human being. As a rule it does not say anything about the nature of the human being that uses it, nor does it reveal anything about the existing concept of the person.

Nevertheless, a name is not only used to indicate an individual. It has the additional function of representing this individual, also when he is not present himself. In the process of naming this representative function of the name is connected with a conception of what constitutes a human being. This conception is presupposed and cannot be introduced ad hoc by a speaker, nor is it solely dependent on the designated object. Four elements can thus be distinguished in the process of naming: an object, a name (a linguistic symbol), a concept of the person and a subject (Langer: 1974, 64).

With respect to the essential and universal characteristics of the object 'individual' I follow H.G. Hubbeling. No human being may be denied self-awareness, will, responsibility for deeds and intersubjective communication. As far as the concept of the person is concerned, however, I would like to start, not from the individual, but from the culture in which this concept exists. Like others, I want to plead for a systematic division between individual and person. 'Individual' should indicate empirical man as object of observation. 'Person', on the other hand, should refer to the set of normative ideas which a society has developed with regard to its members. This approach has recently been resumed and substantiated in the outstanding publication 'The Category of the Person. Anthropology, Philosophy, History' (Carrithers, Collins, Lukes: 1985). It has been inspired by M. Mauss who, in his well-known article 'Une Catégorie de l'Esprit Humain: La Notion de Personne, Celle de 'Moi' (1938; English translation: 'A Category of the Human Mind: The Notion of

Person; The Notion of Self'[1985]) centred his considerations around the Latin notion *persona* (theatre mask). In his the Latin society, like so many others, arrived at the notion 'personnage' by apprehending the individual in the light of his roles in the sacred drama. But they went further than that and established *person* as a legal concept, which later on became connected with the notion of moral consciousness (Mauss: 1985). Many anthropologists have adopted this view.[1] The image of the social drama with its roles is perhaps the most important and in any case the most characteristic metaphor of these anthropological theories. The metaphor indicates that man cannot be 'person' of his own accord. He can only become this by adopting a socially predetermined role. The concept of the person belongs, not to the context of individuality, but to that of the social drama.

One should bear in mind, however, that the object of such studies cannot exist solely in analyses of the concepts of the culture investigated. As a rule the observing and comparing anthropologist must from different and dispersed elements of a culture, reveal a deeper-lying structure that typifies the conception of the person (Lukes: 1985, 286). In addition, information about the category of the person, as it is presupposed in cultures, can emerge in places in which the researcher would not have expected to find them. Something of the sort also used to apply to the clarifications of the social structures of a people. In this field of study, however, disagreement about its relevant subjects of research has ceased to exist for quite some time now, and today no one is surprised when information about a people's social structures are obtained from its collective rites and myths. In spite of the fact that with regard to the concept of the person such an understanding does not (yet) exist, I would like to contend that name systems should be included in a study of the concept of the person.

In the process of naming, the *name* and the conception of the person are connected with each other. The use of a name for a human being always implies such a concept. For a Western observer it is beyond dispute that the relation between name and concept of the person is external and contingent. And in many cases this will indeed be true. But

---

[1] Surveys of these anthropologists and their publications can be found in Carrithers, Collins, Lukes: 1985, 302f, as well as in Michel-Jones: 1974.

there are indications that the relation between name and concept of the person is not external and contingent in all cultures, for a name system can itself be a means to give a human being a role in the social drama. This view was expressed by Mauss. He agreed with M. Leenhardt, who stated: 'Le nom désigne l'ensemble des positions spéciales de l'individu dans son group' (Mauss: 1974, 134). In his article of 1938 Mauss justified this supposition on the basis of the name system of the Pueblos. He typified this system as follows:

> The existence of a limited number of forenames in each clan; and the definition of the exact rôle played by each one in the 'cast-list' of the clan, and expressed by that name.

Like Mauss, C. Geertz (1983) has studied name systems in his search for an example of the categorisation of individuals. In Bali, to identify someone is to assign him a role in the social drama. The terminological systems of the Balinese 'conduce to a view of the human person as an appropriate representative of a generic type, not a unique creature with a private fate' (Mauss: 1977; 1983). Particularly interesting is Geertz's analysis of the *nisba* in Sefrou (Morocco), where he has done some field work. Until quite recently names common to all members of a family did not exist in the Arab world. More likely a string of different indicators was used for the individual: *ism* (personal name), *kunya* (personal surname - abu...), *nasab* (filiation and patronymic - ibn...), *nisba* (indicating origin, profession, school of law, etc., e.g., al-Susi) and *laqab* (nickname, court title, etc., e.g., Nasir ad-Daula = Helper of the Dynasty). It was a flexible system, since Arab persons were known by only one or two in some way conspicuous elements of this string, and sometimes they could adopt or discard names in the course of their lives.[2] The *nisba*, which can be added to a name, tends to be incorporated into the proper name. When a Sefruwi settles in another place the obvious thing to do is to characterise him by means of his origin. As far as this is concerned, however, there is no kind of regularity. There is only one feature that

---

[2] A well-organized treatment of the Arabic (at the same time Islamic) system in Endress: 1982, 175-179.

remains constant: the persons are identified by means of such contextual indicators. They are 'contextualized persons' (Geertz: 1983, 66). The name system is one of the ways in which people can assign to an individual his role in the social drama of a particular culture. These observations reveal that name systems, which in Western thinking are often seen as arbitrary designations for people, can in other cultures allocate a social role to the individual. A name system can have a constraining influence, as was already recognised by Freud (1956, 66f., Brown: 1966, 92).

Finally I would like to discuss the *subjective factor*: the subjects that avail themselves of the names and concept of the person connected with them. From the numerous aspects related to this element I would like to select one which seems to me to be particularly illuminating: the use of names in two ancient *religious communities*. These communities existed within civilian orders, and were bound by civil law as regards the name systems of their members. Nevertheless, they also had the possibility of developing their own name systems. Even if the roles of the individual were prescribed through the name, the bearer of the name, in collaboration with others, could still try to get away from this constraint. Religious communities did not have to display slavish obedience to the laws of the society into which they had been incorporated. They could also develop and use concepts of the person and name systems connected with them which were not shared by the society and culture surrounding them. The civilian names and the concept of the person connected with them (externally or internally) are therefore not of final importance. Just as it is certain that naming classifies a human being, it is certain that, together with others, he can get away from these constraints. With regard to such a theme a stiff dose of interactionistic theory will certainly be productive. 'The individual enters as such into his own experience only as an object, not as a subject...' wrote Mead (1965, 244). To obtain self-awareness man needs the experience of being an object to others. The basis for this is reflexion. B. Babcock summarised this interactionistic postulate as follows:

> Mead, like Lacan, Piaget and others, regards this primary instance of reflexivity, this initial experience of decentering, detachment, and differentiation as the primordial social experience to the development of both self and society (Babcock: 1980, 2).

Religious communities could use reflexion in this sense, and they could offer the individual the possibility of reflecting social constraints. In them the individual could reflect his experience as an object of social forces and identify himself as different from what was prescribed. If there have been conflicts between religious communities and the dominant society, they should be reflected in the name systems and the concepts of the person connected with them.

Political Functions of the Ancient Personal Name

In classical society the name was the most important means to lay down the rights and duties of the individual. When a name was added to a marriage certificate, deed of sale or debt certificate, to the register of population (cf. 2 Macc. 4, 9; Dion Chrysostomos 34, 23), or to genealogical registers (cf. Ezra 2; Neh. 7) or incorporated into the list of tax payers (cf. 3 Macc. 3, 28), this happened on the basis that the name put the bearer under an obligation or gave him special privileges. The use of a name was subject to certain rules, but change of name did occur. When a foreigner joined the Roman army he assumed a Roman name. The Egyptian naval solider Apion informed his father: 'By the way, my name is Antonis Maximos' (BGU II 423 and 632) (Deissmann: 1923, 145-153). Likewise, from 45 B.C. onwards a foreigner who had acquired Roman civil rights had to register with the officially prescribed three-part set of names. *Nomen* and *praenomen* he adopted from the Roman protector who had helped him acquire civil rights. He could go on using his ancestral name as *cognomen* (Harrer: 1940, 19f.). Since the rights and the duties of the indivual laid down through the name were binding, the name could not be changed just like that. The great extent to which the meaning of Greek *onoma* was influenced by this bureaucratic approach to the name was already established by H. Bietenhard: 'In der Sprache der Verwaltung bekommt *onoma* die Bdtg Rechtstitel, Rechnungsposten' (Bietenhard: 1954, 244). The concept of the person in a legal sense developed late in antiquity. It was not until the 3rd century A.D. that Greek *prosopon* acquired this meaning (Lohse: 1959, 771). The Romans used for the first time the notion of the mask (*persona*) to describe the legal role individuals had to fulfil. Only late on did the meaning 'role' disappear (Fuhrmann: 1979) When the rights and duties of a citizen were to be set down the name of this citizen was used. The name was the most important means of representing the individual. That Christian theologians took this for granted has been pointed out by J. Daniélou (1973). In the first three centuries A.D. a unified concept of the person did not yet exist. When people wanted to refer to the Revelation of the Infinite (*aperigraptos*) and Ineffable (*arretos*) God, they used the notion that the Word (*logos*) had defined itself, had given itself a name, and had thus become the Son. Valentinian gnostics expressed this as follows: 'The name of the Father is the Son' (NHC I 38, 6f.). Here the name held the position that the concept of the person was to assume in later times.

The name systems that were used in classical society were not the same in the Eastern and the Western parts of the Roman Empire. The single name system was characteristic of the Eastern part. The Romans, on the other hand, had already adopted a different system at an early time. The Roman historian Appian (2nd century A.D.) states:

> And in earlier days the Romans had one name, like everyone else. Then they got two names. And recently, for ease of distinction, people have began to add a third name on the basis of physical defects (*pathos*) or merit (*arete*) (praef. 13).

This is confirmed by other authors. 'The men have three names', Plutarch writes, Quaestiones Romanae 102 (cf. also Juvenal, Satires V 12; Seneca, De benificiis IV 8) (Doer: 1937, 17-19). In the days of the Principate, however, the development of the Roman name system moved again in the direction of a single name system. I. Kajanto, who has described this development, refers to it in terms of a cycle. At first the Romans had only one name. Then the three-name system developed. Of these three names the *praenomen* was the first to disappear again, and then the *nomen* or alternatively the *gentilicium*. The *cognomen* had won the battle for the personal name (Kajanto: 1977). In the Eastern part of the Empire, however, the single-name system had been used until it had become necessary to add further information. For this Greeks chose the name of the father (in the genitive, depending on the *huios* concerned) and the place of origin (Harder: 1962, 14-18; Menager: 1980).

A similar system was used by the Jews. They too had only one name and they too added the names of fathers and ancestors (filiation and patronymic). This occured with great regularity. The private documents of Murabba'at and Nahal Hever from the first half of the 2nd century A.D.

contain numerous examples: Hadar bar Juda, Simeon bar Joseph, etc., etc. A man did not possess legal personality if he could not prove who his father was. Hebrew *yatôm* referred not only to orphans but also to the 'fatherless', as Lamentations 5, 3 explains (Ringgren: 1982). In the Torah, the fatherless were among those who could not assert their own rights (Deut. 10, 17f., Ex. 22, 20f., Deut. 10, 18f., Ex. 22, 22f., Deut. 24, 17; 27, 19). In the Mishnah the 'silent once', who knew who their mother was but not their father, did not belong to the People of Israel (Qid IV 1-5). The filiation also said something about the legal personality of a Jew. 'In den meisten Vorkommen bildet *ben* einen patronymischen Begriff zur Kennzeichnung des Personenstandes', Fohrer (1969, 342) writes.

In the multiple-name system (polyonomy) as well as in the single-name system, an individual's name represented him before fellow contractors, before the local authorities, before other families or before the imperial authorities. The world of literacy and document registers was evidently of influence here. The name of an individual represented him before others. Moreover, through the name the individual became part of the great social drama. The name was a means of granting the individual certain privileges or imposing serious obligations upon him. Both these occurred. This ambivalent function of the name lay at the root of the fact that religious communities could adopt deviant attitudes towards the civil name.

Name and Person in Ancient Judaism

There is a story in the New Testament which contains many elements that were important for the Jewish name system. I am referring to the story of the naming of John the Baptist, Luke 1, 57-64. Eight days after Elizabeth had given birth to a son, neighbours and relatives came to circumcise him and to give him the name of his father Zacharias. The mother, however, wanted to call him John, which is what the angel had ordered Zacharias to do (Luke 1, 13). 'And they said unto her, there is none of thy kindred that is called by this name.' Zacharias, the father, whom the angel Gabriel had punished with dumbness because of his doubts, wrote on a slate: 'His name is John', whereupon he regained speech.

Already in the Torah the mother, sometimes also the father, was the one who gave the child its name. This was done, not during circumcision, but immediately after the birth of the child (mother: Gen. 29, 31-30, 24; 1 Sam 1, 20; father: Gen. 16, 15; 17, 19; Ex. 2, 22; cf. Gen. 35, 18 [name given by father different from that given by mother]). Many of the names that were chosen in these ancient stories were prompted by the circumstance of the birth.[3] In the Torah, but also later in the Jewish Colony of Elephantine, names were selected particularly on account of their meaning. Here it is possible to distinguish three recurring forms of names: the verbal-sentence name (e.g., z^{e}karya = Qal Perfect with yh designating God = Yah has remembered), the nominal-sentence name (mika'el = Who is like God?), and the word name, which is usually profane (dawid = beloved). An enormous number of names were formed according to these rules. There are 1426 personal names on the list of names compiled by M. Noth (1928). Most of them are theophoric, as semitic names are in general. The Jews continued to be aware of the original meaning of a name also during the time after the Exile, as has been demonstrated in a more recent study of the Elephantine papyri by M.H. Silverman (1985).

After the Exile, names were selected, not only on account of what they expressed, but also for other reasons. It was noted first among the Jews of Elephantine (5th century B.C.) that again and again sons were named after their grandfather or their parents (Buchanan Gray: 1914).[4] From the 3rd century B.C. onwards this *papponymy* also occurred in Judea. In the Gospel according to St. Luke it is taken for granted. The individual lived in the shadow of his ancestors. It is in this context that the *levirate* should also be mentioned, the custom by which the brother or next of kin to a deceased man was bound under certain circumstances to marry the widow. The first son by this marriage should bear the name of the deceased so that his name would not cease to exist in Israel (Deut. 25, 6; Ruth 4, 5;cf. Josephus, Ant. Jud. IV 254).

---

[3] A well-organised discussion of the Old Testament material can be found in De Vaux: 1964, 81-85.

[4] M.H. Silverman has gone through the Elephantine material once more and has arrived at a total of (only) 8% (1985,195); in the Murashu documents from Nippur (5th century B.C.) M.D. Coogan has found even fewer cases (Coogan: 1976, 121f).

To this motivation of the levirate Church Father Julius Africanus (d. 240 A.D.) added an observation which points to an important aspect of this institution. He wrote: 'For because no certain hope of resurrection had as yet been given they portrayed the future promise by a mortal resurrection, in order that the name of him who had passed away might not fail to remain ' (Eusebius, Historia ecclesiae I 7, 2). This is a polemic interpretation of the levirate. Nevertheless, it points to an implication that was connected with the name system. When a son received the name of a deceased, the deceased himself continued to be present in Israel. Not only during his life but also after his death did the name represent the individual before a community.

This representative function of the name must be taken into account in an interpretation of the use of *biblical names* as personal names. The Elephantine papyri from Egypt (5th century B.C.), however, belonged to a past era. With disbelief A.E. Cowley noted:

> Among the numerous names of colonists, Abraham, Jacob, Joseph, Moses, Samuel, David, so common in later times, never occur (nor in Nehemiah), nor any other name derived from their past history as recorded in the Pentateuch and early literature. It is almost incredible, but it is true (Cowley: 1923, XXIII).

It was in Murashu-documents from Nippur (5th century B.C.) that biblical names, which were not used as personal names but as tribal names - Benjamin and Simon - in Hebrew antiquity, were used as proper names for the first time. In the books of Ezra and Nehemiah, Judah (e.g., Ezra 10, 23) and Joseph (Ezra 10, 42; Neh. 12, 14), occur in addition to Benjamin and Simon (Ezra 10, 31f. Neh. 3, 23). In Greek and Roman times Simon, Judah and Joseph were among the most frequently occuring names. What seems to have contributed to the popularity of many a Jewish name is the fact that they were similar in sound to certain non-Jewish names, cf. Hebrew's šim'on and Greek Simon. N.G. Cohen describes this paradox as follows:

> The vogue for certain Jewish names... not only reflects a Jewish identification on the part of the name-giver, but provides an indication of the specific non-Jewish cultural milieu to which the name-giver wished to belong (Cohen: 1976, 97).

People continued to avoid names like Abraham, Aaron and Solomon.

The great names of Pseudepigraphic literature, such as Daniel and Enoch, were also rarely used as proper names for persons.

G. Hölscher tried to explain the appearance of biblical proper names by linking it to 'dem seit der Perserzeit erstarkenden Interesse der Juden an der Reinheit der Abstammung' (Hölscher: 1925, 151). But this explanation has become doubtful on account of more recently acquired understanding of the political situation of the Jews in the days of the Second Temple. Ever since Nehemiah the Jews had formed an autonomous civilian society in Judea, in which they had been allowed, first by the Persian, then by the Greek and finally by the Roman rulers, to live and act politically in accordance with their ancestral laws (*patrioi nomoi*). Jews outside Judea, in Hellenic cities, also laid claim to autonomy. Once they had acquired the right to live according to their ancestral laws they were proud - like their pagan fellow citizens (Josephus, Contra Apionem II 30) - to bear the name of their city. They were called Alexandrians (Josephus, Ant. Jud. XX 281; P. London: 1912; Philo, Legatio ad Gaium 350 and In Flaccum 80) or Antiochians (Contra Apionem II 39) (Kasher: 1985, chapter VII-IX). 'Similarly, those at Ephesus and throughout the rest of Ionia bear the same name as the indigenous citizens, a right which they received from Alexander's successors' (Contra Apionem II 39). Because Jews had been permitted to live in accordance with their ancestral laws in many Near Eastern places, they could regard themselves as citizens of these cities and could claim a Jewish *politeia* (Kippenberg: 1986). The names of the biblical ancestors also belonged to these ancestral traditions. When the civilian names of Jews were taken from these traditions, this happened because the *patrioi nomoi* was interpreted as a comprehensive standard for the political public world of the city as well as for the life of the individual. An ancestral person from early biblical days lived on in the name of the individual. With this name he was at the same time assigned a part in the social drama of classical society. By means of his name his life was associated with the persistent struggle for Jewish autonomy. It is within this political context that the appearance of biblical names should be interpreted and not within the context of purity of descent. The names chiefly served to actualise the great past of the people of Israel and to exercise the right to autonomy.

All this takes place in a society in which social intercourse between citizens of different cities, tribes and religious communities was the order of the day; in a society, therefore, which ethnically was no longer homogenous. In this connection I would like to discuss the Jewish custom of using a *foreign name* in addition to a Jewish one. The Daniel of the Book of Daniel (2nd century B.C.) had both a Jewish and a Babylonian name: Beltshazzar (Dan. 1, 7; 10, 1; Esther also had an additional name). According to J. Lebram (1984, 44) this happened when someone acquired a position at court. M.D. Coogan offers a different explanation: 'The passages [Daniel and Esther] suggest that pious Jews may have had two names: a public (pagan) name and a private (Hebrew) name (Coogan: 1985, 124)'. Something similar can be observed in the Elephantine papyri. There too, Jews had foreign (general Semitic, Persian and Egyptian) names (Grelot: 1972, 352-4; 455-502; Silverman: 1985, 44-88). One and the same person first used the Egyptian name As-Hor, then four years later (416 B.C.) the Jewish name Nathan (AP 20 and 25). Far more popular than any other kind of name, however, were the Greek ones. A survey of this has been provided by E. Schürer (ed. Vermes: 1979, 73f. Cazelles: 1960). In Roman times a kind of polyonomy became common in connection with Roman law. In addition to his Hebrew name, the Roman cognomen Paul seems to have been applied to Saul, not after his conversion, but already from the moment of his birth (Acts 13, 9) (Harrer: 1940). The Acts of the Apostles also mention other persons with Roman names: 'Joseph, called Barsabas, who was surnamed Justus' (1, 13); 'John, whose surname was Mark' (12, 12.25); 'Simeon that was called Niger' (13, 1). It is impossible to determine whether, in all these cases, we are dealing with an official cognomen or just an unofficial surname, an *agnomen*. The only thing that is certain is that as a rule citizens from the Eastern part of the Empire who had become Roman *cives* had to have an additional Roman name (*mutatio nominis*). For this the formula *ho kai* was used, and *he kai* for women, or otherwise their Latin equivalents *qui et* and *quae et* (Doer: 1937; Kajanto: 1967).

I would like to refer once more to Mauss's proposition that the name assigns a role or a social position to the individual using it. The name is more than just an indicator of a human being: it imposes rights and duties upon a human being and it determines other people's behaviour towards him. This proposition is confirmed by the ancient Jewish material that has been discussed. The appearance of biblical names as personal names is connected with the attempts of Jews to live according to their ancestral laws. The Jewish proper name did not represent the individual in an abstract sense. It also implied social interactions in which Jewish citizens of the ancient Hellenic and Roman societies were involved.

The name of the individual represented him not only before the society in which he lived, but also before God. This function of the name is taken for granted in the expositions of Jewish religion in the days of the Second Temple. God's promises to his people only applied to those whose names were listed in the genealogical registers of Israel. The (right) familial-political classifications were prerequisite for salvation, no matter how this was described in detail. The promised salvation applied first of all to the community, and only by derivation to the individual. It is not therefore surprising that in this context reflections on the name of the individual did not occur. This changed with the rise of apocalypticism in the 2nd century B.C. Not every Jew could be saved, for in Israel itself there were righteous and unjust people, and the unjust had lost the right to salvation. Already in the Torah it is said that the godless will be blotted out of the book of the living and will not be listed with the righteous (Ps. 69, 28; cf. also Ex. 32, 32f.). From the Maccabean era onwards this idea began to gain ground in the apocalyptic literature. It was revealed to Daniel that 'at that time' his people would be saved, that is 'everyone that shall be found written in the book' (Dan. 12, 1). In the first Book of Enoch (Ethiop. Enoch) it says in 'the Epistle of Enoch': 'I swear unto you that in heaven angels will remember you for good before the glory of the Great One; and your names shall be written before the glory of the Great One'(1 Enoch 104, 1). In other places in the book of Enoch the 'books of the living ones' (47, 3) and the 'book of all the deeds of humanity' (81, 2) are mentioned. Of the unjust it says accordingly:

> The names of (the sinners) shall be blotted out from the book of life and the books of the Holy One; their seed shall be destroyed forever and their spirits shall perish and die (108, 3 - note the parallelism of name and seed).

At this stage the name has become synonymous with the acts of an individual. The name is therefore often no longer referred to. It is merely mentioned that the deeds of the individual will be written down (1 Enoch 98, 6f. Syr. Bar 24, 1; Apoc. Zeph. 7). In some cases a different metaphor is used. Sometimes it is the register in which the citizens of a town were listed and which guaranteed them civil rights (see Philo, De gigantibus 61). Sometimes it is the black book of a lender (see e.g., Pirqe Abot III

16) (Bousset: 1966, 258f. Volz: 1934, 291f.). In all cases, however, the metaphor presuposes that the name represents the individual before God.

To conclude this section I would like to draw attention to a Greek inscription from a Jewish synagogue in Skythopolis, even though it is of a late date. It was inscribed on a mosaic: 'Gift from those whose name is known to the Lord [written K - a nomen sacrum HGK]. He guards them in the time [that comes, HGK'] (Horsley: 1981, nr.69). The names represent the donors before God. In this respect this inscription links up with the material discussed. But these names no longer have to be made known. Religious identity has dissociated itself from public identity.

Name and Person in Ancient Pre-Constantine Christianity

Just like A.E. Cowley, who to his amazement found that the typical biblical names did not occur in the Elephantine papyri, A. v. Harnack expressed his astonishment at the fact that even though the Church had wiped out polytheism she continued to make unrestrained use of the pagan names common in those days. Among the names of 87 bishops who had gathered for a synod in North Africa in 256 A.D. there was not a single name from the Old Testament and only two from the New Testament: Peter and Paul (Harnack: 1924, 437; Moffat: 1917). Christians continued to use the old pagan names, and even names which had been derived from names of gods. At one time it even happened that a martyr (Apollos) refused to make an offering to the gods whose names he bore himself (Musurillo: 1972,90-105). No fundamental change in this situation occured until the beginning of the 4th century. It is particularly this pre-Constantine attitude of Christians towards the pagan name that I want to discuss and examine for the presupposed concept of the person.

The existing onomastic material from the Roman Empire confirms that pagan names were predominant among Christians. H.-I. Marrou has established that 5-10% of the names of Christians were Christian. In the course of time the percentage of Christian names grew (Marrou: 1977), as is borne out by a historic source. Dionysius of Alexandria (d. 264/5 A.D.) mentions in passing that in his time Christians called their children *Paulos* and *Petros* (Eusebius, Historia ecclesiae VII 25, 14). And in his 'De martyribus Palaestinae' Eusebius reports that during the persecutions of 303-311 A.D. some Christians gave the names of prophets instead of their civil names, because their civil names were derived from the names of pagan gods (XI 8). During the long period that lies between the beginning of Christianity and the Constantine era, Christians had continued to use pagan names unconcernedly. It was not until the second half of the 3rd century A.D. that a change began to take place and that Christians gave their children names of martyrs or from the Scriptures. In the 5th century Theodoret of Cyrus added to this that by naming a child after a martyr Christians hoped to obtain protection for their son or daughter (Graecarum affectionum curatio VIII 67). This development is not really surprising. What is surprising and needs to be explained is why for centuries Christians continued to use pagan, theophoric names (e.g., Dionysius).

The martyrology of Carpus, Papylus and Agathonike records an interrogation that elucidates the prerequisites of this custom. The Proconsul of Pergamum asked Carpus:

> 'What is your name?' The saint answered: 'My first and most distinctive name is *christianus*; but if you want my name in the world, it is Carpus' (Eusebius, Historia ecclesiae IV 15, 48; Musurillo: 1972, 22f.).

If Eusebius' account is to be trusted, this interrogation took place in Asia Minor during the rule of Marcus Aurelius (161-180 A.D.).

A similar incident was recorded by the communities of Lyons and Vienna in a letter concerning the devastating persecutions which hit them in 177/178 A.D. A certain deacon Sanctus from Vienna was terribly beaten up by an angry mob and by soldiers. But

> he resisted them with such constancy that he did not even tell his own name, or the race or the city whence he was, nor whether he was slave or free, but to all questions answered in Latin: 'I am *christianos*'(Eusebius, Historia ecclesiae V 1,20).

This attitude cost him dearly. He was tortured continuously and most gruesomely, but he held on to his statement until he was thrown to the lions in the amphitheatre of Lyons. Christians continued to use their pagan names, but these names could not express their 'self'.

Also connected with this are reports about a spiritual name which was used in addition to the civilian name, and which was received at baptism. In 311 A.D. a Samaritan martyr made the official statement that his paternal name was Balsamus, while his spiritual name, received in baptism, was Petrus' (Harnack: 1924, 441f. Moffatt: 1917, 147).[5] Ignatius' surname 'Theophoros' must probably also be interpreted this way .

In the Roman Empire the name of the individual had had a political function. When Christians continued to use it, it was not because they agreed with this function. In explaining this situation, J. Moffatt refers to an account in the Letter of Diognet (2nd/3rd century A.D.). In this letter it says:

> Christians are not differentiated from the rest of mankind either in locality or in language or in customs...They dwell in cities of Greeks and of non-Greeks as their respective lot is cast, following the native customs in dress and food and the rest of life (5, 1-5).

The fact that Christians went on using their civil names fits in with the Christian attitude towards ancient civic culture.

The civil personal name could not express the Christian's self. The only appropriate term for this was *christianos*. According to the Acts of the Apostles, this designation was applied to the disciples in Antioch in 44 A.D.: 'And the disciples were called Christians first in Antioch' (Acts 11, 26). The words reveal that we are dealing with an official designation for Greek *chrematizein* is an official term. It was applied to the disciples by the Romans. Like Latin adjectives the word had been formed ending in -ianus. It was used in the plural to indicate supporters of a political faction, in our case the followers of a Chrestos or Christos (Sueton, Claudius 25; Tacitus, Annales XV 44, 3). By means of this designation Roman administrative officials distinguished the disciples from other political groups within the Jewish community (the *politeuma*) in Antioch (Peterson: 1959). E. Peterson states that this distinction between *christianoi* and other Jewish groups was made on account of the abolition of their civil rights which the rest of the Jews continued to enjoy in Antioch (Peterson: 1959, 75). The *christianoi* were no longer seen as belonging to the Jewish *politeuma* of Antioch (Grundmann: 1973, 529).

Christianoi was a designation with official implications also in later

---

[5] A change of name with baptism is also confirmed by Syrian documents concerning Persian martyrs, translated by Hoffmann (1880, 25).

times. When in 64 A.D. Nero tried to find culprits for the fire of Rome, his finger pointed to ' a class of men, loathed for their vices, whom the crowd styled Christians' (Tacitus, Annales XV 44, 2f.). And he imposed the death penalty upon them (Sueton, Nero 16). Nero's order to execute every person who confessed himself a Christian was still valid when, fifty years later, Plinius the Younger became governor in Asia Minor (109-113 A.D.). To the governor's own surprise, however, he had to acknowledge that, instead of political conspirators, the Christians were members of a religious sect. 'I found nothing but a degenerate sort of cult (*superstitio*) carried to extravagant lengths' (C. Plinius, Epistulae X 96, 8), Plinius reported to his sovereign. Because of that he had started to doubt 'whether it is the mere name (*nomen ipsum*) which is punishable, even if innocent of crime (*flagitia*), or rather the crimes associated with the name'(X 96, 2). Trajan told him: These people must not be hunted out; if they are brought before you and the charge against them is proved, they must be punished, but in the case of anyone who denies that he is a Christian, and makes it clear that he is not by offering prayers to our gods, he is pardoned as a result of his repentance however suspect his past conduct may be (X 97).

To test them, Christians had to make an offering to pagan gods and renounce Christ. 'True Christians' (*re vera christiani*) did not let themselves be forced into doing this (X 96, 5). They refused to worship the officially acknowledged gods of the Roman Empire. For the Roman officials the *nomen christianum* by itself was enough excuse to take action. Christian apologists bitterly complained about the fact that Christians were persecuted solely on account of their names. Justin (100-165 A.D.) (Apologia I 4, 1), Athenagoras (Plea on Behalf of the Christians, Chs. 1 and 2, addressed to Marcus Aurelius around 177) and Tertullian (160-220 A.D.) (Apologeticum 1; Ad nationes 6) were highly indignant about this situation. This material has recently been discussed by S. Benko (1985) from the point of view of 'The Name and Its Implications'. The name by itself already looked suspicious to the Roman governors and their officials. It is not necessary to assume here that a decree had been issued which was valid throughout the Empire. The existence of such a decree cannot be established and is rather improbable (de Ste. Croix: 1963; Barnes: 1968; Molthagen: 1975, 25-27). The governors of the provinces had the authority to punish violations of public order as they saw fit (*cognitio extra ordinem*) (de Ste. Croix: 1963, 11f). Since Christians refused to acknowledge the established cults of gods as well as the Jewish religion, their behaviour sparked off disturbances. By means of exemplary punishment the governors were allowed to try and restore peace in the provinces (*quies provinciae*) (Barnes: 1968, 48f.).

It was only very gradually that the Christians adopted the designation *christianoi* that was applied to them. In the later writings of the New Testament it is used twice (Acts 26, 28; 1 Pet. 4, 16), whereas Ignatius, Bishop of Antioch (d. 107/8 A.D.), took it for granted (e.g., Magn. 4; 10; Rom. 3, 2). The Martyrium Polycarpi (d. 156 A.D.) contains an account that clarifies the use of the term. After old Polycarp had threatened the Proconsul with eternal hellfire the Proconsul had his herald announce to the crowd that had gathered in the stadium of Smyrna: 'Polycarp has confessed that he is a Christian'. In response to this the crowd of pagans and Jews shouted:

> Here is the schoolmaster of Asia - the father of the Christians - the destroyer of our gods - the one that teaches the multitude not to sacrifice or do reverence (Martyrium Polycarpi 12).

For the citizens of Smyrna the term *christianos* implied a rejection of traditional ancestral religion, and this implication was recognised by those to whom this name was applied as well as by the officials of the Roman Empire. The Christians did not remain strangers to the term, for they abandoned the local laws and cults of gods themselves. The Syrian theologian Bardesanes (d. 222 A.D.) expressed this inner connection of the name with a denial of local tradition as follows: 'We all, wherever we may be, are called Christians after the one name of the Messiah'. After a description of various local laws which the Christians in the correspon-ding places refuses to observe, he sums up:

> In whatever place they are and wherever they may find themselves, the local laws cannot force them to give up the law of their Messiah, nor does Fate of the Guiding Signs force them to do things that are unclean for them (Drijvers: 1965, 60f.).

The concept of the person which underlies these statements about the name is different from that of the Jews which preceded it in history. The

Jewish names represented a self that saw itself as an object as far as social interaction with Jewish and pagan citizens was concerned. The name represented the individual before the surveyable outside world of kinship, religious community and corporate town, from which it was derived. The name *christianos*, on the other hand, expressed a self that was not represented adequately by a name which was derived from the surveyable external world. For this a designation was needed that placed the self in a critical relation to the local traditions, and which at the same time was known throughout the Empire.

Bibliography

Babcock, B.
1980 'Reflexivity: Definitions and Discriminations', in: *Semiotica* 30, 1-14 (Part 1 and 2 have been devoted to the subject: 'Signs about Signs: The Semiotics of Self-Reference') .

Barnes, T.
1968 'Legislation against the Christians', in: *JRSt* 58, 32-50.

Benko, S.
1985 *Pagan Rome and the Early Christians*, London.

Bietenhard, H.
1954 *onoma*. In: *ThWNT V,* Stuttgart, 242-283.

Bousset, W.
1966 *Die Religion des Judentums im späthellenistischen Zeitalter,* 4th ed., Tübingen.

Brown, N.O.
1966 *Love's Body*, New York.

Buchanan Gray, G.
1914 'Children Named after Ancestors in the Aramaic Papyri from Elephantine and Assuan'. In: *Festschrift J. Wellhausen,* Giessen, 163-176.

Carrithers, M., Collins, S. and Lukes, S. (eds.)
1985 *The Category of the Person. Anthropology, Philosophy, History,* Cambridge.

Cazelles, H.
1960 'Onomastique'. In: *Supplément au Dictionnaire de la Bible,* VI, 732-744.

Cohen, N.G.
1976 'Jewish Names as Cultural Indicators in Antiquity', in: *JStJ* 7, 97-128.
Coogan, M.D.
1976 *West Semitic Personal Names in the Murashu Documents* Missoula.
Cowley, A.E.
1923 *Aramaic Papyri of the Fifth Century B.C.*, Oxford.
Croix, G. de Ste.
1963 'Why were the Early Christians Persecuted?', in: *Past and Present* 26, 6-38
Daniélou, J.
1973 *La Notion de Personne ches les Pères Grecs.* In: I. Meyerson (ed.), *Problèmes de la Personne,* Paris, 113-121.
Deissmann, A.,
1923 *Licht vom Osten. Das Neue Testament und die neuentdeckten Texte der hellenistisch-römische Welt,* 4th ed., Tübingen.
Doer, B.
1937 *Die römische Namengebung. Ein historischer Versuch,* Stuttgart.
Drijvers, H.J.W.
1965 *The Book of the Laws of the Countries,* Assen.
Endress, G.
1982 *Einführung in die islamische Geschichte,* Munich.
Fohrer, G.
1969 *huios*. In: *ThWNT* 8, Stuttgart, 340-355.
Freud, S.
1956 *Totem und Tabu*, Frankfurt.
Fuhrmann,M.
1979 'Persona, ein römischer Rollenbegriff'. In: O.Marquard - K.Stiele (Hg.), *Identität.* Munich 1979, 83-106.
Geertz, C.
1983 "From the Native's Point of View': On the Nature of Anthropological Understanding (1974)'. In: C. Geertz: *Local Knowledge. Further Essays in Interpretive Anthropology,* New York, 55-70.

Grelot, P.
1972 *Documents araméens d'Egypte,* Paris.
Grundmann, W.
1973 *chrio*. In: *ThWNT* IX, Stuttgart, 518-576.
Harder, R.
1962 *Eigenart der Griechen,* Freiburg.
Harnack, A. v.
1924 *Die Mission und Ausbreitung des Christentums in den ersten drei Jahrhunderten,* 4th ed., Leipzig.
Harrer, G.A.
1940 'Saul Who also is Called Paul', in: *HThR* 33, 19-33.

Hoffmann, G.
1880 *Auszüge aus syrischen Akten persischer Märtyrer.* Leipzig.
Hölscher, G.
1925 'Zür jüdischen Namenkunde'. In: *Festschrift K. Marti,* Giessen, 148-157.
Horsley, G.H.R.
1981 *New Documents Illustrating Early Christianity. A Review of Greek Inscriptions and Papyri Published in 1976,* New Ryde.
Kajanto, I.
1967 *Supernomina. A Study in Latin Epigraphy,* Helsinki.
1977 'The Emergence of the Late Single Name System'. In: N. Duval (ed.), *L'Onomastique Latine,* Paris, 421-434
Kasher, A.
1985 *The Jews in Hellenistic and Roman Egypt,* Tübingen.
Kippenberg, H.G.
1986 'Die jüdischen Überlieferungen als 'patrioi nomoi''. In: R. Faber and R. Schlesier (eds.), *Die Restauration der Götter,* Würzburg, 45-60.
Langer, S.
1974 *Philosophy in a New Key,* 3rd ed., Cambridge.
Lebram, J.
1984 *Das Buch Daniel,* Zürich.
Lohse, E.
1959 *prosopon*. In: *ThWNT* VI, Stuttgart, 769-781.

Lukes, S.
1985 'Epilogue'. In: M. Carrithers, S. Collins and S. Lukes (eds), *The Category of the Person. Anthropology, Philosophy, History,* Cambridge, 282-301.

Marrou, H.-I.
1977 'Problèmes Généraux de l'Onomastique Chrétienne'. In: N. Duval (ed.), *L'Onomastique Latine,* Paris, 431-433.

Mauss, M.
1974 *Oeuvres.* Vol.2. Paris.
1985 'Une Catégorie de l'Esprit Humain: La Notion de Personne, Celle de 'Moi'<1938>; engl. translation in: M. Carrithers, S. Collins and S. Lukes (eds.), *The Category of the Person. Anthropology, Philosophy, History,* Cambridge, 1-25.

Mead, G.H.
1965 *On Social Psychology,* London (1934).

Menager, L.R.
1980 'Systèmes onomastiques, structures, familiales et classes sociales dans le monde gréco-romain', in: *Studia et Documenta Historiae et Iuris* 46, 147-235.

Michel-Jones, F.
1974 'La Notion de Personne'. In: M. Augé (ed.), *La Construction du Monde,* Paris, 33-51.

Moffatt, J.
1917 'Names (Christian)', in: *ERE* IX, 145-151.

Molthagen, J.
1975 *Der römischen Staat und die Christen im zweiten und dritten Jahrhundert,* 2nd ed., Göttingen.

Musurillo, H.
1972 *The Acts of the Christian Martyrs,* Oxford.

Noth, M.
1928 *Die israelitischen Personennamen im Rahmen der gemeinsemitischen Namengebung,* Stuttgart.

Peterson, E.
1959 'Christianus'. In: *Frühkirche, Judentum und Gnosis,* Rom/Freiburg, 64-87.

Ringgren, H.
1982 *jatom*, in: *ThWAT* 3, 1075-1079.

Silverman, M.H.
1985 *Religious Values in the Jewish Proper Names at Elephantine,* Neukirchen-Vluyn.

Vaux, R. de,
1964 *Das Alte Testament und seine Lebensordnungen,* Vol. 1, 2nd ed., Freiburg.

G. Vermes, F. Millar, M. Black
1979 *The History of the Jewish People in the Age of Jesus Christ (175 B.C. - A.D. 135)* by E.Schürer Vol. 2, Edinburgh.

Volz, P.
1934 *Die Eschatologie der jüdischen Gemeinde im neutestamentlichen Zeitalter,* Tübingen.

THE IMAGE OF THE PHILOSOPHER IN LATE ANTIQUITY AND IN EARLY CHRISTIANITY

Ulrich Berner

Introduction

The compatibility of philosophy with Christian faith was one of the main issues in antiquity in the encounter between pagan philosophy and Christianity. Pagan philosophers referred to the lack of a rational justification of the Christian belief-system (Origen, Contra Celsum I,9). Christian theologians contended that the philosophical and the Christian way of life were not only compatible but nearly identical (Justinus, Dialogus 8,1; Origen, Contra Celsum I,9; cf. Berner: 1982, 123-129).

This controversy between pagan and Christian philosophy is relevant for religious history and especially for the study of religious concepts of personality. For it is the image of the philosopher as one ideal concept of religious personality that is at issue here. In late antiquity pagan as well as Christian philosophers tried to establish a close relationship between religious traditions and rationality. The image of the philosopher included loyalty to a religious faith and the claim to absolute rationality. A comparison of pagan and Christian images of the philosopher shows their similarities and differences, and it can also lead to the question why Christianity prevailed in the end.

It is necessary, however, to focus the discussion on a limited area and to take only one or two examples from each side. We have significant texts from the first half of the third century. They belong, on the one hand, to the revival of Pythagoreanism and, on the other hand, to the emergence of Alexandrian Christian theology.

The *Vita Apollonii Tyanensis* of Philostratus represents a pagan image of the philosopher. The author mentions Julia Domna, the mother of the Emperor Caracalla, in the preface. He says that Julia Domna had asked him to give an account of the life of Apollonius. It is obvious that the *Vita Apollonii* is related to the politics of the Severus dynasty. Therefore it should be considered as a source of third-century religion and philosophy. Most of the research done on the *Vita Apollonii* has however been restricted to the historical problems concerning the sources which Philostratus used and to the figure of Apollonius himself in the first century (cf. Esser: 1969; Petzke 1970; Speyer: 1974; Bowie: 1978) The following discussion concentrates on the third century and compares Philostratus not with the New Testament writers but with the Christian theologians of his time. The comparison focusses on the demand for a rational foundation or justification of a religious belief-system. This demand was made by Philostratus and by the Christian theologians of Alexandria. Clement initiated this development and was succeeded by Origen. Gregory Thaumaturgos describes how Origen integrated philosophy into Christian training.

Philostratus describes Apollonius as a 'philosopher', and his activity as 'philosophizing' (Philostratus, Vita Apollonii (=VA) I,2 (12,6); I,7 (22,17); I,11 (34,12) (Mumprecht: 1983)). Our first task therefore is to explore the meaning of his concept of philosophy and to interpret his image of the philosopher. Other concepts such as 'saint' or 'prophet' are not taken into consideration (cf. Solmsen: 1968, 85; Brown: 1978). Within the framework of an historical interpretation the question whether Philostratus was at all a real philosopher does not arise either. What is important is that his description represents a pagan image of the philosopher which was valid at the time of the Severus dynasty. It is not necessary to presuppose that Philostratus consciously wrote his *Vita Apollonii* in competition with Christianity. It is possible, however, to assume a relationship of indirect competition. For pagan and Christian philosophers had to solve the same problem of establishing a rational foundation or justification of religious belief.

1. *Philostratus and his image of the philosopher*

1.1 The training of the philosopher

Philostratus stresses that Apollonius knew all the traditions of Greek philosophy. He relates that Apollonius studied together with Platonists, Stoics and followers of Aristotle and that he also became acquainted with Epicureanism (VA I,7 (22, 17-21)). So the decision of Apollonius to become a follower of Pythagoras is described as a rational one based on an all-embracing knowledge of philosophy. This rational decision, however, implies the adoption of a special way of life. Apollonius chooses an ascetic way of life called 'Bios of Pythagoras' (VA I,7 (24,14f.)). Philostratus emphasizes this unity of doctrine and life. He relates that the Pythagorean teacher failed to lead such a life and for this reason Apollonius separated himself from him.

Apollonius begins his activities as a philosopher in the temple of Asclepius (VA I,9-11). He must remain silent for a period of time before he is allowed to teach as a philosopher (VA I,14f.). This philosophical training is only the first step. The real philosopher is also obliged to know all the philosophical traditions of the world. So Apollonius has to travel to India and Ethiopia in order to become acquainted with all the famous philosophers in the world.

On his way to India Apollonius meets the Persian magicians. Philostratus describes the encounter as teaching and learning on both sides (VA I,26 (84,8f.)). The same applies to the encounter with the Indian philosophers. According to Philostratus the philosophical attitude of mind implies readiness to learn and a firm will to test every doctrine rationally (VA II,41 (230,4); III,16 (264,7-9)).

In his account of the training of the Indian philosophers, Philostratus emphasizes the unity of doctrine and life once more (VA II,30). This topic is discussed again in the encounter with the Egyptian philosophers. Apollonius explains that he chose a special lifestyle when he became a philosopher. He contends that this choice resulted from his philosophical studies which included all the traditions of Greek philosophy (VA VI,11 (608,16-19; 612,8-12)).

Apollonius is described as the perfect philosopher who knows all the philosophical systems of the world. Philostratus emphasizes the good relationship with the Indian philosophers, and makes it obvious that he sees the philosophy of India as superior to that of Egypt (VA VI,11 (618,3-620,12)).

On the one hand the training of the philosopher means the development of rationality. On the other hand it presupposes the choice of an ascetic lifestyle. Both aspects belong together. The philosophic way of life enables the philosopher to travel all over the earth in order to become acquainted with every philosophy. Real philosophizing presupposes absolute independence.

1.2 The subjects of philosophy

While travelling in Greece, Apollonius very often resides in a temple. Just at the beginning of his philosophical activities he calls together the priests of the Asclepius temple in order to philosophize about the gods (VA I,16 (50,19f.)). Philostratus stresses that human perception concerning the gods is limited (VA IV,30 (418,1-8)). It is evident however that the deity is one of the subjects of philosophy. This part of philosophy may be called 'theology'.

Another subject of philosophy is nature (VA VI,22 (668,7); VI,26 (672,24)). This subject is developed in the discussions with the Indian philosophers. The question as to what elements the world consists of is raised (VA III,34 (308,19f.)). This part of philosophy may be called 'natural philosophy'. The discussions on the immortality of the soul may be numbered among the topics of natural philosophy as well (VA VI,22 (668,6f.)).

Apollonius is interested in political and ethical problems. He discusses at some length the choice of the right political constitution (VA IV,8 (358,15f.); V,34f.). Philostratus mentions that Apollonius speaks about wisdom, bravery, prudence and other virtues (VA IV,31 (418,10-12)). His theory on justice is lengthy and detailed (VA VI,21f.). This part of philosophy may be called 'political philosophy and ethics'.

The philosophy of Apollonius embraces all the subjects of ancient philosophy, with the exception of formal logic. Philostratus wants to correct the traditional image of Apollonius as a magician and wants to describe him as a real philosopher (VA IV,18 (386,8-15); V,12 (486,1-4); VII,17 (764,17f.); VII,39 (824,17f.); VIII,7 (864,10); VIII,19 (946,15-19)). This intention becomes even more evident when his description of philosophical activity is considered.

1.3 The activity of the philosopher

At the beginning of his activities Apollonius changes the temple of Aegae into a place for philosophy (VA I,13 (38,5-7)). Later he corrects the priests when they speak falsely about the gods (VA I,16 (50,20f.)). The philosopher seems to be responsible for the theology of the religious institutions.

Apollonius does not believe in bloody sacrifices. But neither does he consider it his task to criticize sacrificial rites (VA I,31 (94,19-21)). In this respect he shows tolerance towards alien rites. His own form of sacrifice and prayer however is represented by Philostratus as the right and ideal one.

The philosopher has to lead the people to a philosophical way of life. Apollonius gives a penitential sermon during his stay at Ephesus (VA IV,2f.). In Aspendus his sermon focusses on social problems. Philostratus cites the 'message to the grain-profiteers of Aspendus' (VA I,15 (48,3-7)).

Politics is the main area of philosophical activity. Since the philosopher does not have any political ambition himself, he can be an adviser to the Emperor who is above suspicion. Philostratus elaborately describes the good relationship between Apollonius and the Emperors Vespasian and Titus (VA V,28; V,35f; VI,29-33). He also describes Apollonius's struggle with the Emperors Nero and Domitian, in order to show that there is a necessary conflict between the philosopher and the tyrant. Under such circumstances the philosopher must be ready to die for philosophy (VA IV,35-37; VII,1; VII,4; VII,31).

Apollonius is also capable of curing the people of their diseases. He either recognizes the human offences which may be the cause of the diseases or he exorcizes the demons that have caused them (VA I,9 (28,17f.); IV,10; IV,20). In addition to that, Apollonius can explain dreams and omens. He does not need an interpreter because he knows all languages (VA I,21 (64,21f.); I,22 (70,27f.); I,23 (72,22f.)). Philostratus is however very anxious to reject the traditional image of Apollonius as a magician. He stresses that he is a philosopher who is accustomed to solving problems rationally (VA V,39 (562,5)).

The philosopher has an important function in society although he himself stands outside society (cf. Brown: 1978). His authority is based on his rational faculties. His activities, however, are in every respect related to the gods.

1.4 The philosopher and the gods

Philostratus mentions again and again that Apollonius prays to the gods and offers sacrifice. He states that the gods care for the philosopher (VA I,31 (94,11-21); I,35 (108,3f.); II,39 (224,5f.)). It is obvious that he wants to stress the piety of the philosopher and his good relationship with the gods. His description presupposes a line of demarcation between the divine and the human sphere. This also applies to his statement that the gods grant the philosopher the ability to distinguish between divine and human affairs (VA II,39 (224,8f.)). So it seems to be evident that Apollonius himself does not belong to the divine sphere. There is however a problem. Some deeds of Apollonius which Philostratus relates may create the impression that he is a miracle-worker who is closely related to the divine sphere and that he might be considered a god himself. The discussion of this problem is developed in the trial of Apollonius.

The Emperor Domitian asks why the people call Apollonius 'god'. Apollonius replies that every good human being might be called 'god'. Philostratus refers to his account of the journey to India. He declares that this usage of the concept 'god' derives from Indian philosophy (VA VIII,5 (846,9f.); III,18 (270,1-5)). In his apology, which Philostratus claims to cite at full length, Apollonius discusses the possibility of calling human beings 'god'. He contends that there is a congeniality between God and man. This view of the relationship between God and man is substantiated by examples from Greek religion and Indian philosophy. So the proposition seems to have been proved that good human beings participate in the divine nature and might be called 'gods' (VA VIII,7 (878,24-880,19)). This apology gives the impression that in his biography Philostratus wants to demonstrate the possibilities of human development. According to this interpretation Apollonius represents the image of the philosopher as the ideal form of personality that, in principle, any human being can attain. The philosopher has a position between man and God because of his 'supernormal' knowledge (VA VIII,7 (888,1-6)) But that does not mean that the demarcation between the human and the divine sphere has been removed.

However, Philostratus cites some reports on Apollonius which refer explicitly to his superhuman and divine nature. Apollonius was able to free himself from his chains (VA VII,38 (824,7-12); VIII,13 (932,7-9)). He was able to disappear so that the Emperor Domitian could not punish him. Philostratus's accounts of the birth and the death of Apollonius create the impression that there is a unique relationship between Apollonius and the divine sphere. Philostratus uses sources according to which the authority of Apollonius is based on his divine origin. He does not commit himself to a single myth about Apollonius. He keeps his distance by relating all the different and contradictory myths (VA I,4-6; VIII,29f.). But he does not want to dispense with these mythical elements altogether. Thereby the authority of Apollonius seems to rest on both rational and mythical justification. Philostratus supplies both in order to justify the content of his philosophy. His image of the philosopher is not free from contradictions concerning the relationship to the gods.

1.5 The contents of philosophy

Philostratus is not interested in creating a philosophical system. In a few places he states that he is giving an abridged version of the ideas of Apollonius (VA VI,35 (694,17-22)). It is obvious however that he is more interested in giving a comprehensive description of the visible world. His biography of Apollonius includes many geographical details.

Apart from the ideas on ethics and politics the philosophy of Philostratus can be reduced to some elementary statements about the nature of God and man. The main thesis in the field of theology is that the gods are good and just (VA I,11; II,39 (224,5-11); IV,28 (410,19-21)). Referring to the destiny of Hippolytus, he states that this view applies to all the gods (VA VI,3 (582,15-18)). Zeus, Helios and other gods of Greek religion are mentioned. He emphasizes the limitations of human perception as regards the divine sphere, and shows no interest in providing a more detailed description of the gods. He considers it sufficient to sketch a positive image of the deity so that man may have confidence in his fate (VA I,11 (32,18f.)).

The theology of Philostratus could be compared to that of Apuleius. Both systems could be described as 'monotheletic polytheism' (cf. Berner: 1980). There is however an important difference. Philostratus refers to philosophy and tries to give rational reasons for his theology. Apuleius dispenses with a rational justification and refers only to myth and ritual as the basis for his theology.

The main thesis in the field of anthropology is that the human soul is immortal. Philostratus does not give a detailed explanation or proof of this doctrine, but it is emphasized again and again, especially at the end of the biography (VA VIII,31).[1] He considers it sufficient to give an elementary description of human nature so that man may lead his life confident of his fate (VA VIII,31 (970,17-19)).

The image of the philosopher shows the possible development of human nature. Philostratus takes Apollonius as an example to describe his view of the ideal way of life and his concept of personality. The philosopher leads his life in accordance with the demand for absolute rationality and at the same time with confidence in the gods. Philostratus contends that there is no contradiction or incompatibility between religious faith and philosophy. His conception can therefore be compared with the systems of the Christian Alexandrian theologians and perhaps also with the system of Mani (cf. Böhlig: 1986).

2. *The image of the philosopher in the early Christian theology of Alexandria*

2.1 Clement and the image of the Christian Gnostic

Clement distinguishes between the methods and the content of philosophy. He defends philosophy insofar as the principles of rationality are concerned. His criticism refers to the content of philosophical systems. He does not find the whole truth in any of these systems (Clemens Alexandrinus, Stromata VI,154,1; 156,1-3; 160,1). Because he makes this distinction in his judgement of Greek philosophy he is able to solve the problem of discontinuity in the transition to Christianity. It is likely that Clement knew this problem of discontinuity from his own experience since he had been a philosopher himself before he became a Christian (Eusebius, Praeparatio Evangelica II,2, 64).

There is both a discontinuity and a continuity for the philosopher who becomes a Christian. On the one hand he has to learn to obey and follow the commands of the bible (Clemens Alexandrinus, Stromata VI,154,2; VII,21,1). Clement refers to Aristotle in order to give a philosophical explanation of this discontinuity. He contends that Aristotle had already stated that the first principles are to be grasped through

[1] Philostratus relates that someone had a vision after the death of Apollonius and by this means was convinced of the doctrine of immortality.

faith (Clemens Alexandrinus, Stromata II,15,5; VII,95,6). On the other hand philosophy has its place in Christian life. Clement refers to the statements about God's justice and providence in order to give a theological explanation of this continuity. He maintains that God gave philosophy to the Greeks as he gave the Old Testament to the Jews.

The scientific perfection of that faith which has been grasped in obedience is called 'gnosis' (Clemens Alexandrinus, Stromata I,28,3; VI,153,1; 159,7-9; 162,1; VII,11,2; 55). Philosophy is a part of this gnosis. The Gnostic according to Clement is both a philosopher and a Christian. Clement uses the figure of the Christian Gnostic as a model for the ideal lifestyle and personality.

2.2 Origen and the image of the systematic theologian

According to Origen, every Christian should be a philosopher. He knows of course that only a few persons are free to realize this goal. In his refutation of Celsus's argument he contends that philosophy is a part of the ideal Christian life (Origen, Contra Celsum I, 9f; cf. Berner: 1987). The account which Gregory Thaumaturgos gives of his studies with Origen confirms this assertion.

Gregory relates that Origen considered philosophy as a prerequisite of true piety, and that his introduction to Christianity included training in philosophy (Grégoire le Thaumaturge: 1969, VI, 45f [par. 79]). At the beginning Gregory was trained by Origen in dialectics and natural science (VIIf [par. 93-114]). Then he was encouraged by Origen to study all the systems of Greek philosophy with the exception of the atheistic systems (XIIIf [par. 150-173]). Referring to the study of ethics, Gregory emphasizes the unity of doctrine and life in the personality of Origen (IX, 58 [par. 126]). After having finished these philosophical studies he was introduced to Scripture and Christian religion (XV [par. 174-183]).

Gregory describes the theologian Origen as the ideal philosopher who demonstrates the congeniality of man and God (II,32f [par. 13]); XI,18f [par. 136]). His description of Origen is another Christian image of the philosopher.

The combination of philosophy and Christian faith was initiated by Clement. Origen develops this combination by creating a system which includes the possibility of theological research. On the one hand he stresses the obedience to Scripture and to the apostolic tradition in the

Church. On the other hand he insists on the freedom to develop theological hypotheses according to rational principles (Origen, De Principiis, Praefatio 1-3). As a systematic theologian Origen is both a philosopher and a Christian.

3. *Comparison and Summary*

Philostratus, Clement and Origen describe an image of the philosopher which does not show any tension between religious faith and rationality. The image of the ideal philosopher in late antiquity as well as in early Christianity reveals a harmonic relationship between religion and philosophy, faith and reason. Philostratus and the Alexandrian theologians know the limitations of rationality and they consider it necessary for the philosopher to choose a special way of life. Clement refers to the Aristotelian theory of science and thus provides a better foundation for this connection than Philostratus. The basic assumptions about the nature of God and man are almost identical. There are however some differences concerning the rational justification of the theological and anthropological statements.

The image of the philosopher which is given by Philostratus is not free from contradictions. It is not clear whether Apollonius is an ideal representation of human nature or a unique figure belonging to the divine sphere. On the one hand Philostratus seems to be inclined to consider Apollonius as a human being in a state of full development - a conception which could be compared to the anthropology of Buddhism. On the other hand he uses mythical elements in order to establish the divine authority of Apollonius. The relationship between man and God is an unsolved problem in the anthropological foundation of his theological system.

The Christian theologians can shift this problem from anthropology to Christology. For they presuppose that Jesus is a unique figure revealing the nature of God and belonging to the divine as well as to human nature. When a distinction is made between the unique figure of Jesus and the exemplary image of the philosopher, it is easier to give reasons for the basic anthropological and theological statements. The Christian theologians can without any contradiction describe the image of the Christian philosopher in order to demonstrate the compatibility of Christian faith and rational philosophy.

Clement and Origen can refer to Scripture as an authoritative basis for their theological systems. Philostratus does not have such a possibility. He has to create this basis himself by citing, correcting or producing the sources for his biography of Apollonius, whereby he combines various texts (cf. Palm: 1976). Therefore Philostratus can be compared not only to the systematic theologians of his time but also to the New Testament writers.

The comparison of Philostratus and the Alexandrian theologians leads to the question why Christianity won the competition. However, this reflection is to be understood only within the framework of the history of religions. It does not include any theological presuppositions or statements.

Philostratus claims that he was asked by Julia Domna to write Appolonius's biography. His work is therefore closely connected with the political situation of his time. After the proclamation of the Constitutio Antonina the Emperor Caracalla had to face the problem of the lack of a unifying religious system which could be acceptable to all the citizens of the empire (cf. Latte: 1960: 359). Perhaps Philostratus in his work on Apollonius aimed at constructing such a unifying religion, based on rationality, and therefore universally acceptable. The Christian tradition however was a better basis for the development of such a religious system.

Bibliography

Berner, U.

1980 'Trinitarische Gottesvorstellungen im Kontext theistischer Systembildungen', in: *Saeculum, Jahrbuch für Universalgeschichte* 31, 93-111.

1982 *Untersuchungen zur Verwendung des Synkretismusbegriffes.* (Göttinger Orientforschungen, Reihe Grundlagen und Ergebnisse 2), Wiesbaden.

1987 'Origenes und das Synkretismus-Problem'. In: L. Lies (ed.), *Origeniana Quarta* (Innsbrucker Theologische Studien 19), 447-458).

Böhlig, A.

1986 'Denkformen hellenistischer Philosophie im Manichäismus'.

In: *Perspektiven der Philosophie.* Neues Jahrbuch 12, 11-39.

Bowie, E.L.
1978 'Apollonios of Tyana: Tradition and Reality' In: H. Temporini & W. Haase (eds.), *Aufstieg und Niedergang der römischen Welt II,* 16, 2. Berlin, 1652-1692.

Brown, P.
1978 'The Philosopher and Society in Late Antiquity' In: E.C. Hobbs & W. Wuellner (eds.), *The Center for Hermeneutical Studies in Hellenistic and Modern Culture. Protocol of the thirty-fourth Colloquy,* Berkeley, California.

Esser, D.
1969 *Formgeschichtliche Studien zur hellenistischen und zur frühchristlichen Literatur unter besonderer Berücksichtigung der vita Apollonii des Philostrat und der Evangelien,* Bonn, Diss. theol.

Grégoire le Thaumaturge
1969 *Remerciement a Origène,* Paris (SC 148).

Latte, K.
1960 'Römische Religionsgeschichte'. In: *Handbuch der Altertumswissenschaft* V, 2.

Mumprecht, V. (ed.)
1983 *Philostratos, Das Leben des Apollonios von Tyana, Griechisch-Deutsch,* herausgegeben, übersetzt und erläutert von V. Mumprecht, München/Zürich.

Palm, J.
1976 *Om Philostratos och hans Apolloniosbiografi.* Diss. Uppsala. Acta Universitatis Upsaliensis, Studia Graeca Upsaliensia 10, Stockholm.

Petzke, G.
1970 *Die Traditionen über Apollonios von Tyana und das Neue Testament.* (Studia ad corpus Hellenisticum Novi Testamenti 1), Leiden.

Solmsen, F.
1968 'Some Works of Philostrat the Elder'. In: F. Solmsen, *Kleine Schriften II,* Hildesheim (Collectanea IV/2).

Speyer, W.
1974 'Zum Bild des Apollonios bei Heiden und Christen', in: *Jahrbuch für Antike und Christentum* 17, 47-63.

THE SAINT AS SYMBOL

Conceptions of the Person in Late Antiquity and Early Christianity

Han J.W. Drijvers

The third century C.E. is generally viewed both as a crucial age in the history of the Roman Empire and as representing a key stage in the process of Christianization. At the end of the second century Christianity was still confined to a tiny minority consisting of small well-organized communities in a mainly urban context. At the end of the fourth century it became the official ideology of the Empire, although even then the majority of the population was still pagan.[1] It is common in ancient history to link political and economic events with psychological or religious reactions to them, particularly so in relation to descriptions of the third century. In A. Alföldi's view this was the age of a world-crisis in which the barbarians threatened the frontiers and 'der Zusammenbruch der altrömischen sittlichen und religiösen Anschauungen das Reich in tödliche Agonie stiessen' (cf. Alföldi: 1967). E.R. Dodds could call it an 'age of anxiety' and exclaim: 'Where did all this madness come from?', when he looked at the dominance of asceticism as a force in shaping man's relation to the divine and the demoniac world and to his own physical existence (Dodds: 1965, 34; see now Smith & Lounibos: 1984, 13ff.). It was the age that P. Brown called the period of *The Making of Late Antiquity*. In his view, that period brought about a fundamental change in man's relationship with the divine and the rise of what he has called: 'the friends of God' (Brown: 1978a, 56ff. cf. Rouselle: 1985).

These are however impressionistic characterizations; they do not explain single historical facts, but evoke the impression of movements of world historical importance. All these scholars saw what might be termed 'religious' factors as crucial in the process of historical change, whether

[1] There exists a vast literature on the Christianization of the Roman Empire and on the relations between pagans and christians. Of recent publications I mention MacMullan: 1984, Wilken: 1984, and Lane Fox: 1986; for a critical and useful evaluation of some current ideas see Cameron: 1986

they labelled them as superstition, or madness, or the rise of the friends of god. All these designations imply that the third century C.E. was a period more religious than any earlier one. At their heart lies the question why Christianity won and caused fundamental changes in the Roman Empire the foundation of which was laid during the third century. This intriguing question has kept scholarly minds busy for centuries and caused sharp disagreements among students of late Antiquity and early Christianity.[2]

This paper does not pretend to give another version of cultural change during the period 200 to 400 C.E., nor does it intend to deal with the problem of why and how the apocalyptic message of a Jewish rabbi from Nazareth became the leading ideology of the Roman Empire, although that problem will certainly long occupy both scholarly and lay minds in our Christian and post-Christian society. My main question is rather how during that period people wrote about typical representatives of the various parts of society, for it is in their writing that contemporary conceptions of the person come to light. It is a remarkable and certainly not accidental fact that the writing of biographies assumed enormous proportions at that time and indeed partly took over the rôle of historiography (cf. Cox: 1983, 4ff.).

These biographies - acts of martyrs and lives of Christian saints, philosopher's lives and portraits of emperors, originating in pagan circles - are first and foremost the products of literary rhetoric. They do not primarily describe the lives and fates of particular individuals, but put them into the framework of current concepts of the human person; as such they are the expressions of collective perceptions. What Peter Burke wrote on saints' lives : 'One is never a saint except for other people - in other words, the history of the saints is fundamentally a history of collective perceptions' (cf. Burke: 1984, 20), also applies to biographies of sages and philosophers, acts of martyrs and lives of emperors. These biographies, therefore, do not present a mixture of fact and fantasy in the sense that we can extract real historical facts of life from them and dismiss the other, often miraculous, elements as products of the author's fancy. Even what we are inclined to call an author's private fantasy is still culturally determined and part of collective perceptions, since society

---

2 It all goes back to Gibbon: 1776-1788; cf. Momigliano: 1963 & 1980.

controls not only public behaviour, but also emotions and fantasies (Rosaldo: 1984, 141ff.). The various lives, therefore, present concepts of the person and fit individual lives into their framework. These concepts in their turn are embedded in a social context and relate in particular to the degree of institutionalization of offices and the nature of authority (La Fontaine: 1985, 138f.). The concept of the person relates mortal human beings to a social continuum. Ideas about society and the concept of the person are thus interdependent.

The concept of the person is not immediately accessible to us since it is packed up in symbolic language. Symbols are understood here as vehicles of meaning that are socially determined. Social life itself is mapped by conceptions carried in symbols, that is by culture. An analysis of such symbols will make clear that they are a model of as well as a model for the world. In the words of Clifford Geertz, 'they express the world's climate and shape it' (Geertz: 1973, 94f. on C. Geertz's work and theories see Moore & Reynolds: 1984, in particular 71). This applies to every aspect of the contents of our biographies of saints and sages, their food and sexual behaviour, their body and mind, their actions and words. Trying to understand the meaning of these symbols means returning to texts and focussing on their interpretation (Geertz: 1983, 69f.). Interpretation is a way of sorting out the structures of signification and determining their social ground and import, which unavoidably brings us back to the hermeneutic circle. Yet a continuous interplay between detail and generalities is central to every field of study that tries to penetrate into other people's modes of thought, and therefore to history (Geertz: 1973)

The lives of pagan sages on the one hand, and of Christian saints on the other embody specific conceptions of the person expressive of the cultural values of the respective groups responsible for their composition and transmission. Sages and saints represent a type of 'holy man', the *theios aner*. The vast majority of the many modern studies on this subject emphasize the differences between the pagan sage and the Christian saint. They have often been considered totally different personages with little or nothing in common (so e.g., Junod: 1981). The emphasis on the dissimilarities between these two types of holy men results from a view of early Christendom that regards it as a completely new and unique phenomenon in the ancient world which would radically transform classical society, a view common to both apologists and opponents of

Christianity. The first group defends its uniqueness and potential for the salvation of pagans, the second category considers the Christians a band of moral fanatics with often immoral standards and practices which brought about religious coercion and tyranny (so e.g., de Ste. Croix: 1981, 418-452). But Christianity was an integral part of classical culture and in their wrote the Christians reacted to the same situations in the Roman Empire as the pagans did. It therefore falsifies the historical picture of the Roman Empire, if we continue writing about 'Christianity *and* Classical Culture', or 'The Christians *and* the Roman Empire', not to mention the implications of such titles as *Umwelt des Urchristentums* and the like (see e.g., Wilken: 1984; Benko: 1984; Leipoldt & Grundmann: 1965; a typical example of this wrong approach is Grant: 1986; see Cameron: 1987). Like the pagans, the Christians were bearers of classical culture and citizens of the Roman Empire which was their social world. They lived in the same cities and towns, were confronted with the same authorities and calamities, in times of starvation they were all hungry and died, they received the same education, caught the same diseases and spoke the same languages. Pagans and Christians alike produced writings in which their views of man and society were expressed in religious idiom. The biographies of pagan sages and Christian saints ought therefore to be read together as mirrors of their social world.

Yet these lives also function as paradigms of ideal manhood and social ordering, a code through which reality is read and understood by the groups in which these lives originate. They provide us with a metaphysics of human behaviour, a moral that is preached, though certainly not always practised. In P. Veyne's recent formulation of this idea Max Weber can still be heard: 'Toute idée général relative au monde social est un construction, un idéal-type' (Veyne: 1978). It is part and parcel of man's nature that he idealizes the truth of his moral and social constructions: 'le besoin vital de confondre ce qui est et ce qui devrait être'. In other words the image of man and the conceptions of the human person that can be read from these late antique and early Christian texts are culturally determined symbols. We cannot do without such symbols, because 'man is so in need of such symbolic sources of illumination to find his bearings in the world, because the nonsymbolic sort that are constitutionally ingrained in his body cast so diffused a light' (Geertz: 1973, 45). With Clifford Geertz I am of the opinion that 'culture is best seen not as complexes of concrete behavior patterns - customs, usages, traditions, habit clusters - as has, by and large, been the case up to now, but as a set of control mechanisms - plans, recipes, rules, instructions (what computer engineers call "programs") - for the governing of behavior' (Geertz: 1973, 44). An analysis of the figurative language of biographies of sages and saints is particularly suited to the discovery of such 'programs' of human behaviour, in which biological, psychological, sociological and other cultural variables have their part within an overall pattern of synthetic approach.

The type of the holy man is described most extensively by L. Bieler (Bieler: 1976 (1935/1936). Bieler's monograph is a typical product of the German school of religious history which presents a picture of the holy man through the medium of a variety of written sources of different origins and periods. That picture is as valid for late antique paganism as for early Christianity, and still stands, notwithstanding various objections expressed by Christian apologists and anti-Christian polemists (see e.g., Holladay: 1977, 1ff. cf. Betz: 234-312; Cox: 1983, 3ff.). The synthesis created by Bieler, however, never existed. Bieler did not consider the question why and for whom particular individuals represented divine qualities. An inquiry into the social rôle of the holy man is therefore a necessary addition to Bieler's work, for 'the attempt to evaluate candidates for divine status was firmly rooted in social experience' (Gallagher: 1982, 177).

Such an inquiry is beyond the scope of this paper. I shall restrict myself mainly to the relation of mind and body, to sexual and alimentary asceticism, and to the holy man's relationship with wealth and property. I shall draw my examples from a restricted corpus of texts representative respectively of a pagan philosophical milieu and of Syrian Christianity. The latter has been chosen here because it put great emphasis on the contrast between body and mind, propagated asceticism, produced many holy men and their lives, and was permeated with philosophical elements (Drijvers: 1984a; Nagel: 1966). Porphyry's *vita Plotini*, *vita Pythagorae* and *epistula ad Marcellam* will represent the pagan side (Porphyry: 1951; Porphyre: 1982).

The pagan sage represents divine *nous* in bodily disguise on earth and is totally focussed on that divine element in himself. His biography is written as a kind of propaganda for the cult of the divine mind, his interior self, where his wisdom and power are located. Porphyry opens the biography of his teacher Plotinus with the statement:

> Plotinus, the philosopher of our times, seemed ashamed of being in the body. As a result of his state of mind he could never bear to talk about his race or his parents or his native country. And he objected so strongly to sitting to a painter or sculptor that he said to Amelius, who was urging him to allow a portrait of himself to be made, 'Why really, is it not enough to have to carry the image in which nature has encased us, without your requesting me to agree to leave behind me a longer-lasting image of the image, as if it was something genuinely worth looking at?' (Porphyry: 1951; Cox: 1983, 102).

Full emphasis is put on the human mind as the vehicle *par excellence* for defining man's nature. Man's body is no longer the first instrument for expressing of his real character. Man's true nature manifests itself according to the extent to which the mind can tame the body and reign over it. A final denial of man's bodily existence is at the same time the manifestation of his true self. The concept of the 'multiplicity of the self' which goes back to the Greek philosophers of the fifth century B.C., developed into a 'dichotomy between the self and the body' (Brown: 1978, 68). The following passage from Porphyry's life of Pythagoras illustrates this most clearly:

> He (i.e. Pythagoras) practised a philosophy which aimed at redeeming and freeing the mind (nous) that is assigned to us from hindrances and bonds. Without it one is absolutely not able to know or see something that is sound or true irrespective which sense one uses. Because the mind in itself sees and hears everything, and the rest is deaf and blind (Porphyry: Life of Pythagoras, 46).

The body and its needs constitute the main hindrances to and bonds of the divine mind and therefore Pythagoras's philosophy was a process of spiritual purification. At the end of these spiritual exercises the eyes of the mind could see true reality (Porphyry, Life of Pythagoras; cf. Fowden: 1982, 34ff.). A philosophical life consequently implied a form of asceticism, restriction of food and other bodily needs, and especially sexual continence. A well known example is provided by Porphyry's relationship with his wife Marcella. The philosopher married Marcella, a widow with seven children, and almost immediately left her alone to go on a diplomatic mission. Far from home he wrote her a letter with injunctions to embrace wisdom and to say farewell to all passions, for passions are the cause and origin of all disease and evil. Marcella should free herself from her body in order to serve the godhead in and with the spirit, because that is the path to *homoiosis toi theoi* (Porphyry, epist. ad Marcellam, 15-16).

Like most philosophers Porphyry and Marcella belonged to the well-to-do. Porphyry, therefore, took wealth for granted; he could afford to give the useful advice that when somebody was not rich, he should be content with being able to supply himself with the bare necessities of life (Porphyry, epist. ad Marcellam, 1; cf. Brown: 1978, 14 ff.). Apparently it did not occur to him that many people did not have even the barest means to survive (see in general Patlagean: 1977, 17-35; cf. Cameron: 1980). Porphyry and Plotinus, Iamblichus and Themistius, like most philosophers in late Antiquity, belonged to the well-to-do aristocracy, the urban social and intellectual élite, with whom they shared a common education and culture. Their ideal of a fully developed divine mind, which raised man to a divine status and dominated his bodily needs and passions, symbolizes the full command of an upper-class individual over his society. These philosophers were anything but austere and unworldly types who committed themselves to esoteric doctrines far away from the noise and the trouble of their cities. On the contrary, they often served their cities and authorities at embassies or on delicate missions; they were highly valued advisers and mediators. Just because in their spiritual activities they embodied the ideals of their group, i.e. total dominance over the society of which they formed the tiny élite, they could fulfil the rôle of outsider and insider at the same time (Brown: 1978). Their asceticism emphasized the value of the mind and provided them with the essential social distance, so that they could address large groups of the aristocracy with authority. In this way the ideal of humanity supported the effective use of power and authority (Cox: 1983, 17ff. Fowden: 1982, 48-51).

The concept of a divine mind in a perishable body goes back to Plato. The biographies of late antique philosophers put full emphasis on the divine mind and considered their bodies as a mere hindrance. A true philosopher is a divine epiphany and has divine qualities of wisdom and performing miracles (see Tiede: 1972; Kee: 1983). Even his physical appearance, his voice, gestures, eyes, are more than human and are often described as the visible presence of the gods (Bieler: 1976 (1935-1936)).

As *theioi andres* they represent the divine on earth and man's final destiny, the *homoiosis toi theoi* when his mind will be freed from the body and will fly upwards to its eternal destiny.

Like the pagan sage, the Christian holy man is first and foremost an intermediate figure, who represents the divine on earth. His life is, therefore, often patterned on the Gospel story of Jesus's earthly life of which he is the true successor and imitator (Drijvers: 1982). Like his pagan counterpart, the Christian holy man disciplines his mind, tames his bodily and sexual passions such as food and sleep, keeps himself distant from ordinary society, and can function as a mediator (Brown: 1971; cf. Drijvers: 1981; cf. Murray: 1983). But although physical ascesis was a fundamental element both of the Christian holy man's life and of that of the pagan sage, there was one fundamental difference. The Christian holy man did not have a divine mind or spirit *per se*; bodily ascesis transformed his body into a 'holy temple' in which the divine spirit could dwell, as it did in Jesus of Nazareth. As the indwelling of the *Logos* transformed Jesus into God's incarnate son, the indwelling of the holy spirit made the ascetic saint into a divine or angelic being, a son of God (cf. Drijvers: 1988). The Acts of the Apostle Judas Thomas written in Syriac about 225 C.E. in the east Syrian region, the Syriac life of the Man of God at Edessa written about 400 C.E., and Theodoret's *historia religiosa* each picture in their own way the portrait of the Christian holy man (see e.g., Canivet: 1977; Blersch: 1978).

The Acts of the Apostle Judas Thomas symbolize the indwelling of the Holy Spirit as a wedding feast at which the human soul unites itself with the divine spirit, for which asceticism is a *conditio sine qua non*. Judas Thomas, Jesus's twin brother, and in literature a typical representative of the Christian holy man, preaches the gospel of sexual continence to the daughter of the King of Andropolis ('the city of men') and her bridegroom:

> Remember, my children, what my brother (i.e. Jesus) spake with you, and know to whom he committed you; and know that as soon as ye preserve yourselves from this filthy intercourse, ye become pure temples, and are saved from afflictions, manifest and hidden... and ye shall be without care and without grief and without sorrow; and ye shall be hoping for the time when ye shall see the true wedding-feast; and ye shall be in it praisers of God and ye shall be numbered with those who enter into the bridal chamber (Wright: 1968 (1871),

155f. see Klijn: 1962, 38-53; cf. Tissot: 1981; Drijvers: forthcoming).

The Christian saint is not alone with his own spirit; he enjoys the warmth and intimacy of a true marriage and shares those feelings with others, with whom he will be numbered before God's face. All those whose body is pure like a temple form a new body, the Christian community, Christ's body (cf. Drijvers: 1984a, 10ff.). Judas Thomas, Jesus's double, is its centre and represents the highest ideal of man in which God's spirit dwells, as it did in Jesus. When man has been united again with the divine spirit, he symbolically returns to his original state before the fall, in which he was immortal and not yet a sexual being. In a sense he becomes identical with Christ. Just as God's Spirit dwelt in the man Jesus and gave him the power, the wisdom and the will of the Father, so Jesus dwells in those who believe in him in the form of the Spirit that man lost in the beginning, and gives him wisdom, the right will, power, immortal life. Sexual purity is a necessary condition for this. The Acts of Thomas phrases it in the following way:

> Purity is the athlete who is not overcome. Purity is worthy before God of being to Him a familiar handmaiden. Purity is the temple of God, and everyone who guards it guards His temple and the Messiah dwells in him (Acts of Thomas, 85; cf. Wright: 1968 (1871), 220-221; cf. I Cor. 6, 19, a cardinal text in encratism).

It is a Christian variant of the *homoiosis toi theoi* of which the bridegroom in the Acts of Thomas says the following:

> I praise Thee, new God, who by means of a stranger hast come hither. I glorify Thee, God,... who hast removed me from corruption, and hast sown in me life; who hast delivered me from the disease that was abiding in me forever; who hast revealed to us Thyself, and I have perceived in what state I am; who hast saved me from falling and hast led me on to a better state; who hast rescued me from these transitory things, and hast deemed me worthy of those that are not transitory; who hast let Thyself down even to my littleness; that Thou mightest bring me unto Thy greatness,... who didst show me how to seek for myself and to put away from me the things that are not mine; who, when I did not know Thee, hast sought me Thyself (Acts of Thomas, 15; cf. Wright: 1968 (1871). 157f.).

The bride is even unveiled, because she has regained the pure a-sexual state of before the fall:

> And that I am not veiled, is because the veil of corruption is taken away from me; and that I am not ashamed, is because the deed of shame has been removed far from me; and that I am not repentant, is because the repentance, which restores to life, abides in me. And that I am cheerful and gay, is because, in the day of this transitory joy, I am not agitated by it; and that this deed of corruption is despised by me, and the spoils of this wedding-feast that passes away, is because I am invited to the true wedding-feast; and that I have not had intercourse with a husband, the end whereof is bitter repentance, is because I am betrothed to the true Husband (Acts of Thomas, 14; cf. Wright: 1968 (1871), 157).

It is worth mentioning that the Christian symbolism of body and spirit displays a spatial orientation that is different from the pagan one. Man's spirit is not elevated to the world of the divine through asceticism and spiritual exercises; rather the divine spirit descends into his pure body, where the ascetic *kenosis* made room for the indwelling of Christ as God's spirit.

Like the pagan holy man the Christian saint cultivated an ideal of poverty and alimentary asceticism. The Apostle Judas Thomas, who did not taste food or drink, because he came 'for something that is better than eating or drinking, for the King's rest and that I might accomplish his will', used the money that king Gudnaphar gave him to build a palace, to support the poor so that he built a palace in heaven (Acts of Thomas, 17-29; Wright: 1968 (1871), 159-169). In the life of the Man of God at Edessa, who was from a very wealthy family, we are told that the saint spent his days among the poor in the forecourt of the church. He collected alms as an anonymous beggar, but when he had enough for a simple meal he gave the rest to the poor (Drijvers: 1982, 189). Theodoret's *Historia Religiosa* is full of examples of the extreme poverty of the Syrian saints, their restricted alimentary regime, and their care of the poor (Canivet: 1977, 207-233). The diet of the Christain holy man was thus the same as that of the poorest in society with whom he identified himself, as Christ had done (cf. Rouselle: 1983, 205-226).

As *theios aner* the Christian holy man represents the divine, more particularly Christ, on earth and man's final destiny of returning to his original divine state of purity and incorruptibility. The holy man's biography is therefore modelled on the Gospel story of Christ's life. After his death and burial the tomb of the Man of God at Edessa was found empty. Simeon the Stylite spent his nights praying on top of his column in the form of Christ's *stasis* of the Cross. The Man of God at Edessa prayed every night with outstretched arms amidst the sleeping poor of the city, like Jesus in Gethsemane (Blersch: 1978, 42ff. Amiaud: 1889, 5; Drijvers: 1988, 12f.). Judas Thomas healed the sick, expelled demons, and raised the dead as Christ did, and we are told the same about many holy men whose lives were written by Theodoret (Adnès & Canivet: 1967, 56ss).

The pagan sage and the Christian holy man had much in common. Both were representatives of the divine on earth, practised asceticism, performed miracles and healings, possessed special knowledge and wisdom, and lived in a certain social disengagement. However, they did not recognize each other. The controversy between Celsus and Origen over Jesus may illustrate this point. Celsus as a typical representative of the literary élite applied the criteria characteristic of such an élite for conferring the status of divine man - noble birth, rich family, good education and a well-known and respected country of origin. The bastard son of a carpenter, a carpenter himself, did not meet those requirements, since he was born in an out-of-the-way corner of the oikoumene in an insignificant polis. Origen's standards were totally different (cf. Gallagher: 1982, 173-180). The King of Andrapolis, whose daughter embraced a pure life and asceticism, considered the Apostle Judas Thomas a sorcerer, who destroyed existing social relations:

> When the king heard these things from the bridegroom and the bride, he rent his garments and said to those who were by him: 'Go forth in haste through the whole city, and go about, and bring me that sorcerer, whom I introduced with my own hands into my house, and bade him pray over my unlucky daughter. To the man who shall find him and bring him to me, I will give whatever he shall ask' (Acts of Thomas, 16; Wright: 1968 (1871), 158).

The holy men of pagan and Christian origin represent the highest rank in the hierarchy of mankind for their respective groups. In that status they stand for the supernatural and the world of the divine on earth, and consequently, their power and wisdom are pictured as divine qualities. Their leading position on the scale of human values is defined in terms of the relation between body and mind, in which the body stands for the lower principle and the spiritual mind of divine origin for the higher one. Divinity is pure mind, its opposite mere matter. A religious principle, therefore, governs the hierarchy of human society in late Antiquity and gives it its meaning. It should be noted that status in that hierarchy is independent of the actual distribution of political and economic power. A particular saint or sage may represent the ideal of humanity without having any real power or authority. A definition in religious terms, however, does not imply that saints and sages are exclusively religious personalities who sometimes happen to perform a mundane rôle. Their symbolic function is religiously phrased, but nevertheless has a primarily social value, for religion is not a separable and unvarying entity within a culture, but the symbolic way in which a culture designs an image of itself: Society is God (see for this famous Durkheimian saying Douglas: 1970, 161f.).

Given the asceticism that pervades both saints' lives and biographies of sages, it cannot be said that the rise of Christianity in the Roman Empire was itself responsible for an ascetic morality, so that the population of the Empire, when it embraced a new religion also drastically changed its behaviour in streets and bedrooms. Nor is it possible to say that social or psychological reasons caused a fundamental change in the dominant views of man and society, which in its turn brought about the Christianization of the Empire, because Christianity appealed to a special desire for salvation. Biographies of sages and saints show that another, different image of the self manifested itself in pagan and Christian circles from the end of the second century onwards. The models of behaviour were no longer correlated with social status - a senator ought to behave in an appropriate manner, while the behaviour of a female slave ought to be totally different from that of her mistress of noble birth - but were the expression of an ideal of manhood governed by divine principles which can and ought to be realized by every person in his or her physical existence: *une morale des vertus intériorisées* (Veyne: 1978, 56).

P. Veyne has seen a relation between the ascetic ideal of the imperial élite of the second and third centuries C.E. and a fundamental change in the social rôle of the Roman aristocracy from the beginning of the Empire onwards. The existence of the emperor forced a different rôle upon the aristocrats:

> avec le passage d'une aristocratie concurrentielle (sorte de féodalité où les rivalités entre clans sont féroces) à une aristocratie de service, où l'on fait carrière en étant en bons termes avec ses pairs!

In fact asceticism is a kind of psychological reaction to that social shift in which 'répression est autorépression' (Veyne: 1978, 38; see now Veyne: 1985). There is no direct causal link between social change and shift in behaviour; it is a sort of *gymnastique interne* which brings about a form of reaction to such changes. In this way different rules for governing behaviour come into being. Again it should be emphasized that the various texts do not themselves directly mirror actual behaviour, but rather give specimens of these rules.

In this context it must be remarked that whatever changes in cultural values occurred, the relations between the sexes remained fundamentally the same. In traditional society only men had power and authority and consequently could use women, slavegirls, and boys as objects of sexual lust. There was no direct relation between marriage and the experience of sexuality, which was often perceived in isolation from marriage. That pattern of differences in power also found a continuation in the ascetic morality and marriage ethics of a later period. Man exercises power over himself and constrains women to the status of virginity, because marriage and sexuality are two different things. This means, not that asceticism and sexual abstinence was common practice in an average marriage - the opposite was rather the case - but that the cultural value of individual and society was expressed in this manner. The ascetic philosopher was the star of that morality in the élite society of that time. His biography embodies in a symbolic way the cultural values of a small segment of the late antique upper class in the way his pupils formulated them. As the philosopher cherishes and cultivates his divine *nous*, so he represents the *alter ego* of his pupils, an ideal that is formed and proclaimed.

The ascetic morality that the Christians propagated is, therefore, not a Christian discovery, but the expression of an existing pattern. In the words of Aline Rousselle:

> la force de l'argumentation chrétienne: elle reprend une argumentation bien

> ancrée dans les esprits masculins: elle l'applique aux femmes dans une opposition de termes décalée: on passe de l'opposition prostitution ou homosexualité/mariage à l'opposition mariage/virginité (Rouselle: 1983, 176).

It is, therefore, not surprising that the ascetic writings of early Christianity do provide different grounds for the virginal status of men and women. Through sexual continence men regain the original God-given status that they had in paradise. Judas Thomas showed the bridegroom 'how to seek for himself and to put away from him the things that are not his'. But women are persuaded into a status of continence by men, who preach a spiritual marriage with a heavenly bridegroom. They are kept in a subordinate position, a marriage without sex that leaves the traditional pattern of the sexes intact. Women are even constrained to give up their sex and symbolically become men. The last *logion* of the *Gospel of Thomas*, which preaches the same asceticism as the *Acts of Thomas* reads:

> Simon Peter said to them, 'Let Mary leave us, for women are not worthy of Life'. Jesus said, 'I myself shall lead her in order to make her male, so that she too may become a living spirit resembling you males. For every woman who will make herself male will enter the Kingdom of Heaven' (Robinson: 1977).

The moralizing character of Christian belief, whose development ran parallel with an apparent shift in morality in the Roman Empire, provided both a justification of these ideals of asceticism and virginity and an appropriate ideological background. All the treatises *De Virginitate* were written by men about women for the Christian community. The much-debated topic of early Christian virginity has therefore more to do with social relations between man and woman than with the actual practice of sexual continence.

This last point brings us to the question of the social implications of the mind-and-body symbolism which plays such a paramount rôle in Christian as well as in pagan literature. Mary Douglas (1970, 162ff.) suggested 'that philosophical controversies about the relation of spirit to matter or mind to body be interpreted as exchanges of condensed statements about the relation of society to the individual'. Mind-and-body symbolism is a metaphor for social organization. If we adopt that approach for the interpretation of the ascetic symbolism of saints' lives and biographies of sages, the question is not where it comes from, but what it means in a wider context of individual and society (see Gager: 1982).

From such an interpretative perspective the dominance of mind over body as presented in the biographies of pagan sages, means total authority over their traditional society. It is not surprising that notwithstanding their influence, these philosophers did not create new forms of social organization, but corroborated and confirmed the existing ones. Their influence was probably restricted to the educated classes, who were familiar with current philosophical traditions and discussions. They represent the sum of cultural values of pagan society that were embodied in an individual. Their biographies propagate the way of life of that group of the pagan upper-class at the same time as the Christian Church created a new ideal of manhood and society in its writings.

Saints' lives and related literature present conceptions of the person with a specific bodily symbolism that stands for a new relation of the individual to his society. The indwelling of Christ's spirit in each individual transforms him into a son of God, makes him return to his original paradisal state, changes his body into the condition it had before the fall. On the other hand, asceticism creates the necessary conditions for the indwelling of the divine spirit. There is, therefore, a continuous interplay between the individual and the society to which he belongs. Christ as God's spirit governs his bodily existence, but at the same time he is head of the group that all these reborn bodies form. This religious symbolism creates strong bonds and boundaries. Bonds between the members of the group, boundaries of each individual and of the group as a whole (Douglas: 1970, 140ff. Douglas: 1982, 183ff where she expounds on her views given in Douglas: 1970). The strong emphasis on boundaries is also expressed by the severe self-exorcism of the saint and his frequent exorcism of other people. The Manichaean *electus* is another example of this self-exorcism which tried to expel Satan and all evil through a practice of extreme asceticism which went hand in hand with the formation of a closed group, the Manichaean Church. The human body is often symbolized as an army camp which should be defended against the outward enemy (Drijvers: 1984b). As exorcists the saints purify individuals and whole groups and accentuate boundaries between within and without. The human body, therefore, functions as a typical boundary area. In it the specific problems of human existence, food and sex, disease and death, are overcome in a symbolic and exemplary way. The ascetic saint on the one hand 'acted out a ritual of social disengagement' (Peter Brown), but on the other stood in the centre of a new society of which he represented the ideal of manhood, in which the divine had come to dwell. The saint's life is consequently often patterned on the Gospel story of Jesus's earthly life of which he is the true successor as in principle everyone can be.[3] He unites the religiously defined human élite with society in general, for which he functions as a symbol.

The Christian saint has much in common with the pagan sage. Their *lives* represent the same literary genres and the same ideals of humanity tamed through *ascesis* to restore its true essence. Christian writing is not more nor less sophisticated than the texts the pagans produced. Even seemingly popular stories like the apocryphal acts of the apostles with all their miracles and fantastic elements display a high level of symbolism and sophistication (see e.g., LaFargue: 1985). Saint and sage function as symbols, and represent conceptions of the person that have much in common. But the specific body-and-mind symbolism that emerges in the lives of the saints is expressive of new social grouping as well as a strong stimulus to such grouping. Whereas the pagan sage was a typical example of a literate upper-class which could only confirm an existing social order and pattern, but not change it or mobilize its inherent powers, the Christian body social reached the top of Roman society and acquired power in the Empire by creating a conception of the person with such symbolic power that it could embrace not merely one class, but all groups of the population.

Bibliography

Adnès, A. & P. Canivet.
1967 'Guérisons miraculeuses et exorcismes dans 'l'Histoire Philothée' de Théodoret de Cyr', in: *RHR* 171, 56ss.

Alföldi, A.
1967 *Studien zur Geschichte der Weltkrise des 3. Jahrhunderts nach Christus,* Darmstadt.

---

[3] The theme of *imitatio Christi* is a central one in early Christian anthropology and hagiography. Cf. Drijvers: 1984c.

Amiaud, A.
1889 *La légende syriaque de Saint Alexis l'homme de dieu,* Paris.

Benko, S.
1984 *Pagan Rome and the Early Christians,* London.

Betz, H.D.
Art. 'Gottmensch II'. In: *RAC* 234-312.

Bieler, L.
1976 *Theios ANER. Das Bild des 'göttlichen Menschen' in Spätantike und Frühchristentum,* 2 Tle, Wien 1935-1936.

Blersch, H.G.
1978 *Die Säule im Weltgeviert. Der Aufstieg Simeons, des ersten Säulenheiligen,* Sophia 17, Trier.

Brown, P.
1971 'The Rise and Function of the Holy Man in Late Antiquity', in: *JRS* 61, 80-101.
1978a *The Making of Late Antiquity,* Cambridge/London.
1978b *The Philosopher and Society in Late Antiquity,* The Center for Hermeneutical Studies in Hellenistic and Modern Culture, 34th Colloquy, Berkeley University.

Burke, P.
1984 'Making Saints', in: *London Review of Books* 18-31 October, 20.

Cameron, Averil
1980 'Late Antiquity - The Total View', in: *Past and Present* 88, 129-135.
1986 'Redrawing the Map: Early Christian Territory after Foucault', in: *JRS* 76, 226-271.

Canivet, P.
1977 *Le monachisme syrien selon Théodoret de Cyr,* Théologie hist. 42, Paris.

Cox, P.
1983 *Biography in Late Antiquity. A Quest for the Holy Man,* Berkeley/Los Angeles/London.

Croix, G. de Ste.
1981 *The Class Struggle in the Ancient Greek World,* London.

Dodds, E.R.
1965 *Pagan and Christian in an Age of Anxiety,* Cambridge.

Douglas, M.
1970 *Natural Symbols. Explorations in Cosmology,* London.
1982 *In the Active Voice,* London.

Drijvers, H.J.W.
1981 'Hellenistic and Oriental Origins'. In: S. Hackel (ed.), *The Byzantine Saint,* Studies Suppl, to Sobornost 5, London, 25-33 = East of Antioch IV.
1982 'Die Legende des heiligen Alexius und der Typus des Gottesmannes im syrischen Christentum'. In: M. Schmidt (ed.), *Typus, Symbol, Allegorie bei den östlichen Vätern und ihren Parallelen im Mittelalter,* Eichstätter Beitr. 4, Regensburg, 187-217.
1984a *East of Antioch. Studies in Early Syriac Christianity,* London.
1984b 'Conflict and Alliance in Manichaeism'. In: H.G. Kippenberg (ed.), *Struggles of Gods,* Religion and Reason 31, Berlin/N.Y./Amsterdam, 99-124.
1984c 'Athleten des Geistes. Zur politischen Rolle der syrischen Asketen und Gnostiker'. In: J. Taubes (ed.), *Gnosis und Politik,* Paderborn/München, 109-120.
1988 'De heilige man in het vroege Syrische Christendom'. In: A. Hilhorst (ed.), *De Heiligenverering in de eerste eeuwen van het Christendom,* Nijmegen, 11-26.
in press 'Thomasakten'. In: Schneemelcher (ed.), *Neutestamentliche Apokryphen II.*

Fontaine, J.S. La
1985 'Person and Individual: some anthropological reflections'. In: M. Carrithers & S. Collins & S. Lukes (eds.), *The Category of the Person. Anthropology, Philosophy, History,* Cambridge.

Fowden, G.
1982 'The Pagan Holy Man in Late Antique Society', in: *Journal of Hellenic Studies* 102, 33-59.

Fox, R.L.
1986 *Pagans and Christians in the Mediterranean World from the Second Century A.D. to the Conversion of Constantine,* London.

Gager, J.G.
1982 'Body-Symbols and Social Reality: Resurrection, Incarnation and Asceticism in Early Christianity', in: *Religion* 12, 345-362.

Gallagher, E.V.
1982 *Divine Man or Magician? Celsus and Origen on Jesus*, SBL Diss. Series 64, Scholars Press.

Geertz, C.
1973 *The Interpretation of Cultures,* New York.
1973 'Thick Description: Toward an Interpretive Theory of Culture'. In: C. Geertz, *The Interpretation of Cultures,* New York, 4-30.
1983 *Local Knowledge. Further Essays in Interpretive Anthropology,* New York.

Grant, R.
1986 *Gods and the One God: Christian Theology in the Graeco-Roman World,* London.

Gibbon, E.
1776-1788 *History of the Decline and Fall of the Roman Empire.*

Holladay, C.H.
1977 *Theios Aner in Hellenistic Judaism: A Critique of the Use of this Category in New Testament Christology,* SBL Diss. Series 40, Scholars Press.

Junod, E.
1981 'Les vies de philosophes et les Actes apocryphes: un dessein similaire?' In: *Les actes apocryphes des apôtres,* Genève, 209-219.

Kee, H.C.
1983 *Miracle in the Early Christian World. A Study in Sociohistorical Method,* New Haven.

Klijn, A.F.J.
1962 *The Acts of Thomas,* Leiden.

LaFargue, M.
1985 *Language and Gnosis: The Opening Scenes of the Acts of Thomas,* Philadelphia.

Leipoldt, J. & W. Grundmann
1965 *Umwelt des Urchristentums I,* Berlin.

MacMullen, R.
1984 *Christianizing the Roman Empire (A.D. 100-400),* New Haven/London.

Momigliano, A.
1963 'Introduction. Christianity and the Decline of the Roman Empire'. In: A. Momigliano (ed.), *The Conflict between Paganism and Christianity in the Fourth Century,* Oxford, 1-16.
1980 'After Gibbon's Decline and Fall'. In: K. Weitzmann (ed.), *Age of Spirituality: A Symposium,* N.Y, 7-16.

Moore, R.L. & F.E. Reynolds
1984 *Anthropology and the Study of Religion,* Chicago.

Murray, A.
1983 'Peter Brown and the Shadow of Constantine', in: *JRS* 73, 191-203.

Nagel, P.
1966 *Die Motivierung der Askese in der Alten Kirche und der Ursprung des Mönchtums,* TU 95, Berlin.

Patlagean, E.
1977 *Pauvreté économique et pauvreté sociale à Byzance 4e-7e siècles,* Paris/La Haye.

Porphyre,
1982 *Vie de Pythagore, Lettre à Marcella.* Ed. E. des Places, Paris.

Porphyry,
1951 'Vita Plotini'. In: P. Henry & H.R. Schwyzer (eds.), *Plotini Opera I,* 1-41.

Robinson, J.M. (ed.)
1977 'Gospel of Thomas, Logion 114'. In: J.M. Robinson (ed.), *The Nag Hammadi Library,* San Francisco, 130.

Rosaldo, M.Z.
1984 'Toward an Anthropology of Self and Feeling'. In: R.A. Shweder & R.A. LeVine (eds.), *Culture Theory. Essays on Mind, Self, and Emotion,* Cambridge.

Rouselle, A.
1983 *Porneia. De la maîtrise du corps à la privation sensorielle, IIe-IVe siècles de l'ère chrétienne,* Paris.

1985 'Jeunesse de l'antiquité tardive; les leçons de lecture de Peter Brown', in: *Annales ESC* 40, 521-528.

Smith, R.C. & J. Lounibos
1984 *Pagan and Christian Anxiety. A response to E.R. Dodds.*, Lanham N.Y., London.

Tiede, D.L.
1972 *The Charismatic Figure as Miracle Worker,* SBL Diss. Series 1, Scholars Press.

Tissot, Y.
1981 'Encratisme et Acts apocryphes'. In: *Les Actes apocryphes des apôtres. Christianisme et monde païen,* Genève, 109-120.

Veyne, P.
1978 'La famille et l'amour sous le Haut-Empire romain', in: *Annales ESC* 33, 35-61.
1985 'L'Empire romain'. In: Ph. Ariès & G. Duby (eds.), *Histoire de la vie privée I,* Paris, 45-59.

Wilken, R.L.
1984 *The Christians as the Romans saw them,* New Haven/London.

Wright, W.
1968 *Apocryphal Acts of the Apostles,* London 1871.

FEAR OF DEATH[1]

Norbert Elias

There is an old legend about the time when human beings were still in contact with the demon who had created the world. From time to time they sent a delegation to him to ask his advice or to complain. So one day they sent a delegation to him to complain about the weather. They said to him: 'You didn't do that too well, you know. Sometimes there is too much rain in one place and too little rain in another place or too much sun in one place and too little sun in another'. 'Well', the demon said 'I'm sorry you don't appreciate the arrangements I made. We'll soon see what we can do about it, when you tell me what weather you would like'. And so the delegation went back to the people and the people nearly came to blows over it, there was nearly a war, they could not agree at all what weather they wanted. The delegation went up again and said: 'The people can't come to an agreement and so the weather will remain unsatisfactory'. At another time, the delegation went to see the demon to complain about death, and that is why I am telling you the story. 'Why did you have to do that?' they asked. 'It is not very nice of you to arrange that we have to die, that we have to get old and to die'. 'Well', said the demon, 'I made an invention which I hoped you would enjoy, to give you great pleasure when you reproduce yourself, and you enjoy it 'I've been told, like other animals which pass away too. So since you enjoy reproducing yourself, you and the other living creatures, there'd soon be no standing room on earth if death didn't exist'. 'Well, never mind about the other animals', said the delegation, 'we are different, aren't we?'. 'Yes and no' said the demon. 'Yes and no. Of course you're born like the others, you eat like the others, you digest food like the others, and I agree that you die like the others'. 'But we can talk and they can't, and they don't even know about you', they said. 'Yes, that is right', said the demon, 'you have knowledge, you have foreknowledge of death and they don't. I can see that that's difficult. I tell you what. I'll make you a gift so that you won't see it so clearly, so

[1] Lecture, given in Groningen on November 11 1986.

that, if you want to, you can conceal from yourself what you don't like about the world. I'll give you the gift of fantasy. Mind you, it is a double-edged gift. I'll tell you that beforehand. You can use it if you like to disguise death and all the other things you may find unpleasant about the world I have done my best to create. But you can also use it to see how the world really is and then you can use your fantasy to make it better than I did. You can invent things. In fact, that would please me greatly because there're enough other inventions I have to make and you can't leave all the inventing to me. If you made some of them that would really be nice. So I give you fantasy and it's up to you whether you use it more to disguise or more to make a new and better world out of the one I've created'.

Well, that is the story and I think it illustrates one of the central problems one has to consider when one speaks about death and the fear of death. Do we really want to see death as it is, or do we want to cover up this unpleasant fact with our fantasies, our wishes? What do human beings prefer: to see the world as it is, the world which undoubtedly in many respects does not correspond to our wishes, or to cover it up with the cherishted fantasy, or, as the demon put it: 'Use the gift of fantasy to make it a better world to live in'. It is a genuine question and I think it is the key question particularly when one deals with the problem of fear of death. Because one has to ask: are fears fantasies, is there really anything to be feared? Well, as far as we can look back into the development of humanity, people have given in to their wishes to be immortal, to live forever. Socially speaking, it has a great social reality because many of our institutions are designed to give substance to this wish of human beings to live forever, to be immortal. I think that when one discusses the fear of death, one should see that one of the greatest fears, perhaps the core of fear, is indicated by the enormous amount of imagination which human beings have used as regards the desire, the wish, the reality of living forever, even after death. I think the core of that fear is the fear of one's personal extinction, the idea that one no longer exists, that the world may go on but oneself may no longer be there. This fear of personal extinction seems to be one of the main component parts of the fear of death.

The second component part is concerned with what will happen after death, with what would happen if we were immortal, with the punishment which we expect or may expect to be meted out to us for sins committed in this life. It seems to me that the fear of death consists not only of the fear of extinction but also, to a larger extent, of the fear of the uncertainty about what may happen after death, the uncertainty about whether or not we shall suffer terribly for transgressions we commit before our death. So these two components- fear of personal extinction and fear of the uncertainty about the punishments which we shall receive after death - seem to me the two main components of the fear of death. And they are very old indeed. It is quite true to say that the fear of punishment after death has not always been there. In the development of human beings, of human societies, we can follow the path along which human beings gained what we would now call a strong conscience formation. We know that it was in an articulate form that this conscience appeared first, probably in the society of the ancient Egyptians.

There is a book which was once very well known and which is still very readable, i.e., *The Dawn of Conscience*, by the American egyptologist J.H. Breasted. In his view, and I think he is right, the ancient Egyptians were the first to introduce a priesthood and a state doctrine according to which human beings would be punished for earthly transgressions in the hereafter. This is astonishing literature, because in ancient Egypt this conscience formation, this feeling that one must not transgress a certain code, was very closely connected with the feeling for social justice. It was an undoubtedly authoritarian, autocratic society in which the poor were downtrodden, as they were in all societies of antiquity. But there was a feeling that one should not go too far in exploiting the poor and the miserable. This can be illustrated by the following quotation from a text found in a rather sumptuous grave of an ancient Egyptian, approximately from the second half of the third millennium before Christ:

> There was no citizen's daughter whom I misused, there was no widow whom I afflicted, there was no peasant whom I evicted, there was no herdsman whom I expelled, there was no overseer of five whose people I took away for (unpaid) tax. There was none wretched in my community, there was none hungry in my time. ... I gave to the widow as to her who had a husband. I did not exalt the great (man) above the small (man) in anything that I gave (Breasted: 1947, 213-214).

There are hundreds of documents from ancient Egyptian graves with phrases such as 'I was righteous, I never did any wrong, I did not oppress the poor, I did not exploit them, I did not transgress the demands of the gods'. There are alabaster mines with hundreds and hundreds of documents of the 'I'm righteous' type. Of course, one need not believe it. Corruption was great in ancient Egypt and there were certain methods which the priests of ancient Egypt had sorted out to cleanse oneself of transgressions committed. There were, for instance, in one of the big towns of ancient Egypt two famous pools. When you bathed in these pools you were cleansed of all transgressions. So there were various ways in which you could become righteous. I want to add to this that what is translated from ancient Egyptian by the term 'righteous' may be an approximation to the ancient meaning. But it is the best word we have to express the notion that one was cleansed before the gods and need not fear any punishment in the hereafter. This was, of course, very clearly worked out in the mythology of the ancient Egyptians. The ancient Egyptians had a mythology which, for instance, centred on the cult of Osiris. Osiris was killed and his bier was drifting along the Nile, and then his son Horus fought his adversary Seth and offered his eye to the dead Osiris, his father, and Osiris came to life again. There was a spectacle of eight days in which the death and resurrection of Osiris was played as an assurance to people that they too could be resurrected. In fact a gift to the dead was called 'the eye of Horus'. And they clearly had the idea that their heart would be examined in the underworld. This underworld is depicted in one of the pictures from an ancient papyrus. You can see the dead man, Ani, being led in, strangely enough with his wife, both watching anxiously how Ani's heart is put on a pair of scales; you can see the jackal-headed god who operates the pair of scales, and the scribe god, Thoth, standing there, while the high-seated gods are watching the ceremony. It is a vivid representation of what people feared and thought. The next scene shows that Ani's heart has been righteous and that he is welcome. I would also like to draw your attention to the 'Devoureerss', the animal with the head of a crocodile, forequarters of a lion, and hindquarters of a hippopotamus, standing there to devour those who are found to have been unjust. So there really were torments and fears and you can probably see that these dreams were very real, socially speaking.

There is of course the question why at some stage of social

development this conscience-formation came about. It is very different from that of the ancient Babylonians who, as far as I know, did not experience a development such as or similar to this one. It has to do with the whole structure of the state. Even in our time, the whole structure of the state is closely related to the conscience formation of people. And in ancient Egypt a rather authoritarian state with a strong priesthood probably had something to do with it, but I do not wish to discuss this in detail. I just want to draw your attention to the fact that feelings about what happens after death are clearly closely connected with the structure of the society in which they occur.

Perhaps I can illustrate this best by quoting some documents from a totally different society, also from antiquity. Roman society of the first century B.C. had a completely different conscience formation, which lasted for another two centuries, the first two centuries A.D. It was a consience formation in which fear of the afterlife had almost vanished. There was some kind of ancestor-cult, in latin *dii manes*, which had to do with the great value wish, particularly for the Roman upper-classes and the upper-middle classes. They are the classes of whom we know most, who left us some written or stone documents. And in their case they had a vague, not very affect-laden, specific form of ancestor worship. They had the feeling that perhaps one would meet one's beloved in the afterworld. There is a very nice poem by Propertius in which he speaks to his beloved Cynthia, who has died, and he tells her that he hopes to see her again in the hereafter when he himself is dead. I would like to quote two of these passages from a Roman epitaph. We have dozens of epitaphs and not in one of them do we find the slightest trace of fear of the afterworld. We find various forms of a dim belief in meeting one's beloved again, but very often also simple expressions of the idea that this is the only life we have and that we should enjoy it.

> To the revered Spirits of the Dead
>
> ...
>
> Valeria Prima set this up to her
> husband with whom she lived 15
> years 3 months 20 days. He
> deserves well.
> (Beneventum, Italy)

Friends, who read this, listen to
my advice: mix wine, tie the
garlands around your head,
drink deep. And do not deny
pretty girls the sweets of love.
When death comes, earth and
fire consume everything.
(Rome)
(Hopkins: 1983, 228)

So already in antiquity, there was a highly secularised society in which, although the state religion still had a ceremonial value and although ceremonies to the ancestors were commonly performed, the emotional involvement of people was very superficial. It was no longer a deep emotional involvement. And already in Greece, where this process of secularisation started for the first time, we find philosophers like Epicurus who fought the fear of death. Afterwards in the Roman Republic, in the first century B.C. you find one of the famous Epicureans, Lucretius; in his still widely read *De Rerum Natura*, he states: *nili gitur mors est ad nos*: 'Death does not mean anything to us'. And he also says: 'There is nothing to be afraid of after death'. He clearly argues that we have no memory of what happened before we were born, we do not remember the last war, he says, so even if the atoms we are composed of here should after our death be reorganised again into another person, this person would not be you or me, but another person, because he would not have our memory. Once the body disintegrates, memory goes, and if memory goes the identity of the person goes, so there is nothing to be afraid of after death, nor is there any idea of resurrection. One could not express it more clearly. It is worth observing that three centuries later the fear of the afterlife had again become very strong in society and I would like to illustrate this with the following quotation from the fourth century A.D. from a man called Salvianus, who wrote that rich people should give more to the church, that they should leave more money to the church when they died. Then he says: 'Oh, when you will burn in hell, you will cry out: father Abraham, let Lazarus come to wet my dry lips'. So a whole new theology was coming into existence, which lay outside the former Roman tradition. Within three or four centuries the very short spell of secularisation had been broken and a new fear of punishment after death had become not only a personal fantasy but a collective fantasy supported by the institutions of the state. In this sense this fantasy was very real.

You can see that even fantasies of a very negative type, as long as they guaranteed you some form of personal survival, were preferred to the fear of personal extinction. Now the question is how and why beliefs of this kind change in the course of the social development of humanity. There is, as I have said, a very clear connection between conscience formation and the structure of society and I wanted to give you only the facts, not explanations which would carry me too far. But I would like to link it up with some experiences from our own time. In our own time we very often find a conscience formation that is part of a highly individualised form of conscience. We find, for instance, some people who individually are extremely afraid of their own death. Extremely afraid that something terrible will happen to them after death, although they do not have any particular belief. It is a neurotic fear connected with their individual feelings of guilt, the overall feeling that they have committed some kind of transgression, and they are anxious, worried about it. They too are very often in fear of death; they cannot bear to hear of anything that is connected with death.

What used to be an institutionalised belief in former days, is still to a smaller extent an institutionalised belief today. Now, however, we very often find it also among non-believers, as a personal form of neurosis or whatever you want to call it: a personal time of suffering. Very often such persons will in fact try to commit some small transgression from time to time. And when it is not found out, when they are not punished for this small transgression, they are reassured because this means that they will not be punished for the imaginary transgression to which their guilt-feeling is related either. Of course, when they are found out this sometimes increases their fear.

I think one cannot very well consider the problems in our own time without saying that, to some extent, the fear of death is connected with a general attitude towards ourselves, towards what I might call our own animality. Remember the reply of the demon to whom the humans said 'But we are different from animals'. He responded: 'yes and no'. And that indeed is one of the problems which I think we have not clearly solved today. In many respects human beings are ordinary mammals. But they are mammals who have eaten the fruit of the tree of knowledge. They are the only living creatures who know that eventually they will die. And, indeed, that is our great problem. You have probably heard the stories of ape- mothers who carry around their dead baby on their back for some time, not being aware that it is dead. After a time it looses its grip and falls down and the mother is hardly aware of it. Apes do not know what death is. It is only human beings who have this knowledge and in that respect of course we are different from other creatures. We are different from other creatures also in the fact that we can talk in a socially preformed language, not in a way specific to a particular species. We are also unique among all creatures in that we bury our dead. Perhaps the most important aspect of our uniqueness is that we can transmit knowledge from one generation to the other. This is indeed one of the basic elements of our human life. To transmit knowledge also means growth of knowledge. This is quite different from saying that something, a soul, has been added to our body, it is quite different from describing concretely in what respects we - who undoubtedly descend from other animals and yet are different from them - differ having, as it were, made a breakthrough in the biological evolution, which allows us to do things which no other animal can do and which, to put it briefly, has enabled us in the course of time to become the ruling species on this earth. We have gradually eliminated most of our real enemies among the animals. We have transformed the greater part of the earth in a way which no other animal is capable of doing. As societies we have in fact now attained a dominant position on this planet, yet without accepting the responsibility that goes with this new dominant position.

There is, as you may know, a way of describing the more realistic attitude towards death which I have outlined. It is described in some cases as if it were a philosophical belief like any other. One of the names given to the attitude which I have described is nihilism and indeed there is a long movement in our age which proceeds from this recognition that life is final and the end, when one looks at it without covering it up with fantasies. We are indeed living in a period in which the departure of the old beliefs and the arrival of a more fact-related attitude towards death is seen simply as another -ism. And the whole movement, the theatre of the absurd, is as it were devoted to the complaint, to the incessant complaint, that now that we have come to see the world in a more realistic way, now that the old belief in an afterworld has gone, the world has become meaningless. I think that this is a passing phase. One can understand that the shock of being presented with the clear reality of one's own finite existence may for some time have created a void. And so we find people like Camus, Sartre or Beckett - the author of *Waiting for Godot*, which really means waiting for God, who has gone - in misery because this new position seems to be void of any meaning.

I think that sooner or later, we will see that this attitude of disappointment, of mourning for the past meaningfulness, will last only for as long as we are unable to see the new meaning clearly. This is the new task which lies before us. In fact, I believe that what we have today is in part the result of an overgrown individualism. We pay too much attention, we overrate, if I may put it that way, the importance of our individual existence. I know that these are dangerous words to say. I fully agree with all those who fight for human rights in countries in which individuals are oppressed by the state. It is beyond doubt that this has to be done. Nevertheless, I would still like to add that we very often treat our individual deeds or our individual achievements as if they were the end of a process. What is decidedly lacking in our time is the feeling that we are usually more than our reflections tell us, dependent on others and living together with others. In fact, if you think about it, it is a strange form of forgetfulness. In our daily life each of us knows to what extent we are dependent on other people. We live with other people, we are, as individuals, wholly embedded in other people's lives, and the fact of our condition in relation to other people is in actual practice one of the most important aspects of our life. And yet at the level of reflection, the philosophical level or even artistic level we behave or think or represent ourselves as if we were an isolated unit.

I think it has to be said once more that on two levels our individual fate and our individual sense of meaning and fulfilment is entirely dependent on our relations with other human beings. You know that many philosophers, like for instance Husserl, use the word 'meaning' as if meaning were something entirely individual. And yet one can see, when studying words or languages, that a word which does not mean to oneself what it does to others is meaningless. When you listen to another language you hear sounds, but since you receive words on a different wavelength these words are meaningless. So here you have one example of the extent to which meaning is dependent on the reciprocity between people. And so, when we think that the meaning of our life is destroyed because the meaning of afterlife is destroyed, we should pay more attention to the meaning and fulfilment of our life which we can derive from the fact that our life may or may not have meaning for ourselves depending on whether or not it has meaning for others. On two levels: first in space, we live as it were in concentric circles with a series of people in our inner circle, our family, our friends. And the condition of this inner circle for our personal life, for our personal satisfaction is immense. But through a series of intermediary circles we move to mankind. In our time humanity has become, perhaps for the first time, not just an empty word, but a social reality. What happens in Australia is of importance to us. What happens in the Hebrides is important to us. What happens to us is important to people living in distant places. The distances have become smaller. So we are in fact living in a world in which the network of interdependencies has spread in space all over the world. And the same can be said in terms of time. To many people our interdependence with past generations and with future generations may not be as immediately intelligible as our growing interdependence in space with human groups which a century ago might have appeared to our forefathers as groups so distant from themselves that they were virtually of no interest to them.

If one considers the process of our lives as a product over time, in that case too, distances begin to grow smaller. I do think, and I can only speak for myself, that one would have a feeling of an actually fulfilled or satisfied life if, instead of doing only something for one's contemporaries, one also had something, one's own task, one's own knowledge, that, either as a father or a mother or as a learned person, one could pass on to the coming generations. In fact, I can say that one of the afflictions of our time orginates from the fact that the chain of generations has been loosened or broken. One no longer has the feeling that this chain still exists. People believe that they can seek the fulfilment of their own life here and now in our own time. They do not see that none of their tasks is an end, that it becomes meaningless if it is not taken up by the next generation, whose task is also taken up by the generation following them. We live, in fact, to a considerable extent, in an unclear way. The objective social tasks with which we have to cope demand long-term planning. Be it town planning or state planning, both must take one, two, or three generations into account, whereas in our personal life our personal make-up is directed towards the fulfilment of what we want here and now, in our own life. And yet very often it does not come, because more than ever before our world is organised in such a way that it can come only after many generations. I need not tell you that in the sixties - for very good reasons - this chain of generations was to some extent interrupted. There was an older generation that lived with the authority or the authoritarian gestures of the traditional form. There was a younger generation that tried to break down the authority structure of the older one. And this has led to the fact that this reliance on the coming generations is no longer present in our time. I feel that much of the meaning of our personal life depends on the reconstitution of the chain of generations as equals, not as the older generation having authority and the younger generation having to obey. They need each other, they are equal. It is as bad for the older as it is for the younger generation when the chain of generations is broken. But I think the fear of death would diminish greatly if, in the way it used to be in other societies, people in Europe managed to regain the awareness that one does one's task and does one's bit not only for one's own but also for the next generation and this doing one's bit gives a sense of satisfaction and fulfilment- doing it for other people - but only if it is continued critically by the following generations. I say critically because, for instance, in the case of a scholar, my own case, I feel fulfilment to some extent, on account of some of the things I have done. They have meaning, they give me fulfilment. But this does not mean that I expect that everything I say will be adopted by the next generation. I expect that some of it will be adopted and continued in research or artistic work or any other kind of work and I think that this is, if you like, the message with which I want to conclude. The message that we could do more for our own fulfilment in this world if we could be certain of continuity between the generations. Continuity on all levels, on the family level, on the national level, on the European level and above all on the level of humanity. Of course, if we blow ourselves to bits, everything any human being has ever done, becomes meaningless. Because meaning only exists among human beings. So I hope that you will allow me to give you the following to think about. What can we do to make the continuity between the generations stronger again and thus perhaps also render the limited things one can do as an individual more meaningful?

Bibliography

Breasted, J.H.
1947 *The Dawn of Conscience,* New York/London.

Hopkins, K.
1983 'Death and Renewal', in: *Social Studies in Roman History, Vol. 2,* Cambridge.

PART THREE
NON-WESTERN CONCEPTS OF PERSON

INTRODUCTION

After the theoretical and philosophical reflections in our first set of articles and the contributions in the second section of this book on the formation of the Western notion of the person, its archaeology and its history, we now come to studies of the notion of the person in non-Western cultures. These studies, written by Western scholars implicitly or explicitly discuss problems of comparison with Western norms and values and questions of methods and strategies of research.

In his article on contemporary Islamic concepts of the person J.S. Jensen discusses some fundamental theoretical and methodological issues. An Islamic concept of person does not only consist in normative ideas based on theological ideals, it also includes 'the continuous creation of meaning' in cultural reality, where 'human emotions have semiotic preconditions'. The very fact that Islam has spread over many different cultures enables Jensen to discuss the notion of the person as a cultural construct and as a primary instrument in the process of socialization. He also draws attention to another fundamental anthropological problem: the cultural representation of emotions. 'The ways of making a person's emotions a public matter and thereby open to control are further evidence of the social character of emotionality in certain areas of Islamic culture'.

Jensen's views provide a general background for the case-study by F. Leemhuis on the *djinn* as persons. *Djinn* enter into social relations with human beings, they are considered individual persons, legally capable of doing right or wrong.

The study of the notion of the person or the self seems to move away from anthropological associations with social roles and statuses, when attention is focussed on the Indian religions with their tradition of mysticism and metaphysical speculation. The two studies of Indian ideas of the person, however, show the historical limitations of the metaphysical conceptions of the self. L.P. van den Bosch writes on the concept of the person in ancient Vedic texts, while H.T. Bakker traces developments in the image of man in the Hindu world view from the twelfth century to the present day.

In a broad survey of the name-giving systems in ancient Indian texts Van den Bosch stresses the importance in Brahminical ideology of defining a person in his relation to the world. The duties of a person are carefully stated in relation to his sex, estate (*varna*) and stage of life, with a special distinction between the class of serfs and the other three *varnas*. Important rituals help to make an individual a member of one of the three higher *varnas* and to realize the successive stages of his life. These rituals impose layer after layer of personhood upon the individual and help him to acquire his carefully standardized socio-cultural identity.

Besides the various exoteric names and titles, a person has a secret name which indicates his true identity or his divine self, which transcends profane reality. According to Van den Bosch, the hypertrophied urge of the Brahminical class to identify and classify everything while at the same time connecting it with cosmological systems has had paradoxical effects. In the *Upanishads* the divine self or *daiva atman* was no longer considered in connection with the continuity of the family, but came to be regarded as the only eternal reality underlying the whole creation. The attempts to define the *atman* with the help of traditional classifications and categories were doomed to fail, because the *atman* is 'not this, not that'.

Bakker analyzes statements and texts that reflect the self-perception of Indian man over a period of about eighthundred years during which significant changes in the world view of the Hindu took place. Bakker traces a development in which the essence and meaning of an individual is increasingly 'translated' into human emotionality, rather than expressed in otherwordly or transcendent terms. The *bhakti* movement contributed largely to the ideal according to which each individual, irrespective of caste, could attain and participate in the divine, not in a nebulous hereafter, but here and now. *Mokhsa*, 'release', became something that should preferably be experienced in this world.

Nevertheless, in (Northern) India the image of man retained many supra-individual traits. What made the individual into a 'person' was not so much his human capacity to act as a morally autonomous being within social ramifications, but rather his realization of an inner autonomy, i.e., of his potential capacity to transcend his natural as well as his social definiteness in a process of emancipation of his divine soul. To this effect the modern *bhakti* religion offers a set of symbols and archetypes that can be acquired or enacted by the individual, lending him religious and consequently social-esteem and prestige. A central category in this process is the notion of an autonomous eternal self, which forms part of the divine and which is awaiting emancipation. Partly, the degree of this emancipation is thought to be represented by caste, but the institution of renunciation, and the context of popular devotional religion, offer alternative symbol-system which enables man to climb up the rungs of Jacob's ladder.

Philosophical traditions and historical dimension are of minor importance to the last two contributions, which study the notion of person in two non-literate societies.

A.W. Geertz has studied the ritual person among the Hopi indians of Arizona. He approaches his subject by moving from the social situation towards assumptions about the individual. This involves two difficulties: (1.) the assumption that an individual can only know himself through his society's ideal types and evaluates himself and is evaluated by others in terms of those types; and (2.) the Hopi 'ritual person' is an abstraction which suggests that Hopi individuals are far more similar than they in fact are, and which sets a standard that is difficult to live up to.

Geertz shows that the Hopi 'ritual person' embodies all of what being Hopi means. Preparing for ritual activity is in fact a lifetime preparation involving formal initiations as well as the assimilation and practice of Hopi ethical behaviour. Geertz analyzes conflicts between individuals in ritual contexts and the collectivization of this conflict. It turns out that Hopis do indeed evaluate themselves and others by referring to the ideal person, who, by definition, is a ritual person. He also shows that the Hopis, as a people, acknowledge the unavoidable paradox of their ethics by institutionalizing this paradox in several ways. Finally, he proposes a model of Hopi hermeneutics which sketches the dynamics of the concept of Hopi 'ritual person'.

H.A. Witte sketches a model of the West African notion of the person, starting from the assumption that every human being has an awareness of his or her individual self. The cognitive function of this awareness is defined by the overall world view of the culture in which the individual lives. West African views of man as a physical and spiritual being assume that the physical body is not only animated by a spiritual force of life derived from the sky god, but also by an ancestral element that defines an essential interest of every individual lineage as the paradigm for society in general.

To the individual, a society that is modelled on the image of the extended polygamous family with a hierarchical structure of succeeding generations mirrors an image of the self in which age and gender form generations mirrors an image of the self in which age and gender form the basis of his or her social functioning as a person. Witte emphasizes the view that access to personhood, i.e., to the roles and statuses conferred on the individual by society, widens and changes during the successive stages of life. Finally, he argues that ego-awareness and access to personhood is defined by the opposition of the sexes in as far as this opposition is socialized into a complementarity of gender roles which is seen to be vital for the unity and continuity of society as a whole.

TOWARDS CONTEMPORARY ISLAMIC CONCEPTS OF THE PERSON

Jeppe S. Jensen

1.0 *Introduction*

If you want to know something about persons and personality you will probably turn to psychology. Consequently, if you want to know something about Islamic ideas about personality you may turn to Islamic psychology, but this is not easily done. To quote one prominent Muslim psychologist:

> For one thing we may not be able to strictly talk about an 'Islamic theory of personality' in a precise manner. Islam to a Muslim is a revealed religion. It is the Truth. A psychological theory, on the other hand, is simply a set of conventions created by the theorist, in many ways, in an arbitrary creative manner, like an artist or a poet (Badri: 1979, 100).

A bibliographical search for entries like 'psychology' or 'Self' in standard works on Islam is as little rewarding as the search for 'Islam' and 'Muslim' in psychological and psychiatric literature (a notable exception is Racy: 1970). However, this paper is concerned, not with personality as such, but with the cultural and religious conventions and ideas relating to it. Consequently, we turn from psychology to anthropology and the history of religions. Although the lack of success of the earlier-mentioned bibliographical search might even suggest that such concepts are irrelevant to Islam, this can, of course, not be the case. A religious system without concepts of personhood, self and emotion would seem to be an absurdity. In this connection it is interesting to note that in recent works on 'Person' and 'Self' that contain ethnographic, area-defined interpretations of concepts of the person there are no references to Islamic cultures (see Heelas - Lock: 1981; Marsella - DeVos - Hsu: 1985; Carrithers - Collins - Lukes: 1985; Jacobson-Widding: 1983).

1.0.1 The approach

The arguments presented in this paper will be more programmatic than conclusive, a discussion of prospects more than a presentation of results. This discussion consists of a chain of reflections and ideas for further research and contains only a modest amount of empirical data which serve as illustrations of the line of approach taken here and as a basis for discussions of the validity of such an approach. The number of empirical data would be great on the other hand, if one could deduce them successfully from the contexts in which they appear. However, to be able to do so one must have an idea of what one is looking for.

1.0.2 Disciplines and outline

The works of authors from many disciplines have contributed to this eclectic enterprise and it might have been useful to refer to them collectively as The study of Islam, but in my opinion the theories and methods, and the interest behind them are so different that they will be presented and discussed in their own right. Chapther I deals with the sources used for this study. Chapter II introduces some recent reflections concerning the concepts of culture and Self. The general theory and practice of Islam are discussed in Chapter III, which in chapter IV is followed by a consideration of contemporary Islamic interpretations of the ideal paradigm for actual practice, based, first of all, on readings of the Qur'an. Chapter V poses a number of questions concerning the realization of this paradigm in cultural and social practice and reflects on the validity of some theoretical concepts relating the texts of tradition to real-life patterns. A few concluding remarks are offered in Chapter VI.

1.1 *Analysis of Islamic concepts of the person: the aim*

My intention is to present a preliminary account of Islamic concepts of the person, a 'geography' of a concept. This should not be confused with studies of e.g., ethnic identities or personal psychology, i.e., studies of personality traits supposedly prevalent in Islamic countries, cultures or groups (such studies have been severely criticized by Fouad Moughrabi: 1978). The concepts of person should inform us about the ideas inherent in Islam, as an ideological system, concerning the categories that are employed to construe the person as an agent of action and motivation. Thus it is relevant to try to delimit the concept of person: what can the person be associated with and what can the person be distinguished from? Is the person, the 'self', viewed as a bounded unit and what constitutes a concept of personality? Does the self change or is it considered to remain the same? Terminologically I shall not distinguish sharply between 'Person' and 'Self'. However, the Person may be said to be more outwardly and action-oriented, whereas the Self primarily relates to the inner topography of Man. The Islamic concepts should of course be studied primarily from the Islamic point of view, i.e., emically, and instead of starting from some presumed pan-human universals it is necessary to start with what is obviously religious and cultural, and then work towards more problematic questions according to taste. A number of key dichotomies can be applied to the studies on concepts of person, self and emotion to characterize the lines of approach of these studies.[1]

Materialist vs.	Idealist
Positivist vs.	Interpretivist
Universalist vs.	Relativist
Individualist vs.	Social functional
Rationalist vs.	Emotionalist

Western psychology will mostly be located in the left column, whereas the history of religions and anthropology/ethnography tend to represent right-column lines of approach but with numerous variations. Actually any combination of these points of view would be possible, but the system is nevertheless a useful tool for the classification of interpretations of research. I shall emphasize right-column viewpoints and methodologies in the following sections and clarify my reasons for doing so.

1.2 *Scope and Sources*

Another problem is the relation between the normative Islamic expressions and representations of person-concepts in actual social

---

[1] Lutz & White use this schema to classify the lines of approach of the studies of emotions in cultures (1986).

interaction. No one will doubt that there is enormous variation between what is prescribed by religion, here Islam, and the way in which it is put into practice as borne out by ethnographic accounts. But the concepts of the person are of little value to the historian of religion if they do not have implications for earthly life as paradigms, ideals or modes of explanation. This problem is obviously more difficult to solve when one is dealing with a non-ethnic religion like Islam than when one is studying a specific ethnic religion where, all other considerations aside, there is greater overlap between the ideal and social practice. In this connection I will therefore first examine some of the key concepts of the prescriptive (and perpetually reconstructed) tradition, mainly as represented by modern apologetic interpretations and subsequently compare them with real-life patterns.[2]

For both fields of data (inside-views represented by texts and external descriptions/analyses) there is the common positivistic problem of the validity and representativeness of data, but most of the arguments presented here are open-ended considerations and not affirmative dogmas, so no harm will have been done if in due course it appears that our views have been incorrect.

1.2.1 Islamic psychology and philosophy as sources

The *raison de vivre* for the history of religions and anthropology has been to tell Us about Them, the Others, but in the case of Islam, They are talking back! The Islamic world has in fact been talking to the West for quite some time and has acquired the status of a somewhat problematic Other, due to the sharing of the Mediterranean, some themes in Holy Books and cultural patterns to name a few main factors. Islamic philosophy, which traditionally also includes psychology, was developed partly as a response to the West and the same can nowadays be said of Islamic versions of psychology and social science. As life sciences are not

---

[2] I am deliberately excluding Sufism from this context though I am painfully aware that these complex doctrines may hold some keys to the understanding of general concepts of person, e.g., in the context of saint-cults, the powers of *Baraka*, etc. The concept of the *Insan al-Kamil* (Perfected Man) in Sufi-traditions thus also falls outside the scope of this paper.

just descriptions of their objects but just as much interpretive products of the social conditions and cultural forms that give rise to them it may not come as a surprise that the Islamic versions of such studies are radically different from ours. I do not intend to discuss the relative or absolute nature of science here since this has already been done by others (see e.g., Geertz: 1984), but I would like to point out that in my opinion it is important for any science to be crucially critical of its own epistemological basis, and this criterium is hardly met by the disciplines preceded by the designation 'Islamic'. Nevertheless, the Islamic responses to Western scientific and epistemological hegemony are interesting in this connection. In between those Muslims who fully adopt non-Muslim ways and those who reject them there is a group of scholars, Muslims who have been educated in the West and practise a profession there. These scholars experience severe problems in performing their tasks within an Islamic paradigm. In this context one may refer to the title of a small book by the psychologist Malik B. Badri: *The Dilemma of Muslim Psychologists*, i.e., how to reconcile being a modern psychologist with being a devout Muslim (Badri: 1979). In sociology the Western social sciences have been more severely criticized by two Muslim sociologists who among other things refer to the interactionism of G.H. Mead as "fundamentalist Christian logic" (Ba-Yunus - Ahmad: 1985, 10-12). Such scholarship which refers directly to Western paradigms is interesting because a dialogue or refutation is expressly intended but its proposals will mostly remain Islamic texts as it advances common and classical apologetics, in short it deals with theology, not sociology. None the less, it is still doubtful whether we are the ones to give names to things- like Adam in the Qur'an - in what might look like another attempt at epistemological imperialism (if science is a cultural form, etc.).

1.3 *Which Islam? Official or popular?*

Which Islam? The history of religions has sometimes tended to become the Comparative Study of Dogma and anthropology has also had its problems with religions, especially outside those tribal settings where the overlap between religion and social life was, or was made easy to deal with. Popular Islam, the Islam *veçu*, as opposed to dogmatic Islam (*conçu*) used to have an ambivalent status in research, but today it is a major topic (Waardenburg: 1979) in the study of how Islam can actually be recognized in social and cultural life (Gilsenan: 1982; Lewis: 1986, Ch. 6). Waardenburg has aptly distinguished between 1) valid Islam: what Muslims in a certain group consider Islam to be and 2) actual Islam: the way in which it is put into practice. Such a distinction makes sense of the descriptions of Islam in village life given by Lutfiyya (1970) et al. and it coincides with the common notion of claimed vs. real identity. Producing a valid interpretation through description of a certain social situation poses enough problems in itself, so attempts to link normative Islam with popular practice on a wider scale are open to question (e.g. Digard: 1978; El-Zein: 1977), yet necessary if the designation 'Islamic' is to have meaning at all. Regarding the use of apologetic literature it must be emphasized that the writings of prominent Muslim scholars are actually distributed, read and referred to throughout the Islamic world, just like the works of certain writers and intellectuals in the Western world. But in the case of the Islamic world the medium of Arabic facilitates the exchange of ideas among religious scholars, with English serving as a second language on a large scale. In fact one could look upon the religious scholars as a 'society': an elite of 'fuqaha' engaged in a symbolic mediating exchange between the people and the divine. Thus the learned and their culture can be compared to other culturally defined groups. So, in lieu of comparing religious representations in two villages or in Indonesia and Morocco one may compare the interpretations of the elite with local symbolic structures. What we have then is a religio-historical investigation of the role and effect of the Text of tradition along the lines of literary reception theory with an emphasis on the 'reception of the text' (the role of the reader) rather than a study of the work and the author (see e.g., Holub: 1984).

1.4 *Ethnographic sources*

Anthropology has long been sceptical about psychological approaches to the study of person-related problems in non-Western cultures, mostly because of an individualistic perspective that ignores the fact that man is what Lawrence Rosen terms *Homo Contextus* (Rosen: 1984, 179). But according to LeVine (1982) there is a new descriptive trend in psychological anthropology combining a) descriptive ethnography of indigenous concepts of the person, b) case studies of individual adults with contextual material to permit cultural as well as psychological understanding and c) biographical projects and processes (LeVine: 1982, 291ff.) so as to combine ".. the investigation of (1) cultural categories and beliefs concerning the person, (2) individual lives, and (3) the intercultural research relationschip" (LeVine: 1982, 293). This should allow culture and experience to be viewed from an individual perspective rather than from the perspective of a collective system or an external observer (e.g., Crapanzano: 1980; Dwyer: 1982). Recent sociology, too, is taking an interest in emotions under the somewhat unfortunate label of Existential Sociology (Fontana: 1984). Following a time in which severe criticism debunked social functionalism, behaviourism, the 'personality and culture'-school and mechanistic psychoanalysis there is now a tendency towards a renewed recognition of the emotional and psychological in human life, which is borne out by a growing body of literature devoted to these subjects (Lutz - White: 1986; Jacobson-Widding: 1983). But progress is being made through laborious deconstruction of terminology and presumptions and in discussions of methods and terminology. One example of such procedures with reference to our theme is Unni Wikan's treatment of the familiar honour and shame theme (Wikan: 1984). Wikan demonstrates that even within what is thought to be one culture area, the Middle-Eastern Arabic, there are profound differences in the concepts of self and society, in so far as Egyptians and Omanis, and men and women refer to very different conceptual worlds. In my opinion the lesson to be learned from this is that relating interpretations of Qur'anic concepts as constructions of a second order with regard to practice is fundamentally no different from applying anthropology's supposedly etic terms to local variations of a certain theme.

2.0 *Ethnocentricity and relativism*

Cultural universalism proved to be a dangerous path to take in past studies of self and person, e.g., in cross-cultural psychology where standard Western diagnostic techniques were applied to two or more cultures, sacrificing relevance and validity for replicability (Lutz - White: 1986, 414). Rorschach-testing an Eskimo may be an 'etic' enterprise, but the interpretation of the test certainly will not, so what is the use? Recent psychological anthropology is aware of this (psychoanalysis is also interpretation) and instead of being dominated by one single model one may refer to "... a large and loosely organized realm of ideas about the mental background of behavior" (Kiefer: 1977, 104). Another point is that for psychology as an academic discipline religion by convention belongs to a different category. This division is an artefact of our culture and no universal truth (Haule: 1982, 157-158). Yet, there can be no doubt that our ideas about what to search for when we are speaking about person-concepts in other cultures are determined by what we (un)consciously think of when we interact ourselves, this being shaped by psychological, philosophical and other ideas and models of man (see e.g., Hollis: 1977 and Heelas: 1981). So, until we have become wiser we will use our own culture's definitions and apply them somewhere else. Nothing else can be done if the analysis is to have meaning for ourselves and therefore this paper is basically an act of translation of one epistemological matrix into another. This involves the all too familiar pitfalls of ethnocentrism, etc., in general (Ardener: 1982; Crick: 1976; Beattie: 1984) as well as in the study of concepts of person and self (Fogelson: 1982), e.g., by having a view of the concept of person that gives primary importance to inner experiences, an idea that is dominant in most psychological theories because it is consistent with our own highly individual concepts of person and motivation. But even those who have obtained the greatest results by relativistic reflection and dialogue with the Other may be accused of being absolutist in their treatment of Islam and of distinguishing a false from a true Islam, so Geertz on the basis of the reality of experience, Crapanzano on the psychic, Gilsenan on the structure of social relations, etc. (El-Zein: 1977, 249). Talal Asad has accused Geertz of having a modern privatized Christian conception of religion because of his emphasis on the priority of belief as a state of mind (Asad: 1983, 247). This only to remind us of the aforementioned feed-back! There is no privileged neutral Archimedic point from which to describe and interpret Islam. We are forced to consider James Boon's view that a "discourse of cultures confesses its own exaggeration and seeks to control and assess it by becoming interpretive, at times even literary, while remaining both systematic and dialectical" (Boon: 1982, 26).

2.1 *The cultural approach*

Nevertheless, there seems to be only one way to unravel Islamic concepts of persons if we are to include not only normative ideas but also people's perceptions of divergence between what is ideal and what is real: the cultural approach. My view on culture is a semiotic one, defining culture as production and reproduction of meaning, where symbols and meanings are resources but also act as constraints. Culture is not just 'all that is learned', an ideational unity that can be an obstacle or stimulus to other social development. Culture also consists of incomplete projects and fragmentary practices, so that the realm of meaning also includes its own portion of non-sense. This implies that a cultural notion of the person may include an amount of confusion, people do not always agree with one another on everything just because we have ascribed the same culture to them, not even in 'primitive' societies. We have to allow for intra-cultural variations and innovations without having to refer to external causes (Harrison: 1985). Culture is thus not just a fixed text but the continuous creation of meaning intrinsic to a society's formation of institutions.

2.1.1 Religion as signification system

"Meaning here, meaning there, meaning everywhere..." is what one might say in objection to a semiotic interpretation, but it is the content of meaning and not the outward form of cultural expressions that is important. Religions, and here, Islam as signification systems have their own semantics as well as their own syntax and pragmatics. There are certain ways in which things have to be expressed or they will simply not be comprehended. What we encounter is the syntactic realization through time of paradigmatic meaning, which is the constituent of a world-order, lived in and thought of. Every human action is communicative and expressive and may incur an interpretation as long as speaker and listener or the ritual performer and the field-worker share a narrative competence, i.e., as long as they speak the same 'language' when they talk about things. The individual is not an independent master of such narrative competence, since the logic of meaning is already present in social life every time you do or say something. The cultural reality of being and doing is organized narratively, i.e., organized in such a way that it can be talked about. What this also means is that human emotions (which are more than just neurological stimuli) have semiotic pre-conditions and are not just pan-human natural responses superficially susceptible to cultural variations or as Michelle Rosaldo has brilliantly put it: "... culture, far more than a mere catalogue of rituals and beliefs, is instead the very stuff of which our subjectivities are created" (Rosaldo: 1984, 150). So a person is not just someone who intuitively feels that 'I am', it is the way of being that determines how and the extent to which you feel you are a person.

2.1.2 Axiology

Not everything has the same value in culture, in fact culture is hierarchical in structure because axiology places meanings in different orders of being, i.e., a culturally appointed ontology. As a system of meaning culture is teleological, oriented towards goals. This has direct implications for the concept of person, because he or she who is preoccupied with the 'wrong things' is considered to be a pathological case. Culture and not in the last place religion is primarily concerned with things that 'ought to be' and 'ought not to be', and this is exactly where the normative concept of person and its interpretations and uses are of primary importance to the historian of religion.

2.2 *Reflexivity*

Reflexivity is the standard designation of the process by means of which people look upon and understand themselves, or objectify them-'selves' by acting and thinking in ways that make them comprehensible to themselves. And the only possible way of doing so is through the medium of culture as signification, i.e., the system of values and meanings present in society. Thus becoming yourself means to become in some measure the kind of person culture acknowledges. This does not mean that any given person is blueprinted as a replica, but there will be some degree of congruence between public and private selves, between what is thinkable and what is unthinkable, if persons are to be able to understand themselves and others. The concept of person is an axiological-paradigmatic model for self-recognition that serves in the individual autobiographical process which takes place within the confines of narrative competence: people have a propensity for doing things that can be talked about, things that make sense, cf. C.S. Peirce's dictum: "My language is the total sum of my self" (in Singer: 1980, 499). A self-concept is related to how people make sense of events in their lives, primarily through language, though one may doubt whether all knowledge can be expressed in language (Crick: 1982, 288-289). What cannot be doubted, in my opinion, is that man is self-defining and self-constituting.

2.2.1 The corporate self

The perspective of reflexivity may be further developed into the notion of Corporate Self, where the self can be seen as both the product and the agent of semiotic communication. Lately a number of the theses advanced by C.S. Peirce concerning these issues have been re-evaluated, especially the idea of the loosely compacted person: the person's self-hermeneutics as a set of signs, used to communicate ideas, values and strategies for action. In this view the person is not absolutely an individual since his thoughts are what he is "saying to himself" (Singer: 1980, 494). This is a promising point of view in socio-psychological studies, on the one hand, of phenomena like conversion and participation in major religious events where individual motivation is prominent, and, on the other hand, of how this affects the person's interpretation of the self. How much of and what in the person changes in such circumstances? Often a convert expresses the conviction that "I have become a better person...". It is not possible to find out through observation whether a person has more than one self or no self at all, but the theory of the dialogical nature of self-consciousness does make sense.[3] With regard to the concept of Corporate Self, the multiple-identities approach as proposed by Fogelson and Wallace seems useful. They differentiate between 1) real identity, 2) ideal identity, 3) feared identity, and 4) claimed identity (Fogelson: 1982, 78ff.). All of these dimensions of identity interact and motivate in the religious person's conscious and unconscious self-concepts. The awareness of self in relation to others and supernatural powers seems to be a prerequisite of religion.

2.3 *Self as a cultural construct*

Cultural or religious determinism is just as bad as other kinds of

---

[3] The discussion around the application of Peircean semiotics in studies of identity, self-concept etc. can be consulted elsewhere, e.g., in Milton Singer: Man's Glassy Essence, Bloomington 1984 (rev. by W.C. Watt in Semiotica 58, 3/4 (1986), 379-383).

determinism, but discussing the Self as a cultural construct does not entail the notion that individual identity is a projection of collective identity. Personality is not just culture 'writ small', it has to be construed within the cultural matrix. For whatever else a person-concept may be, it certainly is a cultural construct or as Malcolm Crick formulates it: "A 'person' is a semantic construct held together by agreement" (1982, 292). Crick is sceptical about efforts to describe the 'experience' of people in other cultures by means of Western psychological notions, they "often look highly artificial" and he adds: "Of more validity is the effort through the analysis of collective representations to construct each culture's understanding of the human person, his mentality and capacities" (Crick: 1982). Robert A. LeVine has defined the self-concept as "an integral mental representation of the self that includes boundaries between, and identities with, the self and other individuals, groups and ideologies" (LeVine: 1982, 122). One could also say that the culturally constituted self is positioned at the nexus of personal and social worlds (Lutz - White: 1986, 417). Describing and constructing Social Persons in the traditions of Durkheim, Radcliffe-Brown and Mauss (cf. extended discussion of Mauss in Carrithers et al.: 1985) has often implied evasion of the problematics of emotions according to Lutz - White, for which reason they state that: "emotions are a primary idiom for defining and negotiating relations of the self in a moral order" (Lutz - White: 1986), a perspective which is of great importance when describing Islamic notions of persons. Islam is also 'Ethos', the designation given by Bateson to culturally organized systems of emotions. The axiology or value-hierarchy is built upon feelings about what matters, and it need not be seen as being in opposition to cognition, for "the opposites affect/-cognition and personality/culture are central to our way of thinking" according to Lutz - White (1986, 429), who also note that "attention to emotional rhetoric and discourse then, should be a fruitful focus for ethnographic investigations of social life as an active and creative process" (Lutz - White: 1986, 420). Emotions arise in social situations, even imaginary ones, and have implications for future thought and action. Emotional understanding is not just 'thinking about feelings' but is related to how you see yourself and how you build your theory about others. So also within Islam emotion-concepts are a kind of language about the self. Seeing the self as a social, semiotic and hence cultural entity with 'fuzzy edges' and not confined to the inside of the epidermis means overcoming the dichotomy between the personal and the cultural that has pervaded Western ways of thinking (see e.g., Taylor: 1985). Biologically the person is an individual but the concept of the person is cultural and can thus be studied like all other cultural phenomena, including religion.

3.0 *Normativity and reality in Islam*

That religious normativity and social practice differ considerably among Muslims should not come as a surprise to any student of religion. Dogmatic or normative Islamic views seldom fit in with our descriptions of folk categories, belief, etc., and some ethnographic accounts of life in the Islamic world literally refuse to use the label 'Islamic'. It may well be that most of what goes on can be adequately described in what is thought to be etic social scientific categories without reference to Islam - but if the people themselves refer to Islam, then what? Social anthropology has been right in questioning Orientalist views of Islam as monolithic, but Islam can only be discarded if Muslims do so - and they do not. If one wants to find out what distinguishes Islam from all other religions, a study of the central beliefs and actions, as defined and understood by Muslims, is essential. The multiple tensions and outright contradictions between ideals and actual practice should not lead us to disregard or ignore the relations between them, however troublesome and erratic the research may be. Thus, there can be no doubt about the existence in Islamic cultures of ideas being defined as properly Islamic and having some paradigmatic value. A concept of the person is a primary instrument in the process of socialization and in Islamic culture this concept is given authority on the basis of the normative tradition, however heavily any interpretation depends on social circumstances. I shall try to extract some central issues from certain Islamic scriptures, notably from the Qur'an[4] (see also Bouman: 1977), for I agree with

---

[4] The numbering of Qur'anic quotations follows the official Egyptian system, also found in the German translation by Rudi Paret, Stuttgart 1962. The translations of the verses are partly my own and partly taken from a known edition, I have chosen the translation I consider to be closest to the original in meaning not literality. Translation will always be a matter of interpretation.

Jacques Berque that "il est un texte par excellence qui s'impose a quiconque aborde l'Islam, et qui s'impose non seulement par le poids dogmatique, mais par son dégagement existentiel, c'est le Coran" (Berque: 1978, 195). Social fields and texts *are* interrelated.

3.0.1 Islam as a total system

As defined by Muslim theologians Islam as a religion (Din) comprises all aspects of human activity. How this is to be realized is of course a matter of interpretation, and however 'faulty' they may be, most actions can be given an ad-hoc justification yet still within an Islamic frame of understanding. Islam is therefore a very comprehensive system of meaning and signification (Waardenburg: 1974). The system incorporates ideas about its agents and their abilities. Obviously, man is not perfect, for if he were there would be no need for Islam and its prescriptions would not have to be justified. In contrast to some other major world religions Islamic teachings do not focus heavily on the nature of Man as such, it seems rather to be taken for granted and then elaborated on. Consequently, more comprehensive Islamic concepts of the person must be deduced from descriptions of behaviour, values, gender relations and so on.

3.1 *Which Islamic person?*

The fundamental question is: What makes Man human? In Islam the answer that is most often given is: his rational faculties which lead him towards Reason (*Aql*), his ability to think as opposed to animals. Man has the capacity to know about things and about Allah as is illustrated by the account (Qur'an 2: 31-34) of how Adam only, as the first man, was able to name things through what Fazlur Rahman calls the "capacity for creative knowledge" (Rahman: 1980, 18). The quest for knowledge (*ilm*) and divine insight (*ma'rifa*) then takes on different forms according to social conditions (Gilsenan: 1976, 206ff.). What makes man inhuman is going against his primordial nature (*Fitra*) by forgetting that which the Qur'an is the reminder of: his dependency on Allah. In fact, from this point of view the whole of the Qur'an and the guidance (*Hudan*) that it offers can be seen as a lesson in how to become fully human. It therefore contains numerous accounts of, on the one hand, behaviour that is considered to be desirable and, on the other hand, behaviour that is looked upon as perverted and pathological when men become "like cattle, (or) indeed, worse" (7: 179). It is a lesson in how to achieve successful identity (see also Rosen: 1984, 30-34). To get an idea of how this can be achieved, one can for the sake of clarity distinguish analytically between three 'kinds' of person: the Social, the Legal and the Religious person. Although a unified man as a complete and obedient Muslim is the ideal, the various facets of personhood are expressed in different circumstances. One may also argue that, when speaking about Islam and the Middle East, the division between the sexes is too fundamental to be disregarded. I shall nevertheless do so, unless specific reference is made to either sex. The Qur'an states that women are spiritually equal to men (3: 195; 33: 35; 57: 13) and even if men are considered to be the guardians of women (4: 34) I shall take this into consideration only in cases in which the person-concept is specifically different for various social groups.

3.1.1 The social person

Although Islam as a particular body of teachings does not always seem to have an explicit importance in daily life (Lutfiyya: 1970b), it may be referred to to explain a certain practice, since it contains prescriptions that can serve as a basis for interpretations of every aspect of life. Explaining a social act in this way may involve religious evaluation in view of the fact that these aspects may often be inseparable. It is a commonplace, also among Muslim apologetics, that Islam is characteristically a social religion: the emphasis on the idea of a Muslim community, the Ummah, is very strong. The good person is the social person, and the Qur'anic virtues (besides those relating man to Allah directly) are those that further peaceful and harmonious relationships among human beings. In actual practice these and similar virtues are repeatedly stressed in the socialization process where children are taught that a good person is a well-behaved person (*Adib*), someone who has learned etiquette. Such attitudes may, on the other hand, result in a lack of ability to resolve conflicts of interest and may lead to polished superficiality as Hisham Sharabi and Ani Mukhtar point out in a polemic discussion of Middle-Eastern patterns of upbringing (1977). Nevertheless, politeness, generosity and respect for tradition are cherished values in most Islamic countries. The larger part of Islamic teachings in most manuals and catechisms are devoted to questions of social relations and appropriate behaviour. Likewise, in most traditional faculties of theology in the Muslim world major attention is paid to the study of *Fiqh*, the legal system. As a conflict-resolving conceptual system Islam is truly functionalist.

3.1.2 The legal person

Fiqh, the Islamic system of jurisprudence operates with certain conditions that must be met to qualify a person. *Fiqh* is based on uncompromising individualism and it does not accept any social unit beyond the family (except *Ummah*). The sound legal person is *Aqil*, someone who is able to act by motive and consideration, and to whom the commandments and prohibitions of religious law can be applied. The law, *Shari'a*, also sets conditions that vary from group to group, and Muslims do have the highest status, but they are also considered to carry the greatest responsiblilty simply because they have received divine knowledge and are supposed to *know* best. In certain interpretations, like the contemporary Iranian ones, a person without a religion does not qualify as a person, consequently the *Baha'is* are considered heretics guilty of apostasy, which is why they are persecuted. The laws of inheritance and the regulations concerning testimony clearly show a bias towards men, the testimony of one male equals that of two females.

3.1.3 The religious person

The religious person is of course related to the foregoing since it may be said to represent aspects of the religious concept of the person. There are, however, a number of prescriptions which are directly related to man's obligations to Allah. These rules define man as a servant (*Abd*) in relation to Allah as the Lord (*Rabb*), and they are designed to keep man conscious of this. The daily prayers, the food-regulations, the fasting and other rules remind the Muslim of the divine purpose of life. When man does wrong he wrongs himself, the expression *Zulm an-Nafs* means 'wronging yourself', and this happens when man forgets to serve Allah (*'Ibada)*. The ideal is to develop *Taqwa*, usually translated with 'piety', but semantically more related to concepts of guarding, safe-keeping and protecting, i.e., one should protect oneself against the harmful and evil, as pointed out by Fazlur Rahman in his commentary on this central Qur'anic concept (Rahman: 1980, 28-30). The paradigmatic, ideal religious person fulfills his obligations to Allah and by doing so qualifies as a true person, which is not always easy - the fragility of the human spirit is fully acknowledged by the Qur'an: "Verily, man has a restless character; when misfortune touches him he panics and when good things come his way, he prevents them from reaching others" (70: 19-21). Selfishness and greed are vices that are to be overcome: "The successful are those who can be saved from their own selfishness" (59: 9 and 64: 16). If a system of moral teachings is to make sense by way of intra-systemic logic the starting point has to be a feeble soul or self (the word *Nafs* has both meanings in Arabic), rewards for the right efforts have to be great and the required deeds have to be within reach of man. The moral-religious precepts concern man on the road towards perfection. But he should not be too sure of himself: hypocrisy (*Nifaq*) is a major vice of which many are guilty.

3.2 *Morality*

There are only few Western modernist thinkers (cf. Taylor: 1976) who agree with the Islamic notion that the awareness of moral obligations is the most evident contribution to a concept of person. In practice, morality is mostly presented as being Islamic, though it often reflects folk-traditions and sectarian interpretations more than a traditional literal prescription. The problem has been dealt with before: there is no such thing as a pure Islam in operation. In my view, however, it still makes sense to see how people handle the ideals they profess to uphold, and Islamic scholars and clergy come quite close in their interpretations, at least when we confine the discussion to orthodox Sunni-Islam. In the general Islamic view, morality is closely related to being a person because morality is bound by reason and reflection. As Muhammad Abdou put it in his 'Risalat at-Tawhid': "God has given man three faculties, or rather three faculties direct man, make him incomparable to the animals: memory, imagination and reflection" (Abdou: 1965, 52). Morality should not be considered solely as a varnish covering an otherwise unruly human nature, as cultural control of pan-human emotionality. Morality also defines emotions and invests the fabric of social relations with emotional meaning (Luts - White: 1986, 418).

3.3 *Group and Individual in Theology*

The relation between the individual and the group is a central concern of Islam. So central in fact that according to traditional Islamic spiritual medicine there is a natural intimate relationship between health and ethical conduct. In the words of Mehmet Bayrakdar:

> Therefore they (the Islamic physicists) believe that bad ethical conduct can cause in man physical and mental illness, or mental and physical illness can produce in him bad conduct, and they consider that it is possible to heal physical and mental illness by good conduct as well as by psychological conditioning (Bayrakdar: 1985, 1; also Sheikh-Dilthey: 1979).

He adds:

> Thus the conceptions of health and illness can give us a picture of what a normal self/individual is considered to be (Bayrakdar: 1985, 2).

Among the methods for preserving good health are: self-restraint, control of passions, observance of ethical codes, imitation of the way of life of famous personalities and making a distinction between natural and unnatural things (Bayrakdar: 1985, 4), corresponding, of course, to the Islamic codes of purity and impurity. The profound emphasis on law and morality in Islam serves no other purpose than to regulate the lives of people, to solve conflicts and to direct society towards Allah. And as most Islamic theology is also law, it constantly centres on the regulations of social life and notably on the well-being of the group as the major concern, because it is only then that the individual can fulfill his religious, moral and social obligations. Even the aforementioned concept of Zulm an-Nafs 'doing wrong to the self' has social or reflexive connotations, doing wrong not only harms yourself as Kenneth Cragg has pointed out (Cragg: 1973, 99ff.). However, man has of course also a personal responsibility to Allah which he expresses through faith (*Iman*) and personal worship (*'Ibada*). So in strictly theological discourse there is a marked relation between group and individual.

3.3.1 Middle-Eastern patterns of socialization

The religious ideal of group-oriented responsibility accords well with established practices in Middle-Eastern patterns of socialization and interaction. The Arab family has often been classed as patriarchal, trilineal, endogamous and extended, and with its fixed chains of authority and respect it is well prepared to maintain itself as a strongly bounded unit in often perilous social conditions (Gulik: 1983, 203ff.). Through the father as a symbol of family strength and unity the family competes with others for power and respect. This means that a strong I-sense can only be based on a strong kinship-sense, and the process of socialization thus mainly serves to subordinate the new members of the family so that no intra-familial conflicts become visible to the larger society. The fundamental question with respect to socialization is how the personality is shaped so that it motivates the kind of behaviour that society requires. In an extremely critical 'inside' view of child-rearing practices, Sharabi and Mukhtar point out that shaming-techniques are frequently used together with punishment to produce a strong dependence on the family and little individuality in a Western sense (Sharabi-Mukhtar: 1977, 247ff.). In a society in which being alone is considered to be a sickness, the techniques of companionship become highly developed into systems of sociability with countless rules and with sharp divisions between the public and private spheres of life. Islam does not recognize any Original Sin, but in most Islamic societies the concept of shame (*'Aib*) and the fear of gossip greatly influence the construction of strategies for formal behaviour. But where and how shame is recognized and dealt with is a matter of extreme variation, so oversimplification should be avoided (Wikan: 1984).

4.0 *The paradigm for actual practice: Hudan*

The paradigm for human practice as prescribed by orthodox tradition is expressed in the concept of *Hudan*, the right guidance. *Hudan* is extremely comprehensible in that it emcompasses the greater part of the body of religious teachings. Polemic theological debates mostly have had the purpose of establishing the right interpretation of the Guidance provided by in the Qur'an and the Hadith (The Islamic Tradition). The need to follow the right path is strongly felt in many Muslim quarters, e.g., in Saudi Arabia which has its Committees for the Commanding of Good and the Forbidding of Evil who keep vigilant watch over the performance of religious duties of Everyman. In the extreme, *Hudan* may be applied to the minutest detail of life as in Abdur Rahman Shad's *Muslim Etiquettes* which contains descriptions that clearly separate Good from Bad behaviour (Shad: 1980; also Islahi: 1979). The Guidance is very much alive and employed in most situations that call for an evaluation of behaviour. Behaviour may be divided into in four categories:

Human: Islamic and non-Islamic
Non-Human: Animal and non-Animal

There are some peculiarities in this system of classification: animal behaviour is theoretically also Muslim because animals live in accordance with the nature given to them by the Creator. Non-human/non-animal is not just a theoretical experiment, but the classification of apostates (cf. above II1.1), because as one-time Muslims they have been exposed to the right guidance and are therefore held responsible for their conduct. According to the Islamic view there is nothing secular in life and consequently the life of a Muslim could be looked upon as one ritual performance or act of worship. The Muslim interpretation, however, distinguishes between worship proper and *Mu'amalat*, the transactions, i.e., the rules concerning social intercourse. The rituals performed during worship do not only remind man of Allah and of man's cosmological role but they are the necessary prerequisite for right action, and it is essential to consider their role in the transformation of personal experience and its cultural construction. The paradigm for actual practice consequently includes both ritual/religious and secular activities, as they would usually be classed. On the other hand, that which is not quite so 'religious' may also be validated and qualified through the authority of Islamic tradition which in reality is much more flexible than the guardians of this tradition would have us believe.

4.1 *Muhammad as the perfect paradigm*

Throughout Islamic history the prophet Muhammad has retained his status of the perfected human archetype. Modern apologetic versions of the 'Sirat Rasul Allah' (the biography of God's Messenger) often reach panegyrical heigths uncommon in the Western world. One reason why this surprises non-Muslims is their failure to understand the status that the good example has in Muslim life. There is nothing petit bourgeois about it. It is the logical consequence of a conceptual system that can point directly at things that have great value. So, in schools and elsewhere, there is a tradition of telling stories about good and great men, and especially about the Prophet, as examples that are to be imitated. Muslim schoolchildren are bound to know countless stories about the doings and sayings of Muhammad. There are good things and there are bad things: to become a true person you will have to follow in the footsteps of the one man who did not fail, and who clearly demonstrated what man's primordial nature (*Fitra*) is: to be constantly aware of Allah and to carry out his commandments. In the parallel world of popular Islam holy men and women provide other examples that are to be imitated in order to avoid exposing oneself to evil eyes or the influence of the spirits, the *Jnun*.

4.2 *Becoming a person: the hierarchy of values*

Becoming a person in the Islamic sense means to find the right orientation in the hierarchy of values. The legal system operates with five classes of action, ranging from prohibited to prescribed. These five classes are at the same time the religious scale for evaluating the moral consequences of actions and intentions. The desire should be not to side with evil but to seek forgiveness and strive to move upwards. There is a constant dialectic between virtues and vices in the construction of symbols that point to the positive forms of intentionality. Generally speaking, the directions up and down connote good and bad, as in the common conception of the symbolic values of the parts of the body, with the head on top having positive value and the feet down below being the lowest in rank. The concept of the person in this sense implies that everything should be in its proper place and that the classificatory system is based on reciprocal relations between conceptions of what is rightly religious, though it may not always be so from an orthodox point of view. In the concept of the person there may be many different symbolic elements derived from various levels of the value-hierarchy. The 'Idealized Other' is not a single monolithic entity (although Muhammad often serves as *the* archetype), but a complex cluster of symbols that may evoke and sustain a number of attitudes in different situations.

4.3 *Orientation of self*

The proper orientation of the self from *Nafs* to *Aql* is the result of an inner *Jihad* (endeavour, effort), whereby Islam becomes a system of purification and qualification (Charnay: 1977, 145).

> By becoming a self-controlled individual, a *muttaqui* (lit: one who shows regard for something for Allah's sake), a Muslim becomes a member of the community of *saliheens*, the righteous ones (Brohi: 1982, 252).

This struggle is facilitated by the intentionality of the self/soul towards Allah, who when he created man "breathed my own spirit" into him (15: 29 and 38: 72), and even in the midst of temptation man's primordial nature can not be altered, though it may be temporarily disturbed:

> Devote thyself single-mindedly to the faith and thus follow the nature designed by Allah, the nature according to which he fashioned mankind. There is no altering the creation of Allah (30: 30).

Yet, there are weaknesses in man's character. There are numerous remarks in the Qur'an about those who do wrong and revolt against the will of Allah. However, despite man's pettiness and narrowness of mind, which are his basic weaknesses, according to Fazlur Rahman (1980, 25-26), there is always the possibility that he can be awakened to understand the purpose of Allah's creation. The danger consists in letting man alone with his subjective desires because they are apt to let him forget and deceive himself (4:27-28) (Tritton: 1971). One can say that there is a contradictive logic in these views of man's nature. However, instead of discussing this in great detail, I want to restrict myself to drawing attention to the differences between a true conscientious nature and a false one. The true nature is to be cultivated through *Taqwa*, the protection of oneself against the harmful or evil consequences of one's conduct (Rahman: 1980, 29).

4.3.1 *Tahara*: the cultic purity

The condition necessary for the appropriate conditioning of self is cultic purity, *Tahara*, which in fact extends beyond what is usually considered cultic in Western terms. It is no coincidence that the modern English-language 'Manual of Hadith' by Maulana Muhammad Ali deals with the subject of purification right after faith and knowledge. The first Hadith-quotation says: "Purification is half the faith" (Ali: 1983, 41), and Ali's general commentary on the subject runs as follows:

> "The purification of the body is thus made a preliminary to prayer so that by external purification a man's attention may be directed to the purification of the soul which is aimed at in prayer" (ibid: 40).

Whereas purity is necessary before prayer, prayer is needed to purify the mind (and purification of the human soul is salvation (91: 9)). Ali also states that what is acquired by unlawful means is impure, and "the pure and the impure cannot go together" (1983, 42 note 2). Thus *Tahara* is the conceptual means of directing actual practice towards the pure, which is identical to the lawful. It should be noted that the concept of purity creates a link that runs across what is moral, social, physical and spiritual: causes in one realm may have effects in another. This means that individual spirituality is conditioned by social practice and vice versa. The semantic domains are interrelated without the conceptual boundaries of secular thought. Islam is a total system, a traditional world-view. Ritual purification encompasses everything that a Muslim should do including dietary habits which is one of the means whereby a Muslim can interpret his faith. The legal code coincides with the aesthetic code: what is legal (*Halal*) is also good (*Tayyib*), and what is forbidden (*Haram*) is also bad (*Khabith*). In social practice, patterns of behaviour may also be interpreted in this way, especially when it comes to the relations between the sexes. The complex of honour and shame is not directly related to Islamic doctrine, but may at least partially be referred to in Islamic terms.

4.3.2 'The Nature of Man': *Fitra* vs. *Fitna*

As pointed out above the Qur'anic view of man is ambivalent. On the one hand man is with Allah, it is his nature to believe in Allah (57: 9), he is cast in the best mould (95: 4), divine spirit is breathed into him (32: 9) and he is superior to other creations (17: 71). But on the other hand, he is created weak (4: 28), inclined to transgress (96: 6-7), impatient (70: 19-21) and ungrateful (10: 13 and 17: 67). All of these dispositions ought to be classed as natural, but in fact they are not. All that brings man closer to Allah is *Fitra*, nature, because a saying of the prophet states that "Religion is Nature" (*Ad-Din al-Fitra*), and consequently anything that is prescribed by doctrine and tradition becomes 'natural'. In a Hadith from the collection of Al-Bukhari it says that the following five things are in accordance with nature: circumcision, removal of pubic hair, removal of hair in the armpit, paring down of finger and toe nails and clipping moustaches (Sahih al-Bukhari 77: 63). Islam does not recognize original sin, or abominations of the flesh and it does not shun sexuality as long as it is performed under the right cicumstances, i.e., in matrimony. Nevertheless, Islamic culture is oriented away from the body, and most natural functions of the body are tabooed in Islamic culture (Sharabi - Mukhtar: 1977, 248). What diverts man from Allah is *Fitna*, i.e., rebellion, temptation (women are the greatest Fitna according to tradition, e.g., Al-Bukhari 67: 17) and being led from the right course. The concept of person, which is mostly connected with the positive aspects of ideal identity ('The idealized Other') can only materialize against the background of the unruly and the disorderly. *Fitna* covers the aspects of feared identity, all that is uncertain and threatens order and stability. It is man's nature to be religious, but he has to be constantly reminded of this. The guidance and knowledge is present in his nature because the distinction between good and evil is "ingrained in his heart" (Rahman: 1980, 9).

4.4 *Key concepts in tradition*

To delimit the concepts of the person and primarily those of the virtuous or right person further, current interpretations of the traditions emphasize a number of relations between what is proper and what is improper. The following are some of the key concepts that denote such proper relations of men to Allah and their fellowmen; *Hanif* (monotheist) vs. idolaters, *Mu'min* (the believer) vs. the unbeliever, the concept of man's vicegerency on Earth (*Khilafa*), the concept of soul/self (*Nafs*) and the doctrinal ideas about human emotions.

4.4.1 Adam and the prophets: the *Hanif*

Man has the capacity of knowledge and hence of receiving revelations from Allah (15: 29). Those who do not understand the signs are evil, ignorant and harmful to themselves (7: 177). The prophets, who were all *Hanifs*, i.e., monotheists, have a special admonitory status and, according to tradition, it is not allowed to draw comparisons between them. Their bodies are not consumed by the earth after their burial, even though they are considered to be ordinary mortal humans. Yet, their graves are not meant to be places of prayer as they cannot intercede for man with Allah. However, in popular Islam, prophets and especially saints are fervently venerated, the direct relation to Allah being considered impossible by folk-tradition in feudal societies. According to the Qur'an, prophets are sinless (21: 27), they cannot act unfaithfully (3: 164) and they submit themselves to the will of Allah (10: 74). Their purpose is to purify people and lead them to their Lord (79: 18-20). In doing so, however, they may be accused of madness (34: 45) or expose themselves to attempts on their lives (2: 61, 3: 112, 4: 157). The story of the creation of Adam draws a certain picture of the ideas about man and his qualities, though Adam is not to be taken as a *pars pro toto*. The supreme prophet is still Muhammad, Allah's messenger for all Mankind, who possessed perfect qualities (20: 2) and who was the perfect leader (36: 3-4). He was an excellent example for mankind (33: 21) and by following him one can win the love of Allah (3: 20). Quotations concerning the benefits of following in Muhammed's footsteps can be provided *ad infinitum*, and there is not the slightest doubt that the prophet is used as *the* example of a perfect person. The recently published 'Encyclopedia of Seerah' (biography of the prophet) by Afzalur Rahman (1981) opens with a quotation from Iqbal:

> Endeavour to reach (the conduct of) Muhammad, for the Right Way of Life is pursuit in his footprints. If you fail to reach him, all else is falsehood and error.

Such a demand is hard to meet for an average Muslim but nonetheless the ideal is there, and it certainly functions as a paradigmatic concept of and for the person. For mankind as a community, *Ummah*, the prophets are perfected human archetypes.

4.4.2 *Mu'min* vs. *Kafir*

As we have seen above, Islamic doctrine operates with sharp divisions in its semantic constructions. One of the most rigorous divisions is that between believers, *Mu'min*, and non-believers, *Kafir*. The Qur'anic descriptions of these two categories are straightforward and do not have to be elaborated here (see e.g., Rahman: 1980; Cragg: 1973; Wensinck: 1965), but reality is somewhat different. Though not all Muslims are practising *Mu'mins*, no one would like to be accused of *Kafir*-behaviour. Anyone would shudder at the very thought! In reality the distinction is harder to draw and most people will consider themselves Muslims even when, from the clergy's point of view, the way in which they practice their religion leaves much to be desired (Lutfiyya: 1970b). Signs of *Mu'min* behaviour, especially as demonstrated by local sheikhs, is politically powerful and influential (Gilsenan: 1982, ch. 5). Equally interesting is the fact that some are more knowledgeable than others, i.e., they are considered to know *Batin*, to have an understanding of Allah's secret purposes, although it may be very difficult to define how they acquire and display it. The ideas corresponding to proper Muslim behaviour vary according to age and sex. According to Gilsenan, boys from the age of 5-6 may form groups that imitate the ritual practices of their elder brothers. Young men follow the sheikhs in religious study groups and prayer, but older men go on pilgrimage, read during Ramadan and discuss theological matters (Gilsenan: 1982, 123). Obviously, the concept of what constitutes a truely orthodox person varies according to a range of cultural conditions. But as one sheikh once pointed out to me during a conversation: "Do not think that Islam is what Muslims do!"

4.4.3 The concept of *Khilafa*

Most contemporary Islamic apologetic writing stresses the concept of *Khilafa* when discussing man and his obligations to Allah (e.g. Ahmad:

1974, 8-10). The main argument is that Allah has created the earth and man, and has allowed man to become his deputy (*Khalifa*). Allah has entrusted man with the world and thus has given him the responsibility for using it in the right way. This leaves man in the position of servant (*Abd*) with Allah as his Lord (*Rabb*) and this relation determines the forms of reciprocity considered appropriate in carrying out the convenant, or contract, between them. In connection with the earlier-mentioned distinction between *Mu'min* and *Kafir* it should be noted that a *Mu'min* is aware (*Dhikr*) of this relationship, whereas a *Kafir* neglects it (*Ghaflah*). Being a Muslim precisely indicates the realization of this relationship, in which man's worship through his entire culture and works is the prime quality of his existence. Hence history becomes the evidence of the (lack of) fulfillment of his obligations and as Cragg notes: "Archeology is thus a lesson in retribution" (1970: 94).

4.4.4 Soul and self: *Nafs*

The term *Nafs* may be translated equally well with 'soul' as with 'self' (it is also the reflexive pronoun in Arabic). In some parts of traditional and current usage the word *Ruh*, which denotes the life-force of man, and of animals, is used synonymously with *Nafs* (Tritton: 1971). In Qur'anic usage *Nafs* mostly denotes the human self or the human person, but also the human soul, and the passages in question became the cornerstones of later Muslim ethics and psychology, although the later philosophical positions became extremely complicated through the influence of Greek thought and gnostic traditions. In orthodoxy the conscious Muslim will have to watch himself with respect to his soul because as *Nafs al-Ammarah* (the urging or demanding soul) it connects itself with passion and desire (*Hawan*) and may order him to do evil things (12: 53) or cause him to be in doubt (50: 16). The moral struggle within man, the inner *Jihad*, is carried out through the agency of the other part of the soul, the *Nafs al-Lawwamah* which censures and reproves sharply as it is the self-accusing faculty of man (75: 2) which has to be cultivated through *Taqwa*, watchfulness. The soul of the righteous then becomes the *Nafs al-Mutmainna*, the peaceful and confident soul (89: 27). Interestingly enough, these designations are also used by contemporary Muslims with reference to Freudian psychology to denote the Id, ego and super-ego in an attempt to reconcile between Islamic with

Western viewpoints (Badri: 1979, 119-120). In other, mostly popular, interpretations *Nafs* denotes man's 'lower' nature (Tritton: 1971, 493) or that which has to be constrained by *Aql*, of which men have more than women do (Rosen: 1984, 31-34).

4.4.5 Emotions

The soul is closely connected with man's emotional life, as e.g., in the case of the demanding soul and desire. As can be gathered from what has been said before it is to a large extent the emotional life of man that has to be controlled. Emotions are human but some of them are also very dangerous - in the Muslim view ordinary human desire is always dangerous, it is *Fitna*: temptation and disorder. In the third volume of his Revival of the Science of Religion, the great mediaeval theologian Al-Ghazali describes these influences that guide man or lead him astray. There are things that destroy: gluttony, sensuality, envy, arrogance, etc., and there are things that have a saving influence, i.e., those sentiments that are central in positive Islamic morality: kindness, hospitality, humility, patience, etc. As has been pointed out earlier, these emotions, sentiments and attitudes reflect directly man's health. In popular Islamic life there is the same urge to control emotionality and sensuality. There are only a few outlets that have cultural sanction (see e.g., Sharabi: 1977; Wikan: 1984; Lewis: 1986). Expectations as to the range of displayed and socially accepted emotionality vary considerably according to sex, age and status. Women are supposed to be more emotional than men, and, according to Muslim etiquette they should not visit graves of relatives too frequently because they are "weak at heart" (Shad: 1980, 148). The orthodox and mostly also the local traditional ideal is the self-controlled person, especially with regard to men who should demonstrate the ability to control their emotions. The ways of making a person's emotions a public matter and thereby open to control are further evidence of the social character of emotionality in certain areas of Islamic culture. In both classical and modern sources dreams may not just refer to a person's individual inner life. They are frequently considered to be the result of contacts with extra-individual realms or agents, such as the *Jnun*, good or evil spirits (Pruett: 1985; Crapanzano: 1975), and such experiences are then made the subject of public discussion. According to Islahi (1982, 58-62) bad dreams should not be told to anyone, whereas good dreams should be told to friends and one should not relate false dreams, defined as those "conceived by your own imagination" (Islahi: 1982, 61). Though humans are supposed to be cast in the best mould they may easily fall prey to those unwanted desires that are also part of their nature. They are "the forgetful ones" (Rosen: 1984, 33). Islam as submission to Allah is control and cultivation of self.

5.0 *Actual practice: the realization of paradigms*

The religious and social construction of paradigmatic concepts of the person is a way of making sense of human existence (nowadays one hardly dares to say that it has a function in the preservation of society...). Such concepts give value to certain experiences according to the cultural axiology and provide a standard by which thought and action can be measured. In the course of this discussion I have tried to relate doctrinal precepts to social practice in order to present a picture of their interrelatedness. As Ortner has pointed out (1984), one of the major concerns in recent anthropology is to relate actual practice to cultural systems. Orthodoxy is not *the* system but it may be seen as being part of it as the influences of doctrine are ambiguous. There is no doubt that orthodoxy exists and that it is a body of notions which is constantly referred to (Messick: 1986). Although it would be a false interpretation (however) to see either orthodoxy or social conditions as determining cultural discourse, they are both part of the production of culture through human intention and action. Muslims may prefer to refer to each other as 'brothers and sisters in faith' but their monolithic ideal does not fit in well with the fragmented and varied interpretations they present to each other. Nevertheless, in socialization most parents will try to make *their* children good Muslims. Their reasons for doing so may range from pious convictions to economic maximization, though the latter will be given the former interpretation. Adults in Muslim communities may also strive for present identities that coincide with the local view of the paradigmatic person. The concept of person is meaningful and is implicitly present in all forms of discourse relating to a person's behaviour. There could be no social control without gossip (narrated practice) and no gossip without a culturally valid concept of the person.

5.1 *Contributions of ethnography*

But for the contributions of ethnography, anthropology would have been ethnocentric armchair-speculation and the history of religions the comparative study of dogma. As has been outlined above, the Qur'anic and later doctrinal conceptions are interesting objects of study when compared with e.g.,, Western theological and philosophical discourse. However, if they are to be of value for the study of religion 'as lived in' and not just 'thought of' by a priestly elite, the field-work and descriptions of practices are the corrections *sine qua non*. If descriptions of social forms and cultural meanings are to be dependable they must, in principle, be extremely local and as such they can be said to be of little value for the study of religious concepts. In my view, however, such concepts also have to be studied pragmatically if they are to have any relevance, but that is of course a matter of opinion. The problem of representativity of social studies does not necessarily form an absolute hindrance to their application. There are strokes with a wide brush in any culture, there are nuclear semes (i.e. units of meaning) or fundamental structures, and though life in one village will never be identical to that in another we can make some sensible comparisons, provided we leave room for a certain degree of flexibility in our concepts. Any cultural element may have multiple denotations as well as connotations within the emic spheres of evocation, and it is wrong to reify such elements. It is important to contextualize the doctrines of religious traditions. The ethnography of religions therefore can provide us with the pragmatic functions of self-concepts and individual perspectives, however microscopic they seem to be at first, ethnography "can provide data on the interactional and representational worlds of the indvidual... as manifest in individual lives" (LeVine: 1982, 303). But for such a perspective we might have believed that e.g., in accordance with the Qur'an, neither men nor women are allowed to commit adultery, whereas in practice this applies to women only (Lutfiyya: 1970, 510). Or we might have thought that the honour-and-shame complex is what, contrary to fact, anthroplogists believe it to be (Wikan: 1984, 636ff.). However deconstructive the constant relating to ethnographic evidence is for the results of our text-studies, it should be carried out.

5.2 *Anthropological reflections*

Self-concepts, like all other cultural phenomena, should be studied semantically, syntactically and pragmatically, i.e., what do they mean, where are they found, and how are they employed. This has been done in various ways throughout the history of anthropology and the study of religion (Fogelson: 1982). Previous attempts to provide shortcuts via empathy have failed, as Lutz - White have noted concerning the study of emotions, because empathy "presumes what it is often used to prove; which is the universal and transparent nature of an emotional experience construed as internal" (Lutz - White: 1986, 415). The self has become part of culture and culture has become part of the self. Anthropological reflections are as necessary as ethnographic descriptions, or as I would like to add on behalf of the history of religions, as necessary as studies of textual traditions referred to in a given culture. Anthropology has moved beyond the study of 'primitives' to encompass the history of its own culture and segments of 'non-primitive' societies. In tribal societies there need not be cognitive uniformity, but the correspondence between religion and social life tends to be greater and religions are defined by social life, cf. 'Lugbara Religion' whereas in the case of 'world religions' it is religion that defines social life, cf. 'Islamic concepts of person', 'Hindu society' or whatever (Stirrat: 1984, 210). When we are referring to Islamic culture we are confronted with a vast range of ideas and practices that seemingly have very little coherence. Yet, there are common points of reference however disparate the interpretations of them may be. The force of orthodoxy may not be absolute but it is to be reckoned with (see e.g., Messick: 1986).

5.3 *Construction of self and social relations*

The construction of the idea of self through socialization and its relevance to the preservation of social relations need not be questioned. The 'person' is a semantic construct held together by agreement (Crick: 1982, 292), and in conjunction with other cultural phenomena it forms the base for the execution of meaningful practice (Rosen: 1984). Such a performance obviously may include the taking of certain roles, and in connection with static views of culture this observation has led to the notion that the Others of social scientific discourse are simply performing stereotyped parts prescribed by unchanging scripts (see e.g., Kaplan: 1961). A great part of the role-talk in social sciences seems to imply that the performers would act differently if there were not any sanctions in society. This view may lead to an idea of a self unspoiled by group, society or culture. But would such an 'essential' self have any means whereby it could recognize itself? It has been said about the Japanese 'Bildungsroman' that

> it is not so much about the self's discovery of the self, as about the self's discipline of itself into a productive model hierarchically classified and blueprinted in detail by society at large (Miyoshi: 1974, xi).

The observations of Sharabi and Mukhar (1977), and Lutfiyya (1970a, b) et al. would suggest the same for Islamic societies provided we do not object to a comparison between 'Bildungsroman' and the concepts of person. The extent to which individuals are moved by force or interest is then another matter which will not be pursued here. A central concern of the individual and his/her family in Islamic societies is their relation with relatives and neighbours (Lutfiyya: 1970b, 57ff.). The identification with the family unit is also indicated through personal names:

> From birth until death, the Arab villager is always identified with other members of the joint family through the composition of his name (Lutfiyya: 1970a, 506).

Names for children may be chosen with the help of a special sheikh who can communicate with the spirits (Lutfiyya: 1970a, 514). This indicates a custom in which a person is placed within an ordered social and religious field. Family life demands direction of appropriate emotions and the distribution of respect and authority including responsibility for actions of relatives and clansmen in culturally prescribed ways. Michelle Rosaldo has suggested that hierarchical societies, much more than other societies, appear to be concerned with the problem of how society controls an inner emotional self (Rosaldo: 1984). Ethnography will have to confirm this, but the concern is certainly present in Arab societies.

5.4 *Dynamic reflexivity*

A self-concept places the individual in relation to society. It is important to keep in mind that neither the self-concept, the individual, nor society is static, which means that the individual will have to achieve a dynamic reflexivity; there are different ways of thinking about yourself according to what happens to you in life and according to whether you are confronted with positive or negative sanctions, rewarding goals, moral anxiety, social punishment, etc. As far as we know, individuals are capable of having several interrelated identities without necessarily having to be classified as schizophrenic, but the modern Western popular notion of the person as completely bounded and separated from society poses cognitive problems to us. In person-concepts as well as in culture in general there are ideological 'disjunctions' depending on what facets of the person are being expressed and in what context (Harrison: 1985, 128).

5.5 *Islam as narrative competence*

Dynamic reflexivity involves telling the story of yourself to yourself (and others). The framework of this narration depends on the cultural context, the narrative competence acquired by each member of the culture, i.e., the repertoire of symbols, explanations, etc. that can be related in a meaningful way. The self-concept is such a cultural narrative: the reverse autobiography of no one. Being interactive, performance thereby becomes a species of hermeneutics, or in the words of Robert LeVine:

> Viewing custom more as drama than as law, I find it plausible to assume that social performances reflect not merely the dictates of the script but the interpretations of those who enact it (1982, 296).

Also, according to LeVine, there are three modes of communication about the self: 1. face-to-face interaction in routine encounters; 2. public occasions (e.g. rituals) and 3. autobiographical discourse (1982, 297ff.). These are the areas where ethnographic investigations of the Islamic concepts of person could prove to be most useful if we are to examine the nature and extent of Islam as narrative competence with the conventions that make up the framework for the understanding of self and others in Islamic societies.

5.6 *Correspondence between actual practice and normative Islam*

The fundamental issue in Islam is the Qur'an because only through the Qur'an did the will of Allah become accessible to the whole of mankind. And yet it is obvious that not many Muslims live by the book. Does it make any sense to talk about Islam in its normative, dogmatic and orthodox sense and relate this to the everyday life of people who unhesitatingly call themselves Muslims? I think it does. A fine example of how this can be done is presented in B. Messick's article on the role of the Mufti in Yemen (Messick: 1986). A lot of Protestant thinking has fashioned the ways in which we (here) perceive the world, but we should not look upon our question concerning the congruence between words and works as an all-or-nothing business. A Muslim may become more Muslim if he runs for public office or has his child baptized in the belief that it will help the child survive. Here we are deeply enmeshed in the pragmatics of religion, its use or abuse (see e.g., An-Nai'im: 1986), depending on the position one wishes to take. The Muslim religious elite has helped to promote the orientalists' view that there is only one true and absolute Islam, and that all deviations from legalistic orthodoxy represented in folk-religion are aberrations and corruptions. Defining Islam meaningfully is extremely difficult, if not impossible, as well as controversial and it is usually a matter of politics and rhetorics, academic and otherwise (e.g. El-Zein: 1977). Nevertheless, there is little doubt that, in 'Islamic' societies, social life is moulded by religion. Anyone who doubts this can go there and see for himself! But the all too familiar and seductive distinction between the Great and the Little Traditions should be applied very cautiously with regard to the forms of Islamic practice (Stirrat: 1984, 208ff.; Lewis: 1986, ch. 6). To a certain extent orthodoxy and popular Islam represent what Stirrat (1984, 204) calls "two models of the sacred", one of which is concerned with the timeless, spaceless absolute and the other with the here and now. But there are modifications in that orthodoxy is also pragmatic and considered to contain the model for social life, and popular religion of course also has its versions of the transcendent and the sacred (Stirrat: 1984, 209-210). The history of orthodoxy also convinces us that it is not a fixed body of teachings and interpretations, though this is the way in which it presents itself. Both orthodoxy and popular religion have a large repertoire of notions and patterns that become relevant through convention. Like other socio-religious concepts the concept of the person comes to life as *bricolage*, consisting of elements from the entire cultural array of understanding.

6. *Concluding remarks*

Much more needs to be done concerning paradigmatic person-concepts in Islam and Islamic societies but I have given a rough outline of some of the more relevant questions. Some of them have been dealt with only marginally, but such were the conditions. In addition as far as Islamic orthodox tradition is concerned there are great uncertainties as to how its injunctions are interpreted and applied as well as the validity of those classical concepts and notions that I have tried to review in the more empirically oriented parts of this essay. The general theoretical presuppositions are in my view promising enough to deserve to be applied to these problems, which, in turn, are generated by the specific theoretical outlooks. All in all, if we can apply an anti-'Cartesian' model of the person as more loosely composed of what he consciously or unconsciously 'says to himself' through the agency of the available cultural idioms and see the person also as conceptually inter-locked and connected with the social/cultural/religious in multiple ways, we may be gaining ground, because then we shall be able to study not either the person or the religion/culture, but both at the same time in a 'thick' interpretation of social and textual narratives.

Bibliography

Abdou, M.
1965 *Risalat al Tawhid, Exposé de la Religion Musulmane,* Paris.

Ahmad, K.
1974 *Family Life in Islam,* Leicester.

Ali, M.M.
1983 rpt. (1944, 1978 (3)), *A Manual of Hadith,* London.

An-Nai'im, A.A.
1986 'The Islamic Law of Apostasy and its Modern Applicability: A case from the Sudan', in: *Religion,* 16, 3, 197-224.

Ardener, E.
1982 'Social Anthropology, Language and Reality'. In: *Semantic Anthropology,* (ed.) D. Parkin, London.

Asad, T.
1983 'Anthropological Conceptions of Religion: Reflections on Geertz', in: *Man* (N.S.), 18, 237-259.

Austin, R.J.W.
1976 'Some Key Words in the Islamic Concept of Man', in: *Studies in Comparative Religion*, 10, 46-57.

Azzam, S. (ed)
1982 *Islam and Contemporary Society*, London.

Badri, M.B.
1979 *The Dilemma of Muslim Psychologists*, London.

Ba-Yunus, 1. - F. Ahmad
1985 *Islamic Sociology: An Introduction*, Cambridge.

Bayrakdar, M.
1985 'The Spiritual Medicine of Early Muslims', in: *The Islamic Quarterly*, 29, 1, 1-28.

Beattie, J.
1984 'Objectivity and Social Anthropology'. In: *Objectivity and Cultural Divergence*, (ed) S.C. Brown, Cambridge.

Berque, J.
1978 'Sociologies de OU sur l'Islam? (Rev. of Charnay, 1978)', in: *Archives de sciences sociales des religions*, 23, 46/2, 193-197.

Boon, J.A.
1982 *Other Tribes, Other Scribes. Symbolic anthropology in the comparative study of cultures, histories, religions and texts*, Cambridge.

Bouman, J.
1977 *Gott und Mensch im Koran*, Darmstadt.

Brohi, A.
1982 Human Rights and Duties in Islam, A Philosophic Approach. In: Azzam: 1982.

Carrithers, M. - S. Collins - S. Lukes (eds.)
1985 *The Category of the person. Anthropology, philosophy, history*, Cambridge.

Charnay, J.P.
1977 *Sociologie religieuse de l'Islam*, Paris.

Cragg, K.
1973 *The mind of the Qur'an*, London.

Crapanzano, V.
1975 'Saints, Jnun and Dreams: An essay in Moroccan ethno-psychiatry' in: *Psychiatry,* 38, 145-159.
1980 *Tuhami: Portrait of a Moroccan,* Chicago.
Crick, M.
1976 *Explorations in Language and Meanings: Towards a semantic anthropology,* London, Malaby Press.
1982 'Anthropology of Knowledge', in: *Ann. Rev. Anthropol.,* 11, 287-313.
Digard, J.-P.
1978 Perspectives anthropologiques sur l'Islam, in: *Revue francaise de sociologie,* 19, 497-523.
Dwyer, K.
1982 *Moroccan Dialogues: Anthropology in Question,* Baltimore.
El-Zein, A.H.
1977 'Beyond Ideology and Theology: The search for the anthropology of Islam', in: *Ann. Rev. Anthropol.,* 6, 227-254.
Fogelson, R.D.
1982 'Person, Self and Identity: Some anthropological retro-spects, circumspects and prospects'. In: *Psychosocial Theories of the Self,* (ed.) B. Lee, New York.
Fontana, A.
1984 'Introduction: Existential Sociology and the Self'. In: *The Existential Self in Society,* (eds.) J.A. Kotarba - A. Fontana, Chicago.
Geertz, C.
1984 'Anti Anti-Relativism', in: *Am. Anthrop.,* 86, 263-278.
Gilsenan, M.
1982 *Recognizing Islam: An anthropologist's introduction,* London: Croom Helm.
1976 'Lying, Honor and Contradiction'. In: *Transaction and Meaning, Directions in the Anthropology of Exchange and Symbolic Behaviour,* (ed.) B. Kapferer, Philadelphia, 191-219.
Gulick, J.
1983 *The Middle East: An anthropological perspective,* Lanham, MD.

Harrison, S.
1985 'Concepts of the person in Avatip Religious Thought', in: *Man* (N.S.), 20, 115-130.

Haule, J.
1982 'Psychology and Religion: A review of efforts to work at the interface', in: *Religion*, 12, 149-165.

Heelas, P. - A. Lock (eds.)
1981 *Indigenous Psychologies. The anthropology of the Self*, London.

Hollis, M.
1977 *Models of Man, Philosophical thoughts on social action*, Cambridge.

Holub, R.C.
1984 *Reception Theory, A critical introduction*, London.

Islahi, M.Y.
1979 *Etiquettes of Life in Islam*, Delhi.

Jacobson-Widding, A. (ed.)
1983 *Identity: Personal and Socio-Cultural*, Uppsala.

Kaplan, B. (ed.)
1961 *Studying Personality Cross-Culturally*, Evanston, Ill.

Keesing, R.M.
1974 'Theories of Culture', in: *Ann. Rev. Anthropol.*, 3, 73-97.

Kiefer, C.W.
1977 'Psychological Anthropology', in: *Ann. Rev. Anthropol.*, 6, 103-119.

LeVine, R.A.
1982 *Culture, Behaviour and Personality*, New York.

Lewis, I.M.
1986 *Religion in Context, Cults and Charisma*, Cambridge.

Lutfiyya, A.M.
1970a 'The Family'. In: *Readings in Arab Middle Eastern Societies and Cultures*, (ed.) idem, Den Haag.
1970b *Islam and Village Culture*, Ibid.

Lutz, C. - G.M. White
1986 'The Anthropology of Emotions', in: *Ann. Rev. Anthropol.*, 15, 405-436.

Marsella, A.J. - G. de Vos - F.L.K. Hsu (eds.)
1985 *Culture and Self, Asian and Western Perspectives,* New York.

Messick, B.
1986 'The Mufti, the Text and the World: Legal Interpretation in Yemen', in: *Man* (N.S.), 21, 102-119.

Miyoshi, M.
1974 *Accomplices of Silence: The modern Japanese novel,* Berkeley.

Moughrabi, F.
1978 'The Arab Basic Personality: A critical Survey of the Literature', in: *Int. J. Middle East Stud.,* 9, 99-112.

Ortner, S.B.
1984 'Theory in Anthropology Since the Sixties', in: *Comp. Stud. of Soc. and Hist.,* 25, 126-166.

Pruett, G.E.
1985 'Through a Glass Darkly: Knowledge of the Self in dreams in Ibn Khaldun's Muqaddima', in: *Muslim World,* 75, 29-44.

Racy, J.
1970 'Psychiatry in the Arab East', in: *Acta Psychiatrica Scandinavica,* Suppl. 211.

Rahman, A. (ed.)
1981 *Muhammad,* Encyclopedia of Seerah, Vol. I, London.

Rahman, F.
1980 *Major Themes of the Qur'an,* Minneapolis.

Rosaldo, M.Z.
1984 'Toward an Anthropology of Self and Feeling'. In: *Culture Theory, Essays on Mind, Self and Emotion,* (eds.) R.A. Shweder - R.A. LeVine, Cambridge.

Rosen, L.
1984 *Bargaining for Reality: The construction of social relations in a Muslim community,* Chicago.

Said, E.
1981 *Covering Islam,* London.

Shad, A.R.
1980 *Muslim Etiquettes,* Lahore.

Sharabi, H. - A. Mukhtar

1977 'Impact of Class and Culture on Social Behavior: The Feudal-Bourgeois Family in Arab Scoiety'. In: *Psychological Dimensions of Near Eastern Studies,* (eds.) L.C. Brown - N. Itzkowitz, Princeton, N.J.

Sheikh-Dilthey, H.

1979 'Normatives Verhalten und die Gesundheit des Einzelnen, Ein Beispiel aus dem islamischen Bereich', in: *Confinia Psychiatrica,* 22, 81-86.

Singer, M.

1980 'Signs of the Self: An Exploration in Semiotic Anthropology', in: *Am. Anthrop.,* 82, 488-507.

1981 'On the Semiotics of Indian Identity', in: *Am. J. of Semiotics,* 1, 1-2, 85-126.

Stirrat, R.L.

1984 'Sacred Models (Malinowski Mem. Lect. 1983)', in: *Man* (N.S.), 19, 199-215.

Taylor, C.

1976 'Responsibility for Self'. In: *The Identities of Persons,* (ed.) A.O. Rorty, Berkeley.

1985 'The Person'. In: M. Carrithers et al.: 1985, 257-281.

Tritton, A.S.

1971 'Man, Nafs, Ruh, Aql', in: *Bulletin of the School of Oriental and African Studies,* 34, 491-495.

Waardenburg, J.

1974 'Islam Studied as a Symbol and Signification System', in: *Humaniora Islamica,* 2, 267-285.

1979 'Official and Popular Religion as a Problem in Islamic Studies'. In: *Official and Popular Religion, Analysis of a Theme for Religious Studies,* (eds.) P.H. Vrijhof - J. Waardenburg, Den Haag: Mouton.

Wensick, A.J.

1965 *The Muslim Creed, Its Genesis and Historical Development,* London.

Wikan, U.

1984 'Shame and Honour; A contestable pair', in: *Man* (N.S.), 19, 635-652.

CAN YOU MARRY A DJINNI?

An Aspect of the *djinn* as Persons

Fred Leemhuis

Contemporary European concepts of the person are known to be the result of a long development that originated with the Romans and was expanded by Christian contribution to culminate in the now familiar category of the 'self'. The culture of Islam has developed as heir to at least a large part of a shared patrimony, but although Christianity and Islam had similar and related points of departure Islam went its own way.

The history of Islamic concepts of the person may be studied in many different ways, e.g., by studying the Koran and the Apostolic Tradition as well as the large theological and juridical literature. Many useful insights may be gathered from philosophical, ethical and psychological writings of scholars like al-Farabi, Ibn Rushd, al-Ghazali, Ibn Miskawaih, al-Djahiz al-Qazwini and Ibn al-Djauzi, to name just a few. Alternatively, one might try to make explicit what is implied in the large mediaeval dictionaries under entries such as *shakhs* 'person', *nafs* 'soul,'self', *insan* 'human being', *imra'* 'man, person', etc.

Of course in doing so we would mainly be studying normative ideas about and intellectual approaches to the Islamic concepts of the person, which apparently also developed towards making 'the human person a complete entity independent of every other save God' (Mauss: 1980, 77). To determine the validity of these normative expressions for everyday social life we need empirical data about its representations at a given time in a given place, because they may and do differ widely. Most of the time it is of course difficult to obtain these empirical data for a given historical setting.

The aim of this contribution is to present the reflections of a Muslim intellectual of the eighth/fourteenth century on what consitutes a person. He did so more or less indirectly by formulating his reflections in response to a specific social situation in which relations between men and *djinn* had apparently become problematic. The Koran, of course, not only acknowledges the existence of the *djinn* (e.g., in *sura 72: surat al-djinn*), but it also states that at least some *djinn* were believers and started to warn their people (e.g., *sura* 46: 29-32). This indicates that the *djinn* are not *per se* evil and consequently they need not automatically be shunned. And so personal relations with *djinn* are reported to occur and to have occurred throughout the Islamic world. One of the social problems may very well have been that the offspring of a very personal relationship, the union between a *djinni* man and a human woman was very visible whereas the reputed father was not. The response to this social problem also necessitated reflections on the theological and juridical status of the *djinn*. These reflections about what constitutes the personality of a *djinni* are, as a matter of course, expressed in categories that may also be applied to humans, their fellow earthlings. What then were or are these *djinn*?

Even outside the islamic world the *djinn*, these 'sprites or goblins of Arabian tales' or spirits 'able to appear in human and animal forms, and having supernatural power over men' are well-known, at least by those who have relished the 'Tales of a Thousand and One Nights'. Although they are usually represented as malignant and hostile to man, occasionally they are helpful and even when they turn against man, their supernatural powers do not *per se* guarantee that they always gain the upper hand over man. Who does not know the story of the fisherman, who accidentally freed an *'ifrit* (sing. of *'afarit*, a subspecies of the *djinn*) from a copper bottle whereupon the *'ifrit* threatened to kill him. The fisherman, however, outwitted the *'ifrit* by luring him back into the bottle.[1]

The *djinn* were known already in the *djahiliyya*, the pre-Islamic times of Arab paganism. What they were exactly has become known to us only indirectly, from the Koran and other documents from Islamic times. It seems that originally they were 'the nymphs and satyrs of the desert and represented the side of the life of nature still unsubdued and hostile to man... But in the time of Muhammad *djinn* were already passing over into vague, impersonal gods' (Macdonald: 1965, 547). Wellhausen stated it clearly:

> Die Dämonen unterscheiden sich generell nicht von den Göttern. Aber ihre

---

1 Third and fourth night. The story is continued in the sixth and the seventh night. (Alf Laila: n.d., I, 14-16, 23-24; Lane: 1979, 68-75, 86-89).

individualität ist nicht ausgebildet; die Gattung, das Geschlecht bedeutet bei ihnen Alles, die Person sehr wenig (Wellhausen: 1961, 148; cf. Montgomery Watt: 1977, 153).

Wellhausen was apparently quite aware of the fact that statements about how the *djinn* were conceived of, of course, also say something about how humans were looked upon. According to him it may be concluded from the terms with which they are designated that these demons were 'Heerdenwesen', gregarious beings.

Ebenso ist das arabische Hauptwort für Dämon, *Ginn*, ein Collectivum oder Gattungswort; davon erst abgeleitet ist das Einzelwort *Gann*.[2] In dieser Hinsicht gleichen die Dämonen den Menschen, wenigstens den arabischen Menschen, bei denen ebenfalls der Stamm und das Geschlecht wichtiger ist als der Einzelne. *Ginn* und *Ins* (Menschengeschlecht) ergänzen sich wie zwei Hälften, es sind die beiden in betracht kommenden Gattungen von Wesen auf der Welt, alThaqallan' (Wellhausen: 1961, 148).

Leaving alone Wellhausen's etymologically based conclusions about how the ancient Arabs saw themselves, it remains true that the way they conceived of the *djinn* tells us something about how they looked upon themselves.

Actually, Wellhausen's statement that the individuality of the *djinn* has not been developed is at least partially contradicted by some of the instances he mentions of individual relationships between man and *djinn*. A poet had his individual *djinni* who inspired him; the famous pre-Islamic poet al-A'sha Maimun knew his *djinni* by name: Mishal (Caskel: 1960). The most striking of these individual relationships between a human and a *djinni* are the cases of intermarriage (Wellhausen: 1961, 154). Apparently these marriages already took place before Islam and they still occur in contemporary Islam. At the end of the seventies I was told in Luxor in Upper Egypt about the case of a man who lived there and who was married to two wives, one of whom was a *djinniyya*. Every

2 According to both QM and LA s.v. *djinn* is a collective or plural. Ibn Manzur mentions it also as the name of the eponymous ancestor of the *djinn*. Wellhausen may have relied on Lane's dictionary.

Thursday he locked himself up in his room to be alone with his non-human wife, where he was heard conversing with her.[3] Ahmad Amin in his 'Dictionary of Egyptian Customs, Usage and Expressions' mentions the sad story of a taciturn and thoughtful Circassian who through the love of a *djinniyya*, with whom he spent every night, was prevented from marrying (Ahmad Amin: 1953, 141-142). Many stories about these unions were known[4] and it is thus not astonishing that Islamic jurists were particularly concerned with this aspect of the relationships between men and *djinn*.

One of the jurists who dealt with the whole complex of the existence of the *djinn* and their legal status including the permissibility of intermarriage between men and *djinn* was Badr al-Din as-Shibli (b. 712/1312). In 755/1354 he became *qadi* in Tarabulus in Syria where he died in 769/1367 (Brockelmann: 1943/1949, II, 75). Not many further details of his life are known and he would probably have been forgotten but for his *kitab akam al-mardjan fi ahkam al-djann*[5] in which he thoroughly and conscientiously compiled everything he could extract from an impressive number of sources, such as Koran and Hadith commentaries,

---

[3] In the meantime the man's two marriages seem to have prospered. According to Harm Botje, the Cairo correspondent of the Dutch daily *NRC Handelsblad*, he is now living in a three-stored house; his *djinni* wife, by whom he has five children, lives on the top floor, whereas his human wife, by whom he has nine visible children, lives closer to ground level (Botje: 1986). I thank my colleague, W. Jac. van Bekkum, who drew my attention to the analogue of the mediaeval Jewish story of the Jerusalemite who had a human as well as a demon wife. See e.g. Dan: 1967 and Gaster: 1931.

[4] See e.g. Ibn an-Nadim: 1348 A. H., chapter 8, section 1, 428 (Ibn an-Nadim: 1970, vol. II, 723), where 16 books are mentioned that deal with stories about these unions. Cf. also Macdonald: 1965, 547.

[5] See for an appraisal of the first printed edition and a survey of its contents Nöldeke: 1910 and Rescher: 1914. I am inclined to think that the title does not mean: 'The book of coral hills about the legal judgements of (=concerning) the djinn' as Nöldeke and Rescher proposed. In the *Lisan al-ᶜArab* Abu Hanifa is quoted, according to whom *mardjan* is also a spring plant with red twigs and thick round succulent leaves, see LA: s.v. *m r dj*.

Musannaf and Musnad works and biographies of the Prophet.[6] In short, we may conclude that the book is a compendium of what, according to as-Shibli, an orthodox Muslim should know and believe about the *djinn*. Apparently the book became fairly popular, considering the fact that today some twenty-five complete copies and some twenty abridgements are still preserved in manuscript libraries.[7] It was printed in Cairo in 1326/1908.[8]

Although, as has been said above, not much is known of as-Shibli he may, on the basis of his book and his position, be characterized as representing one of the two principal types of educated men existing in his time: 'der Religionsgelehrter bzw. der Vertreter des religiösen Rechts, der Bewahrer und (durch Auslegung) Fortbildner der religiösen Tradition, dem Staat verbunden als Richter oder Notar' (Cahen: 1971, 21).

The book is interesting in many respects, e.g., because it is a rich source of what may be called folkloristic information. To give a few examples:

Djinn or *shayatin* may especially be encountered in dirty and unclean places like baths, latrines, dunghills and garbage heaps. These are precisely the places which old men who associate with *shayatin* frequent as do also those who worship the sun, the moon, the stars or other false

---

6 See Rescher: 1914, 242-245 for a list of the quoted works.

7 See Brockelmann: 1937/1942, II, 75, Brockelmann: 1943/1949, II, 82 and Rescher: 1914, 249.

8 See bibliography: as-Shibli 1326 A.H. As was already stated by Rescher: 1914, 249, it is not a very good edition, as it seems to be based on one, rather corrupted, manuscript, but for the present purpose it is valuable enough, if only it is at least available in printed form.
After reading the proofs of the text, I came across a new edition of as-Shibli's book with a different title (see bibliography). The title means: 'Peculaiarities and curiosities of the *djinn* as representated by the Koran and the Sunna'. The editor states in his foreword that it is 'the most excellent study about the *djinn*, the legal judgements concerning them and the reports about them' and that he prepared the edition 'as a prevention baseless fables and lies and as an announcement of the truth about the *djinn*'.

gods. Of course the graveyard, the outstanding example of a macabre place, also falls within this category. Needless to say these places are forbidden for the performance of the *salat* (as-Shibli: 1326 A.H., 25).

Djinnis may, of course, appear in many forms, human as well as animal, especially as snakes and black dogs. Their change of appearance, however, is said not to be a faculty of their own; they are only able to do this because they possess a word of power which causes God to bring about the change when they pronounce it. Likewise they can travel enormous distances in an instant (as-Shibli: 1326 A.H., 17-19 and 22-23). They cause diseases, especially epilepsy, as is demonstrated by the *hadith*, which among other things is quoted by ad-Darimi in his *Musnad* on the final authority of Ibn Abbas:'A woman brought her son to the Prophet and said to him: "My son has a madness that takes possession of him during breakfast and supper". Then the Prophet stroked the breast of the boy, prayed for him and made him vomit. Something like a black puppy escaped from his body and sped away' (as-Shibli: 1326 A.H., 107).

Of themselves the *djinn* are invisible, that is to most humans, because their bodies are rarefied so that humans cannot see them, or they have solid bodies invisible to us because God did not give us the ability to see them. All the prophets, however, do have this ability (as-Shibli: 1326 A.H., 15-17).

Solomon was the first to make the *djinn* serve him and a bottle which bears his seal may be the prison of a wicked *djinni*, as Musa b. Nusayr, the *amir* of the Maghrib, found out (as-Shibli: 1326 A.H., 90).

Many more such instances can be mentioned, such as that of the devil, Iblis, who by many authorities is considered to belong to the species of the *djinn* and to be their chief, and who usually sits partly in the sun and partly in the shade (as-Shibli: 1326 A.H., 189-190), walks around with only one shoe (as-Shibli: 1326 A.H., 191) and eats with his left hand (as-Shibli: 1326 A.H., 31). The terminology may cause some confusion as Iblis is known to be a fallen angel, but this is only an apparent problem. We are informed by the best authority that the angels are a subspecies of the *djinn* and likewise the *shayatin*, in the same way as Arabs, Negroes and Persians are subspecies of the Adamites (as-Shibli: 1326 A.H., 153-156).

However, what really makes as Shibli's book more interesting than writings on the *djinn* by e.g., al-Qazwini, ad-Damiri or al-Djahiz is not all this, but the author's reason for writing it as well as his treatment of what for him and his contemporaries seems to have been such a central question: Can and may humans marry *djinn*? This is how he presents the matter:

> This is a compendium of information about the *djinn* and of judgements on their legal status and traditions about them. The reason for compiling it, writing it in this strange manner and composing it, was a colloquy that dealt with the problem of the marriage of *djinn*, its possibility and its occurrence. During the session, a conclusion could not be reached, nor could its subject matter be established or precisely formulated. Therefore I thought that this issue required the following introductions:
> I. An account of the existence of the *djinn* against most philosophers, the large majority of the Qadarites (i.e. the Mu'tazilites), all the Zindiq's (heretics or freethinkers) and the perverse words of those who deny the existence of them.
> II. An account of the fact that they have personified (*mushakhkhasa*) bodies, be they rarefied or solid, which evolve and materialize in various forms to make coition possible and feasible, since this is only conceivable between two bodies which touch each other. In this connection I will mention their disposition, their eating and drinking habits and the sexual intercourse they have with each other, because a living being must have a disposition and must partake of what causes his growth, his survival and the survival of his species.
> III. An exposé of their legal capacity (i.e. the duty to fulfil Gods commandments) to contradict to the Hashwiyya (traditionists of little worth). This, because he who permits marriage between men and *djinn* must stipulate that their women believe or that they belong to the people of the Book. Because what is stipulated with regard to the Adamite women applies even more to the female *djinn*, since he who says that it is permissible to marry them does not differentiate. In this connection I will mention the message of the Prophet with regard to them (as-Shibli: 1326 A.H., 2).

This part of as-Shibli's introduction is indeed nothing less than the first part of the book in a nutshell. It clearly shows the general drift of his reasoning: Just like human beings *djinn* are all individual persons, although they are created out of fire and not out of clay (as-Shibli: 1326 A.H., 11-14 and *passim*). Like most human beings they may be considered to be legally capable of doing right or wrong (as-Shibli: 1326 A.H., 34). Unions between men and *djinn* have been trustworthily reported and offspring of these unions are known (as-Shibli: 1326 A.H., *passim*).

Interesting in this respect is of course the question what exactly as-Shibli is referring to when he uses the terms *shakhs*, 'person, individual', and *mushakhkhas*, the passive participle of the D stem of the same root which may be translated as: 'to whom a personal/individual nature may be attributed'. The word *shakhs* may be derived from *shakhasa* 'to stare'. In the *Qamus al-muhit* the word *shakhs* is defined by as-Shibli's later contemporary al-Fayruzabadi (1329-1414) as: *sawad al-insan wa-ghayrihi tarahu min bu'd* or 'a human individual and the like which you (can) see from afar' (QM: s.v. *sh kh s*). However, *as-sawad*, that means something like 'individual' is defined as: *as-shakhs* (QM: s.v. *s w d*)! The same can be found in the *Lisan al-'arab,* the great lexical compilation of Ibn Manzur (1232-1311), but in this lexicon we can also find the remark that *sawad* or, according to al-Asma'i, *siwad* also means: 'features, facial expression' (LA: s.v. *s w d*). To the definition of *shakhs* Ibn Manzur adds: 'Everything of which you can see its body (*djusman* = *djism ar-radjul*, see LA: s.v. *dj s m*) you see its *shakhs*' and also: '*as-shakhs*: every body that has height and visibility. What is meant by that is the establishment of its essence; for this the word *shakhs* is used as a metaphor' (LA: s.v. *sh kh s*).

After having established the existence, individuality and legal capacity of the *djinn* as-Shibli comes to the heart of the matter, i.e., marriage between humans and *djinn*, in the thirtieth chapter (as-Shibli: 1326 A.H., 66-74), which is one of the longest chapters in the book and which deserves somewhat more attention. The chapter is divided into two parts, one of which deals with the possibility and occurrence of marriages between humans and *djinn*, and the other with their lawfulness.

After as-Shibli's affirmation that marriage between a man and a female *djinni* as well as between a woman and a *djinni* is indeed possible he quotes at-Tha'alibi as having said the same, on the basis of Koran 17: 64 and on the basis of the fact that the Prophet said that if a man has sexual intercourse with his wife without pronouncing God's name the *shaytan* is folded up in his urethra and copulates with him. To this as-Shibli adds the words of Ibn 'Abbas who said that when a man comes to his wife while she menstruates the *shaytan* has been with his wife before him. She will become pregnant and produce an effeminate[9] (or: bisexual) child; for the effeminate are children of the *djinn*. The Prophet's prohibition on marrying the *djinn* and the words of the jurists which do not permit it or which loathe it prove the fact that it is nevertheless possible, because something that is impossible does not have to be prohibited by law.

Malik b. Anas is reported to have said, in the concrete case of a *djinni* man who wanted to be lawfully betrothed to a human girl, that from the point of view of religious law he saw no objection, but that he thought it reprehensible (*makruh*), because if the woman were to become pregnant and people were to ask her who her husband was, she would have to say: someone of the *djinn*, and because of that, immorality would increase in Islam.

The author adduces many reports and stories to show that marriages between men and *djinn* occurred before and during his own time. The case of Bilqis, the Queen of Sheba, is mentioned. Of her it is said that her mother was a *djinniyya* with hoofs instead of feet. This was the reason why King Solomon took her with him into his glass palace; the floor looked like water and when she entered it she bared her legs, so that Solomon saw that the legs of Bilqis were slightly hairy. Before they married he had her legs depilated, which made King Solomon the first to apply a depilatory, if only to the legs of his wife.

As-Shibli had been told that a Hanafite colleague of his, called Djalal ad-Dinn Ahmad b. Husam ad-Din ar-Razi, had actually been married to a *djinniyya* for three days when he was on a journey with his father. He visited him with another colleague to have the story confirmed, which was duly done.

As far as the lawfulness of marriages between humans and *djinn* is concerned as-Shibli is less outspoken. Before he can establish this he has to remove three obstacles. The Koran might be interpreted as implicitly forbidding it, as could be and was concluded from a verse
like 30: 21: 'And of His signs is that He created for you, of yourselves (*min anfusikum*), spouses, that you might repose in them, and He has set

---

[9] For the meaning of the two terms *mukhannath* and *mu'annath* which as-Shibli uses here apparently more or less indiscriminately and which may be translated as 'effeminate' and/or 'bisexual' see LA: s.v. *kh n th* and *' n th*.

between you love and mercy. Surely in that are signs for a people who consider'. The words *min anfusikum* might be explained as intended to exclude non-humans. Moreover, a man could not be expected to 'repose in' a *djinniyya* nor were love and mercy expected to occur between men and *djinn*. At best passion and desire could exist between them and that in itself is not sufficient reason for marriage. Especially a juxtaposition of verses 4: 3, 72: 6, 33: 50 and 70: 30 may be seen as proving that the Koran prohibits humans from marrying non-humans. However, as-Shibli does not reveal his opinion concerning this subject. He merely points out that the second objection, which is based on traditions that quote the Prophet as having forbidden the marriage between man and *djinn*, is not valid because these traditions are spurious (*mursal*). The third objection, that the early authorities forbade it, is countered by the opinion of al-A'mash, who permitted it, and that of Malik b. Anas who legally allowed it, but who considered it to be *makruh*.

In short, the *djinn* are seen as something like a foreign tribe. They have all kinds of peculiarities which 'normal' people or at least believing people do not have. They are created beings, but they are created out of fire, not clay. They are individual persons with individual bodies which normally are not visible. They dwell in damp and stinking places and are the cause of fever and other illnesses. They gnaw bones and eat dung (as-Shibli: 1326 A.H., 28-31 and *passim*). They look shamelessly at the pudenda of humans when the latter go to the toilet (as-Shibli: 1326 A.H., 24). And although, as individual persons, they are morally and legally accountable for their deeds, and although cases of believing *djinn* are well documented, in general they are hostile to man or at least so different from man that to marry them does not seem to be advisable, except perhaps on a journey when one has no other companion.[10]

[10] This seems to be suggested by as-Shibli's apparent approval of his colleague Djalal ad-Din having been legally married to a *djinniyya* and by the report on a certain Zaid al-ᶜUmy (?) which he mentions at the end of chapter thirty without further comment: Zaid al-ᶜUmy was said to have prayed: 'Oh God, provide me with a *djinniyya*, so that I may marry her'. It was said to him: 'Oh Abu al-Hawari, what would you do with her?' He said: 'She would accompany me on my travels. Wherever I will be she will be too.'

Bibliography

Ahmad Amin
1953 *Qamus al-ᶜadat wat-taqalid wal-taᶜabir al-misriyya*, Cairo.

Alf Laila
n.d. *Alf laila wa-laila.* The Muhammad 'Ali Subaih edition, Cairo.

Botje, H.
1986 'Onzichtbare zaken', in: *NRC Handelsblad*, Weekend Supplement 26 July.

Brockelmann, C.
1937/1942 *Geschichte der arabischen Literatur,* Supplementbände, 3 vols., Leiden.

Brockelmann, C.
1943/1949 *Geschichte der arabischen Literatur,* 2. den Supplementbänden angepasste Auflage, 2 vols., Leiden.

Cahen, Cl.
1971 *Der Islam II, Die islamischen Reiche nach dem Fall von Konstantinopel* (= Fischer Weltgeschichte, vol. 15), Frankfurt a. M.

Caskel, W.
1960 'al-A'sha'. In: *The Encyclopaedia of Islam,* New Edition, vol. I, Leiden, 689-690.

Dan, J.
1967 'Five versions of the story of the Jerusalemite', in: *Proceedings of the American Academy of Jewish Research,* 35, 99-111.

Gaster, M.
1931 *The Story of the Jerusalemite,* Folklore, 43, 161-178.

Ibn an-Nadim
1348 A.H. *Kitab al-Fihrist,* Cairo.

Ibn an-Nadim
1970 *The Fihrist of al-Nadim. A Tenth-century Survey of Muslim Culture.* Bayard Dodge editor and translator, 2 vols, New York.

LA
1968 *Lisan al-carab lil-imam al-callama Abi al-Fadl Djamal ad-*

Din Muhammad ibn Mukarram ibn Manzur al-Ifriqi al-Misri, Beirut.

Lane, E.W.
1979 *The Thousand and One Nights, commonly called, in England, The Arabian Nights' Entertainments.* A New Translation from the Arabic, with Copious Notes (photogr. repr. of E.S. Poole's new edition of 1859), 3 vols., London.

Macdonald, D.B.
1965 'Djinn'(revised by H. Massé). In: *The Encyclopaedia of Islam,* New Edition, vol. II, Leiden, 546-548.

Mauss, Marcel
1980 *Sociology and Psychology,* Essays translated by Ben Brewster, London.

Montgomery Watt, W.
1977 *Bell's Introduction to the Qur'an,* completely revised and enlarged (Paperback edition), Edinburgh.

Nöldeke, Th.
1910 'Review article of Kitab akam al-mardjan', in: *Zeitschrift der Deutschen Morgenländischen Gesellfschaft,* 64, 439-445.

QM
n.d. *Al-qamus al-muhit li-Madjd ad-Din al-Fairuzabadi,* Cairo.

Rescher, O.
1914 'Ueber das 'Geister und Teufelsbuch' des Schibli', in: *Wiener Zeitschrift für die Kunde des Morgenlandes,* 37, 241-252.

As-Shibli
1326 A.H. *Kitab akam al-mardjan fi ahkam al-djann. Ta'lif as-shaikh al-ᶜallama al-muhaddith al-qadi Badr ad-Din Abi ᶜAbd Allah Muhammad ibn ᶜAbd Allah as-Shibli.* Edited by Ahmad Nadji al-Djamali and Muhammad Amin al-Khandji, Cairo.
1983 *Ghara'ib wa-adja'ib al-djinn kama yusawwiruha al-qur'an wa-l-sunna.* Edition and commentary by Ibrahim Muhammad al-Djamal, Cairo.

Sykes, J.B.
1976 *The Concise Oxford Dictionary of Current English,* sixth edition, Oxford.

Wellhausen, J.
1961 *Reste arabischen Heidentums* (3. Auflage), Berlin.

SOME REFLECTIONS ON THE CONCEPT OF PERSON IN ANCIENT INDIAN TEXTS

Lourens P. van den Bosch

1. *Introduction*

In the history of anthropological research, the application of the concept of person for comparative purposes has led repeatedly to discussions about its cultural implications. M. Mauss (Mauss: 1969, II, 131 f. (= 1929, 124ff.) argued against the one-sided approach to this concept taken by L. Lévi-Bruhl in his book 'L'âme primitive', which especially focuses on the mentality of 'primitive people' (Lévi-Bruhl: 1927).

> Il s'est contenté de l'observation psychologique et de description philosophique, quoique sociologique du fait (Mauss: 1969, II, 131).

In that context he points to the importance of sociological research on systems of name-giving and the ceremonial forms of address in relation to the concept of person. He gives a number of examples in illustration of this and in particular calls attention to New Caledonia, where the name appears to stand for the totality of special positions held by the individual within his group. Mauss (1969, II, 134) makes a stand against Lévi-Bruhl by saying:

> M. Lévi-Bruhl est allé jusqu'à la description du mythe. Je pense, moi, pouvoir trouver la raison du prénom identique à l'âme à travers les faits que je viens de vous indiquer. La personnalité, l'âme viennent avec le nom, de la societé.

With this description Mauss clearly formulates the idea that the attributes and capacities that constitute the 'person' and the signs by which persons may be known are created by society. This cultural conditioning finds its expression in the way in which persons and groups of persons in a society define themselves and each other. In this respect there is a great variation in the cultural coordinates parallel to this definition which is expressed in social action and belief.

Mauss elaborated his ideas in an essay entitled: 'Une catégorie de l'esprit humaine: la notion de personne, celle de moi' (Mauss: 1938, 263ff.). He takes the research methods of social history as tools for his study and writes (Mauss: 1966, 61ff.):

> What I want to show you is the series of form which this concept has taken on in the life of men in societies, according to their laws, their religions, their customs, their social structure and their mentalities.

In this context he studies the 'role' and the place of the 'social person' in various societies in connection with the system of name-giving. He concludes (Mauss: 1966, 73):'It emerges clearly from it that the whole immense set of societies has arrived at the notion of role, of the part played by the individual in sacred dramas, just as he has a part to play in family life'.

However, the idea of 'person' involves more than the notion of role. According to Mauss, this becomes clear when one studies the great ancient cultures of India and China. With respect to India he refers to the *ahaṃkāra*, the I-construction, a concept which is elaborated in the philosophical Sāṃkhya school.

In the course of his essay the author traces the special development of the concept of person in the history of western thinking. This especially concerns the idea of a person as a conscious, independent, autonomous, free and responsible being (Mauss: 1966, 84). Mauss makes it clear that within the western context the concept has acquired a series of specific connotations which make the term unfit for comparitive purposes with other cultures. Nonetheless, he has elaborated in his plan of work possibilities of studying the socio-cultural identity of persons and groups of persons in other cultures.

Following E. Durkheim and M. Mauss, two important representatives of French sociology, L. Dumont stresses the presence of society in the mind of each man (Dumont: 1980, 5). In this context he speaks about 'sociological apperception', i.e.,'the perception by the student of himself as a social being, as opposed to a self-sufficient individual' (Dumont: 1965a, 16). It considers each man no longer as a particular incarnation of abstract humanity, but as a more or less autonomous point of emergence of a particular humanity, i.e., of a society. The implications of this view with respect to the behaviour of individuals are formulated by him as follows (Dumont: 1980, 6):

> In this regard, it is enough to observe that actual men do not behave; they act with an idea in their heads, perhaps that of conforming to custom. Man acts as a function of what he thinks, and while he has up to a certain point the ability to arrange his thoughts in his own way, to construct new categories, he does so by starting from categories which are given by society.

The author accentuates the importance of the study of behaviour in the reconstruction of an ideology, because ideas and values do not exhaust social reality (Dumont: 1980, 36ff.). Both ideas and behaviour, the total situation, must be taken into account. Dumont (1980, 8) observes that 'sociological apperception', which comes about as a reaction to the individualistic view of man, constitutes an important sociological problem, viz., that of the idea of the individual. In a separate publication on the modern conception of the individual he analyzes its development in historical terms (Dumont: 1965a, 13ff.); with which he fulfils a wish of Max Weber (Weber: 1905, 95 note 3). According to Dumont, the expression 'individual' refers in the first place to the individual man, and the notion is characterized by the combination of two elements (Dumont: 1965a, 15):

1. The empirical subject of speech, thought and will, indivisible sample of mankind (viz., the particular man found in all societies and cultures, in virtue of which he is the raw material for any sociology).
2. The independent, autonomous and thus (essential) non-social moral being, as found primarily in our modern (common sense) ideology of man and society, which stresses the values of equality and liberty.

The first element describes the individual as a particular man who is an exclusively socially determined being. It reminds us of Mauss's opinion: 'La personnalité, l'âme viennent avec le nom, de la societé'. The second element has close similarities to the western concept of person (Mauss: 1966, 84ff.). In this context Dumont poses the question as to which functional equivalents are to be found in place of the second element in those societies that do not possess it. He explores this question within the Indian sociocultural system. Fundamental to this system is the idea that global society, which is subdivided into smaller elements by means of the hierarchical opposition of pure and impure, is ontologically prior to any particular man (cf. Dumont: 1965, 99)[1] This implies, among other things, that any particular man has to accommodate himself to the situation in which he is born. On account of this hierarchical system particular human beings are regarded as possessing different and unequal attributes of humanity and are not associated with any normative principle (Carter: 1982, 119). In western ideology, on the contrary, the person is conceived as a monad, ontologically prior to any collectivity and containing within himself all the attributes of humanity. Dumont (1965a, 14f.) contrasts the two systems as holism versus individualism. In elaborating his comparison he suggests 'that the individual, in so far as he is the main bearer of value in modern society, is equivalent to order or *dharma* in classical Hindu society'.

The author elaborates his ideas as to the functional equivalents of the individual in Indian caste society in a separate publication (Dumont: 1965b, 85ff.; cf. also Dumont: 1960 (= 1980 Appendix B., 267ff.)). In this context he deals with the Upanishadic *ahaṃkāra*, the Ego-concept, as described by M. Biardeau (Biardeau: 1965, 62ff.). Contrary to the absolute value which is attached to each particular being in the history of western thinking, Upanishadic thought attaches a negative quality to the idea of Ego as a particular person. Complementary to this idea of particular man living inside-the-world, the ancient Indians developed the religious institution of *saṃnyāsa*, renunciation. The *saṃnyāsin* leaves the world to discover his true identity. Dumont (1965b, 91) proposes to consider this person, in contrast with the western concept, as an individual-outside-the-world. Nonetheless, he admits that the idea of an 'out-worldly individual' is open to criticism and the vocabulary imperfect (cf. Dumont: 1965b, 92 note 9)[2].

---

[1] 'With us, modern westerners, the ontological unit is the human indivisible being. In traditional India it is always a whole, whether big or small, an entirety embodying relations, a multiplicity ordered by its inner, mostly hierarchical oppositions, into a single whole'.

[2] For a criticism see Carter: 1982, 126: 'This distinction between personhood and soul ... cannot be emphasized too much, for to miss it may lead to comparisons of quite disparate phenomena, perhaps missing the Indian concept of person altogether. It is inappropriate, then, to compare the European notion of personhood, individualism,

One of the basic problems in the discussions mentioned above is the fact that words such as 'person' and 'individual' have acquired connotations which are highly idiosyncratic to western ideology. This makes their application to other cultures quite problematic. Geertz (1977, 480ff.) has dealt with this problem from another point of view. He observes that in anthropological descriptions, broadly speaking, two kind of concepts can be distinguished, denoted by such expressions as, e.g., inside versus outside, emic versus etic, experience-near versus experience-distant. He defines an experience-near concept, roughly, as one 'which an individual ... might himself naturally and effortlessly use to define what he or his fellows see, think, imagine, and so on, and which he would readily understand when similarly applied by others.' An experience-distant concept is one 'which various types of specialists ... employ to forward their scientific, philosophical, or practical aims' (Geertz: 1977, 481-482). In his investigations he tries to show the role the two kinds of concepts play in anthropological analysis and their implications for anthropological understanding. He argues for a hermeneutic method in which these concepts are deployed in such a way 'as to produce an interpretation of the way a people live which is neither imprisoned within their mental horizons... nor deaf to the distinctive tonalities of their existence...' (Geertz: 1977, 482).

Geertz (1977, 483) was concerned with the ways in which various people define themselves as persons, what enters into the idea they have of what a self is. He tried to arrive at this notion 'by searching out and analyzing the symbolic forms, words, images, institutions, behaviour, in terms of which, in each place, people represent themselves and to one another'. This research is based on the idea that there is at least some universal conception of what a human individual is, though he is the first to admit that 'the western conception of the person as a bounded, unique, more or less integrated motivational and cognitive universe, the dynamic center of awareness, emotion, judgement, and action, organized into a distinctive whole and set contrastively both against other such wholes and against a social and natural background is... rather peculiar within the

---

either with the Indian notion of the soul or ego (Biardeau 1965), or with the Indian renouncer (Dumont 1965b), for the former is only a component of personhood, while the latter ... has left his personhood behind.'

context of the world's cultures' (Geertz: 1977, 483). He gives concrete form to his ideas by showing how the concept of person can be analyzed in Javanese, Balinese and Moroccan society. He compares his ethnographic interpretation with the interpretation of texts and notes in this context (Geertz: 1977, 491):

> In the same way, when a meaning-and-symbol ethnographer like myself attempts to find out what some pack of natives conceive a person to be, he moves back and forth between asking himself: 'What is the general form of their life?' and 'What exactly are the vehicles in which that form is embodied?', emerging at the end of a similar spiral with the notion that they see the self as a composite, a persona, or a point in the pattern.

With this heuristic approach Geertz tries to overcome the difficulties of the emic versus etic (etc.) attitude in favour of a contextual analysis, in which the various aspects of the concept of person are carefully related to each other according to the pattern of the culture in question (Geertz: 1973, 360ff.).

The method developed by Geertz for the analysis of symbolic structures by means of which individual human beings in particular cultural traditions are perceived and characterized, may be useful for the analysis of the concept of person in ancient Indian tradition. This especially concerns his observation that persons are not perceived as 'mere unadorned members of the human race, but as representatives of certain distinct categories of persons, specific sorts of individuals' (Geertz: 1977, 363).[3] These distinctions are expressed in the attribution of names, sobriquets, titles, and other terms of classification to persons. Thus they play their role in the theatre of life. In this respect Geertz resumes the ideas of Mauss, but places them in a different frame of reference.

---

[3] See also Geertz: 1977, 486: 'To identify someone, yourself or anyone else, in Bali is thus to locate him within the familiar caste of characters - 'king', 'grandmother', 'third-born', 'Brahman' - of which the social drama ... inevitably is composed'... 'The immediate point is that, in both their structure and their modes of operation, the terminological systems conduce to a view of the human person as an appropriate representative of a generic type, not a unique creature with a private fate.'

2. *Names in ancient Indian tradition*

2.1 Introduction

As mentioned above, a good starting point for studying the way in which persons define themselves according to ancient Indian texts may be an investigation of the names and titles which they attribute to themselves and to each other in various situations (cf. also Mauss: 1938). In this context I shall confine myself to the study of Vedic texts, which are regarded by orthodox Hindus as the authoritative religious texts 'par excellence'. They reflect the ideas and customs of the three higher estates (*varṇas*) of ancient Indian society. The male members of these *varṇas* - the brahmins, the *kṣatriyas* and the *vaiśyas* - are characterized as *āryas*, i.e., 'of noble origin'. On account of this they had the right to be initiated in Vedic lore; after their initiation they were qualified as twice-born persons (*dvija*). In this respect they were distinguished from members of the fourth estate, viz., the *śūdras*, whose duty it was to support the three higher *varṇas*. They had no access to the Vedic tradition of their superiors. In their ideology the brahmins assigned a place to the *śūdras* which befitted their position in ancient Indian society, but we do not know much about the ideas and customs of this lowest estate. Therefore one should be aware of the fact that the names and the titles (Geertz: 1973, 368) used in Vedic texts to denote a person in a broader context clearly reflect the cultural traditions of the three higher estates, especially that of the brahmins.

When I restrict myself for the moment to the system of name-giving and refrain from titles and other qualifications, three types of names can be distinguished; viz., 1) personal names, to be subdivided into a public and a secret name; 2) a name derived from one's father's or grandfather's name, the so-called patronymic; and 3) the *gotra* name, the clan name, derived from a male ancestor. The following two examples may serve as an elucidation.

In ṚV. 5.33.8 mention is made of a person called Trasadasyu Paurukutsa, who is further called Gairikitsa.The first name is the public personal name, the second a derivative from Purukutsa (the father's or grandfather's name) and the third one is derived from the *gotra* name Girikitsa. In other words: Trasadasyu is the son (or the grandson) of Purukursa and belongs to the *gotra* of Girikitsa. Similarly, in ChU. 5.3.1

and 7 mention is made of a certain teacher called Śvetaketu Āruṇeya, who is further addressed as Gautama, i.e., Śvetaketu, the son of Āruṇi or the grandson of Aruṇa, belonging to the *gotra* of Gautama. The specimen mentioned above can be multiplied by many others (Kane: 1938, 225ff.). Moreover, both texts illustrate the custom of employing the *gotra* name instead of the personal public name when denoting a person.

Though the pattern of three names is often found and sometimes prescribed (cf. ŚB. 6.1.3.9 ; and DrāhŚS. 1.3.9)[4], a person is usually designated by two names, viz., the public personal name followed by the *patronymic* or the *gotra* name, though names derived from countries or a locality are not uncommon. In BĀU 3.1.1, for instance, one reads about a certain king called Janaka Vaideha, i.e., Janaka from the country of Videha. Sometimes, however, it is difficult to decide whether the second name is a *patronymic* or a *gotra* name because the latter also has the form of a *patronymic*, expressing the relation between a descendent and one of his ancestors (Gubler: 1903, 36f.; Heimann: 1931, 145).

2.2 Personal names: the secret and the public name

The giving of personal names to a child is an important event and forms a part of the complex birth-ceremonies, the so-called *jātakarman* rites (see e.g., Kane: 1974, vol. II, 1, 227-228; Gonda: 1970, 32ff. and 1980, 371ff.). Ten or eleven days after the delivery of the child these ceremonies are generally concluded with the *nāmakaraṇa*, the rite in which a public personal name is given to a child. The *gṛhyasūtras*, a collection of manuals of various brahminical schools, give a description of these ceremonies (see Gonda: 1977, 556; 1980, 364). They are specified as *saṃskāras*, i.e., 'consecratory ceremonies', and are usually regarded as the Indian variants of the rites of passage. Though the authors of these manuals vary with respect to many details, all make a clear distinction between the secret and the public personal name.

The secret name (*guhyam* or *rahasyam nāma*) is usually given to a child on the day of his birth (cf. Hillebrand: 1897, 46). According to some authors this should be done by the father immediately after the delivery and before the umbilicalcord is cut (GobhGS. 2.7.13-17; KhGS. 2.2.28-32.

---

4 It remains, however, unclear which names should be applied.

Cf. ĀpGS. 1.5.2ff.; ĀśvGS. 1.5.4-10). The idea behind this custom was that the child got its own secret identity as soon as it was born. As such, it could not be possessed by all kinds of evil spirits, because the situation of being nameless was considered to be opposed to the right or good condition.[5] Other authorities, however, regarded this question from a different point of view. They were of the opinion that the bestowing of the secret name upon the (male) child should be delayed until mother and child had emerged from the period of impurity, usually after ten or eleven days, when the mother could leave childbed (so e.g., HirGS. 2.1.3 and 4; ŚāṅkhGS. 1.24.6). To protect the nameless child and its mother against the attacks of malevolent demons in this intermediate period, they prescribed special rites (HirGS. 2.1.3.4ff.; PārGS. 1.17.23ff.; BaudhGS. 2.2 (cf. Caland: 1904, 31) and VaikhSmS 3.15.1ff. See also Gonda: 1970, 33ff.). Though both groups of authorities acknowledged that the bestowing of the secret name supplied the child with an identity which impeded possession by demons, the latter group was of the opinion that the secret name should not be connected with the sphere of impurity. In other words, it suggested that the secret name belonged to the realm of purity and the divine.

The idea that the secret name should be used as the real name, indicating the true nature and essence of a person, becomes clear when one considers the situations in which it should be used. Though known to the parents from the time of birth, it was only communicated again to the boy when he was initiated into Vedic lore. The author of the ĀśvGS., for instance, prescribes:

> And let him (the father) also find out a name (for the boy) to be used for 'respectful salutations', which his father and mother alone should know till his initiation into the Veda (*upanayana*) (ĀśvGS. 1.15.8).

The name to be used for 'respectful salutations' is connected in this context with the initiation of the boy, which marks a new stage in his life, viz., that of a student of sacred lore. He is brought by his parents

---

[5] Cf. ŚB. 6.1.3.9: 'Nay, but I am not guarded against evil (*pāpman*); I have no name given to me: give me a name! Hence one should give a name to the boy that is born; for thereby one frees him from evil.' Cf. Gonda: 1970, 36.

to a teacher who initiates him into the Vedas. During this ceremony his secret name is disclosed to him and he should use it when bowing respectfully to his teacher in order to greet him. For this reason the secret name is also called the *abhivādanīya* name, i.e., the name to be used for 'respectful salutations' (cf. Kane: 1938, 299ff.). The ceremonial bowing and proclamation of the name in front of the teacher takes place whenever the student receives instruction in the Vedas. Also in this situation it is clear that the secret name is connected with the realm of the sacred. The secret identity with which the father endows his son after his first (physical) birth is revealed to him during his initiation ceremony, implying a second (spiritual) birth.

The close connection between the secret name and the sacred tradition is also elucidated in the BĀU. During the birth-ceremonies the father should give his son a name with the words: 'You are the Veda', and the texts adds: 'So this becomes his secret name' (BĀU 6.4.26; cf. also ĀśGS. 1.15.3; ŚāṅkhGS. 1.24.4). The secret name is thus equated with the Veda, 'the eternal truth', communicated in the beginning by divine seers and transmitted in the Veda by brahmins. The father places his new-born son in the realm of divine reality by giving him a secret name containing his sacred identity. With his instruction in the Vedas he becomes aware of this identity.

The idea that the pupil at his *upanayana* should be dissociated from his former stage of life and initiated into transcendent reality as revealed in the Vedas is also expressed in the title bestowed on him after his initiation. He is called a *dvija*, i.e., 'twice-born person'. On this account he has access to the sacred reality, but only by presenting himself under his 'true identity', which is represented by his secret name. As such, the use of the secret name seems to be restricted to ritual purposes (cf. also Gonda: 1970, 82). Even nowadays a brahmin keeps his *abhivādanīya* name secret. He only mentions it in praying and in similar religious acts (Masani: 1932, 146).

The close relation between secret name and sacred reality finds expression in the sacrificial cult. The KB. contains an interesting passage on the *dīkṣita*, 'the sacrificer who is consecrating himself so as to be in the right condition for his access to divine reality'. The text informs us that the sacrificer's name should not be pronounced by others and the names of others not pronounced by the sacrificer. According to Gonda (1970, 35ff., who deals with this passage of KB. 7.3), the motivation of this temporary taboo must lie in the fact that the sacrificer during his consecration acquires superhuman powers and belongs to another and distinct sphere: 'he should be silent lest his sacral power should be lost'. By his consecration 'he becomes one of the deities and the gods do not converse with everyone'. During his consecration the sacrificer is transformed into a deity and has access to divine reality; this implies a break with profane reality. Moreover, it is said that the *dīkṣita* 'is considered an embryo ... and embryos have no name'. The comparison of the *dīksita* with an embryo refers to the process of transformation. During the consecration he is 'betwixt and between' the profane and the sacred state and not clearly defined. From this point of view he has no personal identity, but is like an embryo. For this reason he cannot bear a name, but the situation changes when the *dīkṣita* is 'born' in the realm of the divine and is no longer regarded as an embryo. Then he should have a name expressing his new identity. His name should then be inserted in the proclamations of blessing (*sūktavāka*). (For the Sūktavāka formulas see Hillebrandt: 1879, 142ff. and 145 with note 1 and 2). The author of the KB. formulates this idea as follows (KB. 3.8.; cf. Gonda: 1970, 37):

> In that he (viz., the priest) mentions the name of the sacrificer in the Suktavaka formulas, it is because it is the 'divine Self' (*daiva ātmā*) of the sacrificer, which the officiants 'make ready' (*saṃskurvanti*: consecrate or fortify in order to be qualified for the new situation); therefore he mentions his name ...; for there he is born (*jāyate*).

This means, according to Gonda (1970, 37), that when the 'divine Self' is born, it ought to receive a name, which therefore forms an essential part of the consecratory formulas. In the case of the Sūktavāka formulas this implies that one should proclaim the public and the secret name (cf. Gonda: 1970, 26)[6]. From this point of view the sacrificer is during his consecration 'complemented' with a 'divine Self' which makes

---

6 Gonda observes that ĀśvGS. 1.9.5. reads twice N.N., the commentator observing that the priest has to pronounce both the ordinary name and the *nakṣatra* name (i.e. the secret name given to the sacrificer for the duration of the ceremonies, and derived from his lunar mansion, i.e., tutelary deity).

him fit for access to the realm of the sacred. When the Self is born in the divine reality of the sacrificial liturgy, it is represented by the secret name.

Thus far I have indicated in broad outline the context in which the secret name is applied, but I have not dealt with the question of what kind of secret names are used. Vedic texts generally give very scant information in this respect, but most *saṃskāras* are clear with regard to one point. The secret name should be derived from the asterism (*nakṣatra*) under which a person is born, or from the deity who presides over the *nakṣatra*.[7] The word *nakṣatra* indicates a constellation of the stars - an asterism - through which the moon passes; therefore, it is also rendered by the expression 'lunar mansion'.[8] Usually twenty-seven or twenty-eight lunar mansions are distinguished, some of which are auspicious while others are inauspicious. Injunctions concerning the secret name as a *nakṣatra* name are sometimes found in the context of the initiation rites; so e.g., in the KhGS:

> The student, who has been asked by the teacher: 'what is your name', should declare a name derived from (the name of) a deity or a *nakṣatra*, which he should use while bowing to his teacher with the words: 'I am so and so' (KhGS. 2.4.12).

---

7 Therefore the secret name is also called the *nakṣatra* name; cf. ĀpGS. 6.15.1-3; According to GobhGS. 2.10.22-25; HirGS. 1.5.4-6 and KhGS. 2.14.12 the *nakṣatra* name is given to the student at his *upanayana*, but also in the context of the birth ceremonies references to the 'lunar mansions' (*nakṣatras*) are found (see note below); so e.g., ŚāṅkhGS. 1.25.5 ff.; GobhGŚS. 2.8.12 ff. See further MānGS. 1.18.2. (Dresden: 1941, 82).

8 See Van den Bosch: 1978, 31 note 9. The word *nakṣatra* denotes, *inter alia*, an asterism or constellation of the stars, through which the moon passes; hence it is also translated by 'lunar mansion'. See further Weber: 1862 and Kane: 1973 (vol. V, 1), 495f.

Sometimes other prescriptions are added.[9]

The importance attached to asterism and lunar day (*tithi*) is also expressed in another way. Some *gṛhyasūtras* prescribe that the father should perform oblations to the *tithi* of the child's birth and also to the three *nakṣatras* with their presiding deities (ŚāṅkhGS. 1.25.5). The idea behind this custom seems to be that the well-being of the child is thought to depend upon the deities and the divine powers connected with its date and time of birth. One should offer them a sacrifice in order to appease them and avert their malevolent powers. To say this does not imply that a child is totally determined by these powers of *nakṣatra* and *tithi*, because its father can manipulate them with the help of priests by means of rites for the sake of its welfare.

The injunctions concerning *nakṣatra* names seem to be a reflection of the religious conception that time, as structured by asterisms and lunar days, is decisive for the life of the individual; cf. VaikhSmS. 3.30 (Caland: 1929, 92f.). The asterism under which a person is born essentially determines the course of his life and his main characteristics. From this point of view the *gṛhyasūtras* give expression to the conviction that a magico-cosmic relationship exists between the *nakṣatra* under which a person is born and his real nature as indicated by his secret name.[10] The idea that time is a powerful force that acts upon the 'essential' characteristics of a person comes within the scope of this conception.

In their zeal to detect the magico-cosmic relations the brahminical astrologers developed a system of classification for the specific *nakṣatras* and each individual with the aim of influencing and manipulating these relations. One should receive a secret name that corresponds to the lunar mansion in which one was born, thus making one subordinate to the system. Even the gods acquired their fixed place in this system of classification by means of secret names and it was even suggested that

[9] GobhGS. 2.10.21 ff, which mentions as alternative a name derived from the *gotra* name. According to MānGS. 1.18.2 ff.: 'the name should not be identical with the name of a god or with the father's name'. Cf. also Gopal: 1959, 288 note 64.

[10] Cf. Gonda: 1970, 55 and 82 for the secret name given by the father at the name-giving ceremony, or by the teacher (*ācārya*) at the initiation. See further Kane: 1974, vol. II, 1, 246f.

they were determined by their *nakṣatras* and were dependent upon them for their divine powers. According to one text Indra's secret name would have been Arjuna (ŚB. 2.1.2.11. Cf. also Gonda: 1970, 83); this name would have been derived from the Arjunīs, an asterism usually known as the Phalgunīs. In other words: the secret name of Indra, expressing his 'true' identity, is connected with the asterism of the Arjunīs. The secret name not only discloses the 'true' essence of Indra, but also represents it. Therefore, one should not pronounce his secret name, so as to avoid the dangerous manifestation of his power. According to the author of this passage, however, one can also gain profit by an adequate knowledge of 'true essence' of a god. By performing e.g., the *agnyādheya*, the ritual of the spreading of the three sacred fires, under the asterism of the Arjunīs, the sacrificer 'becomes' Indra and derives the benefits of his powers. The brahmins are in this context regarded as mediators essential for the success of the sacrificer, because they can manipulate the divine powers by their knowledge of these magico-cosmic relations. From this point of view the text reveals a devaluation of the gods. The brahmins subordinate them to their astrological classification schemes and deprive them of their powers.[11] The text under consideration in this way reveals how the priests adapted themselves to astrological notions which in the course of time became fairly popular among broad strata of the population.

Though the *nakṣatra* names were regarded as secret names according to most of the Vedic texts, they gradually came to be used as common names and no longer had to be kept secret.[12] Pāṇini, the grammarian of the 4th century B.C., gives elaborate rules for the derivation of *nakṣatra* names (Pāṇini, 4.3.33ff.). Familiarity with a person's date of birth made a reconstruction of his secret name a rather simple affair. For this reason other secret names came into 'en vogue'. Nonetheless, the belief continued that the asterism influenced the course of an individual's life

---

[11] Cf. e.g. ŚB. 2.1.2.6: 'Verily, there are two types of gods; for, indeed, the gods are gods; and the Brahmans who have studied and teach sacred lore are the human gods' (trans. Eggeling: 1882, 309); see also ŚB. 2.4.3.14.

[12] Cf. Kane: 1938, 234f. See further Hilka: 1910, 33f. and Van Velze: 1938, 37f., who mentions whole lists of *nakṣatra* names as personal names.

and was somehow linked with his 'true' essence. Some medieval works on astrology developed new and intricate esoteric codes for the derivation of *nakṣatra* names (cf. Kane: 1938, 238, referring to the medieval Jyotiṣa works and the *Dharmasindhu* (1790 A.D.), which could not be 'cracked' easily by outsiders. Kane notes that even nowadays the *nakṣatra* name is whispered in the ear of the pupil by his *guru* at the initiation ceremony.[13]

In contrast with the secret name the authors give elaborate rules for the public personal name (*vyāvahārika*). This name is bestowed by the father upon the child during the rite of name-giving (*nāmakaraṇa*). This usually happens ten or eleven days after *jātakarman*, when the period of impurity of mother and child comes to an end and both take a bath (cf. Gonda: 1980, 374). According to some ritual authorities it is possible to delay the name-giving rite for a further ten or hundred days, or even a year (so e.g., GobhGS. 2.8.8; KhGS. 2.3.6). Sometimes the advice is given to wait until an auspicious moment (so e.g., JaiGS. 1.9)[14]. As a result of this postponement the child was denied a socially distinct personality and remained impure (see Gonda: 1970, 34). The *nāmakaraṇa* with all its expenses - the invitation of brahmins, etc. - seems to have been regarded as premature if there was a strong chance that the child would die.[15]

The *gṛhyasūtras* make a clear distinction between the public names attributed to boys and girls. Boys should have names with two or four, or at any rate an even number of syllables; girls with three, or at any

---

[13] Kane: 1974 (vol. II, 1) 246 ff. See also Gonda: 1970, 55 (note 19) quoting Russell: 'The higher castes of the Joshi (Central India) have two names, one given by the Joshi (astrologer), which is called the *rāshi-ka-nām* or the ceremonial name, *rāshi* meaning the Nakshatra of the moon's daily mansion under which the child was born. This is kept secret and only used in marriage and other ceremonies, though the practice is now tending to decay. The other is the *chaltu* or current name...' (Russell, Tribes and Castes, III, p. 278).

[14] The giving of a name should take place in the first half of the month under an auspicious *nakṣatra*.

[15] A nameless child was regarded as an embryo. When it died it received a very simple burial. For the funeral ceremonies of children see also Raabe: 1911, 46 f.

rate an odd number of syllables (see e.g., Hillebrandt: 1897, 46f.). The sexual identity should be clearly expressed in the public personal name. This opinion is further stressed by a series of additional rules for the formation of names, which are subject to variation according to the brahminical school. The ĀśvGS., for instance, gives the following rule[16]:

> And let them (i.e., the parents) give him a name beginning with a semivowel in it, with the *visargaḥ* at its end, consisting of two syllables, or of four syllables. Of two syllables, if he is desirous of a firm position; of four syllables, if he is desirous of lustre, but in every case with an even number (of syllables) for men, with an odd (number) for women (ĀśvGS. 1.15.4, transl. Oldenberg: 1886, 183).

Besides the opinion that a person's gender should be made clear by the name in one *gṛhyasūtra* the rule is found that it should also express his or her *varṇa* membership.[17] This idea is further elaborated by later writers on *dharma*. Manu prescribes that the first part of the name of a brahmin should be indicative of auspiciousness, that of a *kṣatriya* of strength, that of a *vaiśya* of wealth, and finally that of a *śūdra* of lowness or contempt. Moreover, the second part should contain expressions suggestive of respectively happiness, protection, prosperity, and of dependence or service (Manu 2.31-32; cf. Bühler: 1886, 35. See also Vi. 27.6-9). With these injunctions, which seem to have had a rather theoretical character if one observes the names collected from ancient Indian texts (cf. e.g., Van Velze: 1938, 37ff.), he embroiders on ideas about the symbolization of differences between the *varṇas*, as already expressed in the *gṛhyasūtras*. These differences are especially stressed

---

[16] Manu 2.33 gives the following prescription for the names of girls: 'The names of women should be easy to pronounce, possess a plain meaning, be pleasing and auspicious, end in a long vowel, and contain a word of benediction' (transl. Bühler: 1886). See further Kane: 1974 (vol. II, 1) 250 and Gonda: 1970, 50.

[17] ParGS. 1.17.10.: '(The name) of a brahmin (should end) in *śarman*, that of a *kṣatriya* in *varman*, that of a *vaiśya* in *gupta*.' See also BaudhGSS. 1.11.14-18, quoted by Kane: 1938, 234f.

during the initiation ceremony, as becomes clear from its detailed prescriptions. The staff of a brahmin student, for instance, should be made of *pālaśa* or *bilva* wood, that of a *kṣatriya* student of *nyagrodha* wood, that of a *vaiśya* student of *bilva* wood.[18] These forms of cultural symbolization seem to express the clearly felt need to distinguish between the *varṇas*, which are believed to have their origin in the cosmic order (so e.g., ṚV. 10.90.12; Manu 1.31 and 87ff.). This concern for clear distinctions is also reflected in the injunctions with respect to the public personal name. From this point of view one can observe that the brahminical authors elaborated a complex and detailed system of symbols to mark the sociocultural identity of members of each of the four *varṇas*.

To recapitulate: the sexual identity of a person should be expressed in the public personal name (*vyāvahārika*) and according to some important brahminical authors also his *varṇa* identity.

2.3 The *patronymic*, the *matronymic* and the *gotra* name

In most Vedic texts a close connection between a person and his male ascendants is suggested by the application of a patronymic to denote him. The patronymic may refer to the father, but also to the grandfather or the great-grandfather, or even to the male ancestor who is supposed to be the founder of the *gotra*, i.e., 'the (exogamous) clan'. Gubler (1903, 8ff.) has made a study of the *patronymics* and their forms in ancient Indian texts. He summarizes their relation to the public personal name, in his terminology the so-called proper name. Proper names are only used when mention is made of a) persons who have a legendary, half-divine or extraordinary character; or b) of mean persons. In the vocative the proper name is usually employed when a person is addressed by his spiritual teacher, his father, his spouse, a superior person or a divine being. Furthermore, this form is employed to address a person in an impolite manner, whereas he deserves the official form of address, namely the proper name together with his patronymic, or only his patronymic. Gubler observed a preference for *patronymics* without the proper name. In the vocative the patronymic is usually employed when a person is

---

[18] See e.g., Gonda: 1980, 378f., with reference to the texts; Gonda: 1964, 262ff. Cf. also Van den Bosch: 1978 index for various kinds of wood, *sub voce*.

addressed in a lofty way, but also high-born persons are often designated by their patronymic. Mostly the patronymic form functions as a *gotra* name; in this respect the person in question is connected with the ancestor who is supposed to be the founder of the clan. The individual person is conceived here within the broader context of the clan, in the honour of which he shares.

The tendency to avoid the use of a proper name, together with the custom of using two names for polite forms of address, is also reflected in the custom of denoting a person by two *patronymics*, viz., by the *gotra* name, which is used as a kind of proper name, and by the patronymic in the strict sense (Gubler: 1903, 10f.; 25). In this manner the person thus addressed is defined in relation to his clan and his father (or grandfather). Pāṇini gives precise rules in his grammar about the derivation of *patronymics* and their meaning. The following paradigma may elucidate the gradations (Pāṇini 3.1.93-94; for the trans. see Renou: 1966, vol. I, 304):

1) Gargaḥ
2) Gārgiḥ
3) Gārgyaḥ
4) Gārgyāyanaḥ

The proper name Garga is used to denote a person. Gārgiḥ, 'son of Garga', is the patronymic form *strictu sensu*. Gārgyaḥ, 'a descendant of Garga from the third generation onwards', is a *gotra* name which indicates a specific category of grandsons, great-grandsons, etc. of Garga.[19] The term Gārgyāyanaḥ is also used as a kind of *gotra* name. It denotes 'son of Gārgyaḥ' in a broad sense. However, a careful distinction is made between the application of the names Gārgyaḥ and Gārgyāyanaḥ. The last form is called in Sanskrit the *yuvan* form, i.e., 'the younger one'. It is used to denote a person if one of his ascendants in the male line is still alive. The *gotra* name Gārgyaḥ is in that case specified as the *vṛddha* form, i.e., 'the elder one'. This implies that in an (extended) family only that person is designated by the *vṛddha* name who (on account of his age) is invested with the final authority in the family. After the death of his father the eldest son receives the *vṛddha* name on

[19] Pāṇini 4.1.162. 'Le descent à partir du petit-fils porte le nom technique de *gotra* (ou patronymique)'. Transl. L. Renou: 1966, I, 316. Cf. also Pāṇini 4.1.166f.

account of his right of primogeniture while the younger son(s) are denoted by the *yuvan* name (Pāṇini 4.1.163ff.).

Pāṇini notes that in daily life the *yuvan* name is often applied if one wishes to honour someone who actually has the right to the *vṛddha* name. In this way his modesty is praised. Contrarily, the *vṛddha* name is sometimes used to denote a person who is only entitled to the *yuvan* name. By applying in the presence of others the *vṛddha* name, the speaker uses a form of speech which enables him to criticise the person concerned for his arrogant behaviour. The person criticis is at the same time reminded of the fact that a superior member of his family is still alive (Pāṇini 4.1.66ff.). With this rule Pāṇini refers to the etiquette of his days, which governs the relations between persons belonging to the same *gotra*. Gubler, however, concludes that the personal data of individuals mentioned in ancient Sanskrit literature are so scanty that it is often difficult to make adequate distinctions between the *gotra* and the *yuvan* name (Gubler: 1903, 37). Nonetheless, it becomes clear that the authority relations between persons can be expressed by the application of specific names which indicate their position in the hierarchy of the family and clan.

In this context a few words may be devoted to the addition of the *matronymic* to a person's proper name. According to Kane (1938, 227 and 239ff.), it was used to show that the person thus described was endowed as well with a high and pure descent on the side of the mother. Sometimes this purity of the mother's lineage was stressed when the lineage of the father was not totally blameless. Moreover, a son received the *gotra* name of his mother when the father was not known (see e.g., ChU. 4.4.1-2).

2.4 The application of names in the cult of the ancestors

The importance of male ascendants in the definition of personhood is also affirmed in the cult of the ancestors, called *śrāddha* (see e.g., Caland: 1893, 1ff.; Kane: 1973 (vol. IV), 334ff.; Gonda: 1960, 130ff. and 1980, 441ff.). Essential to this cult are the oblations offered monthly in the afternoon on the day of the new moon by the head of the household (*gṛhastha*) for his three immediate ancestors, viz., his father, his grandfather and his great-grandfather. An important feature of these monthly *śrāddhas* is the invitation of an odd number of brahmins,[20] who

---

20 For specific qualifications of the brahmins see Gonda: 1980, 444.

are supposed to represent these three ancestors (*pitṛs*). The reception of the *pitṛs* as honoured guests is enacted upon the brahmins, who are addressed by their names. In other words: the ancestors are represented as respected persons. As 'consociates' (Geertz: 1973, 364f.), they are especially invoked to use their influence for the multiplication of male progeny in order that the continuity of the family line will be guaranteed.[21] They are regarded as persons and are respectfully addressed by their public personal name (*vyāvahārika*) and by their *gotra* name (cf. Caland: 1896, 77. For the later texts see e.g., Vi. 76.23; GarP. 10.60; 11.28). The central part of the *śrāddha* ceremony consists of offerings of *piṇḍas*, lumps of flour, to each of the three ancestors. The three *piṇḍas* are placed upon a layer of *kuśa* grass[22], while benedictions are pronounced together with the names of each of the *pitṛs*. When the essence of the oblations has been enjoyed, their remains are added to the food which is to be eaten by the brahmins (see also Gonda: 1980, 445f.). At the end of the rite the living take leave of the dead and send them away to their own realm.

As is clear from the preceding, the living and the dead form a strong community with reciprocal obligations. The living should offer *piṇḍas* for the welfare of the dead. This offering to the three male ancestors can also be regarded as a paradigm by means of which the relations in the male line are defined with respect to each other.[23] The common sharing of one or more ancestors is made clear by the proclamation of their names in the *śrāddhas* rite. Related householders are called *sapiṇḍa* if they offer lumps of flour to a common male ancestor up to the third generation (see also Kapadia: 1947, 123). In this respect, persons qualified

---

[21] Cf. also Gonda: 1960, 138: 'Schon aus dem im vorherigen Gesagten geht klar hervor, dass nach vedischer Vorstellung nicht etwa eine 'Seele', sondern die ganzen Person des hingeschiedenen - obwohl nicht von Natur unsterblich - ins Jenseits hinüberging'.

[22] For *kuśa* see Van den Bosch: 1978, 12 note 3. See further: Gonda: 1986, 29ff.

[23] Cf. Basham: 1967, 156-157. He considers the *śrāddha* a most potent force in consolidating the family.

as *sapiṇḍa* are regarded as relations belonging to the same family-group.[24] This definition of *sapiṇḍa* relationship broadly coincides with that of the joint-family, consisting of three generations. Brothers share three male ancestors, assuming that they would both perform *śrāddha* offerings; cousins two, having different fathers; and second-sons one, having two different ancestors.[25] In various later texts the definition of *sapiṇḍa* relationship is extended up to the fifth or even the seventh generation. This extended definition is especially used in the case of exogamy.[26] Moreover, it is analogically applied to matrilineal relations for which the exogamy rules are relevant (see Kane: 1974, vol. II, 452ff.).

It would go beyond the scope of this paper to deal with the various implications of *sapiṇḍa* relationship, but they are of special importance in three fields, viz., a) impurity (*aśauca*) in the case of birth and death, b) marriage and c) inheritance. The special rules which are formulated with regard to these three areas contribute to an individual's awareness with respect to his family identity and to his place in the family hierarchy.

In this context a few words may be devoted to the relation between father and son. Most *gṛhyasūtras* mention in the context of the birth ceremonies two interesting stanzas which may elucidate the relationship between father, son and Veda. The father should say to his son (MānGS. 1.17.5 and 1.18.6)[27]

---

24 Basham: 1967, 156: 'The family, rather than the individual, was looked on as the unit in the social system; thus the population in a given region was generally estimated in families rather than in heads'.

25 For a detailed definition of *sapiṇḍa* relationschip see Kane: 1974 (vol. II), 452ff.

26 In ancient Vedic texts, however, mention is made of the prohibition against marrying within the third or fourth generation; so e.g., ŚB. 1.8.3.6 (see note 1 Eggeling: 1882 (vol. I), p. 238); AiB. 7.13.12-13 (see Rau: 1957, 40). Cf. also Kapadia: 1947, ch. on marriage.

27 See also Dresden: 1941, 84 note 13 with references to many other texts. Cf. J.J. Meyer: 1953, 151 and 203.

Be a stone, be an axe, be insuperable gold; you are indeed the Veda called 'son': so live a hundred autumns.

From every limb you are produced, out of the heart you are born; you are indeed the self (*ātman*) called son; so live a hundred autumns.

The first stanza points to the identity between the Veda and the true 'essence' of the son. For this reason the secret name indicating his true and sacred identity can be denoted by referring to the Veda; see 2.2 and note 27. With the birth of a healthy son the continuance of Vedic lore within the domestic circle is guaranteed for another generation. The second stanza suggests that the *ātman* of the father has found a firm foundation in the son. In these two stanzas the *ātman* and the Veda correspond with each other, so that it is clear that the *ātman* is connected with the sacred dimension of existence which is continued in the son. In other words: the idea behind these stanzas is that the sacred essence - the true self - of the father is essentially reborn in the son. This idea of identity between father and son is also formulated by the authors on *dharma* (Manu 9.8) and has ancient roots, as may be clear from the ŚB. (See also Kapadia: 1947, 87ff.):'The father is the same as the son, and the son is the same as the father' (ŚB. 12.4.3.1.)

In the ancient story of Śunaḥśepa the divine teacher Nārada instructs King Hariścandra about the necessity of male progeny (see AiB. 7.13). The king has no sons, though he possesses a hundred wives. The sage explains that a man without a son has no firm foundation in this world because the father lives on in the son, or to use the words of the text, 'the self (*ātman*) is born out of the self (*ātman*)'. Moreover, by the procreation of a son a man pays a debt to his ancestors and guarantees their continuity in heaven. Finally he secures the performance of his own funeral rites, necessary to gain entry into the realm of the ancestors. In some stanzas Nārada refers to the regeneration of the father in the son. By means of his seed he enters into his wife and is born out of her as his son. He places his seed (the embryo) in the womb, she develops (feeds) it and sends it forth into the world as a child.[28]

The importance of a son for the continuity of the cult of the ancestors is stressed in many books on *dharma* (see Kane: 1974, vol. II, 560f. with references to the texts).

> Because he (the son, *putra*) delivers (*trāyate*) his father from the hell called Put, he is therefore called *put-tra* (i.e. a deliverer from Put) by the Self-existent (*Svayambhū*) himself (Manu 9.138; transl. Bühler: 1886).

A son thus secures the continuity and well-being of the patriline in this world as well as in the other one.

Ideas concerning male generation return in a rite connected with the consummation of marriage, which is performed after the couple has passed three nights in sexual continence.[29] Sometimes this rite is described as the placing of the embryo (*garbhādhāna*) (see Gonda: 1980, 367ff.; Kane: 1974, vol. II, 205). During the first sexual intercourse[30] the newly-married man should recite stanzas to his wife to bring about the

---

[28] In the passage of AiB.7.13 the whole series of stanzas concerning the procreation of sons is attributed to Nārada. So e.g.: 'Fathers always overcome great difficulties through a son. (In him) the Self is born out of the Self. The son is like a well-provisioned boat, which carries him over' (st. 3). 'His wife is only then a real wife, when he is born in her again. The seed which is placed in her, she develops to a being and sends it forth' (st. 7). For the sage Nārada see Van den Bosch: 1978, 109 note 1. For the ideas in ancient Indian texts concerning conception see Meyer: 1953, 359ff.

[29] The so-called *caturthīkakarman*; Cf. e.g., Hillebrandt: 1897, 68. The custom of living the first three nights in sexual continence is also found among many European peoples.

[30] For an ancient description see also BĀU. 6.4.20ff.

generation of male progeny, such as for instance:[31]

> May a male embryo enter your womb, as an arrow the quiver; may a man be born here, a son after ten months.
>
> From the auspicious sperm which men produce for us, you should produce a son; be a well-breeding cow.

The necessity for male progeny is further stressed by the performance of a special rite, the *puṃsavana*, in the third or fourth month of pregnancy which aims to secure the birth of a son (see Gonda: 1980, 369). As may be clear, all these rites and injunctions illustrate the cultural importance attached to male progeny. With the birth of a son a man has essentially fulfilled a deep-rooted cultural obligation and thereby achieves complete personhood. In the application of the patronymic in the strict sense all these notions are implicitly expressed.

2.5 The system of *gotra* and *pravara*

As mentioned before, the *gotra* name is often used when a person is addressed (Brough: 1953, 5f.). The term *gotra* initially denoted 'a herd of cows', but in the course of time it came to designated 'group of persons living within the same walls'. In that capacity it also referred to a family denoted by a family-name (so, e.g., Kapadia: 1947, 56f.). In conformity with this meaning mention is sometimes made of many thousands of *gotras* (cf. Kane: 1974, vol. II, 484 referring to BaudhGŚS. See also Pāṇini 4.1.162 note 18). In the later Vedic literature, however, the term is used for the eight primeval *gotras* of the 'divine seers' (*ṛṣis*) who were

---

31 Some of the stanzas mentioned in ŚāṅkhGS. 1.19.6. Cf. e.g. HirGS. 1.7.24.4ff.; MānGS 1.1.4.16ff. for similar stanzas. See further Gonda: 1980, 368; Kane: 1974 (vol. II), 195.

originally regarded as eight exogamous groups.[32] In the course of time these primeval *gotras* would have been multiplied by the insertion of many other sages (see e.g., Basham: 1967, 154f.). The term was therefore applied as well to a subdivision (*gaṇa*) of the primeval *gotras*, to subsections (*pakṣa*) of these subdivisions, or even to individual *gotras* (see Kane: 1974, vol. II, 486). Brough has defined the individual *gotra* as an exogamous sibship whose members trace their descent back to a common ancestor (Brough; 1953, 5). It would be beyond the scope of this paper to deal with the intricate problems connected with the *gotra* system, but it becomes clear that individual persons, when addressed, are defined in terms of those ancestors by whose name their families have been known for generations.

According to the texts, the *gotra* system was of fundamental importance with respect to marriage and the laws of inheritance. It was strictly forbidden to marry a girl belonging to the same *gotra*; the property of a man without male progeny should go to a relation within the *gotra*. In this respect the injunctions concerning *gotra* exogamy partly coincide with those of *sapiṇḍa* exogamy, but they are narrower because they exclude all persons having the same *gotra* ancestor (Kane: 1974, vol. II, 499). Because the meaning of the term *gotra* was quite elastic, the rules with respect to *gotra* exogamy were felt to be inadequate.

In later brahminical works a precise system is introduced by adding to the *gotra* name the names of the mythical divine seers with whom one was supposed to be related. This list of remote ancestors (*pravara* lists) was employed by the brahmins not only to show that they were descendants of worthy ancestors, but also to legitimate themselves as proper priests for the perfomance of sacrificial rites. They extended the rule of *gotra* exogamy to *pravara* exogamy, which implied that the sharing of a

---

32 As such, mention is made of the seers who have founded the 'hymn-families' of the ṚV. and Agastya, the sage who is said to have spread the Vedic religion beyond the Vindhyas. The progeny of each of these seers is said to constitute a *gotra*; see further Kane: 1974, 484f.; Brough: 1953, 4.

common *pravara* seer formed an impediment to marriage as well.[33] This rather theoretical *pravara* system is mainly restricted to the higher levels of the brahminical estate; therefore I shall not discuss it here.[34] The introduction of these lists with respect to exogamy stressed the status of a person and legitimated his role as a capable and respectable (hieratic) functionary.

2.6 The life-cycle and the acquisition of status and titles

An important part of the *gṛhyasūtras* is devoted to the description of the *saṃskāras*. They are regarded as the Indian variants of the rites of passage. They should be performed in the course of the life of an individual and 'were expected to bring a person's personality to higher stages of development'(Gonda: 1980, 365). By means of them a person became consecrated and was supposed to overcome the risks of a new stage of life (Gonda: 1977, 556f.; 1980, 364). Sometimes mention is made of eighteen so-called 'bodily consecrations'.[35] The most important ones are the birth-rites, the ritual tonsure of a child, the initiation into the study of the Vedas, and the wedding-ceremonies.[36] On the whole these

---

[33] MānGS. 1.7.8: 'He should marry a girl of a (good) family, who is a virgin, who belongs to the same *varṇa*, who has not the same *pravara*, who is younger; (a girl) who has not yet reached the age of puberty, (is) best'. See Dresden: 1941, 28 notes on this prescription with references to other texts.

[34] See for a detailed discussion Brough: 1953, 17 ff.

[35] In this context the expression *śārīrāḥ saṃskārāḥ* is used; see Kane: 1974 (vol. II), 201f.; Gonda: 1980, 365ff.; Pandey: 1949.

[36] The relatively late VaikhSmS (1.1), orginating in Kerala (cf. Caland: 1926, 273 f.), gives the following enumeration of *saṃskāras*:

1)seminal infusion for the first time in marriage (*niṣeka*)

2)cohabitation twelve or sixteen days after the wife's menses (*ṛtusaṃgamana*)

3)the rite to secure conception (*garbhādhāna*)

4)the rite to secure the birth of a male child (*puṃsavana*)

5)the rite in which the wife's hair is parted (*simāntonnayana*)

rites are comparatively simple and they take place in the domestic circle or in the house of the *guru* (cf. Gonda: 1980, 366)[37] They are regarded as a family affair; by means of them a person is supposed to be qualified for the complex of duties (*dharma*) that is characteristic of this new stage of life (see also Lingat: 1973, 4).

The ritual authorities make a clear distinction between males and females. The *saṃskāras* are primarily destined for male persons.[38] Those performed on behalf of females mainly have reference to their incor-

---

6)the worship of Viṣṇu by means of a mess of rice in the eight month of pregnancy to ensure an easy delivery (*viṣṇubali*)
7)the birth ceremonies (*jātakarman*)
8)the getting up from child-bed after ten or twelve days (*utthāna*)
9)the name-giving rite (*nāmakaraṇa*)
10)the first feeding with solid food in the sixth month (*annaprāsana*)
11)the ceremony performed by a householder after returning home from a journey (*pravāsagamana*)
12)the ceremonial feeding of the boy together with his relatives and learned brahmins, who should proclaim benedictions (*piṇḍavardhana*)
13)ritual tonsure in the third year (*caula* or *cūḍākaraṇa*)
14)the initiation ceremony with the investiture of the sacred thread and the recitation of the *sāvitrī* stanza by the pupil (*upanayana*)
15)the boy's undertaking of the observances relating to the study of the Veda (*vedavrata*)
16)the opening of the annual course of study
17)the taking of a bath at the end of studentship and the returning homeas *snātaka*, i.e., as 'one who is fit for marriage' (*samāvartana*)
18)the wedding ceremonies (*vivāha*)
See further Caland: 1920, 1 with notes and Carter: 1982, 188ff. for a contemporary description of the *saṃskāras*.

[37] Many *saṃskāras* are supposed already to have existed in a more or less institutionalized form from an early date.

[38] With the exception of the *simāntonnayana* (see Gonda: 1956) the authors of the *gṛhyasūtras* always take the *saṃskāras* of a male person as point of departure for their exposition.

poration in their husband's family and their essential though 'passive and subordinate' role in procreation. The line of the family of the man should be continued by means of male offspring and women are considered subsidiary to this paramount aim (cf. Kane: 1974, vol. II, 206).

The asymmetrical relation between male and female persons is already expressed in the rules concerning the rite of name-giving. Only one *gṛhyasūtra* mentions the possibility of a *nāmakaraṇa* rite for girls, but this should be performed without Vedic *mantras* (ĀsvGS. 1.24.5).[39] This specific injunction becomes clear when one bears in mind that women have no access in their own right to Vedic lore. In this regard they have the same status as *śūdras* (Kane: 1974, vol. II, 367), but by their marriage with 'twice-born' men they can participate in Vedic tradition, though in a modest manner, and only in a way complementary to their husbands (Kane: 1974, vol. II, 365f., 428, 535). Their marriage is regarded as their initiation.[40] From a sociocultural point of view a wife receives a new identity on account of her wedding-ceremony, namely that of her husband. She becomes a member of his family and as such can acquire respectability by giving him a (multitude of) son(s).[41]

---

[39] The later authors on *dharma* prescribe the performance of the *saṃskāras* from *jātakarman* up to *caula* also for girls, but then without Vedic *mantras*; see Kane: 1974 (vol. II), 265.

[40] GobhGS. 2.1.19 prescribes the wearing of the sacred thread by a bride, when she is introduced to the sacrificial fire in the house of her husband. This thread is a characteristic attribute with which boys are endowed at their *upanayana*. According to Manu 2.67: 'the nuptial ceremony is stated to be the Vedic sacrament for women (and equal to the initiation), serving the husband (equivalent to) the residence in (the house of the) teacher, and the household duties (the same) as the (daily) worship of the sacred fire'. Transl. Bühler 1886, 42. See further Kane: 1974 (vol. II), 294f.

[41] The dependence of women in all matters concerning men is clearly attested in many ancient texts; see Rau: 1957, 40f.; Kane: 1974 (vol. II), 577f.; In as much as they were generally considered to be the moral property of their father, husband or son, they could not take any decisions in the legal sphere. They were not partners in the marriage negotiations, nor were they entitled to inheritance. For a classic formulation see e.g., Manu 5.148.

One of the most important *saṃskāras* (see Kane: 1974, vol. II, 188f.) for a male member of the three higher *varṇas* is his initiation in Vedic tradition (*upanayana*). VāśDhS. 2.6., quoting a certain Harita, mentions in this context:[42]

> Up till the investiture with the girdle of *muñja* grass (viz. until *upanayana*) there is no action that is obligatory for him; as long as he is not born again for Vedic study he may be in his conduct like a *śūdra*.

According to the brahmins the *śūdra* is only physically born and in that capacity is called *ekajāti*, 'having (only) one birth'. A man of one the three higher *varṇas* who has been initiated in Vedic lore is qualified as *dvijāti*; 'having two births', or as *dvija*; 'twice-born'. The *yajñopavīta* - a thread consisting of three strands and usually worn over the left shoulder and under the right arm (Kane: 1974, vol. II, 296) - is the characteristic attribute of a twice-born person. In the course of time the title *dvija* acquired a broader meaning and was also used to denote a member of the three higher *varṇas*. From comparitively early times, however, the *yajñopavīta* came to be regarded as the peculiar indicator of membership of the brahminical estate (Kane: 1974, vol. II, 296).

The initiation of the pupil is characterized by the instruction in the Veda. During this period he is called a *brahmācārin*, 'one who is practising the sacred study (*brahman*), whilst observing chastity' (cf. e.g., Gonda: 1960, 119f. and 1965, chapter 9). The polluting effects of sexual intercourse made a person unfit for contact with the sacred reality. Sexual intercourse with women was therefore regarded as a most reprehensible act, defiling the stage of *brahmācārya* (Kane: 1974, vol. II, 374). The *gṛhyasūtras* give specific rules for each of the *varṇas* with respect to the initial phase (Kane: 1974, vol. II, 274f.). The age of the initiand is eight years for a brahmin, eleven years for a *kṣatriya*, twelve years for a *vaiśya*. Moreover, a distinction is made between the attributes with which each of the *varṇas* is endowed. Each estate should wear garments of different colours or materials (Kane: 1974, vol. II, 278f.). The stage of *brahmācārya* was regarded as of paramount importance for

---

[42] See for parallels ĀpDhS. 2.15.19; GautDhS. 1.10; 2.4-5; BaudhDhS. 1.3.6; Manu 2.171 and 172; Vi. 28.40.

the brahmins (Kane: 1974, vol. II, 105ff.)[43] because it was their first duty to preserve the sacred tradition:

> At birth every brahmin is indebted with a threefold debt, viz., of *brahmācārya* to the sages (*ṛṣis*), of sacrifice to the gods and of offspring to the ancestors; he indeed is freed from his debts who has a son, who sacrifices and who dwells with the teacher as *brahmācārin* (TS. 6.3.10.5. Cf. also ŚB. 11.3.3.1ff.).

In the course of time the title *brahmācārin* was used for an unmarried brahmin, if he was conversant with the Veda and practised sexual continence (see e.g., Monier Williams, Dictionary).

During the stage of *brahmācārya* a student was initiated into the Vedas and was subject to many restrictions (Kane: 1974, vol. II, 304ff.), but these were lifted when he finished his study and took the ceremonial bath which marked the end of this stage of life. He was then called a *snātaka*, 'one who has bathed'. He returned to his family as a person fit for marriage (Kane: 1974, vol. II, 678f). The wedding-ceremony introduced him to the next stage of life, namely that of a householder (*gṛhastha*). From the day of his marriage he was to worship the domestic fire twice a day by means of the *agnihotra* sacrifice in the evening and in the morning.[44] The importance of marriage was stressed in many ancient texts, because a man was not regarded as a 'complete person' without a wife[45].

> The wife is indeed half of one's self; therefore as long as a man does not

---

43 With references to the various texts, such as e.g. Manu 4.147: 'A brahmin should always and assiduously study the Veda alone; that (Veda study) is the highest *dharma*; anything else is inferior to this'.

44 The *agnihotra* sacrifice is an offering consisting of clarified butter poured into the sacrificial fire.

45 See further AiĀ. 1.3.5.6; Manu 9.45. Cf. also BĀU. 1.4.17 where the traditional idea of completeness of a person is contrasted with the idea developed in the passage of ŚB. 5.2.1.10: the ignorant man thinks that he is incomplete without a wife, sons and possessions. See further Kane: 1974 (vol. II), 428.

secure a wife he is not regenerated; but when he secures a wife he is regenerated, for then he is complete.(ŚB. 5.2.1.10)

When a man is supplied with a lawful wife he is regarded as a 'complete person' and is able to produce legal sons; from this point of view he is 'regenerated'. The wife enables the man to perform his religious duties as a 'complete person' and cooperates with him in sacrificial worship, which is an essential requisite for success. When a man is therefore qualified as *gṛhastha* it implies that he is regarded as a whole person.[46]

In Vedic texts the *gṛhastha* is denoted by a number of titles which often have reference to his status as sacrificer. In the first place a clear distinction is made between two groups of sacrificers, viz., those householders who have set up the three sacred fires and follow the official *śrauta* cult, and those who confine themselves to the performance of the relatively simple offerings in the household-fire according to the *gṛhya* cult.[47] The first category of persons is qualified as *āhitāgni*, i.e., 'who have not spread the (three) sacred fires', and the second one as *anāhitāgni*. The *āhitāgni* is further classed according to the types of offerings he has performed. The VaikhSmS. prescribes that a *gṛhastha*, after the establishment of the three sacred fires, should accept a name which proclaims the highest grade of sacrifices accomplished by him, beginning with the rite in which the three sacred fires are spread (*agnyādhāna*).[48] The householder who, for instance, has a soma sacrifice performed may add to his name the title *somayājin*, thus expressing his

---

46 See also Winternitz: 1920, 6ff.; 13f.; 16; etc.

47 This distinction between the *āhitāgni* and the *anāhitāgni* returns in the funeral ceremonies. The first one is usually cremated with the help of his three sacrificial fires, while the latter one is burnt with his household fire.

48 See VaikhSmS.: 3.19 'After the establishment of his three sacred fires he should accept a (third) name, which proclaims the highest grade of the sacrifices accomplished by him, beginning with the establishment of his fires'. Trans. Caland: 1929, 92. See also HirGS. 2.4.15, which has been misunderstood by Oldenberg according to Caland.

high status in the sacrificial cult (see Kane: 1938, 224). In the funeral ceremonies these distinctions are clearly expressed.[49] The householder is commemorated by virtue of his status as sacrificer (cf. Van den Bosch: 1986, 209ff.). He is burnt on the funeral pyre with the help of the three sacred fire(s) after the arrangement of his sacrificial utensils upon his dead body. These utensils function in this context as 'labels', which express the level he has reached in the hierarchy of the sacrificial cult.[50]

From the few preceding observations it is clear that the development of personhood should be understood in relation to sexual and *varṇa* identity. With due regard to these data man has to pass the successive stages of life according to predestined patterns which help him to appropriate his *varṇa* identity and the rights and obligations connected with it, to distinguish himself from the other *varṇas*, and to take his specific place in the whole of ancient Indian society. Thus pieces of personhood are imposed as it were layer after layer upon the individual human being, which helps him to define his sociocultural identity and to present himself in the presence of other persons. By marrying according to the Vedic rules and by the establishment of the sacred fire(s), a man acquires the status of a 'complete person'. In this way he contributes to the maintenance of the socio-cosmic order (*dharma*). The following of the complex *śrauta* instead of the *gṛhya* cult is optional and adds extra status to the householder and his family, thus legitimizing his high and respected position in traditional Aryan society.[51] To summarize: the

---

[49] For a comprehensive description of the various traditions see Caland: 1896; Kane: 1973 (vol. IV), 214f.

[50] The collection of sacrificial utensils becomes proportionately more extensive as the sacrificer performs more complex sacrificial rites. Moreover, specific utensils which are characteristic of a certain type of rite indicate that the deceased man had this rite performed during his lifetime. For the arrangement of these utensils on the corpse see Caland: 1896, 49ff. (par. 27 Das 'Schichten der Opfergeräthe', *pātracayanam*).

[51] In the course of time the *śrauta* rites have become restricted to the brahminical estate, and especially to a restricted number of brahminical families, who define themselves in this manner as the heirs of ancient Vedic tradition and as 'true Aryans'.

titles which are employed to classify persons according to their stage of life and social position clearly reflect brahminical ideology with its hierarchical division of the traditional society.

Finally, in this context a few words may be devoted to the position of *śūdras* according the ideology of the brahmins. As mentioned before, they are clearly distinguished from members of other *varṇas*, who are qualified as *ārya*. The *śūdras* are *anārya* and for this reason they have no access to Vedic lore (see e.g., GautDhS. 10.50ff; Kane: 1974, vol. II, 35). The following passage is illuminating with respect to their position:

> After it (viz. a series of various other creations) ... from man the *śūdra* was created, and from cattle the horse; therefore these two, the horse and the *śūdra*, are dependent on others. Therefore, the *śūdra* is not fit for sacrifice, for he was not created from any (of the Vedic) gods. Therefore they depend on their feet, for they were (only) created from the feet (of the god Prajāpati).(TS. 7.1.1.6; cf. PB. 6.1.11)[52]

Unlike the three other *varṇas*, the *śūdras* were not thought of as having a divine counterpart and were therefore excluded from sacred reality and regarded as impure. Though they might be rich in cattle, they were only qualified for menial duties. In the course of time they were partly incorporated into Aryan society and were accorded low positions (see Kane: 1974, vol. II, 34). This gradual incorporation is illustrated in the brahminical instruction with respect to the *saṃskāras* for *śūdras*. Though they remained excluded from the *upanayana* and related rites, the other important ceremonies could be performed, but only by proxy and without Vedic stanzas (Kane: 1974, vol. II, 34, 159). Instead of these, non-Vedic *mantras* were applied. To summarize, the conclusion seems to be justified that in brahminical ideology the *śūdras* were credited with a sociocultural identity, but a sacred identity was denied to them.

---

52 The creation of the world by Prajāpati has its analogy in the creation of the world by Puruṣa; see ṚV. 10.90.

2.7 The concept of person in the Upaniṣads

In the preceding pages I have dealt in broad outline with the name-giving system in ancient Indian texts with regard to the concept of person and its sociocultural coordinates. This approach has necessarily been to a certain extent one-sided, because it presupposes the importance of names with respect to the reconstruction of this concept. For a long time, however, there have been important intellectual trends in Indian tradition which opposed the traditional brahminical ideology with its rigid orientation towards the sacrificial cult. Though the representatives of these groups did not deny the importance of this concept for traditional society, they criticised it from a metaphysical and soteriological point of view. In the *upaniṣads* this criticism is clearly formulated. The central theme is a reflection on the 'self' (*ātman*) within the broader context of its liberation. What is the true essence of man when he is stripped of the traditional names and roles used in traditional society? This is no place to deal extensively with this question, so I shall confine myself to a few remarks on the *ātman* and its relation to the idea of the social person.

In the BĀU the 'self' (*ātman*) is sometimes equated with the *puruṣa*, i.e., 'the (cosmic) person in the beginning'. The passage in translation runs as follows:[52]

> In the beginning the self (*ātman*) was this all in the shape of the *puruṣa*. Looking around he saw nothing else except himself. He first said: 'I am' (*aham asmi*). On account of this name 'I' (*aham*) arose. Therefore, even nowadays a person who is called says first: 'Here am I (*aham*)'; then he proclaims the other name which belongs to him (BĀU. 1.4.1).

The *ātman* manifesting himself in the form of the *puruṣa* proclaims his omnipresence in the beginning with the words: 'I am'. This ubiquity in the whole creation is further deduced by the author of this text from the fact that each man presents himself first with the personal pronoun 'I'; then mentions his name. In other words: the name is secondary with respect to the *ātman* which is present in each individual. The *ātman* is

---

[52] For an alternative translation see Senart: 1934, 10:'L'atman existait seul, à l'origine, sous la forme de Puruṣa'.

his 'true essence'. The text goes on with a discourse on the relation between the primeval *puruṣa*, 'being *per se*', and the origin of creation. The lonely existence of the *puruṣa* is characterized as joyless and for this reason he desires a second person. According to the text this is shaped by a division of the *puruṣa* into two parts:

> He was as large as a woman and a man in close embrace. He divided himself into two parts. From that arose husband and wife. Therefore, as Yajñavalkya used to say, this (body) is (one half of) oneself, like one of the two halves of a split pea. Therefore, this space is filled by a wife. He became united with her. From that human beings were produced (BĀU. 1.4.3. See also 4.2.21).

With the differentiation between male and female the process of creation starts. The universe becomes differentiated by names and forms (*nāmarūpa*); so BĀU 1.4.7.[53] In spite of the differentiation the *ātman* is always present as a whole in all manifestations of creation. Therefore, one should not restrict oneself to the study of just names and forms, but meditate upon the *ātman* as undivided, because the manifest things become one in him. The text continues:[54]

> That self (*ātman*) is dearer than a son, dearer than wealth, dearer than everything else and innermost. If one were to say to a person who speaks of anything other than the self as dear: 'he will lose what he holds dear', he will

---

[53] For *nāmarūpa*, i.e., 'name and form (or shape)', which together make the individual see e.g. Radhakrishnan: 1969, 167.

[54] See also the important passage of 4.4.22: 'Verily he is the great unborn Self... On knowing him, in truth, one becomes an ascetic. Desiring him as their only worlds, monks wander forth. Verily, because they know this, the ancient (sages) did not wish for offspring. What shall we do with offspring, we who have attained this Self, this world. They, having risen above the desire for sons, the desire for wealth, the desire for worlds, led the life of a mendicant. For the desire for sons is the desire for wealth, is the desire for worlds; both these are, indeed, desires only. This Self ... is not this, not this. He is incomprehensible, for he cannot be comprehended. He is indestructible, for he cannot be destroyed...' (Transl. Radhakrishnan: 1969, 279). See also ChU. 8.1.5.

> very likely do so. One should meditate on the self alone as dear. He who meditates on the self alone as dear, (should know that) what he holds dear, verily, will not perish (BĀU. 1.4.8, transl. Radhakrishnan: 1969, 167 with minor emendations).

In these passages traditional ideas with respect to the concept of person receive a new interpretation. The ancient creation myth with the primeval (cosmic) person is used for this purpose. From his body the whole world is created by means of a sacrifice. *Puruṣa* is in this context described as an androgynous being who divides himself into a male and a female part for the sake of joy and for the progress of the creation. These parts together form the original complete *puruṣa*. In traditional brahminical ideology a man is regarded as a 'complete person' when he has supplied himself with a wife (and with progeny); then the progress of the creation in principal is guaranteed. Though the relative truth of this ideology is not denied, it is criticised because it neglects the *ātman* as the 'true essence' of a person. According to the various authors of the ancient *upaniṣads* the primacy of the *ātman* should be defended, because he precedes the manifest creation and is the only eternal reality behind it (see also e.g., BĀU. 2.4.12; ChU. 6.9.1-6.16.3). Only by the realization of the understanding that the *ātman* is omnipresent does one become one and thus complete (see e.g., BĀU. 2.4.1ff).

The concept of person is discussed in the JUB. from a slightly different point of view. When a deceased man reaches the entrance of the hereafter he should answer the question: 'Who art thou?'. The text continues:

> If he answers with his personal or his *gotra* name he is subject to the law of *karman*. If he responds with the words: 'Who I am is the light thou art. As such I have come to thee, the heavenly light'. Prajāpati (the lord of creatures) replies: 'Who thou art, that same am I; who I am that same art thou. So come in' (JUB. 3.14.1-4. For the text see Limaye and Vadekar: 1958, 444-445).

Only a person who knows his 'true identity' reaches liberation, but he who mentions the names referring to the social person 'falls down' and is subject to reincarnation, because these ephemeral names do not reveal his 'true identity'. They have no meaning from the soteriological point of view of the *upaniṣads*.

In the ChU. the oneness of *ātman* is taught by a certain teacher Uddālaka to his son Śvetaketu by means of a whole series of examples (ChU. 6.1.4). The teaching reaches its culmination in the frequent recapitulation of the famous text:[55]

> That which is the subtle essence, this whole world has for its self. That is the true. That is the self. That art thou Śvetaketu.

With this expression: 'That art thou', a new metaphysical dimension is added to the concept of person. The 'true identity' of a person should not be confused with the social person as designated by temporal names and titles, but it is divine, eternal and beyond words.[56]

3. *Conclusions*

An analysis of the system of name-giving discloses various notions with respect to the concept of the social person. These notions are dependent on the type of names which are used in specific situations. The public personal name (*vyāvahārika*) is given to a child during the official ceremony of name-giving. It should at least express the sexual identity of a human being, and according to the ancient authorities on *dharma*, also the *varṇa* identity. Though this name is often used in everyday life, it should not be used by everyone. When a person is only addressed by his personal name this may point to an informal or intimate relationship between the two parties, or to an asymmetrical relationship in which a superior person gives expression to his higher position by ignoring the intimate sphere of life of the addressee. The application of the public personal name points to the right of access to the personal sphere of life. As such it is only to be used by the in-group. From this point of view, a superior can be regarded as belonging to the in-group of his subordinate, but an inferior person, on the contrary, has no right to

---

55 The expression: *sa ya eṣo'nimā aitadātmyam idaṃ sarvam, tat satyam, sa ātmā, tat tvam asi, Śvetaketo, iti*, returns in many passages of Uddālaka's teaching concerning the oneness of the self. So e.g., in ChU. 6.13.1 ff. (the illustration of salt and water).

56 For an elaboration of these ideas see e.g. Radhakrishnan: 1969, introduction.

address his superior by his public personal name; he does not belong to the in-group of his superior. He has to use the polite forms of address.

The official form of address between two persons who do not belong to the same in-group consists of the *vyāvahārika* name together with a *patronymic*, which may function as a *gotra* name. This implies that in an official context a person should be defined in terms of his personal name as well as of the group to which he belongs. There is, however, a clear tendency in the texts to avoid the application of the personal name in the conventional forms of address between two persons who do not belong to the same in-group. This may be explained in connection with the idea of privacy of the person in question. A person is then denoted by the *patronymic*, or by the *patronymic* and *gotra* name. This implies that in official situations he is defined in relation to his father and the 'clan' to which he belongs.

A further nuance in the classification of persons is introduced by the distinction of two types of *patronymics*, the so-called *vṛddha* and *yuvan* form. By the application of one of these forms the position of the individual within his family is carefully indicated. The rules with respect to the application of these forms seem to point to a refined etiquette, in which the hierarchical position of the individual within his family and *gotra* is carefully regulated. If a man does not know his place he can be subtly reprimanded by the application of a specific *patronymic* which contributes to the awareness of his real position.

In ancient Indian texts a person is not only defined in relation to his living contemporaries, but also with respect to his deceased ancestors. In this respect the synchronic point of view is supplemented by the diachronic one, though one should relativize these positions because the three immediate ancestors are considered as real persons. Once a month they are invoked using their public personal and *gotra* names in the ancestor cult, called *śrāddha*. In that context they communicate as 'consociates' and are supposed to exert their benevolence. The invitation is usually restricted to the deceased father, grandfather and great-grandfather and they are honoured with offerings consisting of lumps of flour (*piṇḍa*). This offering of *piṇḍas* functions as a paradigm by means of which the relationships in the male line are implicitly defined: the measure of kinship can be deduced from the common offering of *piṇḍa(s)* to one or more ancestors. In this case the relationship between two persons is qualified as *sapiṇḍa*, which implies that they have (at least) one ancestor in common to whom both offer a *piṇḍa* (in common). In this view a person is thus defined in relation to his three male ancestors. The definition of *sapiṇḍa* relationship broadly coincides with that of the joint-family, which often consists of three generations. Moreover, it functions, among other things, as an important criterion in the case of exogamy.

The *gotra* name has from early times had a complex meaning, but usually the term denotes an exogamous sibship, whose members trace their descent back to a common ancestor. By the application of the *gotra* name a person is defined in terms of his sibship. The definition of a person in terms of the *gotra* is regarded as essential in the case of exogamy and inheritance.

The close connection between father and son becomes apparent from the frequent use of the *patronymic* in the strict sense. In many texts this relationship is elaborated in an ideology which suggests that the self (*ātman*) of the father is regenerated in the son. This 'self' is regarded as essential for his identity and is equated with the Veda. As such the son is the new link in the patriline and has the obligation to beget male progeny. By designating the son by means of the *patronymic* it becomes clear that the father has fulfilled his obligation with respect to his ancestors. The state of being without lawful sons is regarded as a disaster because the continuity of the family-line is broken and with that, the continuity of the Veda, which guarantees continued existence of the divine order. From this point of view it becomes clear that the son delivers his father from chaos or hell, and contributes to the well-being of the family.

In brahminical ideology a person is defined in his relation to the world. He has to maintain the socio-cosmic order which has its foundation in creation, but this does not mean that each man has the same obligations.These duties are carefully defined in relation to the sex, estate (*varṇa*) and stage of life of a person. From the beginning male and female human beings have always had different tasks. With the creation of the world the four *varṇas* came into existence and with it, the allocation of specific tasks to each of them. A principal distinction was made between the *śūdras*, the class of the serfs, and the other three *varṇas*. The first category was qualified as *anārya*, which implied that they had no access to Vedic tradition. A sacred identity was denied them. The male members of the other three estates regarded themselves as *ārya* and could participate in Vedic lore after the initiation rite. This distinction between *ārya* and *anārya* broadly coincides with qualifications such as *dvijāti* and *ekajāti*, but a member of the three higher estates who has not been initiated before a certain age is also classed on the same level as a *śūdra*, because he has 'only one birth'.

The *saṃskāras* form important ritual events in the life of an individual. They are especially destined for male members of the three higher *varṇas* and help them to realize the successive stages of life successfully. As such, these rituals impose pieces of personhood upon individuals layer after layer, which helps them to appropriate their carefully standardized sociocultural identity. The realizations of the most important rites of passage can be expressed by means of special titles conferred upon the person in question such as *brahmācārin*, *snātaka* and *gṛhastha*. This attribution of personhood reaches its peak in the first instance in the wedding ceremonies. A man realizes complete personhood by his marriage, because he is then supplemented by a better half. In that capacity he is regarded as a productive unit for the procreation of children, especially sons. He is a householder (*gṛhastha*) and as a 'complete person' is entitled to perform the Vedic rituals for maintaining the world in order to ensure the well-being of the family.

In brahminical ideology the close relation between the concept of person and status has been elaborated in a refined way. The sacrificial cult is characterized by a hierarchy of rites, which become more and more complex. The qualified householder has the right to perform the various sacrifices in due order during the course of his life and acquires by the performance of them specific titles and a connected status. These titles, such as e.g., *somayājin* (i.e., 'he who has the *soma* sacrifice performed'), are sometimes added to the official names of a person. In the funeral ceremonies these titles seem to be quite important, because in that sad context a person is commemorated by virtue of his status. The complexity of the funeral cult with its mourning customs essentially gives expression to the status of the deceased person and should not be seen primarily in connection with individual grief (see Van den Bosch: 1986, 215ff.).

Besides the various names and titles mentioned above, a person is also endowed with a secret name, which would indicate his true identity. Sometimes this name is equated with the Veda, which suggests that it points to the sacred dimension of personal existence. From a metaphysical point of view a person is more than merely names and titles used in various daily roles, though these may be adequate for the designation of the social person. The true person should be defined in relation to the divine; for this reason, he should present himself in communication with that reality with his true identity. This identity ideologically precedes the concept of the social person. Immediately after his birth the father gives a secret name to his son and places him as it were in the realm of the divine. The secret name represents, therefore, his sacred identity. This is the name the son should use for respectful salutations, that is to say in formal contact with representatives of the divine order. As such, the *abhivādanīya* name is used for the first time by the pupil in his official acquintance with the *guru* who initiates him into the Vedic tradition and reveals to him the 'eternal truth'.

The idea that the secret name refers to the divine identity of a person is also found in the sacrificial consecration rites, which prepare the sacrificer for his contact with the sacred reality. This contact is possible because he makes himself known with his 'divine Self', which transcends profane reality. For this reason the sacrificer should proclaim his public personal name together with his secret name, which indicates that he should present himself with his 'total' identity to the other participants in the ritual concerned. The *śūdra* does not have a secret name, because he has no access to the Veda. From this point of view he has no divine identity - he is not created after any of the Vedic gods - and in this respect he is dependent upon others. For this reason he can be put on a par with cattle and is only defined as a human being in connection with ordinary reality.

The secret name is often denoted in Vedic tradition by the *nakṣatra* name. This indicates that the brahmins have tried to define the true identity of a person in connection with the conjunction of moon and stars. As such, a person was made subordinate to a reality structured in the last resort according to abstract laws of time functioning in practice as fate. Even the Vedic gods and their powers were determined in connection with these laws and made subordinate to them. Nonetheless, this constraint and submission to fate did not lead to helplessness, because the brahmins knew how to manipulate fate by their apprehension of these cosmic laws. By connecting the secret name with astrology they seem to have adapted themselves to opinions which must have been fairly popular.

In the traditional ideology of the brahmins expression is given to a detailed system of classifications by means of which a world-view is developed in which everybody and everything is ordered according to well-defined categories. This ideology also holds good for the concept of person, which is placed in a complex hierarchical framework. This becomes clear from the attribution of names, titles and other qualifications in various situations. A person is always controlled by various groups to which he is related in different situations. It seems to me that this subordination of a person to the whole has led in general to a weak ego identity. In this context one example may suffice. The conception that the *ātman* of the son is the same as the *ātman* of the father, because the father is regenerated each time again in the son, does not plead for a high valuation of the individual as an unique human being, but for a deep-rooted estimation of the family and its traditions.

The ancient brahminical ideal of Indian society described in Vedic texts can be characterized as belonging to the type of 'strong grid/strong group'.[57] The highly intricate ritual practices fit very well in this picture. The efforts of the brahmins to fix the ritual system down to the minutest details and to explain them in relation to their cosmological implications were regarded by other intellectuals as useless. The 'externalization' of the ritual with its redundant repetition of the same patterns on smaller scales led to a new reflection on the main premises of the sacrificial cult with, as a consequence, an 'interiorization' of sacrifice. The metaphysical speculation focussed on the eternal and true essence of man. The hypertrophied urge of the brahminical class to identify and classify everything and to connect it with cosmological systems led to something that was diametrically opposed to it. The divine self (*daiva ātman*) which was connected with the secret name was one of the starting points of this reflection. In the traditional ideology the true essence of a person was determined in relation to the progress of creation and in relation to time. With the idea of regeneration of the *ātman* in each generation the *ātman* was considered in connection with the continuity of the family and its well-being in the future, which in turn was dependent on the continuity of the Vedic cult. The dimension of time finds expression in the *nakṣatra* name. The conjunction of moon and

---

[57] For the distinction of cultures according to a group axis and a grid axis see Douglas: 1973. For a discussion of this position see Van Baal en Van Beek: 1985, 158f.

stars was of paramount importance for the specification of the true identity of a person. In the *upaniṣads* this development is interrupted because the *ātman* as the true self of a person is no longer explained in connection with the ideas mentioned above. The *ātman* is the only eternal reality underlying the whole creation and as such it forms the only basis for a correct contemplation of the 'true' identity. The attempts to define the *ātman* with the help of traditional classifications and categories, characteristic of manifest creation, is doomed to failure, because the *ātman* is 'not this, not that' (*neti neti*). From this point of view the traditional beliefs, values and rituals are meaningless. The sages who know their true identity do not crave any more for male offspring, wealth and the prestige in this world. With the conception that a person cannot realize his true identity within this fugitive world, which is no more than 'vanity fair', the tradition of the *saṃnyāsin*, the religious mendicant who drops out, acquires a new metaphysical legitimation.

Bibliography

Baal, J. van - W.A.E. van Beek
1985 *Symbols for Communication. An Introduction to the Anthropological Study of Religion*, Assen (second revised edition).

Basham, A.L.
1967 *The Wonder That Was India. A survey of the History and Culture of the Indian Sub-continent before the Coming of the Muslims*, London (third revised edition).

Biardeau, M.
1965 '*Ahamkāra*, the Ego Principle in the Upanishads', in: *Contributions to Indian Sociology*, vol. VIII, Paris/The Hague.

Bodewitz, H.W.
1969 'Der Vers *vicakṣaṇad ṛtavo*... (JB. 1.18; 1.50; KausU. 1.2)', in: *Zeitschrift der Deutschen Morgenländischen Gesellschaft*, Supplementa I (XVII Deutscher Orientalistentag, Vorträge, herausgegeben von W. Voigt), Wiesbaden.

Bosch, L.P. van den
1978 *Atharvaveda-pariśiṣṭa, Chapters 21-29. Introduction, Translation and Notes*, Groningen (Thesis Utrecht 1978).

1986 'Dood en Religie: over funeraire riten, in het bijzonder in het oude India', in: *Nederlands Theologisch Tijdschrift*, vol. 40, 3, The Hague.

Böthlingk, O.
1887 *Pāṇini's Grammatik*. Herausgegeben, übersetzt, erläutert, Leipzig.

Brough, J.
1953 *The Early Brahminical System of Gotra and Pravara*, Cambridge.

Bühler, G.
1886 *The Laws of Manu*, Oxford (SBE. XXV).

Caland, W.
1893 *Altindischer Ahnenkult*, Leiden.
1896 *Die Altindischen Todten- und Bestattungsgebräuche*, Amsterdam (Royal Academy, N.R., I, 6).

1904 *Ueber das rituelle Sūtra des Baudhāyana*, Leipzig (Abh. für die Kunde des Morgenlandes, repr. 1966).
1922 *The Jaiminigṛhyasūtra belonging to the Sāmaveda*. Edited with an Introduction and translated into English, Lahore (reprint Delhi 1984).
1926 'Over het *Vaikhānasūtra'*. In: *Mededelingen van de Koninklijke Nederlandse Academie van Wetenschappen*, afd. Lett. deel 61, serie A nr. 8. Amsterdam.
1929 *Vaikhānasasmārtasūtram*. The Domestic Rules and Sacred Laws of the Vaikhanasa school belonging to the Black Yajurveda, Calcutta (BI. 251).

Carter, A.T.
1982 'Hierarchy and the Concept of Person in Western India'. In: *Concepts of Person: Kinship, Caste, and Marriage in India*, ed. by A. Östör - L. Fruzetti - S. Barnett, Cambridge (Mass.).

Douglas, M.
1973 *Natural Symbols: Explorations in Cosmology*, Harmondsworth.

Dresden, M.J.
1941 *Mānavagṛhyasūtra, A Vedic Manual of Domestic Rites. Translation, Commentary and Preface*, Groningen (Thesis Utrecht 1941).

Dumont, L.
1960 'World Renouncer in Indian Religions', in: *Contributions to Indian Sociology*, IV (is Appendix B. 1980, 267 sqq.), Paris/The Hague.
1965 'The Modern Conception of the Individual. Notes on its Genesis', in: *Contributions to Indian Sociology*, VIII, 13-61, Paris/The Hague.
1965 'The Functional Equivalents of the Individual in Caste Society', in: *Contributions to Indian Sociology*, VIII, 85-99, Paris/The Hague.
1980 *Homo Hierarchicus, the Caste System and its Implications* (third revised edition), London.

Eggeling, J.,
1882-1900 *The Śatapatha Brāhmaṇa, according to the text of the Mādhyandina school*, transl. 5 vols., I, 1882; II, 1885; III, 1894; IV, 1897; V, 1900 (SBE. XII, XXV, XLI, XLIII, XLIX), London.

Geertz, Cl.
1973 *The Interpretation of Cultures*, New York.
1977 'From the Native's Point of View': On the Nature of Anthropological Understanding'. In: *Symbolic Anthropology, a Reader in the Study of Symbols and Meanings*, ed. J.L. Dolgin - D.S. Kemnitzer - D.M. Schneider, New York.

Gonda, J.
1956 'The *simāntonnayana* as described in the Gṛhyasūtras', in: *East and West*, vol. 7, Rome.
1960 *Die Religionen Indiens, I. Veda und älterer Hinduismus*, Stuttgart (repr. 1978).
1964 'A note on the vedic student's staff', in: *Journal of the Oriental Institute of Baroda*, vol. 14, Baroda.
1965 *Change and Continuity in Indian Religion*, The Hague.
1970 *Notes on Names and the Name of God in Ancient India*, Amsterdam (Royal Academy, N.R., vol. 75, no. 4).

1977 *The Ritual Sūtras*, Wiesbaden (A History of Indian Literature).
1980 *Vedic Ritual, The non-Solemn Rites*, Leiden (Handbuch der Orientalistik).
1986 *The Ritual Functions and Significance of Grasses in the Religion of the Veda*, Amsterdam (Royal Academy, Letter., N.R., vol. 132).

Gopal, R.
1959 *India of Vedic Kalpasūtras*, Delhi.

Gubler, Th.
1903 *Die Patronymica im Altindischen*, Göttingen (Thesis Un. Basel).

Heimann, B.
1931 'Zur Indischen Namenkunde', in: *Studia Indo-Iranica, Ehrengabe für Wilhelm Geiger*, Leipzig.

Hilka, A.
1910 *Beiträge zur Kenntnis der indischen Namengebung*, Breslau (Indische Forschungen, Heft 3).

Hillebrandt, A.
1879 *Das altindische Neu- und Vollmondsopfer*, Jena (1977 Graz).
1897 *Ritual-Literatur, Vedische Opfer und Zauber*, Strassburg.

Jolly, J.
1880 *The Institutes of Vishnu*, Oxford (SBE. VII).

Kane, P.V.
1938 'Naming a Child or a Person', in: *Indian Historical Quaterly*, vol. 14, Calcutta.
1973 *History of Dharmaśāstra, Ancient and Medieval Religious and Civil Law*, vol. IV and V, 1, Poona (Bhandarkar Oriental Research Institute).
1974 *History of Dharmaśāstra*, vol. II (two parts), Poona.

Kapadia, K.M.
1947 *Hindu Kinship*, Bombay.

Lévi-Bruhl, L.
1927 *L'âme primitive*, Paris.

Limaye, V.P. - R.D. Vadekar
1958 *Eighteen Principal Upanishads*, vol. I., Poona.

Lingat, R.
1973 *The Classical Law of India*, Berkely.

Masani, R.P.
1932 'Customs, Ceremonies and Superstitions Connected with the Naming of Children in India', in: *Actes du XVIIIe Congrès intern. des Orientalistes (1931)*, Leiden.

Mauss, M.
1938 'Une catégorie de l'esprit humaine: la notion de personne, celle de 'moi', un plan de travail', in: *Journal of the Royal Anthropological Institute*, 68, pp. 263-282, London (Huxley Memorial Lecture).

1966 'Category of the Human Mind: the Concept of Person, the Idea of a 'Self''. In: *Sociology and Psychology*, London (transl. publ. 1938).

1969 'L'âme, le nom et la personne. Intervention à la suite d'une communication de L. Lévi-Bruhl: 'L'âme primitive', in: *Oeuvres*, II, pp. 131-135, Paris. Originally published in: Bulletin de la société française de philosophie, 29 (1929), pp. 124-127.

J.J. Meyer
1953 *Sexual Life in Ancient India*, New York.

Oldenberg, H.
1886-1892 *The Gṛhyasūtras, Rules of Vedic Domestic Ceremonies*, 2. vols., I, 1886; II, 1892 (SBE. XXIX and XXX), London.

Pandey, R.B.
1949 *Hindu Saṃskāras*, Banaras.

Radhakrishnan, S.
1969 *The Principal Upaniṣads*, London.

Rau, W.
1957 *Staat und Gesellschaft im alten Indien, nach dem Brahmana-Texten dargestellt*, Wiesbaden.

Renou, L.
1966 *La Grammaire de Pāṇini. Texte Sanskrite, Traduction Francaise avec Extraits des Commentaires*, Paris (2 vols.).

Senart, É.
1930 *Chāndogya-Upanisad, Traduite et Annotée*, Paris.

1934 *Bṛhad-Āraṇyaka-Upaniṣad, Traduite et Annotée*. Paris.

Velze, J.A. van
1938 *Names of Persons in early Sanskrit Literature*, Utrecht (Thesis Utrecht 1937/1938).
Weber, A.
1862 *Die vedische Nachrichten von den Naxatra*, Berlin (Abh. der Berl. Ak. der Wiss.).
Weber, M.
1930 *The Protestant Ethic and the Spirit of Capitalism* (transl. by T. Parsons), London (Germ. ed. 1905).
Winternitz, M.
1920 *Die Frau in den indischen Religionen, I, Die Frau im Brahmanismus*, Leipzig.

Abbreviations

AiĀ	Aitareya-Āraṇyaka
AiB.	Aitareya-brāhmaṇa
ĀpGS.	Āpastamba-gṛhyasūtra
Āśv.GS.	Āśvalāyana-gṛhyasūtra
BaudhGS.	Baudhāyana-gṛhyasūtra
BaudhGŚS.	Baudhāyana-gṛhyaśeṣasūtra
BĀU.	Bṛhadāraṇyaka-upaniṣad
ChU.	Chāndogya-upaniṣad
DrāhŚS.	Drāhyāyana-śrautasūtra
GarP.	Garuḍa Purāṇa
GautDhS.	Gautama-dharmasūtra
GobhGS.	Gobhila-gṛhyasūtra
HirGS.	Hiraṇyakeśi-gṛhyasūtra
JaiGS.	Jaiminīya-gṛhyasūtra
JUB.	Jaiminīya-upaniṣad-brāhmaṇa
KB.	Kauṣītaki-brāhmaṇa
KhGS.	Khadira-gṛhyasūtra
Manu.	Manusmṛti or Mānava-dharmaśāstra
MānGS.	Mānava-gṛhyasūtra
PB.	Pañcaviṃśa-brāhmaṇa
ParGS.	Pāraskara-gṛhyasūtra
Pāṇini	Pāṇini
ṚV.	Ṛgveda
ŚB.	Śatapatha-brāhmaṇa
ŚāṅkhGS.	Śāṅkhāyana-gṛhyasūtra
TS.	Taittirīya-saṃhitā
VaikhSmS.	Vaikhānasa-smārtasūtra
VāsDhS.	Vāsiṣṭha-dharmasūtra
Vi.	Viṣṇusmṛti

AN INDIAN IMAGE OF MAN

An Inquiry into a Change of Perspective in the Hindu World-view

Hans T. Bakker

Introduction

In his 'Einleitung in die Geschichte der Philosophie' ('lectures on the History of Philosophy') Hegel wrote:

> Dieses Hervortreten des Geistes hängt nach der geschichtlichen Seite damit zusammen, dasz die politische Freiheit aufblüht; und die politische Freiheit, die Freiheit im Staate, hat da ihren Beginn, wo das Individuum sich als Individuum fühlt, wo das Subjekt sich als solches in der Allgemeinheit weisz, oder wo das Bewusztsein der Persönlichkeit, das Bewusztsein, in sich einen unendlichen Wert zu haben, zum Vorschein kommt, - indem ich mich für mich setze und slechtin für mich gelte [...] Da fällt uns zuerst der Orient auf; [...] denn [...] der Geist geht wohl im Orient auf, aber das Verhältnis ist so, dasz das Subjekt, die Individualität *nicht Person* ist, sondern als untergehend im Objektiven bestimmt ist. Das substantielle Verhältnis ist da das Herrschende. Die Substanz ist da teils als Übersinnliches, als Gedanke, teils auch mehr materiell vorgestellt. Das Verhältnis des Individuums, des Besonderen ist dann, dasz er nur ein Negatives ist gegen das Substantielle. Das Höchste, wozu ein solches Individuum kommen kann, ist die ewige Seligkeit, welche nur ein Versinken in dieser Substanz, ein Vergehen des Bewusztseins, also Vernichting des Subjekts und somit des Unterschieds zwischen Substanz und Subjekt ist. Das höchste Verhältnis ist so die Bewusztlosigkeit. Insofern nun die Individuen diese Seligkeit nicht erlangt haben, sondern noch irdisch existieren, so sind sie aus dieser Einheit des Substantiellen und Individuellen heraus; sie sind im Verhältnis, in der Bestimmung des Geistlosen, sie sind Substanzlose und - in Beziehung auf politische Freiheit - Rechtlose. Der Wille ist hier kein substantieller, sondern ein durch Willkür und Zufälligkeit der Natur (z.B. *durch Kasten*) bestimmter, -ein Wesen der innerlichen Bewusztlosigkeit.[1]

---

[1] G.W.F. Hegel 'Einleitung in die Geschichte der Philosophie' (Vorlesungen 1825/26), 225ff. In later lectures Hegel considerably modified his views, though he stuck to his own conviction that the determinism entailed by the birth within a

Though, admittedly, long as a quotation, this passage from Hegel's 'Lectures on the History of Philosophy' presents in a nutshell a central idea in modern European understanding of man: the concept of person or individuality and how it may account for the Western ethos as being apparently fundamentally different from the Indian. And when it is objected that the view quoted is an early nineteenth century one, and worse, one of Hegel, let me draw your attention to Marcel Mauss' treatment of the history of the notion of 'the person', in which he needs only one paragraph to explain that our notion of person, though it would not seem to have been completely absent from the ancient Indian mind, "was dissolved (again) almost irrevocably": the 'self' (i.e. the ego) is according to one school of Indian thought ('Brahmanists') an "illusory thing", to another, the Buddhists, a "separable compound of *skandha*", the annihilation of which is to be sought (Mauss: 1980, 75f.).[2] What a sad world we must be prepared to arrive in when we pass through the customs at Delhi Airport!

M. Mauss' student, Louis Dumont, fully envisaged the intricacies and limitations of comparing the experience of existence ('Existenzerfahrung') in two entirely different socio-cultural contexts. At the outset of his *Homo Hierarchicus* Dumont warns the reader never to lose sight of an ambiguity in our notion of 'the individual': (1) "l'agent empirique", (2) "l'être de raison, le *sujet normatif* des institutions" (Dumont: 1966, 22). Whereas the individual in the first sense is virtually co-existent with the human race, the second seems more peculiar to our society "comme en font foi les valeurs d'égalité et de liberté, c'est une représentation idéelle et idéale que nous avons" (Dumont: 1966, 22). To designate this second category we should employ, unlike Dumont, the word 'person' and use it as an operational definition of an individual who somehow conceives, or is supposed to conceive of himself, rightly or wrongly, as an (ethical) value *sui generis*, "la mesure de toutes choses" (Dumont: 1966, 23), and end in

---

distinct caste precludes true morality (Sittlichkeit). See my 'Die indische Herausforderung' (in press).

[2] Cp. Sanderson: 1985, 190f.

itself.[3]

As Dumont has argued, the idea of an individual as 'person' is an ideal and sociologically speaking an impossible one, since hierarchy appears to be "une nécessité universelle" (Dumont: 1966, 300). It is not our intention to give an assessment of Dumont's work[4], nor to focus on the caste system and its counterpart, 'renunciation' (*saṃnyāsa*), social institutions that, despite some modifications, seem to be giving way but slowly (cp. Dumont: 1966, 289f.). In view of the overall religious setting which encompasses Indian society, we intend to give an appraisal of the traditional Hindu understanding of individual man by focusing on some religious currents that made their appearance in northern India from the 12th century onwards. From it we may gain an impression of whether Indian thought approximates and appraises our ideal of 'personhood' or develops its own categories.[5]

---

[3] By taking this definition as our point of reference we align ourselves with the concept of person as current in post-Kantian Western philosophy, a tradition that is understood in Hubbeling's concept of 'person$_c$' and 'person$_{c'}$'. On the other hand, we refer to 'man' by the term 'individual', conceiving of him as characterised by self-consciousness and/or will - that is without any implication of moral and aesthetic categories. To avoid misunderstanding, it may again be stated explicitly, that we consider these definitions 'operational', hence neither propositions concerning the 'real' nature of human beings can be derived from them, nor value judgements.

[4] For a critical evaluation see i.a. Burghart: 1983, in particular with respect to Dumont's concept of the 'renouncer', which appears sociologically and religiously to be a more complex phenomenon. Though, undeniably, the ethos of the renouncer and the householder differ in several important aspects, it would seem to me that Richard Burghart's view, developed in reaction to Dumont's simplifications, that householders and renouncers operate through "two different conceptual universes" is too much a theoretical construction (Burghart: 1983, 650). Cp. also Van der Veer: 1986, 61-67.

[5] It cannot and should not be the aim of this paper to assess the Indian image of man in terms of 'true' and 'false', or 'inferior' of 'superior' with regard to our own notions. What we do aim is to point out some significant differences between the Hindu and our own cultural traditions in respect to the conception of the world and hence of man.

To speak of Indian society and culture without unwarranted generalisations inevitably means limiting the scope of investigation to a particular milieu. Of the four main social and religious groups in north India- Muslims, Sikhs, Jainas, and Hindus - we shall chiefly be concerned with the last, though the Muslim impact cannot be ignored. Another complication lies in the fact that European influence since the 18th century has significantly altered the traditional worldview, which has led to new departures in Indian philosophy. We shall leave them aside as far as possible. Yet, we shall begin by presenting a contemporaneous instance of the 'empirical agent' in virtue of his being the 'raw material' or "matière première principale de toute sociologie" (Dumont: 1966, 22). In order to minimalizc distortion caused by modern influences it is taken from a traditional, orthodox, and conservative Hindu milieu.

The 'Raw Material'

On one of my tours around the holy places of Ayodhyā accompanied by my aged host, a learned and devout brahmin who is held in high esteem by the local priesthood and monks, the city magistrates, and the populace alike, I spoke to him:

> Pandit ji! One of the essential differences between us Europeans and you Indians is, it seems to me, that, suppose that we would believe that we were to be reborn on earth, we would be happy and rejoice at this good prospect, whereas you take quite the opposite stance, considering it a punishment from which one has to liberate oneself as soon as possible by subduing one's individuality or *karma*.

My guide fully disagreed with the view. He, convinced that he will come back on this earth, explained to me that the idea of being born again as a human being was attractive to him just as to me, since it would enable him to live in and experience the proximity and love of god.

For the ordinary Hindu of today god is experienced through his presence in certain landscapes, the temple and the heart. To this I may add what everyone knows who has visited Hindu temples, viz. that the atmosphere there is usually one of great joy and exuberance, which strengthens the individual and makes it worthwhile to be present in the flesh and in the company of fellow devotees. There can be little doubt that many a Hindu experiences a great measure of liberty and solidarity, though perhaps not equality, in the daily routine of his religion. To understand this ethos in its genesis we should consider the religious currents that informed it.

The Sufis

The extent to which Islam and the spread of Sufism influenced the patterns of religiosity in northern India is a matter of much debate and appears to be difficult of define. That this influence has been considerable, especially on the level of popular religion, cannot be denied but is too easily underestimated due to one-sided attention to the higher written expressions of Indian culture.[6] Although the notion of 'direct influence' itself is opaque and mostly not explicitly defined we would subscribe to the view expressed by Charlotte Vaudeville who notes:

> Even when the influence of Islam does not appear to have been direct, it certainly acted as a catalyst, helping to release and bring to the fore deep undercurrents which were already present in the lower strata of Indian society, as they reflected the culture of the masses and their own religious aspirations (Vaudeville: 1974, 118. Cp. Schimmel: 1980, 38).

We are even inclined to go one step further and maintain that the impact of Islam/Sufism, whether 'directly' or not, has been one of the main factors in effecting a significant change in the image of man in north India.

The central notion of Sufism, viz. that of *fanā'* or 'passing away' (i.e. evanescence of all awareness of an empirical ego and hence of that ego itself) as propounded by Abū Yazīd of Bisṭām (better known as Bāyazīd), although not entirely unknown to earlier Sufis[7], may or may not have

---

[6] Gonda: 1960-1963, II, 102: "Der direkte Einflusz des Islam auf den Hinduismus ist - von den nachher zu erwähnenden Erscheinungen abgesehen - sehr gering gewesen, jedenfalls beträchtlich geringer als die Veränderungen, die er selbst erfuhr."

[7] The Koran commentary ascribed to Djaᶜfar al-Sādik (d. AD 765) describes the phenomenon of *fanā'* with reference to the passage of Moses in the burning bush. 'Next to [God] is no room for Moses' (Gramlich: 1965-1981 II, 330). Cp. Crollius: 1978,

not have been developed in the middle of the ninth century under the influence of Indian thought which had reached Bāyazīd via his teacher Abū ᶜAlī al-Sindī (Zaehner: 1960, 93ff. Cp. Gramlich: 1965-1981 II, 317), yet when it was imported into India again by the Sufi holy men of the 13th and 14th centuries it bore the mark of Islamic monotheism. Mystic enrapture (*sukr*) of the kind that led Bāyazīd to exclaim: "Glory be to me, how great my glory!" or "I sloughed off my self as a snake sloughs off its skin: then I looked into my essence (or self) and lo! I was He!", or al-Husayn b. Manṣūr al-Ḥallādj's renowned heresy "*ana 'l-ḥaḳḳ*" ('I am the Truth (or God)'), though by no means completely alien to Sufism, appears, nevertheless, to have been an exception rather than the rule; it should, probably, not be interpreted in terms of complete identity of god and human soul[8]. If, at all, a comparison with Indian mystic illumination is apposite, the Sufi experience should be compared with theistic shools within Hinduism rather than with monistic ones such as that of e.g., Śankara (cp. Crollius: 1978, 89f.).

The theory of *fanā'* was supplemented by the characteristic concept of *baḳā'* or 'continuance in god'. Admittedly, all individual features of the human soul are believed to be lost in the process of *fanā'*, but the soul as such, as unconditioned receptacle in which and through which god reveals his own true nature remains essentially different from the divinity itself. In other words, it would be better to think of an inward transformation of the human individual when he enters into a supra-natural mode of subsistence which, however, is not fully detached from the ordinary conditioned (empirical) state, since the mystic falls back to it whenever his ecstasy ends (often thought necessary in order to fulfil the injunctions of the Koran). Hence there is no question of merger or total

---

28f.

[8] Nicholson: 1963, 152ff.; Rizvi: 1978 I, 58; Gramlich: 1965-1981 II, 321. "Aber es bleibt immer ein Letztes und Höchstes, für das man immer noch dableibt, dem man sich nicht entziehen kann, weil es niemals tiefer steht als der Entwerdende. Mag man auch für sonst nichts mehr da sein, für Gott ist man immer noch da. Ein radikales Zunichtewerden, das einem selbst vor Gott zu einem puren Nichts werden lässt - ein *fanā'u ᶜani llāh*, ist für den Sufi undenkbar" (cp. o.c. 324ff.).

absorption in god or the absolute once and for all[9], and theoretically it remains even possible that the mystic would be damned on the Day of Resurrection. In this respect Islamic/Sufi eschatology differs fundamentally from the classical Hindu concept of *mokṣa* which designates an irreversible permanent state. Accordingly, for the Muslim the individual retains a value per se, as a means by which god steers the created world and a medium through which he sees or loves himself.

The relationship of soul and god is mostly expressed in terms of love (*ᶜishḳ*) - renunciation of the empirical ego (*nafs*), and turning towards god is conceived of as an act of love - and the human being appears as a vital element in the divine plan when Sufis answer the question as to the meaning of creation by referring to the words: "I was a hidden treasure and I desired to be known; therefore I created the creation in order that I might be known" (Nicholson: 1963, 80 (Ḥadīth ḳudsī)). It is necessary to distinguish explicitly the spirit expressed in this Tradition from the idea underlying the conception of the world as illusion (*māyā*) or play (*līlā*) of god as taught by Śankara or Rāmānuja respectively. Though in neither conception the individual is an end in itself, the Muslim's view attaches a greater significance to the individual human being by accrediting him with a certain measure of responsibility for the course of history, which is conceived of as linear, heading towards a last judgment[10], thus opposing

---

9 Cp. the doctrine of Abu 'l-Ḳāsim al-Djunayd of Baghdad summarized by Zaehner: 1960, 152: "The relationship between God and the *rūh*, or higher soul, is an eternal one in which God is *mustaulī*, 'absolutely predominant' and *musta'thir* - he appropriates each elected soul to himself in a manner that is peculiar and individual to each and every soul so elected. In mystical experience this relationship will be revealed to the soul in a flash of intuition in which it not only realizes that it has its being outside time, but that it has forever a unique relationship with God. When the vision passes the soul suffers bitter anguish...".

10 Cp. Böwering: 1980, 165f. describing the tradition of Sahl At-Tustarī: "Tustarī's range of mystical ideas depicts man as being driven in his inner dynamics to his ultimate destiny, described by the events of the Day of Resurrection. This post-existential Day, beyond the phenomenal existence of man in the world of creation, introduces man to his final and lasting state in the eternal presence of the Transcendent, and opens up for him the life of paradise, gratified by the bliss of

the predominantly anti-historical Hindu view which conceives of time as a cyclic process which conforms to an immutable law and tends to render all idiosyncratic effort as futile and transient. It is evident that the Muslim world-view fosters a more dynamic attitude towards the environment (Entwistle: 1985, 6, 10).

The doctrine of divine love (*ᶜishḳ*), on the other hand, referring to an emotional experience that enables the mystic to approach god personally, with or without his help (and this question has divided the Viśiṣṭādvaita of Rāmānuja into two schools), though generally believed to be of Christian origin (Nicholson: 1963, 10f.), is one of the central ideas of Sufism that concurs so much with the Hindu conception of (emotional) *bhakti* that it may account partly for the successful accomodation of Sufism in India.

Notwithstanding that it shared, besides some ritualistic practices that we shall note below, asceticism, mysticism, and several religious ideas with theistic currents in medieval Hinduism, the entry of Islam in India, even when mediated by its main vehicle, i.e. Sufi holy men, meant the introduction of another system of belief, that is to say another image of man, which was *sui generis* in spite of the fact that it had imbibed many elements from neighbouring religions. Its specificity finds expression in the relationship that is thought to exist between man and god, and it may be best illustrated by the way the figure of the prophet as the perfect man, the archetype, came to be considered in Sufism.

In discussing the theological differences between the figure of Christ and of Muhammad with regard to the concept of personality, Nicholson observed:

> Allah is the Creator; and though the metaphor of 'creation', which implies His transcendence, is often exchanged for 'emanation', which implies His immanence, yet all beings, including Mohammed himself are on one side of their nature His creatures, His slaves, absolutely inferior to Him. And Allah in His essence is One. In His essence there can be no interplay of personality. The Islamic conception of plurality in the Divine Unity signifies not the relation of persons

---

theophanic encounter [...] The theophany, as the perpetual self-manifestation of the divine Reality, thus transfigures man through its irradiation, transforms him through its illumination, and brings his life of ultimate destiny and final glory to fulfilment". Cp. o.c. 264f.

> within that Unity, but the relations existing between the Unity and the manifold aspects in which it reveals itself. All these aspects are reflected in the Perfect Man, who may therefore be considered as the personified Idea in and through whom the Divine nature makes itself known. While the Christian doctrine expresses 'the realisation of human personality as characterised by and consummated in the indwelling reality of the Spirit of Christ, which is God', in Mohammedan theology the main stress falls on Revelation (Nicholson: 1964, 95).

We may add that in Hindu theology as reflected in Sanskrit literature up to the time of the introduction of Islam in India the main emphasis fell on merging into god.[11]

The expansion of Sufism in India was largely due to the order of the Čishtīs. Although there had been earlier contacts, the actual history of Sufism in South Asia started with the arrival of Khwādja Muʿīn al-Dīn Čishtī (d. 1236) in Lahore (AD 1161) and the subsequent foundation of his *khānḳāh* (monastery) in Ajmer (1194). The *khānḳāhs* became the centres through which Sufism diffused. It was probably the most organised form of religion extant in northern India in the 13th century and as such may have had an impact on the evolution of monasticism within rival Hindu sects (see below p. 258). The Čishtī order obtained its expansive character as a result of the policy of Shaykh Niẓām al-Dīn Awliyā (d. 1325), the third in (spiritual) descent of Muʿīn al-Dīn, whose *khānḳāh* was in Delhi and who ordained that the apprentices (*murīds*) of a *shaykh*, or head of the *khānḳāh*, as soon as they were given the status of *khalīfa* (spiritual successor), had to move together with their own disciples to another city, generally their native place, in order to found a new centre (Mujeeb:

---

[11] This may be illustrated by examples taken from two texts the *Bhagavadgītā* (14.27; 6.20-27; 12.9-10; 11.54; 6.31) and the *Agastyasaṃhitā* (23.46; 20.24; 20.29-32; 5.38-39; 19.23-24). Both teach primarily the doctrine of devotion to a personal god (Kṛṣṇa/Rāma), yet acknowledge two methods (*yoga*) of reaching him: worship of a god who loves his devotees for whose sake he has descended to earth, and meditation on the absolute divinity. Though both texts declare that the method of devotional service and activity (*bhakti*) is to be preferred in the present circumstances, the ultimate state attained by both methods is more or less the same, viz. union, that is submersion into the divine. The *Bhagavadgītā* stands at the beginning of devotional Hinduism, the *Agastyasaṃhitā* concludes, as it were, the pre-Muslim era of north India.

1967, 138; Schimmel: 1980, 26f; cp. EI II, 51).

As a matter of course the Sufi orders did not meet with the same impediments from the government as their Hindu counterparts, but the individualistic attitude of the Sufis on the one hand, and their continuous suspiciousness in the eyes of the ᶜ*ulamā'* on the other, largely prevented the majority of them from engaging in politics. Up to the time of Muḥammad b. Tughluḳ, the middle of the 14th century, they remained generally aloof from political power and often criticised officials or even the sultan (Mujeeb: 1967, 139ff.; cp. EI II, 51), whereas the egalitarianism of Islam made the Sufi movement the first one to defy the caste system, on principle.

In order that the Sufi *shaykh* could sustain his authority, against the ᶜ*ulamā'* on the one hand and the people on the other, the possession of *karāma*, supernatural power, became essential (Mujeeb: 1967, 118). It appears that by the second half of the fourteenth century Sufism was firmly established. By that time succession to the *shaykh* was becoming hereditary and the *khānḳāh* evolved into an institution of vested interests (Mujeeb: 1967, 162). A debate with Hinduism ensued. As far as metaphysics was concerned, Indian Sufism accepted on the whole the doctrine of the immanence of god, or 'unity of phenomena' (*waḥdat al-shuhūd* (Mujeeb: 1967, 289; McGregor: 1984, 23; Schimmel: 1980, 23, 41f.). The austerity tended to slacken and the status of the *shaykh* was increasingly seen in terms of divine grace or favour rather than of self-discipline. The esteem in which he was held gradually began to assume enormous proportions like that of his Hindu counterpart, the *guru*. In sum, Sufism became integrated in the course of development of north Indian society and religion as a whole in which it remained a dynamic factor (Mujeeb: 1967, 290).

This is not the place to deal with the forms of popular syncretistic religion that ensued on the periphery of Islam among the lower strata of society where large groups had nominally embraced the new faith and that made for instance the cult of saints (*pīr/shaykh*) and tombs ubiquitous (see Crooke: 1926 I, 201ff.; Ahmad: 1964, 155ff.; Herklots: 1975, passim). There are two Sufi practices of great consequence that deserve to be noted: *dhikr* and *samā*ᶜ

Among the traditional orders that were established in India the Čishtī order was the only one that accepted *samā*ᶜ ('audition'), i.e. listening to song and music, as a legitimate (not contrary to the *sharīᶜa*) means to pursue spiritual aims. Music seems to have been able to bridge the gap between Hindus and Muslims more than anything else, and its acceptance by the Čishtīs greatly contributed to their success.[12] Early Indian Sufi literature (14th century) provides ample evidence of the ecstasies evoked by Hindi songs and refrains, and the tradition mentioned by Vaudeville that Shaykh Niẓām al-Dīn "is supposed to have said that God himself had spoken to him in the *purbī* ('Eastern', i.e. Avadhī?) language!" is to be seen in this light (Vaudeville: 1974, 90; cp. McGregor: 1984, 26f.; Lawrence: 1978, 31f.; Mujeeb: 1967, 167f.). The prestige attached to *samāᶜ* was no Indian innovation but goes back to the early days of Sufism as it was often seen as homologous with *fanā'* itself (Nicholson: 1963, 59ff.).

Of all the observances the Sufis brought with them into India none found such fertile soil as *dhikr* ('recollection'), which involves the practice of repeating the name of god or some religious formula like e.g., *lā ilāha illā 'llāh* ('there is no god but Allah'). Like the concept of *ᶜishḳ*, the practice of *dhikr* is generally thought to derive from Christian origins (Nicholson: 1963, 10; EI II, 223f.), but in Sufism it became the main means of concentrating. Communion with god (or interiorization of god) evolves from uninterrupted (mechanical) repetition of the syllables that constitute his Name, which is gradually spiritualized.[13] The practice resembles the one known in Hinduism as *nāmajapa* or *nāmakīrtana*. It can hardly be a coincidence that the cult of the Name, as *inter alios* promulgated by the Sants (see below), was so fervently adopted in that part of India and in that very period that witnessed the introduction and establishment of Sufism.

From all that has been said it ensues that the greatest impact was

---

12 Mujeeb: 1967, 167: "By the time of Shaikh Gēsū-darāz (d. 1422) Indian music had been studied and Hindi devotional songs had come to occupy a very significant position in the *samāᶜ*" (cp. McGregor: 1984, 23f.; Schimmel: 1980, 14, 24).

13 Gramlich: 1976 II, 379: "Der Ḏikr kann eine rein äusserliche und mechanische Repetition eines Namens Gottes sein. In dieser Form ist er kein mystisches Phänomen. Aber er ist seinem Wesen nach dazu angelegt, in mystische Sphären überzugreifen". For a description of this process see. o.c. 378ff.

felt on the popular level. Sufism largely contributed to the (religious) emancipation of the lower strata of society and it was there that it found its most competent rivals. Already the first Sufis to settle in India are reported to have been forced to measure their *karāma* against the *siddhi* (occult power) of the Yogis.[14] Both parties frequently claim to have won over the champions of the other to their own creed (cp. Vaudeville: 1974, 94).

The appearance of 'Warrior Sufies ', on the other hand, may shed a more grim light on their relationship with the Yogis (Eaton: 1978, 19ff.; cp. Farquhar: 1925, 440f.). It does not seem improbable that the Sufi *fakīrs* imparted a stiff dose of Islamic self-assertiveness and militantism to their Hindu counterparts.

The Yogis

The frequent mention of Yogis in medieval Indian texts refers to a rather ill-defined group of practitioners of *yoga* which may range from itinerant charlatans, conjurers, and wonder-workers of all sorts to sincere ascetics who through rigorous self-discipline endeavoured to transcend the human condition, to attain a state of complete autonomy by defying the laws of nature. In many cases they would not have belonged to any particular school or organisation, and attempts to unite the various and often legendary traditions of individual adepts into one framework, like that of the 84 *siddhas* or of the 9 *nāths*, were certainly made in retrospect. The yogis of the 13th and 14th centuries were the heirs of a rich and long tradition of uncompromising experiments with human physiological and psychological processes. Physiological exploration of the human body had led to a system of discipline that is usually designated as Haṭhayoga. In addition to the current that sought complete control over mind and body by means of self-restraint, there had evolved a school of alchemy (*rasāyana*) which developed proto-chemical theories with respect to the effect of chemical compounds (in particular of

---

[14] Shaykh Safī al-Dīn of Uch (Bahawalpur dstr. Pakistan) (middle of the 11th century) is said to have defeated a Yogi in a super-natural contest (Rizvi: 1978 I, 111f.) and similar stories are told of later Sufi *shaykhs* as for instance Khwādja Muʿīn al-Dīn (Rizvi op. cit. 117; cp. Vaudeville: 1974, 94) and many others (Mujeeb: 1967, 165).

mercury, *rasa*) on the human body. Its aim was to immunize the body, to prevent its decay and to facilitate yogic techniques.

In the centuries under discussion a group of wandering Yogis appeared on the scene who cultivated the 'sciences' of Haṭhayoga and Rasāyana, and considered themselves to be the descendants of the semi-mythological preceptors Macchendranāth and Gorakhnāth. These so-called Nāth Yogis or Gorakhnāthīs stood outside the pale of orthodoxy and must have enjoyed great popularity. Nothing is known about the earliest form of their organisation, but the oldest centres or monasteries (*maṭhas*) may date from the 14th century (Briggs: 1938, 86; Unbescheid: 1980, 197). They were not the first sect within Śaivism to be organized into monastic orders (cp. the Dasnāmī (Sarkar: 1958) and Kālāmukha (Lorenzen: 1972, 103f.) orders), yet their organising may have found a stimulus in their Sufi antagonists, as has been suggested above.[15]

Reason why attention is paid to the Nāth Yogis in the present context is that they represent an influential and significant popular phenomenon that contributed largely to the image of the perfect man in the eyes of the common people. The Nāth Yogis embody the belief that the individual human being, irrespective of caste, can attain perfection in this body, here and now. As inheritors of the alchemic tradition the Yogis tend to identify the supra-natural or 'divine body' (*divyadeha*), which is attained in the highest state of perfection (i.e. when identity with Śiva is realised), and the natural body that is transmuted to perfection by *yoga* (*siddhadeha*). In this connexion they subscribe to the position expressed in the alchemic text *Rasārṇava* (1.8-9):

---

[15] The abbots (*mahant*) of the Gorakhnāth monasteries, for instance, are frequently called *pīrs* (Briggs: 1938, 8; Vaudeville: 1974, 95). Ghurye: 1953, 157 makes some interesting remarks: "First, the most important centres of the Nāthapanthīs are situated in predominantly Muslim localities [...] Second, the partiality of the Nāthapanthīs for the goddess Hingalaj on the Makran Coast (see Bakker-Entwistle: 1983, 73-85) must have brought them in close contact with Muslim population. Third, we know it from history that the Nāthapanthīs had repeated trouble with the Muslims. The temple of Gorakhnātha at Gorakhpur is known to have been destroyed by the Muslims twice or thrice, the Nāthapanthīs having rebuilt it every time. The daily course of life that is lived at Nāthapanthī centres, typically in the past, approximates the life of the Muslim Pir".

> Release during life-time (*jīvanmukti*), i.e. realisation of one's identity with Śiva, is attained by him whose body is no longer subject to decay and death, O Great Goddess. Even for gods this is a precious thing (*durlabha*). But release (*mokṣa*) that is accompanied by the break-up of the body, that kind of release is useless, for, O Goddess, even a donkey is liberated when his body falls apart.

Accordingly, the Nāth Yogis claim, by means of iatro-chemical methods and yogic techniques, i.e. through a course of bodily perfection (*kāyasādhanā*), to be able to rejuvenate the body, to make it immutable, and consequently to postpone death *ad libitum*. If he wishes, the Yogi may, at a certain point, decide to dematerialize his body and to assume a divine body. The divine body (*divyadeha*), which can be obtained within the material frame, although it is considered to be nothing else than Śiva's own nature (*śivatādātmya*), is, paradoxically, accredited with some individuality of the empirical Yogi.[16] Thus the (divine) bodies of the great preceptors, as e.g., Gorakhnāth, are believed to be eternally present in order to assist the yoga aspirants in their pursuit, which, again, recalls the notion of the Boddhisattva and may testify to a Buddhistic background (notably the Sahajiyā school of Vajrayāna) of the Nāth cult (cp. Das Gupta: 1969, 220, 253; McGregor: 1984, 21). Unlike the Buddhist, however, the Yogis believe in the immortality of the body (*kāyasiddhi*) and, consequently, are concerned with physiological and psycho-chemical processes rather than with the psychological intricacies of meditation (Das Gupta: 1969, 247f.).

The Yogi adepts consider themselves, and are considered, as individuals who have succeeded in transmuting their bodies, and thus to have won over time and death. They have gained perfect control over their nervous system, including the autonomic nervous system, and by so doing have attained the status of perfect man as well as of 'perfect

---

[16] The paradox between the retained individuality in the state of *jīvanmukti* and the simultaneous realisation of Śiva-hood may be and is explained away by postulating a second ultimate state of release (*parāmukti*). This state is described as *sahaja*, i.e. 'natural', in which the all-encompassing form of the Yogi manifests itself. See Das Gupta: 1969, 169, 220f.

instructor' (*sadguru*); in other words, they are conceived of as true gods on earth. The sturdy and austere character of the Yogis accounts for the many (occult) powers ascribed to them. Like their modern congeners, the adepts of body-culture, they inspired awe and veneration in the general public, and often would not have desisted from using their bodily prowess to lend force to their cause. The Nāth Yogis were the first Hindu sect that took to arms[17], possibly in imitation of their Sufi brethren.

The Sants

The cultural forces, exemplified by Yogis and Sufis, which manifested themselves in northern India during the 13th and following centuries, the tendency to reassess the position of the individual in the socio-religious context and to make a stand against orthodoxy in favour of the religious sentiments of the masses, the spirit that fostered egalitarianism in defiance of the caste system - this crucial shift in the Indian cultural pattern reached its acme in the movement of the Sants. The Sants, i.e. saints, are the pivot of cultural developments in northern India during the period under consideration (the 14th to 16th centuries). For the first time the lower classes, cotton-printers, weavers, cobblers, barbers, and butchers raised their voices, and soon the country resounded with their devotional vernacular poetry, which rapidly attained to an astonishingly sophisticated level. We may conceive of the Sant movement as the first successful reaction of the indigenous genius against the foreign domination to which it had become exposed.

As a matter of fact, the Sant movement was deeply influenced by Islamic attitudes. Its uncompromising monotheism and devotion towards one transcendent god, its rejection of idol worship, and its refusal to attach much significance to caste distinctions are not conceivable without the incitement of Islam. These concessions went so far that the Sants can hardly be considered as pertaining to Hinduism in the traditional sense. In

---

[17] Lorenzen: 1978, 68. There is a spurious verse in the *Kabīr Bījak* in which a Yogi carrying arms is criticised (ibid. 61). The earliest hard testimony to Yogis behaving as warrior ascetics seems to be the armed clash between Yogis and Nāgas of the Dasnāmī order that was witnessed by the emperor Akbar (1567) (ibid. 68f.).

fact its exponents were individualists who rejected the traditional precepts and practices of Islam and Hinduism alike and who created a cultural synthesis that stood on its own. They were zealots, hankering for god, and they harnessed their lives in order to contact him. Socially they were neither wandering ascetics nor settled monks or householders. The orthodox division of the four stages of life did not concern them. They were unorganized and exalted laymen, who renounced as much of their social and religious duties as possible in order to devote themselves to singing the Name of god. Their world-view was basically puritanical and in several respects they resembled the protestant movement of the 16th century Europe. Their enthusiasm may have inspired the masses, but the following they attracted became organized only after their death. This was the case, for instance, with Kabīr who, more than any of his contemporaries, embodies the movement of the Sants.

Kabīr, a weaver of Islamized stock (*julāhā*), active in the mid 15th century, promulgated devotion to an unqualified (*nirguṇa*) ultimate being that reveals itself graciously to the devotee through its Name. The Name of god (mostly 'Rām') is the mystical schema that connects the ineffable being with those who love him (it?). By repeating the Name of god the devotee becomes imbued with it, unites with god.[18] Though the god of the Sants can hardly be called personal, the relationship between god and soul is, paradoxically, described in terms of love (*prema-bhakti*). It may be clear how much this movement owed to Sufism. Not only the doctrine of love and grace as the medium between this and the transcendent realm, but especially the only ritual acknowledged to celebrate god, the repetition (*japa*) and singing (*bhajan*) of his Name, in solitude or in communal sessions (*saṃkīrtana*), are in harmony with Sufi conceptions.

We would be mistaken, however, if we attributed the spread of this type of devotion exclusively to Sufism. Its success is as much, or probably more, due to ideas that had already emanated within Hinduism

---

18 "Repeating 'Thou, Thou', I became Thou;
in me, no 'I' remained.
Offering myself unto Thy Name,
wherever I look, Thou art".
(Kabīr, quoted in Tulpule: 1984, 143).

itself.[19] The foundations of emotional devotionalism (*bhakti*) were laid in south India in the second half of the first millennium of our era, and northern India was on the verge of embracing this new form of religion when the course of history took a new turn with the Muslim invasions. The belief in the efficacy of sound in the process of religious emancipation is an old all-Indian phenomenon which had its theoretical basis in the 'Platonic' theory of the eternity of phonic archetypes constituting, as it were, a realm of 'phonic ideas' which underlies the phenomenal reality (*śabdabrahman*). This conception was common property of Yogis, Sants, and Bhaktas alike. I have shown elsewhere (Bakker: 1986 I, 72, 78) that this doctrine of sound was reformulated in a devotional framework in north India during the 12th century and that the repetition (*japa*) of god's Name (Rāma) was already recognized as a means of release a century before the Sants declared it to be the only one.[20]

The rise of the cult of the Name appears to be characteristic of religious developments in northern India where, initially, Muslim authority had prevented the growing stream of devotionalism from taking shape in the sensuous 'materiality' of idol worship and temple cult. Here as contrasted with southern India, the resources of popular religiosity, explored by the emanicipating forces at work, were primarily led into individualistic and non-visual aesthetic channels. Gatherings where the ordinary devotee could participate in recitation and singing the praise of god, where he could indulge himself in music and songs in his mother tongue, and where the gap between god and votary was bridged not only by the enrapture provoked by these performances but also by the proximity of god-men who were not separated by hieratic distance - these experiences were new departures which would inform Hinduism in the

---

[19] Cp. Ahmad: 1964, 142: "Thus, most of the ideas underlying all varieties of the Bhakti movement such as religion of love, monotheism, revolt against the formalism of orthodoxy and the basic principles of egalitarianism are of Hindu origin. They were brought into relief by Muslim example, stimulus, and challenge".

[20] This theoretical background explains the schematic function attributed to the Name of god by the Sants. The Name is a sort of cosmic force that can be appropriated by the devotee rather than a sign that conveys god's personality. It embodies the quintessence of his being, but this quintessence is devoid of personality (*nirguṇa*).

following centuries and would put the Name of god on the tongue of the masses (cp. Vaudeville: 1974, 54).

All authors who have dealt with the Sants, and especially Vaudeville (1974, 120), have pointed out how much this movement was indebted to the Yogis. Although Vaudeville exaggerates the Yogis' contribution, since much that she ascribes to Nāth influences may actually be attributed to the common stock of esoteric mumbo-jumbo developed in Vaiṣṇava Saṃhitās, Śaiva Āgamas, and Śākta Tantras, the important point to note is that the Sants shared with the Yogis this anti-brahmanical individualistic self-asserting ethos. Unquestionably, the verses of the Sant poets generally contain a stronger moral and social emphasis than those of the Yogis, yet also in the teachings of the former one would look in vain for a philosophy that establishes the ethical value of the individual per se. Kabīr's god, despite being conceived of as the 'perfect instructor' (*sadguru*), a concept borrowed from the Yogis, is no person and hence no ethical substance. The greatness of Kabīr lies in his waywardness, in his courage to break with conventional codes, in the superb manner in which he interprets the deepest religious sentiments of the ordinary people. As the greatest of the Sant poets, the personality of Kabīr epitomizes the self-esteem of the lower castes whose exalted voice he was.

The Bhaktas

However, there was a more down to earth, pedestrian strand in this outburst of devotion. It seems, a priori, very unlikely that the majority of devotees, who since time immemorial had approached god through an idol, i.e. who had worshipped his visual manifestations (*saguṇa*), would give up the habits under the influence of such ecstatics like Kabīr. The Sant owed his popularity to his charisma, to the fact that he was recognized as the embodiment of perfect man, but this does not imply that his followers shared his view of the absolute. Moreover, it could well be that many of the Sants themselves were in reality more closely affiliated to Vaiṣṇava *bhakti* as the doctrine of *nirguṇa* would suggest. There seems to be sufficient evidence for the view expressed by me earlier (Bakker: 1986 I, 123) that, from their inception, the Sant movement and the cult of the Name were in constant touch with Vaiṣṇava religion from which they partly derived and into which sections of them would eventually be reabsorbed. This view receives support from Friedhelm Hardy's observations which led him to infer: "that a simplistic usage of terms like *nirguṇa*, *sant*, *advaita* etc. creates lines of demarcation which, by using a different type of conceptual framework, reveal themselves as artificial" (Hardy: 1983b, 149).

The soil on which an emotional type of *bhakti* directed either to Kṛṣṇa or to Rāma could grow was prepared before the Muslim conquest. The germs of devotion towards Rāma were still couched in an intellectual and ritualistic framework peculiar to the Pāñcarātra tradition, but remarkable concessions to popular demand were already made. The *Agastyasaṃhitā* (12th century), for instance, acknowledged the singing of god's Name, Rāma, and the 'remembering' (*smaraṇa*) of his exploits as suitable methods, open to everyone, for realizing god (Bakker: 1986 I, 67ff.). Somehow the strongly pedantic and hieratic 'higher' Hinduism of the North interacted with the more personalistic emotional forms of Viṣṇuism of the South, but exactly how this process operated remains largely unsolved. The growth of the *bhakti* movement during the 13th to 15th centuries is eclipsed by that of the Sants.

This is not the place to dwell at length on the early forms of Vaiṣṇava *bhakti* that evolved in south India. A most significant contribution to its understanding was recently made by Friedhelm Hardy (Hardy: 1983a). From it we learn that the earliest Vaiṣṇava mystics, the Āḻvārs, started from anthropocentric premises. A positive world-view rooted in the self-awareness of the individual as a psychosomatic being combined with aesthetic sensibility. From it arose the aestheticizing attitude towards the natural environment which was employed 'to visualize and savour' human emotions (Hardy: 1983a, 444). Mystic experiences were expressed by means of symbols derived from sensuous experiences and sexual imagery was used to express and evoke intensity of emotions. The awareness of the limitations of the human condition turned god into a distant beloved, which made feelings of separation (*viraha*) the emotional cornerstone of this type of *bhakti*. The relationship between god and Bhakta was basically an interpersonal one. But though god as another, as 'you', is fundamentally different from the ego, he, being as Kṛṣṇa the personification of beauty and love, allows a meeting halfway through his incarnations "in a variety of concrete forms available to the I's senses and emotions: in the temple *vigrahas* (i.e. images), and similarly in poetry and in the heart" (Hardy: 1983a, 443).

The main vehicle in which the emotional and sensuous *bhakti* of the Āḻvārs was exported to the North was the *Bhāgavatapurāṇa* (9th century/ early 10th century). It conveyed a religious attitude that was basically anthropocentric, maintaining "the validity of the whole person (body, senses, emotions, mind)" (Hardy: 1983a, 553). Intrinsically related to this self-awareness is the conception of an absolute being that is avowedly personal, endowed with qualities such as love, grace, beauty, and compassion. In later centuries poems deriving themes and inspiration from the *Bhāgavatapurāṇa* began to circulate in northern India. It would seem that in particular Bengal, where a Vaiṣṇava-sahajiyā cult[21] developed by integrating elements of Kṛṣṇa-bhakti and 'Tantric' *sādhanā* (the latter we already encountered while discussing the Nāth Yogis), played an important role in the transmission of the spirit of southern devotion into the northern realm.

Another, indirect, channel through which the *bhakti* movement was infused into upper India was the Viśiṣṭādvaita and kindred schools. From the 10th century onwards learned brahmins of the South, trained in Vedantic philosophy, were engaged in coming to grips with popular devotion which tended to undermine their position. By far the greatest figure that emerged from this encounter was Rāmānuja (late 11th century). Rāmānuja succeeded better than anyone before or after him in coming to terms with *bhakti* - on the one hand by transforming the abstract absolute of Advaita into a personal god endowed with (ethical) qualities who contains the world and the souls within him (*advaita*), yet remains distinct from them (*viśiṣṭa*), thus leaving scope for a personal relationship between god and man, the latter's liberation being ultimately dependent on the former's grace (*prasāda*) - on the other hand by reformulating *bhakti* in intellectual terms, thus providing it with a theological basis that made it eventually acceptable for the brahmins of the North. The order in which Rāmānuja's followers were organized, the Śrīsampradāya, seems only to have slowly penetrated into the North, but other southern Ācāryas, founders of orders (*sampradāyas*), like Nimbārka (12th century?) and Madhva (13th century) also contributed to the

---

[21] For reasons of space this interesting cult should presently be passed over. The reader is referred to Dimock: 1966, Das Gupta: 1969, S.K. De: 1961.

(organized) spread of *bhakti* all over India.[22]

In this context an idea propounded by Hardy seems to me to have a particular relevance. He points out that inherent in the *bhakti* experience of separation (*viraha*) is the urge to overcome the spatial and temporal distance from god: "a *bhakti* that defined itself by reference to space and time began to use space and time to 'materialize' itself" (Hardy: 1983b, 144). The spatial interval was crossed when the southern Bhaktas moved northwards and recovered the putative sites where Kṛṣṇa's amorous adventures had taken place according to the texts. In this way the mythical spatial realm elaborated in the *Bhāgavatapurāṇa* was reified in Vṛndāvana and its surroundings, Vraja, and one of India's most important pilgrimage centres sprang into existence.

But something more happened. As we have seen, the North with its growing individualism was well prepared to receive the subjective emotionalism of the South and so the ecstatic cult of the Name was easily harmonized with the sensuality of southern devotion as soon as the political situation had stabilized and the socio-religious atmosphere became less tense.[23] But the northern attitude of not being satisfied with halfway solutions, the unquestioned belief that the individual could ultimately transcend his limitations and unite with god - be it in his own immortalized body as aspired to by the Yogis, or in a spiritual state of total merger as aimed at by the Sants and, to some extent, by the Sufis - this disposition contrived a means of crossing the 'temporal' separation as well. The tendency of the Āḻvārs to substitute aesthetic experience for spiritual illumination was brought to its logical conclusion.

A trend to identify *bhukti* (enjoying the world of the senses) and *mukti* (release from the pangs of the human condition) could already be indicated in the *Agastyasaṃhitā* (Bakker: 1986 I, 74), and a similar thought was expressed in the *Rasārṇava* quoted above (see p. 258). The social and religious condition that had evolved in northern India in the 15th and 16th centuries was ripe for a theory which proclaimed that,

---

[22] Apart from the Vaiṣṇava orders the Śaiva Dasnāmī order seems also to have contributed to diffusion of Viṣṇu *bhakti* in the North (see Hardy: 1974; cp. De: 1961, 23ff.).

[23] Outstanding exponents of the blending are e.g. Caitanya and Tulsī Dās. Cp. Bakker: 1986 I, 124.

although Viṣṇu's *avatāra* as Kṛṣṇa in Vraja had happened a long time ago, his subtle presence in the places of dalliance (*līlā*) had not vanished at all. To experience his presence and to participate in his eternal sports only required the special eye and disposition of the Bhakta. The state of auto-suggestion pursued by the devotees allows them to perceive in the impoverished copses, pointed out to them by local pandits, the luxuriant forests in which Kṛṣṇa sported. The holy sites were no longer seen as 'souvenirs' of a far past, but as actually imbued with divine presence. The whole sacred complex of Vṛndāvana, like the city of Ayodhyā for the Rāma Bhakta (Bakker: 1986 I, 139ff.), turned by the end of the 16th century into a 'mega-avatāra' of the realm of myth. Sacred sites became conceived of as true replicas of paradise and god's eternal *līlās* as being enacted simultaneously on two planes, unmanifest (*aprakaṭa*), i.e. in heaven, and manifest (*prakaṭa*), i.e. cognizable in the phenomenal world. The Bhakta needed only to cultivate this hyper-sensitivity, this faculty to envisage, through the profane, the underlying divine aesthetic quality in order to realize communion with god.

In order to explain this possibility of transcendental rapture, poetic aesthetical theory was reformulated in a theological context of *bhakti-rasa* (De: 1961, 166ff.). God himself and his divine retinue are the containers of sublime emotions (*rasa*) that are pursued by the Bhaktas. The soteriological effect of the earthly holy places is due to their underlying divine beauty which, when perceived by the eye of the Bhakta, evokes in him the very emotions that identify him with the archetypal divine actors. In his phantasy the devotee plays the role of one of god's intimates.

In this way someting of a revolution was accomplished in the Indian world-view as represented in more literate forms of so-called higher Hinduism. Instead of seeking release from this world the Bhakta plunges into it. Instead of hoping to reach heaven and not to be born again the Bhakta intensifies his earthly experience and hopes to prolong it in a subsequent life. The ideal Bhakta transcends the limitations of the human condition which are invigorated by the laws and rules of caste and society. Hence the *bhakti* movement contributed largely to the ideal that emerged in the first half of the second millennium according to which each individual, irrespective of caste, could attain to and participate in the divine, not in a nebulous hereafter, but here and now. At the same time it led the masses safely back into the fold of Hinduism. In this respect the *bhakti* wave that rolled through northern India in the 16th and 17th centuries may be seen as a successful restoration. But the background from which this movement emanated, the religious compound of Sufis, Yogis, Sants, and popular religion had effected a lasting change of perspective. *Mokṣa*, release, became something that should preferably be experienced in this world. As we have seen this new ethos was anticipated by the Āḻvārs (cp. Hardy: 1983a, 484, 430, 448ff.) and in several Sanskrit texts datable before the Muslim period, but its full growth only took place in 16th century north India. It is here, where the vernacular tended to fuse with the Great Sanskrit Tradition, that in an outburst of devotional poetry lyrics such as the following could be produced:

> What shall I do, once I have arrived in Vaikuṇṭha (Paradise),
> where there is no banyan where Kṛṣṇa plays the flute, no
> Yamunā river, no moutain Govardhan, [or] cow of Nanda;
> Where there are none of those bowers, creepers, and trees, and
> no gentle fragant wind blows, no cuckoo, peacock, or swan
> sings; what is the joy of living there?
> Where Kṛṣṇa does not place the flute on his lip and fill it
> with sound; no thought, word, or deed gives rise to the
> thrill and rapture of love, my friend!
> Where there is no earthly Vṛndāvana, father Nanda, [or] mother
> Yaśodā
> Govinda says: 'abandonning the Lord and the joy of Nanda's
> homestead (i.e. Braj): living there (i.e. Vaikuṇṭha) [would
> be] a misfortune![24]

---

24 A poem (Pada 574) ascribed to Govindasvāmī and datable in the 16th century. Another version of the same poem is found in Paramānanda-Sāgara (Pada 1371). Cp. the famous poem of Raskhān quoted in Entwistle: 1987, 71):

"Should I be a man, then let me, Raskhan,
mingle there with the herdsmen of Gokul.
If as a beast, then how should I live
but ever grazing among the cows of Nanda?
If a stone, then one of the very hill that he made
an umbrella for Braj against the torrents of Indra.

This brings us back to the pandit of Ayodhyā, i.e. the 'raw material'. It has become evident that the attitude towards life assumed by this devout brahmin adheres to the Hindu tradition that culminated in the 16th century. For him, as a sincere Bhakta, experiencing the proximity of god consists in cultivating the emotions that are evoked in the practice of worship and in participating in god's divine play as enacted every day in his temples and the landscape of his holy sites.

Epilogue

Let us return to our initial question with respect to the concept of 'person' in the traditional Indian context. Despite the value attached to each individual soul, to the concrete human being of flesh and blood as the ultimate medium through which the divine play (*līlā*) is enacted, we are reluctant to designate the self-perception of the ideal Bhakta in terms of 'personhood' in the Western sense as defined at the outset. In fact, north Indian *bhakti* has removed itself from the 'humanist' or anthropocentric world-view of the Āḻvārs in inverse proportion to its ambition to attain union with god. In this respect it is indifferent as to whether union is pursued by means of aesthetics or *yoga*. What makes an individual in traditional Hindu culture a 'person' is not so much his supposed intrinsic human capacity to act as a morally autonomous being within social ramifications[25], as his realisation of an inner autonomy, i.e. of his potential capacity to transcend his natural as well as social definiteness by appropriating a system of religious symbols; in other words, his acknowledgement as a person in the Hindu context rather depends on the measure in which he succeeds in manifesting himself as enacting or personifying these symbols, or to cite Witte (elsewhere in this volume), his personhood, rather than something given, is something that can be acquired by degrees.

To give an example, the Bhakta, for instance, aspires to emancipation

---

If as a bird, then let me dwell for ever
in the boughs of a kadamba on the banks of the Yamuna".

[25] For the development of ethical thought in Neo-hinduism under Western influence see especially Hacker: 1978.

by evoking an emotional state (*bhāva*) that is traditionally ascribed to one of the archetypes affiliated with god. Thus he may identify himself with the milkmaids (*gopīs*) who develop their erotic feelings for Kṛṣṇa (*mādhurya-rasa*), or , he may assimilate to Hanumat, the servant of Rāma, in order to experience god's proximity through sentiments of service and submission (*dāsya-rasa*). By integrating his religious and social life as much as possible his endeavour and zeal may be translated into social esteem and prestige.

A central category in this process is the notion of an autonomous eternal self or soul essential to each human being, which forms part of the divine and which only awaits emancipation. Partly, the degree of this emancipation is thought to be represented by caste, however, the institution of renunciation (*saṃnyāsa*) as well as the context of popular devotional religion offer alternative symbol-systems, which may lead man up the rungs of Jacob's ladder. All this amounts to what is already almost an intellectual cliché, viz. that, rather than promoting the ideal of Homo Aequalis, traditional Hindu culture fosters man as a Homo Hierarchicus.

Bibliography

Ahmad, A.

1964 *Studies in Islamic Culture in the Indian Environment,* Oxford.

Bakker, H.

1986 *Ayodhyā* Pt. I 'The History of Ayodhyā from the 7th century BC to the middle of the 18th century; its development into a sacred centre with special reference to the Ayodhyāmāhātmya and to the worship of Rāma according to the Agastyasaṃhitā'. Pt. II 'Ayodhyāmāhātmya. Introduction, Edition, and Annotation'. Pt. III 'Appendices, Concordances, Bibliography, Indexes, and Maps', Groningen Oriental Studies Vol. I, Groningen.

(in press) 'Die indische Herausforderung. Hegels Beitrag an einer europäischen kulturhistorischen Diskussion', in: *Annalen der internationalen Gesellschaft für dialektische Philosophie-Societas Hegeliana* (1989)

Bakker, H. - A.W. Entwistle (eds.)
1983 *Devī The worship of the goddess and its contribution to Indian Pilgrimage,* Groningen.

Barthwal, P.D.
1978 *Traditions of Indian Mysticism based upon Nirguna School of Hindi Poetry,* New Delhi.

Böwering, G.
1980 *The Mystical Vision of Existence in Classical Islam. The Clur'ānic Hermeneutics of the Sūfī Sahl At-Tustarī (d. 283/896),* Studien zur Sprache, Geschichte und Kultur des Islamischen Orients, Neue Folge Bd. 9, Berlin/New York.

Briggs, G.W.
1938 *Gorakhnāth and the Kānphaṭa Yogīs,* Calcutta.

Burghart, R.
1983 'Renunciation in the religious traditions of South Asia', in: *Man* (N.S.) 18, 635-653.

Crollius, A.R. SJ
1978 'Die islamische Transzendenzerfahrung im indischen Kontext. Zur Beziehung zwischen Sufismus und Bhakti'. In: *Tranzendenzerfahrung, Vollzugshorizont des Heils.* Herausgegeben von Gerhard Oberhammer, Wien, 81-96.

Crooke, W.
1926 *The Popular Religion and Folk-lore of Northern India,* 2 Vols, Oxford.

Das Gupta, S.
1969 *Obscure Religious Cults,* Calcutta (3rd ed.).

De, S.K.
1961 *Early History of the Vaisnava Faith and Movement in Bengal from Sanskrit and Bengali sources,* Calcutta (2nd ed.).

Dumont, L.
1966 *Homo Hierarchicus. Essai sur le système des castes,* Paris.

Eaton, R.M.
1978 *Sufis of Bijapur 1300-1700. Social Roles of Sufis in Medieval India,* Princeton.

EI
The Encyclopaedia of Islam. New Edition, 5 Vols. & Suppl., Leiden.

Entwistle, A.W.

1985 'An Introduction to Indian Historiography', in: *Groniek* 92, 4-15.

1987 *Braj. Centre of Krishna Pilgrimage,* Groningen Oriental Studies, Vol. III, Groningen.

Farquhar, J.N.

1925 'The Fighting Ascetics of India', in: *Bull. of the John Rylands Library, Vol. 9,* Manchester, 431-452.

Ghurye, G.S.

1953 *Indian Sadhus,* Bombay.

Gonda, J.

1960-1963 *Die Religionen Indiens.* 2 Vols. Die Religionen der Menschheit Band 11, 12, Stuttgart.

Govindasvāmī

Sāhityik viśleṣan vārtā aur pada-saṃgraha. Edit. by Brajabhūṣaṇa Śarmā and Kaṇṭhamaṇi Śāstrī and Gokulānanda Tailaṅga, Kankroli VS 2008.

Gramlich, R.

1965-1981 *Die schiitischen Derwischorden Persiens.* Erster Teil: 'Die Affiliationen'. Zweiter Teil: 'Glaube und Lehre'. Dritter Teil: 'Brauchtum und Riten'. Wiesbaden 1965, 1976, 1981. 3 Vols. Abh. für die Kunde des Morgenlandes Bde. XXXVI, 1, XXXVI, 2-4, XLV, 2.

Hacker, P.

1978 'Schopenhauer und die Ethik des Hinduismus'. In: Paul Hacker *Kleine Schriften.* Herausgegeben von Lambert Schmithausen, Wiesbaden, 531-564.

Hardy, F.

1974 'Mādhavêndra Purī: a link between Bengal Vaiṣṇavism and South Indian bhakti', in: *JRAS,* 23-41.

1983a *Viraha-Bhakti. The early history of Kṛṣṇa devotion in South India,* Delhi etc.

1983b '*Viraha* in relation to concrete space and time'. In: *Bhakti in current research, 1979-1982.* Edit. by Monika Thiel-Horstmann, Berlin, 143-155.

Hegel, G.W.F.

System und Geschichte der Philosophie. Vollständig neu nach den Quellen herausgegeben von Johannes Hoffmeister,

Leipzig 1940, Hegels sämtliche Werke band XVa 'Vorlesungen über die Geschichte der Philosophie. Einleitung' (= Der philosophischen Bibliothek Band 166).

Herklots, G.A. (Tr.)
1921 *Ja^c far Sharīf 'Islam in India or Qānūn-i-Islām'*. Transl. by G.A. Herklots, Edit. by W. Crooke, Oxford.

Lawrence, B.B.
1978 *Notes from a Distant Flute. The Extant Literature of pre-Mughal Indian Sufism*, Tehran.

Lorenzen, D.N.
1972 *The Kāpālikas and Kālāmukhas. Two lost Śaivite sects*, New Delhi.
1978 'Warrior Ascetics in Indian History', in: *JAOS* 98, 61-75.

Mauss, M.
1980 *Sociology and Psychology*. Essays translated by Ben Brewster, London.

McGregor, R.S.
1984 *Hindi Literature from its Beginnings to the Nineteenth Century. A History of Indian Literature* Vol. VIII Fasc. 6, Wiesbaden.

Mujeeb, M.
1967 *The Indian Muslims*, London.

Nicholson, R.A.
1963 *The Mystics of Islam*, London (first publ. 1914).
1964 *The Idea of Personality in Sufism. Three lectures delivered in the University of London*, Lahore (repr.).

Paramānanda-Sāgara
Paramānanda-Sāgara. Edit. by Prabhūṣaṇa Śarmā, Kaṇṭhamaṇi Śāstri, and Gokulānanda Tailaṅg, Kankroli VS 2016.

Rasārṇava
Rasārṇavamor Rasatantram. A semi dialogue between Parvati & Paramesvara. Edit. with 'Rasachandrika' Hindi Commentary by Indradeo Tripathi, Varanasi 1978.

Rizvi, S.A.
1978 *A History of Sufism in India*, 2 Vols., New Delhi.

Sanderson, A.
1985 'Purity and power among the Brahmans of Kashmir'. In: *The Category of the person. Anthropology, philosophy, history.* Edit. by M. Carrithers, S. Collins, and S. Lukes, Cambridge, 190-216.

Sarkar, J.
1958 *A History of Dasnami Naga Sanyasis,* Allahabad.

Schimmel, A.
1980 *Islam in the Indian Subcontinent.* Handbuch der Orientalistik, zweite Abt. 'Indien' 4.Bd. 3. Abschnitt, Leiden-Köln.

Schoonenberg, P. SJ
1978 'Gott als Person und Gott als das unpersönlich göttliche. Bhakti und Jñāna'. In: *Tranzendenzerfahrung. Vollzugshorizont des Heils.* Herausgegeben von Gerhard Oberhammer, Wien, 207-234.

Tulpule, S.G.
1984 *Mysticism in Medieval India,* Wiesbaden.

Unbescheid, G.
1980 *Kānphaṭā Untersuchungen zu Kult, Mythologie und Geschichte Śivaitischer Tantriker in Nepal,* Wiesbaden.

Vaudeville, Ch.
1974 *Kabīr,* Vol. I, Oxford.

Veer, P. van der
1986 *Gods on Earth. The management of religious meaning and identity in a North Indian pilgrimage centre,* Utrecht (diss.).

Zaehner, R.C.
1960 *Hindu and Muslim Mysticism. Jordan Lectures in Comparative Religion V,* London.

HOPI HERMENEUTICS

Ritual Person Among the Hopi Indians of Arizona

Armin W. Geertz

Our approach to the topic of religion and person diverges significantly from that of our colleagues in the psychology and sociology of religion. Whereas their challenge is the establishment of cross-cultural validity, the challenge for the historian of religions is to move from valid statements about a religion to valid statements about religious persons. And if we wish to retain our own disciplinary profile, we must do this without recourse to Rorschach, the sentence completion technique, Picture Frustration Study, or questionnaires.

Let us briefly reflect upon a few of the problems at hand by examining George Herbert Mead's theory of the self. Being a behaviorist, Mead was of the opinion that this characteristic of the self as 'being an object to itself' comes into being through the mechanism of behavior and not because of an 'alleged possession of a soul or mind with which he, as an individual, has been mysteriously and supernaturally endowed' (Mead: 1934, 137 note 1). This basically materialistic explanation does not mesh with Hopi psychology, which postulates significantly more than Mead's social core. The Hopi individual has for example *hikwsi*, 'breath', understood as 'spirit', *soona*, 'vitality', and *unangwa*, 'heart', understood as being the seat of the emotions and of ethical behavior.

This does not necessarily disprove Mead's theory. The problem lies in the fact that Mead's theory of the self is an expression of his philosophy of humanity, a philosophy which by its very nature is universal in scope. But its applicability in an absolute universal sense is reduced when confronted with evidence which by its very nature stems from another and 'alien' universal philosophy of humanity. We cannot, as impartial students of religion, decide from the outset that our particular philosophy and its resultant postulates applies in all cases. Nor does the fact that we are interested in cross-cultural problems, and therefore prefer to conceive of ourselves as having a trans-cultural status, make our postulates different in principle than Hopi postulates or our results more adequate.

A fruitful endeavor might be to analyze the two philosophies as two models in comparison.

However, in this paper I am interested in the assumptions of the Hopis through an analysis of a Hopi social event. In other words, instead of applying Mead's model to the situation, I choose to interpret the situation on the basis of the *a priori* assumptions of the Hopis. This solution is admittedly not without its problems. As a matter of fact, Mead's theory demonstrates the dimensions of the problems at hand, for our texts go no further than the *image* of the self among the Hopis, both for the individual and for the group at large. The use of the 'generalized other' in Mead's sense is evident in our examples, and therefore advises caution in the complete rejection of Western analytical models. And although I feel hampered by the problem, it is by no means unique and is probably irreconcilable in the long run. But once again, I wish to emphasize that I do not consider the problem so much in terms of theory as opposed to fact, as in terms of theory as opposed to theory.

The anthropologist or ethnographer, on the other hand, is generally, and I might add *per se*, interested in reproducing the institutions and general organizational principles of a given society. The individual appears in an anthropological analysis only insofar as that individual illustrates the workings of identifiable organizational principles. The anthropologist by necessity has to start with the individual in his actual field work, but the goal of his interest in the individual is to move on to a comprehensive understanding of the whole society in question. This is of course a generalization, but it illustrates the state of the art in Hopi studies. The analysis needed at this point in Hopi studies would be to move from the comprehensive viewpoint back to the individual viewpoint, even to a point *behind* the facade of the ideal individual to the private or 'internalized' individual. Another way of putting it is that we are studying the functional role of religion at the individual level: we wish to understand the religious person by studying his religion and we wish to understand his religion by studying the religious person.

What can a historian of religions contribute to a field firmly anchored in the expertise of the social anthropologists and a topic firmly anchored in the rules and terminology of social psychologists? There can be no doubt that these are matters central to historians of religions as well. The first contribution which in my opinion is in line with our research tradition is text methodology, and the second is the methodological explication and exploration of the religious dimensions of humankind.

Concerning the first contribution: just as the study of scriptural religions is beginning to find new inspiration in field studies, so too is the study of non-scriptural religions beginning to find renewed inspiration in text studies. The history of religions, which is traditionally text orientated has something to teach as well as to learn from social anthropology and ethnology. One thing we must learn here is that if we lack the proper textual data, then we must go out and get them - with all due use of proper field techniques, of course. Another thing that we must learn is that the study of native peoples has moved beyond the Frazerian age - a fact which many historians of religions seem to be unaware of.

Concerning the second contribution: it is the traditional interest in *religion* and the epistemology upon which that interest builds that characterize our science. Our interest is in the religious individual, conceived and perceived. But this 'contribution', as I choose to call it, leads to a host of problems which are in part created by scholastic and national boundaries. The hermeneutics of the Eliade school would not have the same epistemological difficulties with the topic of identity or person as a European positivistic-historistic school would have. In Denmark, the history of religions received its greatest impetus during the decades of the 1920's to the 1940's from Wilhelm Gronbech, a scholar who combined the use of texts with an interpretation of religious man in various epochs and places. The ideal, in my opinion, is to pursue such a combination of the two approaches by attempting to understand religious humanity as a global phenomenon, and religious man both as an ideal as well as a historical type, on the basis of stringent historical-philological text apparati. I do not wish to advocate the hermeneutics of the Eliade school nor the strict positivism of the historical schools. I wish to elucidate through my field material *Hopi* hermeneutics as far as this is humanly possible.

The problem of definition

The psychological literature on the subject of the person is characterized by a great diversity of opinion and by an emphasis on isolated issues connected with the topic. This state of affairs is hardly conducive to a unified definition of 'person'. There seems to be a general agreement that personality integrates various traits, a type of organizing consistency of behavior which can be investigated and described. However, a more precise definition depends upon whether you choose the Stimulus-Response, the Trait and Factor, the Organismic, the Neoanalytic Personality, or the Self theories. In any case, one can expect diversity of opinion within the same theoretical framework as well.[1]

Besides the problem of the variety of definitions based upon school affiliations, there is also the very serious problem of the nature and the actual extent of psychologists' contribution to personality theory. Without anthropological training, especially field work, it is doubtful that a psychologist can make cross-culturally relevant observations.[2] In Gustav Jahoda's opinion 'there are extensive and important areas of behaviour about which academic personality theory has little if anything to say' (Jahoda: 1982, 96). In other words, we as historians of religions should not make the mistake of assuming that 'the psychologist has access to a store of universally valid generalizations relating to complex aspects of personality and behaviour' (Jahoda: 1970, 38), which are not available to us in our texts or in the field. Advances are being made, of course, but even in the much vaunted *Handbook of Cross-Cultural Psychology* attempts at defining universals is still only tentative (see Lonner: 1980). It is probably not insignificant that the chapter on 'Attitudes and Beliefs' contains not a single reference to an anthropological or a religio-historical study (Davidson and Thomson: 1980).

Given this confusion concerning basic definitions and assumptions, we have no choice in our cross-cultural study but to approach our picture of the Hopi ritual person by moving from the social situation towards assumptions about the individual. As far as I can see, this approach

---

[1] See the chapter on 'Varieties of Personality Theory' in Marx and Hillix: 1962, 367-411. P.E. Vernon mentions other theories as well in Eysenck, Arnold and Meili: 1972 and in the German edition as well (1980). For the social sciences, a similar 'growing convergence' is mentioned with a diversity of definitions in Gould and Kolb: 1964.

[2] A useful introduction to the theories and research of culture and personality can be found in Singer: 1961, and can be supplemented with later works such as Honigmann: 1975 and Jahoda: 1982.

involves at least two problems. In the first place, as previously mentioned, the very status of our text material leads us to behavioristic *a priori* assumptions, a working hypothesis which states that any individual in any given society can only know himself through his society's ideal types and evaluates himself and is evaluated by others on the basis of those types, with perhaps a mitigating code of acceptable deviance. How can the case-study evidence, by its very shortcomings, prove or disprove this hypothesis? This remains to be seen below. Perhaps an application of the epidemiology of representations espoused by Sperber would prove fruitful here (Sperber: 1985).

In the second place, it should be noted that an abstraction such as a 'Hopi ritual person' is not without problems of relevance. This abstraction corresponds with Ruth Benedict's configurational theory, a theory which coincides with the implicit historiographical assumptions of the history of religions. The theory operates with an ideal type or types of personality in a particular culture which is then applied to generalizations about that culture. It should be added that Benedict emphasized that most individuals are plastic to the moulding force of their society even though she also speaks about the interdependence between society and the individual. Later scholars cast serious doubt about the concept of ideal or model personality and its relation to cultural influence. The argument is that even though model personality characteristics exist, all individuals interact with their cultures and are not simply passive recipients. In fact, individuals seem at the outset a good deal more similar than they really are.[3] This important modification is amply confirmed by my field observations, and therefore I must emphasize that this paper assumes the paradox that the Hopi society postulates an ideal personality, more or less dogmatically, which due to its ideal nature hardly exists within the social reality, or, to put it less incontrovertibly, this postulated personality is difficult to live up to.

Thus I will exemplify problem situations in ritual contexts for individuals and then explore, on the basis of those elements which

---

[3] Kaplan: 1954, 31-32. His study of individuals from the Zuni, Navajo, Mormon, and Spanish American ethnic groups indicated that personality differences *within* each group were greater than the differences *between* the groups. However, it should be mentioned that the method of analysis slurs cultural differences.

dominate the problem situations, how Hopis as a society of individuals give expression to their collective existential situation.

The background

There are about 10,000 Hopis living in 12 pueblo villages, most of which are perched atop the southwestern mesa tips of the Colorado Plateau near the edge of the Painted Desert region of northeastern Arizona. Hopi society consists of a number of loosely organized matriclans with each their own religious traditions, sacred objects, village buildings, and clan holdings. The clan mother owns the material and non-material possessions of the clan, and her brother uses these possessions. The rights and possessions of each clan are documented in their clan traditions, and these rights are based upon knowledge and cultic power.

The modern Hopi society is governed today by an uneasy combination of independent village entities (a village chief in cooperation with a group of other important village leaders) and a tribal council. The economy is based upon agriculture, cattle and sheep raising, and wage earnings, which means that Hopi society is developing from an agriculturally based economy to a pluralistic economy with the consequent disintegrative tensions which such changes entail. The Hopi language is still dominant, but many of the young people have an imperfect knowledge of Hopi and are in general caught in an acculturative process.

Hopi religion is also undergoing change, but since the evidence points to a dynamic history of change, we must refrain from moralistic judgement and simply state that the integrative cycle of the major recurrent agricultural ceremonials is disintegrating in all but one of the villages and is being replaced more by Katsina masked dances than by any interest in Christianity. In fact, many Hopis are non-participatory believers in the Hopi religion, by-standers to their own cultural disintegration, which incidently coincides with their eschatological expectations.

Despite the changes, Hopi ethical statements have remained constant. The socialization processes still remain, although with certain modifications. The Katsina cult is one of the main socialization factors; gossip and the fear of witchcraft are two other factors.

The posture of shame: crisis and confession

Our first example involves one of the major agricultural ceremonials still being practiced at the village of Hotvela on Third Mesa.[4] It is a little known ceremonial which is held during the lunar month of March, the month marking the end of the winter, the first signs of spring, and the beginnings of the dry season. It is the month of Katsina Night Dances which follow the spring ceremonial, called Powamuya, of the preceding month. The ceremonial involved in this example is a puppet ceremonial using the Koyemsihoya ('The little Kooyemsi, or Mudhead') as its main figure. This ceremonial lasts sixteen days and emphasizes the themes of warmth, germination, human fertility, the health of children, and individual bravery.

The many days of preparation and activity culminate in a public procession of all the masked dance groups from each *kiva* (brotherhood meeting house), a communal meal, and a series of evening dances in each kiva performed by the participating groups in turn - giving a round of about 6 performances which are repeated at least once more during the evening. The main performance involves the manipulation of the puppet to the beat of the drum and the rhythm of the songs, sung by anywhere up to a dozen masked performers.

The Koyemsihoya looks as though it is standing all by itself, stepping and dancing to the music and shaking its gourd rattle. But it is actually built onto a box. There are strings inside the puppet which are tied to the feet and which are threaded through the legs to the arms. The strings are then weighted inside the box. The manipulator has simply to pull the strings attached to the system in order to make the puppet move.

One last detail before we move on to our example: these dolls are

---

[4] The Hopi texts quoted in this paper represent the majority dialect of Third Mesa where I carried out my research. I use the orthography developed by Ekkehart Malotki, Northern Arizona University, Flagstaff. The texts were taped, translated roughly in the field, and then subjected to the process of transcription and analytical translation by Michael Lomatuway'ma and myself. Concerning the ceremonial cycle see A.W. Geertz: 1987a, 1-15 and Hartmann: 1978, 80-90. Concerning the Hopi calendar see Malotki: 1983, 451-480. Concerning the puppet ceremonials see A.W. Geertz: 1982 and 1987b.

considered to be animate superhumans, and dangerous in the ritual context. In non-ritual contexts, they are treated as members of the family capable of revealing themselves as living Hopis. Having such animacy, it is imperative that the manipulator maintains a proper attitude towards the doll.

We must leave this fascinating topic and describe the setting of our conflict situation. The text before us was directly elicited in 1982 after the topic was uncovered in an open-ended interview during 1979. I had originally hoped to record the story from the main actor, who is named TÖ here. He was reluctant to tell the story, and asked me to get it from his wife. This was not possible, so I asked one of the other performers to tell the story. It is very important to note that the narrator is none other than one of TÖ's uncles: a mother's brother, the traditional Hopi administrator of sibling justice and moral up-bringing. The narrator is a man of high ritual standing in the community, one of the last initiates of the highly esoteric Kwaakwant Brotherhood in Hotvela.

The situation

TÖ's group had brought the puppet in at the proper time under the proper circumstances and proceeded to repair and repaint the doll. Everthing was checked and rechecked, and the group practiced their piece until the doll 'performed well'. The narrator concluded that 'there was nothing at all that could bring us bad luck. There was nothing at all that could go wrong'.

But during the first performance, which is always held in the home kiva, the puppet began malfunctioning during the second set of songs. It did not move its arms correctly and consequently did not dance correctly. Everyone saw it and was troubled by it.

After the performance was over, the group retired to a secluded room and examined the puppet. It was discovered that the weight had become untied from the string and had fallen into the bottom of the box. During repairs, pointed remarks about TÖ's *intentions* were brought up, which caused TÖ to break down and cry while he was working on the doll.

Then the oldest of his mother's brothers approached him and said:

> You are performing this dance with aggressiveness. You want to be foremost. You are dancing while thinking like that, with these intentions, with your

> vanity, and that is why this thing is being stubborn with you. So you must confess to us: what are you doing, why is this thing doing as it is doing?

And TÖ answered:

> Yes, I thought that if it were me doing it, then it would perform very well. This is how I thought. I did not intend to do it that way, it was only after we had reached the dance day that I acted like that. It is true, I (am doing it) with vanity. I will tell the truth... I admit it.' His uncle then replied: 'Now, do not be like that, you must pray to it! Pray to it again. It will certainly hear you. Because it is alive just like us.

The narrator then continued by relating the moral of the story:

> For sure, whenever one performs something with vanity and with aggressiveness, it becomes completed in a most unfortunate way. It is very difficult performing things because one is performing for life... A thing becomes right only through humbleness. When one humbles oneself to something, one completes an endeavor beautifully... He made us all very unhappy that time, but being forced to really humble himself to it, nothing else happened when he again went back to perform it, and he finished the ceremonial (the original text and translation in A.W. Geertz: 1987b, 171-174, 347-349).

Analysis

This example illustrates a number of Hopi *tutavo*, 'instructions, traditions', in practice and effect.[5] TÖ, being the most important ritual person, is unquestionably named as being the cause of the trouble. There is a serious breach of ethics here, and there is no question of blaming the uncles who were involved in preparing the doll for ritual use. A sponsor is expected to act in a certain way, and TÖ evidently did not do this. The Hopi ritual person is expected to be the ideal person, embodying all of what being Hopi means. Preparing for ritual activity is in fact a lifetime preparation involving formal initiations as well as the assimilation and practice of Hopi ethical behavior. The fact that we discover the

---

5 Voegelin and Voegelin: 1960, 53. They translate the term 'didactic ethics'.

model person within the ritual context is important for sociology and is one of Durkheim's central points. I have documented this relationship elsewhere and will therefore not repeat it here (A.W. Geertz: 1986).

But what exactly is TÖ accused of? He is accused of improper thinking (*wuuwankya*) and improper intentions (*tunatya*), aggressiveness (*a'ni unangwa*), wanting to be foremost (*pasniqey*), and vanity (*kwiivi*). The aggressiveness and vanity are reflected in TÖ's thinking and intentions, two processes which are of immense importance to the mechanics of Hopi ceremonials. The participants of the ceremonial, and especially the sponsor, must nurture a state of mind which maintains a holistic image of reality and which focusses on particular aspects of that image, be it rain, fertility, health, and so on. In fact the Hopi term for sponsor is *tunatyay'taqa*, 'he who has an intention'.

As our text notes, performing dances are difficult because their whole aim is to secure life, understood here as the reality of the holistic image mentioned above. But whereas the reward may be the good of all people, the danger lies in self-promotion. This means that the Hopi ritual institution gives the opportunity to test and reconfirm the strength of the model person. At the same time it acknowledges the paradox of good behavior resulting in social gain, and provides an ethical trap for those who fail.

Our text illustrates that another difficulty with performing ceremonials lies in the fact that the success of a performance is measured by the behavior of the participants, especially the sponsor. This means that if something goes wrong everyone goes about finding fault, and unless the sponsor has a good excuse, he becomes the butt of endless criticism not only during the ceremonial but for a long time afterwards. This is something that all Hopis expect: when one sponsors a ceremonial, one is exposed to public criticism. I call this type of gossip 'narrated ethics'.

Turning now to aggressiveness, wanting to be foremost, and vanity, these three traits are intrinsically related according to Hopi thought, as Voegelin and Voegelin discovered in their linguistic analysis of random utterances of persons-in-the-culture and of chain-reaction utterances. The *tutavo* in question is stated in the following manner: 'One does not have a mean personality and reciprocally people do not feel hostility toward one' (Voegelin and Voegelin: 1960, 73-74). This *tutavo* involves all of the characteristics of a model personality, one who behaves circumspectly, is other-oriented, and avoids 'the kind of cultural imbalance which inevitably brings angry criticism to *mean* persons' (ibidem, 57). In other words we are in the ethical area of what it means to be Hopi. *Hopi* means 'well behaved, well mannered'. Its opposite is *qahopi*, 'not-Hopi, ill-behaved, bold'. The very name of these people invokes the ideal personality, and every member of this society judges himself and all others on the basis of this ideal personality. For example: *hopi'iwta*, 'he's well behaved, well adjusted'; *hopivahana*, 'honest white man'; *pam pahaana qahopiqay put u'uyi*, 'that white man who is improper (not-hopi) stole it'; *qahop'unangway'ta*, 'he deliberately wants to be naughty, improper (has a non-hopi heart)'; *pam qahopintiqay put ep hamanti*, 'that one who acted improperly (not-hopi behavior) became ashamed of it'.

There are of course specific terms for a whole variety of negative traits, but space allows only mention of the cluster of traits exhibited by TÖ. These are *tota'tsi*, 'bossy, domineering person'; *tsomo*, 'braggart'; *pam taaqa nu'an tsomo hiita kwivilalvayngwu*, 'that man is a blow-hard, he's always bragging about something'; *mongwiwuwanta*, 'he thinks of himself as if he were chief'.[6]

Hopis cannot stand bossy people filled with self-importance. I have seen their expressions of disgust in many field situations. On the other hand, we might rightly ask whether TÖ's intentions were so bad. And if so, exactly how bad were they? TÖ was proud of what he was doing. The anticipation was tangible. He even claims that his intentions were proper up until the last day. Being a sponsor carries with it the responsibilities of a chief, in fact a sponsor actually functions as the village chief during his tenure as sponsor. Why therefore did TÖ feel the need to affirm himself and why did his group feel the need to constrain him?

At this point our text tells us nothing more, only field data can help. I first became acquainted with TÖ in 1978. His wife became my assistant by providing a first rough translation of my tapes. I lived in the house of a member of TÖ's family and later in a trailer on his clan lands. TÖ and I attended dances at the other villages, I served as assistant for his dance groups, and even made a few pilgrimages with him. TÖ is a talented young man in his late thirties, a silversmith of repute. His wife is a very talented medicinewoman from the most prestigious clan in Hopi

---

6 These examples are drawn from Voegelin and Voegelin: 1957 and 1960, with adjusted orthography.

society. They are well-to-do, have all the modern conveniences, a happy and healthy family which finds itself comfortable in Anglo as well as Hopi society. In short, TÖ is an obvious target for envy and jealousy. Indeed, TÖ's wife spends a lot of energy warding off attacks by sorcerers and witches.

But there are two more facts about TÖ which are significant: 1) he is not initiated into any of the brotherhoods which perform the Wuwtsim Ceremonial and is therefore not a Hopi with full status. Even though no one in TÖ's age group on Third Mesa is initiated because of political factors, the narrator of the story is. 2) TÖ is a member of the Piikyas Clan, and even though it was an important clan in Orayvi, there is a stigma attached to that clan in connection with events in the primordial past. TÖ therefore does not measure up to Hopi standards despite all of his talent and success. He is not a full Hopi in the traditional sense of the term and therefore he must be doubly humble in order to be *hopi*.

How serious then is his transgression? Its seriousness is evidenced by the text. Our text constitutes an eye-witness description of a formal confession: interrogation by the mother's brother, confession, absolution, and penitence. The permanent paradox, noted by Hepworth and Turner between 'the ideal of confession and the practical obligation to confess' applies here (Hepworth and Turner: 1982, 78). It is clear that TÖ has the desire to confess, but it is equally clear that the 'institution of confession and the culture of guilt' have produced the need to confess.[7] TÖ has himself (if we can depend on our narrator) labeled his transgression by using the verb *nakwha*, 'he admitted it'. Hopis have three forms of confession, and *nakwha* is the term used when confessing to a crime. Chances are, then, that his transgression was perceived of as being a crime.

The crime was rectified through confession to his human ritual partners and through prayer to his superhuman ritual partner. His crime was therefore twofold: a socio-ethical transgression on the one hand and a ritual transgression on the other. In both cases the crux of the problem

---

[7] Hepworth and Turner: 1982, 77. I cannot agree with Pettazzoni's evolutionistic distinction between 'savage' and Christian confession which overemphasizes the 'magical character' of the confession of sins among native peoples (see Pettazzoni: 1954). As this example indicates, ethics is the primus motor in Hopi confession.

was TÖ's inability to live up to the model personality. The social mechanism of control is transacted through a posture of shame.

The posture of guilt: mask and punishment

One could multiply such examples of conflict in ritual (as well as non-ritual) contexts, but they would only serve as variations on the same theme. I wish to briefly present the next example because it involves a conflict with the ideal personality in a situation where the judging peers are absent and the transgressor pronounces judgement on himself. The narrator ST, is the very same person who accused TÖ of his transgressions in our previous example. ST is a man dedicated to the Hopi way, but he is also a man caught in a web of personal conflict. He is originally from Hotvela but has spent his mature life pursuing a career in forestry in the Flagstaff area. One of his major sources of concern is his family: his wife has political views which are the opposite of his own, and his son is married to a Navajo girl - the Navajos being the traditional enemies of the Hopis. Thus he is often at his mother's home in Hotvela in order to avoid the conflict at his own home. And unless he is participating in a dance or ceremonial, he goes off on drinking bouts. Although he was 55 at the time, he is not an initiate of any of the Wuwtsim brotherhoods and, as with TÖ, he is also a member of the Piikyas Clan. On the other hand, he is very active religiously and is frequently asked to help others paint their paraphernalia and to compose new songs for them. His father was the oldest living member of the Kwaakwant and his mother was a one-time leader of the Maraw Sisterhood. When people criticize him, it is not for boasting or ambition, but for his non-Hopi excessive drinking.

During 1978 ST told me during an open-ended interview that during a Navan (Velvet Shirt) Katsina Dance one time, he wasn't paying proper ritual attention. He did not practice well, nor did he make serious plans about his participation. On the day of the dance, the katsina dancers were about to climb up the ladder through the roof, which provided the exit from their kiva, when ST put on his mask.
He related the following:

> As we were about to go, I put my mask on. But it suddenly cut my breath short! It felt like someone had tied my throat. No, it felt like somebody had

> wrapped my head in something, that is how I felt. I had not even reached the ladder yet. We were still at the bottom getting ready to climb up to the (entrance) ledge.
>
> I tried to pull it off, but I could not at first. Then it finally came loose and I got my mask off real fast. I waited until I was ready to step on the cornmeal path. Then I prayed to my mask, 'Please don't do this to me! Please don't!' I prayed for his forgiveness. For him not to bother me so that I could enjoy myself. I wanted to perform the dance well. This is what I thought to myself, what I thought to my mask, as I put it back on.
>
> It started doing it again, but it was now my turn to go up, so I did not dare take a breath until I reached the top of the kiva. When I came out, everything was bathed in a bright light! And then I realized that there was nothing choking me. I could breath easily! Then I wondered how I was going to make it through this day - my friend had punished me for neglecting him.

Needless to say, ST danced all day without getting tired and he sang loudly without losing his voice. He finished the narration with the moral:

> And my grandfathers used to tell me, even though the mask is made of leather, it will become a spirit, so you can pray to it. It is a spirit even though it does not look like much. It is nothing but leather, but the spirit takes over. They (the katsinas) are the ones that help you along your life path. If you really believe in it, it will help you throughout your life.[8]

Again the problem was that ST had the wrong intentions (*tunatya*) and he was disrespectful to the ritual preparations and to his mask. The result was the same as with TÖ: the superhuman ritual partner refused to cooperate. The penitence was the same: humble prayer. But the mechanism of social control in this case was the conscience of the sinner alone. The posture of guilt in this example is equivalent to the notion of self-monitoring which Shweder reintroduced from Tylor and Freud (Shweder: 1980, 62). The constraints of tradition were effectuated through a superhuman agent, but the interpretation of the event was based upon ST's understanding of the model personality and its relationship to superhuman beings. The problem was remedied by ST conjuring up in his

---

8 From my unpublished tape material.

mind, during his prayer, all of the proper attitudes and traits of the correct ritual person.

Shame, guilt, and eschatology: Nuutungk Talöngvaqa

The foregoing examples derive from extraordinary situations which reveal normal people confronted with their own impulses and personalities in conflict with the ideal personality type. Other examples could have been included: the startling phases of the socialization of Hopi children, the more positive mechanisms of social control with built-in correctives such as consultation with persons of authority and the formal ritual pipe-smoking, or the highly negative mechanisms of witchcraft and all that it entails. In each case it could be shown that the basic cause of an illness, a mishap, a drought, or an ineffective ceremony is a Hopi person who either willfully or by omission fails to embody those ethical traits which fall within the compass of *hopi* behavior. This is a tremendous burden for any individual to bear, and it is no wonder that many Hopis break down and exhibit a variety of abnormal actions. One could even say that our first example illustrates a limited breakdown within a strictly controlled context. In any case, all Hopis are held accountable for a variety of extrahuman conditions, not the least of which being the weather, in greater or lesser degree depending on the individual's standing in society. This means that conditions are right for considerable criticism, conflict, and anxiety, the only safe recourse being to behave in a *hopi* manner. When everyone starts behaving in a non-*hopi* manner then the end of the world is nigh, according to Hopi belief. This is exactly the key element in Hopi ideas about Nuutungk Talöngvaqa, 'The Last Day'.

Hopi eschatology is an integral part of the Hopi conception of the cyclical world eras and especially of the myth of the emergence of humanity from the womb of the earth (see A.W. Geertz: 1984). Their emergence was actually an escape from the confusion and evil of the prior world, a situation which the Hopis constantly compare to their present situation, and this they have done, as far as our ethnographic material can tell us, for at least the last 100 years. They were received during primordial times after their emergence by their tutelary deity, Maasaw, who gave them their lands on lease with the admonition that they must live in the *hopi* way despite the new values of the long-awaited White Brother. Maasaw warned them further that when they have realized all of their worldly ambitions to the fullest, then he will return to cleanse and punish them and to usher in the destruction of the present world, which will lead to a subsequent world renewal.

Thus the present state of affairs of the Hopi Nation and of the world at large are interpreted by the Hopis as signs of the immanent Last Day. There are diverging viewpoints as to how one should live in the face of disintegration, and these viewpoints are a partial cause of the ever-present political strife between the Progressive and the Traditionalist factions. Most Hopis are convinced that their present discontent is the prelude to Maasaw's return and that the social and political turmoil is a sign that the Hopis as a people have failed to live up to their ideals. The old men were and are so convinced of the truth of their expectations that they have intentionally withheld their ritual secrets, taking them with them to their graves in order to speed up the disintegration of Hopi religion, and thereby Hopi life, so that destruction will lead more quickly to renewal. The Hopis are living in a type of preludian state, a purgatory on earth, and have probably been in that state ever since the arrival of the Spanish conquistadores.

As one of my middle-aged informants put it:

> If they did not carry on in such a manner, maybe things would become right again. That we may again renew and reveal the aims of our fathers, but I suppose that we can no longer do it that way. So it is in vain that they keep attempting to do what is right and sponsoring dances. They display to others things that will put them to the fore. Our goals are all broken down, and this is true of everyone. And there is no possibility of this becoming right anymore (the original text and translation in A.W. Geertz: 1987b, 142, 361).

The post-Nuutungk Talöngvaqa era is briefly characterized in the following manner: 'From then on, we will live again as we should. There will be no illness. We will sustain ourselves without any hardship. Nobody will hold anything against anyone, no animosity against anyone' (the original text and translation in A.W. Geertz: 1987b, 139). In other words, the whole world must collapse before the Hopis can practice their central ethical statement, restated in the last sentence of the above quote. Once again it is individual behavior which destroys and rectifies: the reflection of the model personality in a nutshell.

There are a number of formal ritual songs which reveal these eschatological ideas. These songs may very well be the main vehicle of eschatological tradition. They at least contribute to the institutionalization of the Hopis' collective crisis. A number of the songs are fittingly sung during the esoteric Wuwtsim Ceremonial, a ceremonial which is intimately linked with the Emergence Myth and its accompanying eschatological statements. But the two examples chosen here from my tape material are sung within other ceremonial contexts.

The first song is sung by the Maswik Katsinas during the Nevenwehekiw Ceremony (the gathering of the greens in May). These katsinas have the function of bringing Maasaw himself to the new Wuwtsim initiates and their girl friends. Even though the themes are fertility and bountiful crops, the Nevenwehekiw functions as a last ritual of the initiations which began in November (see Titiev: 1944, 139-141). I will quote the first verse:

> Aaw yahaa'aa, aaw yahaa'aa
> My father went to fetch the hard prayerfeather,
> My father went to fetch the hard prayerfeather.
> To the west, to Köqva, to Hopor'ovi, you went to fetch those who possess the knowledge of the Hopi way of life.
> It appears that your way of life is going to disappear,
> Because there is forever nothing but arguing going on.
> I wonder whose intentions will stand up here at the south, at Tunöstutukwi?
> Various things are always being asked at this place
> that will backfire on you.
> Therefore, the wanton girl at Aatutuskya is meting out her demoralized way of life to this place.
> Why do you people enjoy this kind of life?
> So the Masawkatsinas, those who are to make you see the light, have picked up their whips and have descended to here.
> Tomorrow you have no choice but to go about crying with your children, my fathers,
> Iyaya'aa'a'hay aahaa'aa'a'ay'ay yaa'aa'a'a'aa'aa'aa'a ayan uma'a.
> This is how you make your children tired of Hopi life.
> Because of them you will have to go around weeping,
> Haayaa haayaa, hiyay aaw yahay'aa.
> People, you have no alternative but to put this way of life away forever.
> You wanted to get rid of the Hopi way of life.

As a result, you poor things, you move towards summers that are always uncertain,
Haayaa haayaa, hiyay aaw yahay'aa
Haayaa haayaa, hiyay aaw yahay'aa.

Aaw yahaa'aa, aaw yahaa'aa
Wiktama huruvaho ina'a
Wiktama huruvaho ina'a
Ayo' teevenge köqvami hopor'omi hopiqatsit tuwiy'taqamuy
wiktama uma'a
Pay sumataq umuuqatsi lewtiniqw'ö
Oovi sutsepsa yep lavaynangwungwutiwa
Maataq haqawatuy tunatya'am taatö tunöstuutukwiy hongvaniwniqat'a
I' hapi yantaqa umumi yep ahoyniwtiniqa sutsepsa pew lavaymaqaptsitiwa
Oovi aatutuskyave honaqmana honaqqatsiy tuuhuylawu pewi
Eenoq uma kwangwuu'ey unangwa sinomö
Oovi ummuu'unangway taalawnaniqa wukotupqave masawkatsinam
wuvaapiy ömaatotat oomi pew yayvaqw'ö
Nawus uma qaavo yep umuutimuy amumum tsaykinumni inamu
Iyaya'aa'a'hay aahaa'aa'a'ay'ay' yaa'aa'a'a'aa'aa'a ayan uma'a
Yanhaqam uma umuutimuy hopiqatsit aw maamangu'a
Nawus amutsviy tsaykinumni yep'e
Haayaa haayaa, hiyay aaw yahay'aa
Nawus uma yantaqat sutsepsa qatsivöötotani sinomu
Pay nawus uma hopiqatsit ii'ingyalya
Oovi hintaniqat tal'angwuy awsa hoyoyotima okiwa
Haayaa haayaa, hiyay aaw yahay'aa
Haayaa haayaa, hiyay aaw yahay'aa.[9]

Without going into detail about the difficult passages of the text (several of which, by the way, could not be explicated by my informants), it is sufficiently clear that the text describes the confusion and disintegration of Hopi life and casts it into eschatological terminology. And while the new Wuwtsim initiates await with some trepidation the entrance of the Maswik Katsinas and the much feared Maasaw, their hopeless

---

9 From my unpublished tape material.

cultural situation as well as the actual cultic situation are described and interpreted eschatologically. Thus the threat of immanent destruction serves to warn the youths against the very real dangers of forsaking the Hopi way of life - a way of life which only the fully initiated truly can pursue. As the singer of our text told me afterwards:

> It had been known long ago how life was to be in the future. Therefore songs like this were made from that time... They used to say that one who had the knowledge of the Hopi way of life [meaning Maasaw] would be summoned. We are now at that stage of time.

Thus the song is considered to derive from primordial times, casting it and its contents in the paradigmatic aura of those times.

The next song was sung by the Maraw Sisterhood during the Maraw winter ceremonial in 1979. The women usually compose songs for this occasion called *tawsoma*, 'song-tie', which specifically criticize individual members of the corresponding Wuwtsim Brotherhood and other brotherhoods as circumstances allow. These songs name the men by name and describe some activity of theirs which rumor has uncovered. The songs always point out the non-*hopi* behavior of the accused in a ridiculing manner. The following song draws the additional connection between individuals, the perfect primordial past, and the troublesome future.

> Aahaahaa'aa iihiihii'ii, aahaahaa'aa iihiihii'ii
> Alright, you Tsoryamtiwa (a kiva group), you are our fathers.
> What happened to your sand altars and their cornhusk flowers?
> And where are the yellow bird boys and their chirping?
> Now listen, think about your old selves,
> Lii'ii'ii ihiilaa'aa.
> Yes, you, KY (a person), you are our father.
> What happened to your sand altars and their cornhusk flowers?
> And where are the yellow bird boys and their chirping?
> Now listen, think about your old self.
> Lii'ii'ii ihiilaa'aa.
> See, a long time ago, remember the Wuwtsim's hearts were united throughout the land with the sunflower patches and the flower covered plains?
> See, a long time ago, the Wuwtsim's hearts were united throughout the sunflower patches with the beautiful and pleasing hearts of the yellow bird boys

who go along chirping.
These things are so, you life path is obliterated, too bad!
Oo'oo'oo'oo'oo'oo hi'oo'oo'oo o'oohi'oo'oo'oo
O'oohoo'oohoo'oohoo'oohoowaa, ee'eeheelooy (the sound of weeping).

Aahaahaa'aa iihiihii'ii, aahaahaa'aa iihiihii'ii
Ta'a um'i tsoryamtiwa, uma yep itananmu
Haqami umuutuwapongyay sinkwa'ata
Piw haqami sikyats'itiyotuy töötöki'amu
Ta'a naawuwaya huvamu
Lii'ii'ii ihiilaa'aa
Ta'a um'i kyarhongiwma, uma yep itana
Haqami uumutuwapongyay sinkwa'ata
Piw haqami sikyats'itiyotuy töötöki'amu
Lii'ii'ii ihiilaa'aa
Meh ura hisat'o, wuwtsimtuy unangwvasyamuy sunsayangwutniqw tuuwapongyava aqawqölö siitalngwu ura'a
Meh ura hisat'o, wuwtsimtuy unangwvasyamuy sunsayangwutniqw aqawqölönawit sikyats'itiyot kuwan'ewunangqway töötökimangwu
I' hapi yaayantaqa umuuqatsi pöötavi tuuvoy'iwma ohii'ii'ii'ii
Oo'oo'oo'oo'oo'oo hi'oo'oo'oo o'oohi'oo'oo'oo
O'oohoo'oohoo'oohoo'oohoowaa, ee'eeheelooy.[10]

Thus, we find that the songs quoted above are specific exercises of the 'generalized other' which are meant to provoke shame and guilt through ridicule and fear. It is worthy of note that these exercises are mobilized in ritual contexts where one expects to find model personalities, and that the songs are clothed in eschatological imagery, that is, clothed in the language of collective sorrow and threat.

Individual weakness, when written large on the backdrop of cataclysmic dimensions, is the very cause of collective destruction. Abandoning the Hopi way is equivalent to knowledge lost, and this knowledge can first be regained when humankind has been cleansed by ordeal and is once again worthy to emerge on a new virgin world.

---

10 From my unpublished tape material.

Superhuman Entities   Tradition   Social Group

Ethics   Ritual

Eschatology

T h e   I n d i v i d u a l

A diagram of Hopi hermeneutics

A diagram of Hopi hermeneutics

As stated at the outset of this paper, the main goal was to make valid statements about religious persons and to combine the methodological tools at hand and produce an ethnohermeneutic. All of the examples in this paper have shown Hopi religion in action on the personal level. We have seen the dynamic tension between individuals attempting to live up to and match their personal identity with the model Hopi personality.

The accompanying diagram illustrates the mechanisms involved in this dynamic confrontation and aspires to be a statement of Hopi belief as I see it. The obverse pyramid equation suggests that the two main sources of Hopi tradition are the superhuman entities in interaction with the clan group. These two sources can of course be directly revealed to the individual and, in turn, can be affected by the individual. But the main road of influence, forming the identity and personality of the individual and continuing the on-going socialization of the individual, is a one-way thoroughfare of ethics, ritual, and eschatology.

I have concentrated on the model personality in this paper because of the fact that the model personality is identical to the ideal ritual person.

By focussing on conflict situations, I have indicated the on-going interaction between demands and urges as well as the corrective mechanisms involved. I have not delved into a description of the private individual for a number of reasons. In the first place, another set of texts would be needed. In the second place, we can never really be sure whether the 'individual' revealed in the texts is a truly private one or whether it is just another model personality, however deviant. A statement such as the following from ST creates more problems than it solves: 'Even though we are clearly the Hopi people, by doing things like that, we reveal that we are evil people. We are hiding ourselves with that name' (the original text and translation in A.W. Geertz: 1987b, 145, 310). Is this simply a tirade against bothersome neighbors, a formulation of the imperfect model personality, expectations about a foreign interviewer seeing through an informant's ethnic pride, or a revelation of the inner person? The dividing lines are not clear-cut. A truly complete analysis of Hopi hermeneutics would require the addition of an opposing, submerged pyramid in our diagram, if such a mirror balance exists.[11]

---

[11] One should not leave this topic with the impression that nothing of this type has been attempted. Dorothy Eggan's work is of particular interest here, although she did not live long enough to complete her promised psychobiography through dream analysis of one Hopi man. See Eggan: 1943, 1952, 1955, 1956, 1961, and 1966. Aberle's analysis (1951) of this same Hopi's autobiography (see Simmons: 1942) comes closest to a mapping of the internal equation. Earlier studies by Joseph, Thompson, and Dennis as well as modern studies by Schlegel have all concentrated on external matters such as the model personality and socialization. See Thompson and Joseph: 1943; Thompson: 1945 and 1950; Dennis: 1940 and 1943; and Schlegel: 1973 and 1977. Granzberg's brief attempts to draw conclusions about Hopi personalities based upon the test scores of Hopi children raises serious questions of the validity of his approach. See Granzberg: 1972, 1973a, and 1973b. Matchett's experience as a psychiatric consultant with the Indian Health Service can provide a basis for more relevant study (Matchett: 1972). None of the authors mentioned here have elicited or worked with material in the native tongue. Any attempt to map the Hopi psyche without access to the Hopi language must be doomed from the start.

Conclusion

This paper has presented a few methodological reflections concerning the role of the history of religions in the study of the concept of person and has suggested that a fruitful approach is through the application of a hermeneutics which combines indigenous statement with academic analysis.

Two main problems were identified: 1) the problem of applying a behavioristic hypothesis on texts which go no further than the image of the self among the Hopis, and 2) the problem of working with the abstraction 'Hopi ritual person'. The case material seems to have vindicated both problems through an analysis of conflict situations in ritual contexts between individuals and through an analysis of the collectivization of this conflict. It was shown that the Hopis do indeed evaluate themselves and others by comparison with the *ideal* person who, by definition, is the *ritual* person. It was also shown that the Hopis, as a people, acknowledge the unavoidable paradox of their ethics and institutionalize this paradox in several ways. All of the evidence led to a proposed model of Hopi hermeneutics which sketches the dynamics of the concept of Hopi ritual person.

Acknowledgements

This paper was read in part at the XVth Congress of the International Association for the History of Religions in Sydney, Australia, 1985. I wish to thank the Danish Council of the Humanities which has provided funds for my field trips during 1978-1979 and 1982, and which has made the subsequent processing of my field data possible. My gratitude extends to the memory of my friend and colleague Michael Lomatuway'ma, formerly at Northern Arizona Unversity, Flagstaff, who played a crucial role in my work with Hopi texts. A special thank you goes to my other Hopi assistants and informants in the field, and gratitude for helpful criticism is extended to Karl W. Luckert at Southwest Missouri University, Springfield, Hans J. Lundager Jensen and Ole Riis both at the University of Aarhus, Denmark, and the Groningen Working Group for the Study of Religious Symbols, Groningen, The Netherlands.

Bibliography

Aberle, D.F.
1951 *The Psychosocial Analysis of a Hopi Life-History,* Berkeley.

Davidson A.R. and E. Thomson
1980 'Cross-Cultural Studies of Attitudes and Beliefs'. In: Triandis and Lambert: 1980, vol. 5, 25-71.

Dennis, W.
1940 *The Hopi Child,* New York, rpr. 1972.
1943 'Animism and Related Tendencies in Hopi Children', in: *Journal of Abnormal and Social Psychology* 38, 21-36.

Eggan, D.
1943 'The General Problem of Hopi Adjustment', in: *American Anthropologist* 45, 357-373.
1952 'The Manifest Content of Dreams: A Challenge to Social Science', in: *American Anthropologist* 54, 469-485.
1955 'The Personal Use of Myth in Dreams', in: *Journal of American Folklore* 68, 445-453.
1956 'Instruction and Affect in Hopi Cultural Continuity', in: *Southwestern Journal of Anthropology* 12, 347-370.
1961 'Dream Analysis'. In: Kaplan 1961: 551-577.
1966 'Hopi Dreams in Cultural Perspective'. In: von Grunebaum and Caillois 1966: 237-265.

Eysenck, H.J., W. Arnold, and R. Meili
1972 *Encyclopedia of Psychology.* London.

Geertz, A.W.
1982 'The Sa'lakwmanawyat Sacred Puppet Ceremonial among the Hopi Indians in Arizona: A Preliminary Investigation', in: *Anthropos* 77, 163-190.
1984 'A Reed Pierced the Sky: Hopi Indian Cosmography on Third Mesa, Arizona', in: *Numen* 31, 216-241.
1986 'Typology of Hopi Indian Ritual', in: *Temenos* 22, 41-56.
1987a *Hopi Indian Altar Iconography,* Leiden.
1987b *Children of Cottonwood. Piety and Ceremonialism in Hopi Indian Puppetry,* Lincoln.

Gould, J. and W.L. Kolb
1964 *A Dictionary of Social Sciences,* London.

Granzberg, G.R.
1972 'Hopi Initiation Rites - A Case Study of the Validity of the Freudian Theory of Culture', in: *Journal of Social Psychology* 87, 189-195.
1973a 'The Psychological Integration of Culture: A Cross-Cultural Study of Hopi Type Initiation Rites', in: *The Journal of Social Psychology* 90, 3-7.
1973b 'Note on Delay of Gratification Among the Hopi', in: *The Journal of Social Psychology* 91, 151-152.

Grunebaum, G.E. von and R. Caillois, eds.
1966 *The Dream and Human Societies,* Berkeley.

Hartmann, H.
1978 *Kachina-Figuren der Hopi-Indianer,* Berlin.

Hepworth, M. and B.S. Turner
1982 *Confession. Studies in Deviance and Religion,* London.

Honigmann, J.J.
1975 'Psychological Anthropology: Trends, Accomplishments, and Future Tasks'. In: Williams 1975: 601-626.

Jahoda, G.
1970 'A Psychologist's Perspective'. In: Mayer 1970: 33-50.
1982 *Psychology and Anthropology. A Psychological Perspective,* London.

Kaplan, B.
1954 *A Study of Rorschach Responses in Four Cultures,* Cambridge.
1961(ed.) *Studying Personality Cross-Culturally,* Evanston.

Lonner, W.J.
1980 'The Search for Psychological Universals'. In: Triandis and Lambert 1980, vol. 1: 143-204.

Malotki, E.
1983 *Hopi Time. A Linguistic Analysis of the Temporal Concepts in the Hopi Language,* The Hague.

Marx, M.H. and W.A. Hillix
1962 *Systems and Theories in Psychology,* New York, 2nd ed. 1973.

Matchett, W.F.
1972 'Repeated Hallucinatory Experiences as a Part of the Mourning Process Among Hopi Indian Women', in: *Psychiatry* 35, 185-194.
Mayer, P., ed.
1970 *Socialization. The Approach from Social Anthropology.* London.
Mead, G.H.
1934 *Mind, Self, and Society. From the Standpoint of a Social Behaviorist,* Chicago 1962.
Pettazzoni, R.
1954 'Confession of Sins: An Attempted General Interpretation'. In: Pettazzoni, *Essays on the History of Religions,* Leiden.
Schlegel, A.
1973 'The Adolescent Socialization of the Hopi Girl', in: *Ethnology* 12, 449-462.
1977 'Male and Female in Hopi Thought and Action'. In: Schlegel, ed., *Sexual Stratification. A Cross-Cultural View,* New York, 245-269.
Shweder, R.A.
1980 'Rethinking Culture and Personality Theory Part III: From Genesis and Typology to Hermeneutics and Dynamics', in: *Ethos* 8, 60-94.
Simmons, L.W., ed.
1942 *Sun Chief. The Autobiography of a Hopi Indian.* New Haven.
Singer, M.
1961 'A Survey of Culture and Personality Theory and Research'. In: Kaplan 1961: 9-90.
Sperber, D.
1985 'Anthropology and Psychology: Towards an Epidemiology of Representations', in: *Man* 20, 73-89.
Thompson, L.
1945 'Logico-Aesthetic Integration in Hopi Culture', in: *American Anthropologist* 47, 540-553.
1950 *Culture in Crisis: A Study of the Hopi Indians,* New York.
Thompson, L. - A. Joseph
1943 *The Hopi Way,* Chicago.

Titiev, M.
1944 *Old Oraibi. A Study of the Hopi Indians of Third Mesa,* Cambridge.
Triandis H.C. and W.W. Lambert, eds.
1980 *Handbook of Cross-Cultural Psychology,* Boston, 6 vols.
Voegelin, C.F. and F.M. Voegelin
1957 *Hopi Domains. A Lexical Approach to the Problem of Selection,* Chicago, rpr. 1974.
1960 'Selection in Hopi Ethics, Linguistics, and Translation', in: *Anthropological Linguistics* 2, 48-78.
Williams, T.R, ed.
1975 *Psychological Anthropology,* The Hague.

EGO-AWARENESS AND THE PERSON IN THE WEST AFRICAN WORLD VIEW

Hans A. Witte

1. *Introduction*

In Western reflection on the human being the concept of the person has become a central issue. In a lengthy process outlined by Marcel Mauss, Western philosophy slowly developed a conception in which the 'person' (*personne*) becomes 'more than an organisational fact, more than a name or right to assume a role and ritual mask' (Mauss: 1985, 14). From a socially imposed and socially accepted role the notion of the person becomes 'synonymous with the true nature of the individual'; it has become 'the category of self (*moi*)'. Mauss summarizes the development as follows:

> From a simple masquerade to a mask, from a 'role' (*personnage*) to a 'person' (*personne*), to a name, to an individual; from the latter to a being possessing metaphysical and moral value; from a moral consciousness to a sacred being; from the latter to a fundamental form of thought and action - the course is accomplished (Mauss: 1985, 22; cf. Hubbeling in this volume).

In this final view the fulfilment of individual human life is a 'personal' affair and it leads to an ethical and juridical reflection on the rights and duties of the individual as a person with regard to the community and society in general. In this volume J. Oosten underlines the formal character of this notion of the person, which in a certain sense also indicates its static nature. Every human individual is a unique person from birth, whatever his or her place, role or status in the community.

Mauss (1985, 14) himself remarked that 'those (nations) who have made of the human person a complete entity, independent of all others save God, are rare' and Clifford Geertz (1983: 59) observes that this Western conception of the person is 'a rather peculiar idea within the context of the world's cultures' (cf. also Y. Kuiper in this volume).

Shweder and Bourne (1984: 168) recall that

> Geertz, Mead and Dumont contrast Bali, New Guinea, and India with a Western mode of social thought in which the 'individual' is abstracted from the social role, and the moral responsibilities of this abstracted, inviolate individual are distinguished from his/her social responsibilities and duties.

This article on the West African notion of the person starts from the assumption that every human being has an awareness of his or her individual self. Abundant evidence from non-western cultures indicates, however, that the cognitive functioning of this awareness is defined by the overall world view in which the individual lives. I hope to show that West Africans have a 'sociocentric conception of the relationship of individual to society' (cf. Shweder and Bourne: 1984, 190) and that their notion of the person cannot be described in terms of a given quality of the autonomous individual, but is seen and experienced in the perspective of the essential relation, differentiated by gender and age, of the self to society.

Our orientation towards West Africa, an enormous region running from Senegal to the Cameroons and inhabited by people living under vastly different ecological, linguistic and cultural circumstances, needs some reflection. Is it possible to speak of the West African world view and the corresponding notion of the person? Many anthropologists familiar with one West African culture or even a few would deny this. In my opinion, however, this is a matter of perspective.

In this volume we try to compare fundamental orientations as regards the notion of the person and the self and the accent is not on local detail. It is, I think, possible to outline a model of West African world view, that is not based on sweeping statements that cannot be verified. Nor should such a model represent a generalization of 'local knowledge' on which it is based, to be applied to other cultures. It tries to detect basic underlying characteristics and values common to the different West African world views and cultures. Such a model can, of course, only serve limited purposes. It facilitates comparison of basic orientations, but it cannot go beyond its abstract character. It does not provide an acceptable picture of reality for someone unfamiliar with its manifold actualizations in West African cultures.

Looking for a West African equivalent of the notion of the person, I adopt the starting-point indicated by Hubbeling in this volume, i.e., the fact that every human being is conscious of himself or herself, implying, for my purpose, consciousness of ego. Hubbeling shows that in Western thought this starting-point leads to a whole range of notions of the person, in accordance with affirmation or denial of possible implications.

The traditional West African cultures did not develop a writing system, neither does one find a caste of priests or an intellectual elite dedicated to philosophical reflection. Consequently we do not find an abstract philosophical tradition concerned with the ego-consciousness of the human individual (cf. e.g., Fortes: 1981, 284).

> In 'primitive' societies we do find 'thinkers', but the absence of writing as an instrument to analyse 'discourse' in an abstract, detached and decontextualized manner prevents the development of a tradition of critical thinking that frees itself from the immediateness of oral communication (Lemaire: 1984, 117; my translation).

The noted aversion to abstract speculation is a general characteristic of West African mentality (cf. e.g., Kenneth Little: 1970, 112-113). Under these circumstances scientific research into the concepts of the person and the self of West Africans is necessarily oriented towards the symbolic representation of man in the wider context of his world view.

In comparison with Western views we certainly find a general unity among West Africans in the ways the individual experiences him/herself. On reflection, however, we find significant differences between the different cultures in the possibilities for development of the individual self within the scope of a general model. Young men of the Tallensi, the Yoruba and the Ibo will all submit to the authority of the elders. A Tallensi knows also that, whatever his personal talents, he will fully realize his personal possibilities only if he respects the strict limitations defined by his age and his sex, which the cultural system of his people impose on the expression of the self and the person. The Yoruba has more space for personal ambitions within the framework of family and compound. Finally among the Ibo 'a forward-moving and talented young man who can acquire wealth and 'convert' it into the traditionally valued status symbols (such as title-taking) is allowed to wield power over his peers and elders' (Uchendu: 1965, 20). Apart from the differences between the West African cultures, there are, of course, within each culture different ways in which each individual experiences himself. Although the autonomous ego is far less emphasized in West African value systems than in the Western world view, we must remember Lienhardt's warning (1985, 145) that 'one can lay too much one-sided stress on the collectivist orientation of African ideas of the person'.

The preceding reflections lead to the distinction of three levels at which our question of West African awareness of the self can be directed: 1) the level of an overall model of West African cultures; 2) the level of the specific cultures and 3) the psychological experience of each individual. Insight into the last two levels implies knowledge of the first, to which this article will limit itself. The global consonance of ego-awareness of West Africans is probably less striking for themselves than for Western observers, who in their turn and because of the cultural distance that separates them from West Africa, may have many difficulties in evaluating important local differences. However much one tries to adopt 'the native's point of view', it is impossible for a Western observer to avoid an implicit or explicit comparison with Western values.

Ego-awareness with all individual differences has immediately to do with the opinions one holds about the nature of man as a physical and spiritual being, with representations and ideas about human ideals and destiny and finally with the way reality is observed and understood. All these opinions, representations, ideas and understandings, which all together express the nature of a culture, indicate the space that it allows for the ego-awareness of the individual. For this reason it is, in my opinion, necessary to sketch the structure and nature of the West African conception of cosmic and social reality and of man. In this outline a certain simplification for clarity's sake will be hard to avoid.

2. *The human being as a physical and spiritual individual*

It is important to examine the different components that together are said to make up the human being, because this vision of the self determines the auto-experience of the individual. A rewarding start to discover these components lies in the examination of creation-myths. A brief overview of West African creation-myths shows that these myths do not concentrate in the first place on explaining the origin of the human being, but on the creation of society. The Yoruba version of the creation of man is nothing but an appendix to the story of the creation of the civilized world. The divinity Obatala, who in certain versions fails as the creator of society because he becomes drunk and cannot fulfil his mission, is afterwards afforded some compensation in becoming the creator of man. He models the body of each human being and not only those of the first human couple. The priority of the creation of the civilized world over that of man already suggests that the human individual is defined much more according to his place within the relational fabric of society than according to his private individuality.

In most West African cultures it is the sky god or one of his ministers who models the human body from clay or mud (cf. Bascom: 1969, 81; Mercier: 1970, 222; etc.). The sky god animates the clay body through the gift of his vital power. In many cases the vital power is described as the breath of the sky god; for that reason this power is often seen as a part of the creator-god that is housed in each human being, as G.K. Nukunya (1981, 124) reports from the Anlo Ewe, Idowu (1962, 21) and others from the Yoruba, K.A. Busia (1970, 197) from the Ashanti and Mercier (1970, 227) from the Fon. This inherence does not indicate an intimate personal relationship between the human being and the sky god. The latter is in all cases a *deus otiosus* who hardly interferes with his creation and who receives virtually no cult. Even in those West African cultures which developed a pantheon of lesser divinities who are the object of a cult and who can be seen in a certain sense as ministers or limited manifestations of the sky god, these divinities are not interested in the weal and woe of human beings. Humans must try to use the power of divinities for their own benefit, or avoid them.

The vital power manifests itself in the human being through respiration, blood and sexuality. In some regions this power, which originates from the sky god, is also said to express itself in emotions. Elsewhere, however these are connected with the ancestors.

The human body houses not only vital power, but also an element that comes from the ancestors. The ancestors were once part of the community of the living and their very essence is still oriented towards this community. This is not the place to revive the discussion of the question in how far death forms an essential barrier between the living elders and the ancestors (cf. Kopytoff: 1971; Brain: 1973; Meyer Fortes:

1976), or of the distinction between on the one hand the dead who are still personally remembered and who manifest themselves first of all through warnings and punishment, and anonymous benevolent ancestors on the other (cf. William H. Newell: 1976). I want to stress here that there is a continuous interaction across death between the living and the ancestors and that without this interaction the community and its members could not exist.

Ancestors are much more important in the religious world view of West Africans than gods or divinities (cf. e.g., M. Fortes: 1966, 69). Only a few West African peoples such as the Fon, the Yoruba and the Bini, and to a much lesser degree the peoples of the Mande and the Akan, have developed a clearly articulated pantheon under the sky god. The lesser divinities manifest themselves in natural phenomena such as rain, thunder, lightning, rivers and storms, and also in diseases.

Divinities have a certain character or temperament, they are imagined as tempestuous or benign, their behaviour is described as hot, hard, or cool, and symbolized by colours such as black, white or red. One could say that they are not seen as persons, but as personalities. They are cosmic forces with their own laws, field of action and character. This makes their manifestations and behaviour to a certain degree predictable and thus their power can be manipulated for the benefit of the society by elders or specialized priests.

In contrast to the gods and divinities, the ancestors are very much interested in the well-being of the community, because they have never ceased to form an essential part of it. Without the ancestors giving protection and fertility the community would cease to exist.

In spite of the important role that the ancestors play in the community, the representations of their existence are extremely vague (cf. M. Fortes: 1965, 126-127). For the Yoruba the ancestors exist as 'ancestral material', that is represented as formless clay (cf. Witte: 1982a, 125-133).

The meaning or the fulfilment of life is not drawn from representations of life after death or inspired by such images. A meritorious life on earth is not rewarded by admission to a heaven or paradise, nor is there a hell to punish the wicked (cf. e.g., Busia:1970, 207; Le Moal: 1981, 196). Anti-social behaviour like sorcery and witchcraft may be punished by exclusion from society during life and after death, but the object of such punishment is to protect the community of the living against a bad person, and not to exclude a criminal individual from a better world in the beyond.

It is true that sometimes we hear descriptions of a more or less ideal society of ancestors, a community of peace and justice where everyone exercises his old profession within the same hierarchical framework that we find among the living. Such an eternalized ideal, which would make life after death enviable, does not answer to the West African world view and seems to be adopted from christian or islamic examples. It may serve as a model for life on earth, not as a model of life after death. Existence as an ancestor is only enviable in so far as it eliminates the ultimate catastrophe of being definitely excluded from the community without hope of return among the living.

In spite of the power of the ancestors and the influence they exercise on the community, existence as an ancestor is not regarded as the fulfilment of a human life. Every human being hopes to reach eventually the status of a true ancestor, because this is the condition necessary if one is to remain oriented towards society and to return, in a sense, among the living. This requires that after death one passes from life as an individual to the collective existence of the ancestors. Through the passage of death the orientation towards the community that is essential for the individual, is as it were absorbed in the collectivity of the ancestors, which in its turn enlarges and fortifies the community with new individuals.

Certain human beings never reach ancestorship after death. Those who die young or childless (e.g., M.D. McLeod: 1981, 37) or who die a violent death or succumb to certain illnesses (e.g., G.K. Nukunya: 1981, 122-123; Meyer Fortes: 1976, 8) are excluded. Criminals and witches who already during their lives have placed themselves outside the community by their anti-social and ego-oriented behaviour, remain excluded, as we have seen, after death, and will never attain the status of ancestors. An essential prerequisite is also that funeral rites have been performed for the deceased. Through these rites the community helps the deceased to take his leave, provides him (or her) with the possibility of joining the ancestors and sanctions his manifesting himself afterwards in the community in the orderly traditional ways (e.g., R.E. Bradbury: 1966, 100; W.H. Newell: 1976, 19; Anita Glaze: 1981, 149-150). All this means, in fact, that to become an ancestor, one has to have grown during one's life into a complete adult person with a legitimate offspring, and that, after death, this status of full personhood in the sense of a social concept, is ultimately confirmed by society through funeral rites. If we use the term 'person' as 'a label for the social representation' (La Fontaine: 1985, 125), the completed person in West Africa is indeed the product of a whole life (La Fontaine: 1985, 132).

After death the human *compositum* falls apart. The physical body decays in the earth; the vital power or breath returns to the sky god. The only element that does not altogether disappear from the human community is the ancestral element. This element is expected to be assimilated into the collectivity of the ancestors and eventually to be reincarnated among the living in one or several descendants. The fact that one can hardly speak of a personal reincarnation can be demonstrated with the example of Yoruba opinions. When a child is born the question whether a certain ancestor has returned in this child is determined on the basis of its physical characteristics and consultation of the oracle. The same ancestor can, however, return in several children, even of both sexes (e.g., Bascom: 1969, 71). Lalèyê (1970, 10) reports that a newborn baby may even be regarded as the reincarnation of a living parent! If we would ascribe personhood to the ancestors, this would mean that we forget that it is always 'an individual (that) is invested with the capacities of personhood specific to defined roles and statuses' (Fortes in: La Fontaine: 1985, 132).

If we recall the three components of the human individual, i.e., the body, the vital power and the ancestral element, we have no reason to relate the ego-awareness of West Africans to one of these elements in particular. During life they form a solid unity and it is difficult to distinguish the three components in daily experience. The vital power and the ancestral element are experienced in the body and they are symbolized by parts of the body or related phenomena such as the shadow, breath, the heart or the intestines.

At the moment of death the ego-awareness ceases to exist once and for all, because even the ancestral element, the only component that has some persistence, can only 'reincarnate' after it has been assimilated into the collectivity of the ancestors. Although we often hear that a certain ancestor has returned in a child, this only means that the deceased continues to fortify the community with children even after his death, but now in the manner of the ancestors. It is easy to understand that the anonymous collectivity of ancestors is represented from the point of view of the living by the face of an ancestor that is still remembered.

3. *The individual and the descent groups*

Although the ego-awareness of West Africans cannot be specifically tied to the ancestral element, yet the presence of such a component in the human being reveals a fundamental characteristic of that awareness, i.e., the essential role that is reserved in it for an orientation towards the community, i.e., the extended family and from there on society in general. I have already indicated that in the creation myths the origin of the civilized world takes priority over the creation of the human being. The presence of the ancestral element indicates moreover that the orientation towards the community of parents forms an intrinsic constituent element of every human being.

In every culture the margin for individual realisation of ego-awareness is determined by the ideas on man and society that have been developed in that culture. These ideas are not only concerned with man as a spiritual and physical being, but also with that culture's views on society and reality.

Evidently the orientation towards society, so essential for each individual in West African thought that it is marked by a special ancestral element, will make for important variations in the ego-awareness of West Africans in as far as they live in different cultures. Indeed, the cultural divergence stretches from the isolated peasant villages in Southern Burkina Faso or other small rural groups, to the well-organized kingdoms of the Akan and the densely populated cities of the Yoruba.

These profound differences do not alter the fact that West African cultures share a world view in which the extended family is *fons et origo* and the symbol of society. I do, of course, recognize that West Africa shows a whole scale of kinship systems. I only want to put forward the idea that the image of the family defines the ideal of society. The larger and structurally more complicated West African societies are based on a fabric of lineages held together by political and economic ties.

Probably an essential and intrinsic orientation of each individual towards society can only be maintained if that society is ideally modelled on the image of the family. The family forms a framework within which the life force circulates in a regulated manner between individuals and between the generations. A world view that is centred on the civilized world, which is modelled on the ideal of the family and first of all structured by lineage ties, regards all people outside this civilized world as *barbaroi*, who belong to the domain of untamed nature which, limits and menaces culture, and which also, in certain respects, makes culture possible.

Through this concept of society as coextensive with the civilized world but not with the human race, access to personhood (i.e., the socially generated 'assemblage of roles and statuses' that is conferred on the individual by society, cf. La Fontaine: 1985, 132) is not open to outsiders and strangers, unless they are somehow adopted. On the other hand the West African notions of the person and of the individual must be distinguished, but cannot be separated. The social category of the person is not imposed as it were from the outside on the individual, it corresponds to the intrinsic orientation on society that defines the individual.

To the individual a society that is modelled on the image of the extended polygamous family, with a hierarchical structure of succeeding generations, mirrors an image of the self in which age and gender form the basis of social functioning. These elements indicate the place of the individual within the community. The hierarchical character of West African lineage structure entails an outlook in which knowing your place, giving and receiving respect according to age and gender, are fundamental values for the ego-awareness of the individual.

4. *The life cycle of the individual*

The place one occupies within the familiy defines, of course, a dynamic situation that changes and develops. Growing older entails new responsibilities and a new relationship to the rest of the family. Such a dynamic vision of the self corresponds very well with the general attitude from which West Africans approach and understand reality. Roughly speaking this attitude is less inclined to define things and essences, and more to describe forces, powers and potentialities. This means for ego-awareness that one experiences oneself as a developing link in the dynamic whole of succeeding generations.

The extended family is a corporate whole that is closer to the individual ego than the indifferent society described by economic and political structures. Mutual solidarity within the family group provides the individual with a self-evident image of ego that is in accordance with his or her sex.

During his life the individual passes through successive periods of increasing social responsibilities. He or she slowly grows into personhood. Real responsibility can only be borne when one is no longer a child, but an adult who strengthens and renews society with children of his own. In a later stage one joins the elders, who are the living proof of the validity of the world view of the culture, because no man becomes old if he does not know how to handle the cosmic forces. Preoccupation with fertility lends the younger adults an ego-oriented attitude that widens in the later stage of the elders into a consciousness of responsibility for the community as a whole (cf. Witte: 1982b).

A growing responsibility also brings with it the benefit of increased respect and status. Helen Ware (1983, 30) indicates that the status that goes with age differs in West Africa for men and for women.

> Where old men just grow older, gradually accumulating respect and losing physical strength, old women attain a new status as honoured and sexless beings (...). For the very young and for the old there is little difference between the respect shown to males and females.

The difference in status lies in the phase of young adulthood, when married couples are having children. According to Ware (Ware: 1983, 30) the difference is mainly caused by 'the practice of polygyny, the age-gap between the spouses and the implications of patrilineal descent (which is found over most of the region)'.

Finally there is a fourth period after death, when the ego gradually fades away into the sexless collectivity of the ancestors and the remembrance of the deceased slowly disappears among the living.

The accent on age underlines the diachronic nature of the West African concept of the person. Children and married people without children have not yet attained full adulthood, and for that reason are not regarded by society or by themselves as complete persons. Personhood requires the role of a parent with legitimate children. In West African iconography small children are represented as small adults, because the individual is only significant as a person. The West African concept of the person implies a mutual relationship between the individual and the community, a social consciousness within the framework of the lineage.

An important consequence is the necessity to have legitimate children that strengthen the lineage and assure its future.

People without children are not given a complete funeral with all the required rites. They have no access to the ancestors; they are eliminated after death from the community, lest they further endanger the fertility of the lineage (cf. Cole and Aniakor: 1984, 16). For them the life cycle of child-adult-elder-ancestor is broken.

In West African thought personhood grows with increasing social responsibilities. As a person the individual becomes more and more part of the community and thus he or she is assimilated into the cycles of the generations.

Responsibility for the community means that one has as many children as possible, who will form the next generation in which the community, and in a way, their parents' person (though not their parents' ego) lives on. Putting things this way, however, leads to confusion, because it introduces a notion of the person that lacks ego-awareness. In the West African life cycle of child-adult-elder-ancestor the individual disappears after death, and the only continuity that runs through this life cycle is the orientation towards the community, which is the essential element corresponding in the individual to personhood. The West African world view assures continuity to the collectivity, not to individuals.

I come to the conclusion that the West African concept of the person expresses an essential orientation of the ego towards the community, based on the ancestral component in the individual and mirrored by the image of growing personhood that the community presents to the individual.

Within the community of the living the individual ideally grows into the status of elder and then as an ancestor gradually loses his or her individuality and personhood for the living. What remains is a collective ancestral power that guarantees the well-being and fertility of the lineage.

5. *Ego-awareness and gender*

Social responsibility implies not only the element of age, but also that of gender and sexuality.

West African societies are modelled on lineage structures, which already implies an accent on the complementarity of the sexes. Ivan Illich

(1982: 99) observes:

> Kinship primarily structures gender domains in their complementarity. (...) Kinship presupposes the two genders, which it relates to one another. Gender not only tells who is who, but it also defines who is when, where, and with which tools and words; it divides space, time and technique.

West African men and women live indeed in two distinct but strictly related worlds. In a way one can say that men - as nearly everywhere else - dominate public life, but in West Africa this does not mean that women are constricted to the homestead (cf. e.g., Mona Etienne: 1983). Eleanor R. Fapohunda (1983, 33) observes:

> Generally, West African women of both agricultural and pastoral traditions cannot expect to be completely supported by their husbands, especially in polygynous societies, and must find independent ways to support themselves and their children (also Fapohunda 1983, 52).

The important commercial role of women, which often gives them a certain economic independence (and sometimes makes men dependent, cf. e.g., Hagan: 1983, 195-196), already denies a simplified picture of male dominance in the public field (cf. Ware: 1983, 17; Sudarkasa: 1973). Helen Ware (1983, 21) resumes:

> It is now commonplace to state that women's limited access to public roles results from the inevitable conflict with their all-important domestic and child-rearing roles. In the West African case it would be more reasonable to argue that the combination of child-rearing and economic roles leaves little time for public roles. Yet even that statement is an oversimplification which ignores the facts that some women do play important political roles (...), and that there are many traditional women's groups with political roles of their own (...) (cf. Kwame Arhin: 1983; Kamene Okonjo: 1983).

More recent economic developments, showing a shift from agricultural to non-agricultural occupations and from village to town, bring with them, as Fapohunda (1983, 35) states, 'a modern sector occupational status (...) based on educational qualifications and reflected in a widening of income differences. As women tend to have lower educational opportunities than men, they become relegated to low-status, low-income occupations'. The sexual inequality in the modern sector of work seems to confirm Illich's thesis that loss of gender roles is a prerequisite of sexual inequality.

In spite of these modern developments we can say that West African men and women still live in two separate worlds defined by gender, each with its own social space and its own experience of time, punctuated by different events. There is a strict division of work and social functions. Women perform 60-80% of the agricultural labour (Ware: 1983, 21). Even when men and women both work the fields, there is a clear division of labour (e.g., Ottenberg: 1983, 78). Each gender has its own vocabulary, its own social behaviour, its own etiquette. Men and women have their own way of walking, sitting, dancing, and gesticulating (e.g., Fapohunda: 1983, 44). Corpulence of women is appreciated as an indication of fertility; young men have to give evidence of efficient muscularity as a sign of vital power; elderly men have to express their sense of social responsibility in patriarchal dignity. Among the Yoruba both women and young men prostrate themselves before dignitaries, but the men stretch out on their stomachs, while women lie on their right sides (Thompson: 1983, 16).

In this context we should not forget that gender differences are not only expressed in material behaviour, they also define underlying ways of observing and perceiving reality, because each gender has its own affinities with the cosmic forces that manifest themselves in the world. In other words, the division of the human world into two complementary parts is not merely the consequence of an efficient labour division according to physical strength and ability. The gender division of the human world reflects the existence of two cosmic domains, symbolized by sexual opposition.

This is not the place to go into a full consideration of the differences between the male and female universe (cf. Sudarkasa: 1973; Lowery-Palmer: 1980, 147-148; Ware: 1983; Fapohunda: 1983; etc.). What is clear, I think, is that both ego-awareness and the roles and statuses that confer personhood on the individual are rigorously determined in West Africa by the fact that men and women live in separate gender worlds, each with its own symbolic affinities. Identification with one's own sex and distinction from the other sex 'is part of a child's earliest empirical, but not yet verbal, growth' (Illich: 1982, 127).

In general women are supposed to have a more intrinsic link than men with the forces of fertility, by reason of the phenomena of menstruation and pregnancy. This opinion has important consequences for the ego-awareness of West African men and women, and counterbalances the submissive attitude to men that women are supposed to show in public. For the Yoruba the vital power of women is far stronger than that of men, and women are expected to keep this power 'cool' by controlled behaviour, lest it should become destructive (H.J. Drewal: 1977; Witte: 1985/1986). In the whole of West Africa women form the sterner sex (Helen Ware: 1983, 30). On the other hand it should be remembered that the male and female world are not opposed to each other, as we hear e.g., from certain South American Indian cultures; they form, to use Illich's words (1982, 99), an 'ambiguous and asymmetrical complementarity'.

The fact that in West Africa the male and the female world are complementary can be demonstrated on the level of gods and divinities and on that of the human world. Certain sky-gods have a male and a female component, as Mercier (1970, 219), among others, reports from the Fon, and Anita Glaze (1981, 53-54) from the Senufo. In the pantheon of the Yoruba, divinities change their gender if symbolic connotations make that necessary. In central Yoruba-land Odudua is a male divinity of the sky, but in the south-western region he is a female earth spirit (Witte: 1982a, 84-87). The river goddess Oya is assimilated, as faithful wife of the thunder god, into the male domain of divinities of the sky (Witte: 1982a, 110-111), whereas the male hunter Erinle is transformed into a river god and thus becomes part of the symbol-complex of female earthspirits (Witte: 1982a, 103-106; 1987). The messenger and trickster god Esu is a stranger in both domains and can be symbolized in Yoruba iconography in male and female forms (Witte 1984).

Although ambiguity of gender on the human level is firmly rejected in West African societies (because, among other things, it endangers fertility), the social function (we could say: the person) of some women brings them into the male world of public office. Among the Yoruba the female head of the market is one of the most influential dignitaries in the city state (Bolanwe Awe: 1977); in Ondo certain female office-holders are counted among the chiefs (Jerome O. Ojo: 1976, 36). Speaking of the Iyamode, one of the principal 'Ladies of the Palace' of the court of Oyo, Kamene Okonjo (1983, 214) says:

> The king's unprecedented respect for her exalted position was evident in the manner in which he addressed her, calling her '*baba*' (father), since she was the official representative of the departed kings, and saluting her on his knees.

It is not difficult to find analogous examples from the Mende, the Hausa, the Bini, the Igbo and from elsewhere in West Africa (eg. Okonjo: 1983).

It seems that these crossovers to the gender domain of the opposite sex are the consequence of public function and are thus linked to the person. The fact that the public domain is considered to be male territory could explain why most such examples have to do with women. Examples of men associated as social persons with the female domain can probably be found among the priests of certain cults. An example of more or less socially accepted gender crossing based on individual preference or tendencies, and not on social function as a person, is perhaps found in the homosexual and bisexual transvestite Hausa men who live in 'houses of women' (Renée Pittin: 1983, 297-298), but such cases seem to be extremely rare in West Africa.

Although sexuality is only one aspect in which the complementarity of gender expresses itself, it is an important one in cultures in which the notions of lineage, community and fertility are of central interest. Consequently sexuality becomes a major aspect in symbolic representation. If we consider the four phases of the life cycle from the point of view of sexuality, we observe that it is absent in the fourth phase, that of the ancestors. Ancestors that are no longer remembered are sexless. As to the living, children and elders belong as individuals to the male or female world according to their sex and this fact defines to a large degree their ego-awareness, although sexuality is not yet, or not any more, an important preoccupation of the ego. This is only the case in the adult phase of life. One can hardly exaggerate the oppressive interest in fertility which is focussed on married couples, and the dramas that sometimes result from this. The impact of the cultural accent on gender, narrowed to the importance of fertility for the lineage, bears fully on people in the adult phase of life.

Fertility requires that the marriage partners be unambiguously male or female. Circumcision, and sometimes clitoridectomy, are meant to remove what is considered to be a rudimentary characteristic of the other sex and an impediment to clear sexual distinction. Before the operation the child has in a sense the physical indications of an androgynous being, but far from being an ideal state, this makes the child as it were locked up in itself and incapable of entering into social relations. Lacking the orientation towards the other sex, it cannot yet take its place in society. We find a good example of these ideas in the rituals of the N'domo society of the Bambara (Zahan: 1960). Such a society for uncircumcised boys is extremely rare. The N'domo rituals underline not only the social insufficiency of the child, but show it also as a symbol of the unity of society in which both sexes are integrated. Social responsibility, which among adults is very largely oriented towards their own fecundity and care for their children, widens with elders into a responsibility for society as a whole. The Bambara symbolize this renewed responsibility by initiation into the Koré society. Elders continue to belong to the gender world of their physical sex, but the element of opposition between the sexes tends to recede before the evidence that the male and the female world have to collaborate to make up one lineage and one society.

In the context of West African cultures we should, I think, avoid speaking of an androgynous ideal in the sense of the gnosis of late Antiquity. This would mean not a extension of social responsibility over society as a whole, but a spiritual integration transcending the opposition of the sexes, as an ideal for the human individual.

Elders have to prepare themselves for the loss of ego and personality after death in the sexless situation of the ancestors, where only an anonymous orientation towards the society of the living remains. It is difficult to see the sexless anonymity of the ancestors as the pinnacle of individual life. It is equally inadequate to describe the ancestors as androgynous beings. It is true that they are supposed to manifest themselves in descendants of both sexes, but that is not sufficient reason to call them *utriumque sexus*. They do not represent a human ideal in which sexuality is brought onto a higher, integrated level.

6. *Summary and conclusion*

The creation myths already show that the West African world view is centred on the community of the living. Society is not seen as made up of separate, independent individuals, linked by lineage ties, social relations and common interests. Through the ancestral material that is a core element of every human being, the individual destiny of the latter is essentially focussed on the well-being and the continuation of society and cannot be separated from that collective perspective. The ancestors themselves only exist to ensure the continuation and prosperity of the community of the living.

Individual life emanates from the ancestors and after death fades away again into this collectivity. Through the succession of generations it is society, not the individual, that vanquishes death. Properly speaking there is no continuous life-cycle for the individual as individual, but only for the living as a group, supported by the ancestors.

The society of the living in general is structured along a 'vertical' axis of age and a 'horizontal' axis of gender. Roles and statuses, and social responsibilities in general, which confer personhood on the individual, have to be in accordance with these basic data. This means that a child, who is in the process of learning to bear social responsibility in a later stage, cannot yet be called a person. In West Africa personhood is a growing reality, differentiated by gender and ideally increasing with age.

On the other hand personhood should not be restricted to those with very special roles and statuses. Every adult who tries to live up to his or her responsibilities, raising a family and having children, should be called a person.

The ego-awareness of each individual, from child to elder, is, of course, also formed and defined by age and gender. In West African cultures the innate orientation towards society that every individual feels as belonging to the definition of the self, makes it necessary to conform to the behaviour and attitudes according to age and sex that the community expects. In general this means that very individual ambitions can only be consciously pursued, or even formulated by the self, within the limitations imposed by age and gender. Individualistic ambitions that would ignore these limitations not only lead to a disregard for social values, they are seen as an attack on the very structure of society, which needs to have every individual in his or her hierarchical place. Cut off from society and from his own ancestral soul, the individual would be in a position where no one can survive.

Bibliography

Arhin, K.
1983 'The Political and Military Roles of Akan Women'. In: Oppong: 1983, 91-98.

Awe, B.
1977 'The Iyalode in the Traditional Yoruba Political System'. In: *Sexual Stratification, a Cross-cultural View,* ed. A. Schlegel, Columbia University Press, 144-160.

Bascom, W.
1969 *The Yoruba of Southwestern Nigeria.* Holt, Rinehart and Winston, New York.

Bradbury, R.E.
1966 *Father and Senior Son in Edo Mortuary Ritual.* In: African Systems of Thought, ed. M. Fortes and F. Dieterlen, Oxford University Press, London, 96-121.

Brain, J.
1973 'Ancestors and Elders in Africa - further thoughts', in: *Africa,* 43/2, 122-133.

Busia, K.A.
1970 'The Ashanti of the Gold Coast'. In: Forde: 1970, 190-209.

Cole, H.M. - C.C. Aniakor
1984 *Igbo Arts - Community and Cosmos. Museum of Cultural History,* Los Angeles

Dieterlen, G. (ed.)
1981 *La notion de personne en Afrique noire.* C.N.R.S., Paris.

Drewal, H.J.
1977 'Art and Perception of Women in Yoruba Culture', in: *Cahiers d'études africaines,* 68-17/4, 545-567.

Etienne, M.
1983 'Gender Relations and Conjugality Among the Baule'. In: Oppong: 1983, 303-319.

Fapohunda, E.R.
1983 'Female and Male Work Profiles'. In: Oppong: 1983, 32-53.

Forde, D. (ed.)
1970 *African Worlds. Studies in the Cosmological Ideas and Social Values of African Peoples.* Oxford University Press, London.

Fortes, M.
1965 'Some Reflections on Ancestor Worship in Africa' In: *African Systems of Thought*, ed. M. Fortes and G. Dieterlen, Oxford University Press, London, 122-144.
1966 *Ödipus und Hiob in westafrikanischen Religionen*. Suhrkamp, Frankfurt a.M.
1976 'An Introductory Commentary'. In: *Ancestors*, ed. W.H. Newell, Mouton, The Hague, 1-16.
1981 'On the Concept of the Person Among the Tallensi'. In: Dieterlen: 1981, 283-320.

Geertz, Cl.
1983 *Local Knowledge. Further Essays in Interpretive Anthropology*. Basic Books, New York.

Glaze, A.
1981 *Art and Death in a Senufo Village*. Indiana University Press, Bloomington.

Hagan, G.P.
1983 'Marriage, Divorce and Polygyny in Winneba'. In: Oppong: 1983, 192-203.

Idowu, E.B.
1962 *Olódùmarè God in Yoruba Belief*. Longman, London.

Illich, I.
1982 *Gender*. Pantheon Books, New York.

Kopytoff, I.
1971 'Ancestors and Elders in Africa', in: *Africa*, 42/2, 129-142.

La Fontaine, J.S.
1985 'Person and individual: some anthropological reflections'. In: *The category of the person*, ed. Carrithers, Collins and Lukes, Cambridge University Press, Cambridge, 123-140.

Lalèyê, I.P.
1970 *La conception de la personne dans la pensée traditionelle Yoruba, 'approche phénoménologique'*. Herbert Lang & Cie, Berne.

Lemaire, T.
1984 'Antropologie en schrift. Aanzetten tot een ideologiekritiek van het schrift'. In: *Antropologie en ideologie*, red. T. Lemaire, Konstapel, Groningen, 103-126.

Le Moal, G.
1981 'Quelques aperçus sur la notion de personne chez les Bobo', in: Dieterlen: 1981, 193-204.

Lienhardt, G.
1985 'Self: public, private. Some representations'. In: *The category of the person,* ed. Carrithers, Collins and Lukes, Cambridge University Press, Cambridge, 141-155.

Little, K.
1970 'The Mende in Sierra Leone'. In: Forde: 1970, 111-137.

Lowery-Palmer, A.
1980 *Yoruba World View and Patient Compliance.* U.M.I., Ann Arbor.

Mauss, M.
1985 *A category of the human mind: the notion of person, the notion of self.* Transl. W.D. Halls, in: The category of person, eds. Carrithers, Collins and Lukes, Cambridge University Press, Cambridge, 1-25.

McLeod, M.D.
1981 *The Ashante.* British Museum Publications, London.

Mercier, P.
1970 'The Fon of Dahomey'. In: Forde: 1970, 210-234.

Newell, W.H.
1976 'Good and Bad Ancestors'. In: *Ancestors,* ed. W.H. Newell, Mouton, The Hague, 17-32.

Nukunya, G.K.
1981 'Some underlying beliefs in ancestor worship and mortuary rites among the Ewe'. In: Dieterlen: 1981, 119-130.

Ojo, J.O.
1976 *Yoruba Customs from Ondo.* Acta ethnologica et linguistica, Wien.

Okonjo, K.
1983 'Sex Roles in Nigerian Politics'. In: Oppong: 1983, 211-222.

Oppong, C. (ed.)
1983 *Female and Male in West Africa.* Allen & Unwin, London.

Ottenberg, S.
1983 'Artistic and Sex Roles in a Nimba Chiefdom'. In: Oppong: 1983, 76-91.

Pittin, R.
1983 'Houses of Women: a Focus on Alternative Life-Styles in Katsina City'. In: Oppong: 1983, 291-302.

Sanjek, R.
1983 'Female and Male Domestic Cycles in Urban Africa'. In: Oppong: 1983, 330-343.

Shweder, R.A. - E.J. Bourne
1984 'Does the concept of the person vary cross-culturally?' In: *Culture Theory, Essays on Mind, Self, and Emotion,* ed. Shweder and LeVine, Cambridge Unversity Press, Cambridge, 158-199.

Sudarkasa, N.
1973 *Where Women Work: a Study of Yoruba Women in the Marketplace and in the Home.* University of Michigan Press, Ann Arbor.

Thompson, R.F.
1983 *Flash of the Spirit. African and Afro-American Art and Philosophy.* Vintage Books, New York.

Uchendu, V.C.
1965 *The Igbo of Southeast Nigeria.* Holt, Rinehart and Winston, New York.

Ware, H.
1983 'Female and Male Life-Cycles'. In: Oppong: 1983, 6-31.

Witte, H.A.
1982a *Symboliek van de aarde bij de Yoruba.* U.M.I., Ann Arbor.
1982b 'Initiation à la responsabilité dans la société: le modèle Ogboni chez les Yoruba', in: *Réseaux,* 35/37, 57-66.
1984 *Ifa and Esu. Iconography of Order and Disorder.* Luttik, Soest.
1985/1986 'The Invisible Mothers. Female Power in Yoruba Iconography', in: *Visible Religion,* IV, 301-325.
1987 'Images of a Yoruba Water-Spirit'. In: *Efficies Dei,* ed. D. van der Plass, Brill, Leiden, 130-141.

Zahan, D.
1960 *Sociétés d'initiation bambara: le N'domo et le Koré.* Mouton, La Haye.

PART FOUR
SPECIAL ISSUES

PERSONA NON GRATA

The Case of *Zwarte Piet*

Barend P. Hofstede

And I am black, but O my soul is white!

William Blake (1757-1827) 'The Little Black Boy'

A mythic dyad

In the history of religion, the duality of good and evil, light and darkness, plays a persistent role, as it does in modern psychology, psychiatry, and the social and political sciences, such as criminology and polemology. With Freud, Durkheim, who saw the person as 'homo duplex, split... between angel and beast', shared the conviction that there is 'a true antagonism between the demands of social life and those of his individual, organic nature' (Lukes: 1985, 286).

The Latin *persona* as a ritual mask can represent the good as well as the bad person or, *persona grata - persona non grata*. The present case-study deals with the former, in the shape of 4th century Bishop Nicholas of Myra, in Asia Minor, who became a highly popular medieval saint, and more particularly with the latter, in the shape of his mythological servant, who under different names and disguises according to time and place, originally personified the domesticated devil.[1]

---

[1] In Roget's Thesaurus, *persona non grata* comes under the entry of 'bad person'; other expressions that qualify are 'sons of Belial', 'limbs of Satan', 'children of darkness'. *Persona grata* is found under 'good person' with terms like 'pillar of the church', 'true Christian', 'holy man', and 'saint' (Roget: 1977, items 986, 985).

The mythic dyad - a pair of units considered to be one - of St. Nicholas and his dark companion, *persona grata* and *non grata* respectively, remind 20th-century Europeans of the ancient struggle between good and evil, between the god of light and the god of darkness, as well as of the old Hebrew dilemma: how to combine the essential principle of monotheistic religion with the evil side of the godhead called the Devil. The Devil, not prominent in the Old Testament, gained stature in the Apocryphal, Apocalyptic, and New Testament literature. He has his genesis in the Godhead himself. He is a counterpart, and doublet of the good Lord. He is the shadow of God (Russell: 1979, 251).

Even a saint would be incomplete and inhuman without both his psychological and his physical shadow. As A.D. de Groot, who wrote a psycho-analytical study of St. Nicholas, puts it:

> Taken together, St. Nicholas and Black Peter can be seen as representing - as does the Saint riding his white horse - the dyadic unity of flesh and spirit, of animal and man, the integration of animal, man and moral mastery (De Groot: 1965, 175).

Saint Nicholas

Nikolaos was a person of such precocious piety, the legend records, that on the day of his birth he stood up in his bath with his little hands joined in thanksgiving, and that, while still being breast-fed, he refused to be suckled on fast days (Hall: 1979, 222). He became the patron saint of children, sailors and travellers, the guardian of nubile maidens, the worker of miracles, the feeder of the starving, known for his charity and for the power to reanimate the dead. Being a man after the people's heart, Nikolaos became the perfect personification of the good.

As early as the 16th century, the Roman Catholic Church, influenced by macro-processes of transition - Reformation, Counter-Reformation and Enlightenment - decided no longer to promote the cult of a primitive saint and miracle-worker. However, it took another four centuries before the Vatican finally removed Nicholas from the Calendar of Saints (1969). Due to the combined efforts of the Church of Rome and the Protestant Churches to reduce him to a minor saint or to abolish him altogether, most countries switched from the old Nicholas cult to that of Christmas. In both Germany and Britain, Reformed preachers reached their goal with reasonings such as 'All things good come from God only; so that if gifts are received at all, they must come from the Christ-child' (De Groot: 1965, 22). St. Nicholas became the prototype of Father Christmas and Santa Claus, in England and the United States of America respectively.

In the Low Countries, orthodox Calvinists took action against the cult when they came to power in the 16th and 17th centuries. In the name of true religion they banned the old naive customs. During and after the Reformation, as a consequence of this repression, St. Nicholas not only refused to disappear, but also managed to become a kind of popular 'resistance hero' of traditional Dutch family life confronted with the rational, no-nonsense regime of the Calvinists. After all, through the ages people had been cherishing him and had been asking for his support during almost all vicissitudes of life.

Comparably, in recent times, St. Nicholas has managed to survive the secularization and bureaucratization of Dutch society. Amid a radical uprooting of beliefs and values, and a growing disenchantment with the world, with a large number of people, many of whom belong to the younger generation, terminating their church membership - both Protestant and Roman Catholic - the Dutch maintain the yearly celebration of their *Sinterklaasfeest* on a national scale. The Dutch *Sinterklaas* still makes his yearly call on December 5 and not without his regular companion.

Why has the ancient Nicholas cult survived in the Netherlands? In order to find an appropriate answer, we have to consider that in Calvinism there were two main tendencies, an orthodox and a liberal Protestant one.

The former, which mainly controlled the countryside, struggled in vain to conquer the latter's strongholds in the cities. As a patron of the seafaring trade Sinterklaas was a typically urban saint, e.g., he was the patron of the town of Amsterdam, the main harbour and merchant city of the Dutch Republic, and the leading trade centre of the Western world during the 17th century. His patronage was so much sought after, that it gradually came to include almost all trade, commerce, and transport over sea and over land.

The Dutch historian Johan Huizinga ascribes the unity of the Dutch in the first place - not to their collective 'struggle against the water' as the current stereotype wants it - but to their 'bourgeois' (*burgerlijk*) character. Their national culture is bourgeois in every sense of the word, and their history consistently reflects genuine bourgeois aspirations (Huizinga: 1985, 13-14). Cornerstones of Dutch society, from the 16th century onwards, were such primordial bourgeois characteristics as stability of family life and the role of women as faithful housewives and caring mothers. The ruling clergy who tried to get rid of the Nicholas cult were men. Since Nicholas met the requirements of an all-round bourgeois saint, his most loyal adherents were women. According to a survey conducted by the present author in co-operation with the Dutch newspaper *Trouw*, women are still the ones who attach the greatest value to keeping Sinterklaas alive without altering the trusted symbols (Marktresponse: 1986).

The survey also revealed that almost two-thirds of the Dutch population participated in the Sinterklaas celebrations of 1985. The festivities mainly took place in families with 3-to-10-year-old children, but also in more than half of the childless households. Notwithstanding his Catholic origins, Sinterklaas appeals to people of different denominations, with or without religion. He also appeals to people from all layers of society, even to the cultural and educational elites, reared in the Enlightenment tradition of 'delegitimizing' traditional human experiences of mystery, awe and transcendent hope. Most Dutch children are raised in the firm belief that Sinterklaas and Zwarte Piet really exist.

In the Netherlands Sinterklaas customarily gives not only bountifully, but also more or less anonymously. Children receive their present from *Sint* but they also give each other presents accompanied by home-made rhymes and poems, at least quasi-anonymously. The idea behind this is not that the giver's identity must never become known to the recipient, 'nor is there much anonymity in St. Nicholas's dealings with the children. He is their dearest uncle himself, who gives from the fullness of his warm, human heart' (De Groot: 1965, 178-179).

So the fairy tale of Sinterklaas creates a link between autochthonous Dutch people from their primary socialization years onwards, regardless of religious, social or political controversies. Every year somewhere about November, adults start conspiring to bring it to life again. Children also, as soon as they reach the age at which they no longer believe in Sinterklaas, consciously join the game in order to keep it going for the little ones. It is a genuine rite of passage, the first symbolic step into the adult world, and such a persistent national custom that Dutch migrants take Sinterklaas with them to overseas countries, preferring their own version of the Holy Man to Father Christmas or Santa Claus.[2]

---

2 In order to explain a minority custom to a majority audience, the Canadian anthropologist David S. Moyer made a detailed ethnographic study of the St. Nicholas rituals on Vancouver Island among Dutch immigrants in 1983 (Moyer: 1984, 57-62). For a better understanding of the Sinterklaas phenomenon, I will offer some extensive quotations from his careful description: '...a child of four or five will have a distinct set of impressions of St. Nicholaas and Zwarte Piet. A major factor will be the way the family has chosen to interpret the general symbols of Sinterklaas. In particular, the degree to which he is seen as both a rewarding and punishing figure, as opposed to an entirely benevolent one, will have a significant impact on the child's perception. In contrast to the believing child there is the unbelieving teenager who still participates in Sinterklaas celebrations, sometimes as a Zwarte Piet but more often on the receiving end of barbed familial poems. As an adult one may be involved in the work place party where, under the guise of Sinterklaas, gift and poems point out an irritating personal habit of the recipient. The recipient is obliged to read the poem aloud and then say: "Dank u Sinterklaas"'. Here is the author's description of the official arrival in Victoria, British Columbia: 'By one o'clock a crowd of about three to four hundred people has gathered. About half are Dutch, and they are usually the closest to the roped-off area where the dancers and the musicians perform. At about 1:15 the Seaspan International tugboat bringing St. Nicholaas from nearby Esquimalt appears in the distance. As the tugboat approaches one can easily see St. Nicholaas and the Zwarte Piets standing on the foredeck. One can also see a large sign draped across the tugboat's bow. The sign, in three-foot-high letters, says "SPAIN". As soon as the tug is secured to the end of the dock the president of the Vancouver Island Netherlands Association helps St. Nicholaas ashore and introduces him to his wife. The president, his wife and St. Nicholaas proceed towards the shore followed by the two Zwarte Piets. At the ramp connecting the dock and shore St. Nicholaas is welcomed by children in Dutch costume, who are for the most part members of the children's dance group. Once ashore, an official welcome is extended by the Acting Mayor of Victoria. (...) Meanwhile, during the less serious moments, the Zwarte Piets are throwing 'pepernoten" (ceremonial cookies, BPH).

Moyer's description of the Sinterklaas evening party - for grown-ups only - at the Dutch club in Victoria shows the Zwarte Piets at work: 'Each 'child' is called and escorted to St. Nicholaas by one of the Piets. Occasionally, the escorting Piet rides the 'child' to the front of the hall. The 'child' kneels before St. Nicholaas and listens to

At the end of the 16th and at the beginning of the 17th century St. Nicholas may have had a hard time defending his tradition. In the Netherlands today the position of Sinterklaas, with a few minor exceptions which are not relevant here, is hardly under attack. The same cannot, however, be said of his dark companion *Zwarte Piet* (Black Peter).

Zwarte Piet: the origins

Already in the Greek tradition Nikolaos was known for his struggle with devils and demons, resulting not in mere exorcism but in his taming and subduing them. The point is that, since the very basic conditions of life such as potency, fertility, and procreation were part of his business, he was faced with the necessity of coming to grips with the dark powers behind them. That is the reason why, in folk tradition, the Evil One has become his inevitable companion. The German authority on St. Nicholas, Karl Meisen, has no doubt that the Bishop's servant is the Devil, conquered and rendered harmless by his holy master (Meisen; 1931).

During the 13th century, the Golden Age of St. Nicholas, the belief in Satan reached a corresponding peak, which enabled the Saint to perform lots of striking - and in later centuries almost forgotten-miracles.

Controlling and taming ancient paganism with its emphasis on instinct and libido was the first historic task of militant Christian doctrine. There was Pan, a phallic deity, born hairy and goatlike, with horns and cloven hooves, the very incarnation of sexual desire. Also, the early Christians

---

the mock serious speech and is given a small present. The general tone is one of comic uproar, (...) At one point one of the Piets, while looking for a present, gets lost in his sack and has trouble either finding the present or extricating himself from the sack. Later a Piet tells a kneeling 'child' that he has a present in there. At this point he sticks his hand into his oversized Spanish breeches. He then proceeds, amidst total uproar, to rummage in his drawers. Finally, he extracts a small, neatly wrapped package. At another point the wife of one of the men dressed up as Zwarte Piet is called to the front. When she is kneeling before St. Nicholaas he says, 'I hear you have been fooling around with one of my Piets'. The innuendo is unmistakable and very funny. After about 30 minutes of such antics St. Nicholaas and the Zwarte Piets depart.'

rejected chthonic fertility deities as demons, which again were to be particularly feared because of their association with the wilderness and sexual frenzy (Russell: 1979, 126).

In Christianity, as in Zoroastriansm and Manichaeism, the forces of evil are powers of darkness. In all sorts of common words and phrases blackness and darkness connote evil. Black also implies dirt and foulness, by contrast with white, which is the colour of cleanliness, purity and innocence (Cavendish: 1975, 91). It is one of the most ancient and powerfully biased symbols in the human psyche. Blackness possesses an immense range of negative and fearful associations (Russell: 1979, 65-66).

The Devil himself was frequently described as black or dark. His blackness mirrors the darkness of sin, which led to the fear of the demonic qualities of people with black skins and strange, 'heathen' customs. The African Negro and Satan had this in common; they were both identified with heathenism. De Groot agrees with Meisen's identification of Zwarte Piet with the Devil, but insists that the dark companion of Sinterklaas should be identified more specifically with the Devil's quality of a phallic, heathen lust-seeker and seducer. Such characteristics - outsize genital equipment and lustfulness - have of old been projected onto black men in white people's fantasies.[3]

Cavendish reminds us that in early Christian literature, the Devil sometimes in this kind of manifestation, frequently occurred in legends and visions. For instance, in an episode of St. Brendan's voyage, probably written in the 9th century, the saint sees a demon take on the form of a little Ethiopian boy trying to tempt a monk. Four centuries later, a French Dominican, Etienne de Bourbon, who fiercely disapproved of dancing and thought that all dances had been invented by Satan, said that the Devil had been seen leading a dance in the form of a small Ethiopian (Cavendish: 1975, 92). Apparently the Middle Ages already kept Zwarte Piet in store for use by later generations. The dark shadow had cast itself over times to come.

---

[3] We have no account of women's sexual fantasies in the 16th and 17th centuries other than from witch trials, during which copulation with the Devil was frequently 'confessed' under torture. But we may expect that e.g. among sailor's wives in Antwerp and Amsterdam, with husbands at sea and black he-men strolling about town, erotic fantasies and whispered tall stories were not uncommon.

The Devil's image as a composite, zoomorphic creature belongs to ancient Persian and Egyptian religion. Western medieval art modified Satan's image, making it essentially human but retaining numerous bestial appendages such as claws, tail, and limbs entwined with serpents (Hall: 1979, 272). Following F. Redl's and B. Bettelheim's description, this was more or less the appearance of *Krampus* (or *Grampus*), as they called St. Nicholas's companion in Roman Catholic Vienna, where both authors spent their youth. Krampus quite clearly was the Devil, or at least his emissary. He was black, had horns, a mephistophelian countenance, a long tail, and preferably hooves or their equivalent. Redl describes Krampus's activity as follows:

> He cannot really act on his own, unless Saint Nicholas tells him to go ahead; but upon St. Nicholas's sign he will be ready to beat you, catch you and chain you, and carry you off for good. Whereto can only be speculated upon; it is rarely directly mentioned.[4]

---

[4] F. Redl, 'Free and not so free - associations after reading De Groot's Sinterklaas'. De Groot's original study appeared in Dutch shortly after the Second World War. The Austrian psychologist F. Redl wrote a letter to the author commenting on it. The English version of this letter was published in 1965 (De Groot: 1965, 190-191). Another account of Krampus's role in Austrian culture emphasizes his significance as an integrated symbol belonging to our human personality (Bettelheim: 1987, 371-371). 'When I was a child in Austria, Saint Nicholas's Day was celebrated, there as in many other countries, and as it is still celebrated now. On this day, two male adults visit the homes of children. One is dressed up as bishop, playing the role of Saint Nicholas; the other either his helper and servant, of his counterpart - a figure variously dressed and named, depending on local custom. He is often called Ruprecht when he is merely a servant carrying a bag of presents, but more frequently he is called Black Peter, Krampus, or Grampus, in which case his face is blackened and he represents the devil. Then he wears a mask with horns, a tail, and even hooves; he is dressed in black and carries a sack or some other receptacle. Black Peter's sack, however, does not contain gifts - it is there to carry away bad children. But while this evil figure looks and acts ferocious, he is in the power of the good bishop Saint Nicholas, who always stops him and - as in the legend - rescues the children.

On Saint Nicholas's Day these two, who are neighbors appropriately dressed up, go from door to door, asking the parents (who have expected them) whether their children

Only in the Low Countries did the companion of Saint Nicholas change from devil into Negro. Also characteristic of the Dutch version is

---

have been good or bad. In most cases the answer is 'mostly good, though not always'. At this the devil steps forth and tries to grab the child to give him a few strokes with his birch, but the child nearly always manages to escape with great shrieking. In any case, after a perfunctory effort on the part of the devil to punish the child, the good saint comes to the rescue and puts the devil in his place, making it clear that he will protect all children. Then Saint Nicholas admonishes the child to be good and gives him small presents, usually some pieces of fruit and candy. But one of his more traditional gifts is particularly meaningful: branches like those which were made into Krampus's birch, but Saint Nicholas's are covered with gold or silver glitter, and from their branches hang small fruit candies. Saint Nicholas's branches are turned into a token candy tree; they are a close parody of the instrument with which children are occasionally punished, a transfiguration of the instrument of punishment into one giving pleasure that is much appreciated by the children. Thus, on Saint Nicholas's Day, through a little drama much enjoyed by all, first the negative side of parental ambivalence and children's guilt about their bad behavior (if not also bad thoughts) are satisfied by the threats or token punishment meted out by the devilish figure, and then the positive side of this ambivalence wins out, and the gifts are given which are much more immediate and real than was the symbolic punishment. (...)
The two characters of Saint Nicholas's Day always appear as a pair, reflecting the two sides of our personalities in a way that everyone understands. They symbolize that in the child as also in adults, neither the good in us nor the bad exists in isolation. The parents' answer to their query shows they know that their child is neither all good nor all bad, and thus the child can enjoy his small presents to the fullest without guilt. Of course, the impressive bishop's costume with his miter and staff and the flamboyant and ingenious get-up of Black Peter (Ruprecht or Krampus) add a great deal to the fun, as does the red costume of Santa Claus at Christmas. Since adults dress and act this way for children with full parental cooperation, they thus give body and reality to the child's fantasies, both the fearful and the wish-fulfilling ones, according them obvious adult approval'.

the belief that Sinterklaas lives in Spain and travels from there by boat.[5] In search of explanations, De Groot makes the following conjectures:

> Through many centuries the Netherlands were closely associated with rich, powerful Spain, not only politically - ending up with the Eighty Year's War of independence - but also through various kinds of trade relations. A 'ship from Spain' was apt to bring a rich cargo of common goods' worthy of Saint Nicholas. The final step in this connection may have been due to Black Peter, who was sometimes called 'the Moor'. Of course Moors came from Spain, and Spanish lords often had black valets; so whoever had a black valet must be a Spanish lord - but this is sheer speculation, of course (De Groot: 1965, 50).

Here De Groot tries to explain why Sinterklaas comes from Spain (because he has a Moorish servant), but he does not make clear when and where the servant changed from a Krampus-like companion into Zwarte Piet. Since there are no clear historical data available, we can only guess.

Would it be too far-fetched to suppose that the metamorphosis was somehow inspired by the phenomenon of the slave trade? Rich trading families, originating in Spain and Portugal and living in Antwerp, were in the habit of importing slaves from Africa as domestic servants. In this large inland port, located in the southern Netherlands more Negro

---

5 The 'boat from Spain' may perhaps be associated with the legend of the 'Narrenschiff' (*Nef des Fous*, as described by Michel Foucault: 1975). The 'Narrenschiff' - Ship of Fools - was a literary form, which probably goes back to the old Argonaut stories, and manifests itself among the most important Renaissance myths in the Rhine area and Flanders. It sailed rivers which flowed into the North Sea: a long, symbolic boat trip, bringing its passengers and crew - imaginary heroes, ethical models or social typifications - to a certain destination and connected truth. The ship itself symbolizes unrest and agitation as they appear on the European cultural horizon at the end of the Middle Ages. Added to the fact that Nicholas happened to be the patron saint of sailors and merchants, this may have contributed to the myth of the 'boat from Spain'. There may also have existed a mythical mixture of 'Narrenschiff' and slave-ship. After all, the slave-trade was one of the main economic and sociopolitical engines on the road toward modernization: the old world gone mad and the new one promising the ultimate destination and its truth, Utopia.

children were baptized during the 16th century than anywhere else in Europe (Preedy: 1984, 27). For nearly two centuries, from 1637 to 1830, Dutch merchant associations officially took part in the African-American slave trade, but there is evidence that individual entrepreneurs were involved in the highly profitable business much earlier. After the Spanish conquest of Antwerp in 1584, Amsterdam took over its main harbour functions, which also meant that it became a staple for negro slaves. In the official acts of those days, they are referred to as 'Moors'. As Preedy puts it, the silent, dark witnesses to the Dutch overseas territories had already been present in the Netherlands for a long time, their status varying from free citizen to domestic slave, from church minister to heathen that could be converted, from curiosity to living toy (Preedy: 1984, 12-13; Menkman: 1947).

The slave trade brought enormous profits to the Dutch society of the 17th and 18th centuries, stimulating all kinds of other economic activities. The rationalization which permitted a Christian nation to play a leading role in this type of commerce was that as long as they were heathens, Negro slaves could be considered to be objects, not human beings, let alone persons. They could be bought and sold for profit without damaging the soul of the Christian merchant. The early Christians had known a form of slavery, but in those days slaves still formed a social class of human beings; they could eventually become free citizens (and most of them were of European origin). With the arrival of the colonial age, the ancient Roman principle was revived, i.e., slaves were excluded from the right to the *persona* as synonymous with the free nature of the individual. *Servus non habet personam*, the slave has no personality. He does not own his body, nor does he possess any ancestors, names, or personal belongings. In old Germanic law he could at least own his body (*Leibeigen* = 'body-owner'). It was Christianity that later on gave the *Leibeigen* a soul (Mauss: 1985, 17).

The return of pre-Christian social ethics concerning slavery may be considered as a grave moral regression. In the wave of optimism marking the cultural renaissance of Europe in the 15th and 16th centuries, however, it was embraced in a socially and politically, and even morally accepted disguise; a disguise cleverly used by early capitalism on the road towards Western world domination. Non-European populations, mainly from Africa, were looked upon, not as a low social class of human beings with potential freedom, but as outcasts without legal rights:

objects of profit for the merchant nations of Western Europe.

We may safely assume that in its own days, the transformation from devil to Negro was a logical process, fitting within the changing theological and political frames of reference. It can also be seen as a commercially influenced step towards cultural modernization, in a symbolic way selling the slave trade to the Dutch community. After all, Zwarte Piet embodied the converted black heathen. On the 'archetypal' level, he personified the controlled Devil in ourselves.[6]

The act of transformation in itself was the kind of thing one could expect. The Devil was known for not being restricted to one distinct form or outward appearance. He had the power to change his shape at will, and in order to deceive people he might appear as a handsome youth, a beautiful girl, or an angel of light (Russell: 1979, 254), or, less deceiving to the public eye, as a Zwarte Piet.

A Dutch dilemma

Since 1974, half of the population of Surinam - former Dutch Guiana on the north-east coast of Latin America - (i.e. half of a total of 380.000) has emigrated to the Netherlands, the two largest ethnic groups among them being descendants of slaves brought from West Africa and India respectively; other slave imports came from the Dutch East Indies (Java) and China. Slavery was abolished in 1863. In a wider politico-economic sense, however, the colonial period, initiated two centuries earlier when a Dutch admiral conquered Surinam on behalf of his superiors in Holland, did not end before 1947 (Braam: 1973, 18). In 1975, the former colony finally became independent. From that time on the young nation has been struggling with social, economic and political problems. In the Netherlands many people from Surinam were confronted

---

[6] When analyzing dreams of white 20th-century Americans, psychologist C.G. Jung found the demon in the self frequently represented by a Negro or an Indian. The 'shadow', as Jung used to call the animal-like, instinctive, primitive creature which is normally masked by the outward *persona*, appears in dreams as a degraded, unpleasant and unwanted person: a clear case of *persona non grata*. Yet the shadow was regarded by Jung as a necessary component of the personality (Cavendish: 1975, 94).

with unemployment and problems of adaptation to Dutch society in general. This resulted in a negative public image which seems to have stigmatized the younger generation in particular.

Though taking pride in an age-long tradition of hospitality to foreigners, to the oppressed and the persecuted, Dutch society when it unexpectedly became multicultural during the sixties and seventies (there were also large numbers of workers from the Mediterranean who preferred to stay) started to show signs of discrimination and growing racism (Tennekes: 1984, 113; Scheepers: 1986). As a reaction to this, an anti-racist activist movement manifested itself, which received support from the political left. About 1980 radical non-white activists opened attacks on Zwarte Piet as a 'key symbol of racial oppression'.

Each year, Sinterklaas's official arrival is broadcast by national television (NOS, the Dutch equivalent of the BBC). Taking into account the rapidly growing numbers of black immigrants and their children, the organizing committee decided to adapt Zwarte Piet's television image to the changed demographic situation in the Netherlands. Formerly, Zwarte Piet used to display about the same stereotyped *non-grata*-behaviour as manifested by the Viennese Krampus. Now the burlap sack was thrown overboard and the rod was taken from Zwarte Piet; an effective disarmament or rather a castration, which opened the way to evolving from bogey to buddy, no longer inspiring fear.

The TV-directors also put an end to Zwarte Piet's double-Dutch, thus disposing of the childish image and changing Piet's role to that of an equal partner of Sinterklaas. The master-slave relationship lost its sharp edges. Zwarte Piet acquired a more autonomous TV-role of his own. Even his blackness is no longer what it used to be: in order to meet the technical demands of colour TV, his face has acquired the brown tan brought home by millions of Dutch tourists from their holiday exposures to the Mediterranean tan, particularly the Spanish tan sun.[7]

---

[7] In due time, mass media examples find their way into society. In November 1987, the secretary of the local *Sinterklaas Comité* in Enschede, a provincial town in the eastern part of the country, was reported - in a national newspaper - to have told the press: 'Our Piets are not that black, you know, just a tiny little bit, and they don't behave like underdogs. In fact, they're more like Swiebertjes ('Swiebertje' being a hilarious tramp-like hero from a popular children's TV-programme, BPH). Also, there's

But the activists are not satisfied by what they consider to be only marginal corrections. Each year during the weeks preparatory to the feast of St. Nicholas they renew their attacks by means of publications in the press, interviews on radio and TV, the distribution of posters and folders, or the production of video information films, to be shown at schools. Their main arguments, gathered from a number of these sources are:

1. To justify the exploitation and oppression of black people, white men long ago invented a theory that Negroes are lazy, stupid and bad; they will therefore have to obey the superior white race forever. In Dutch culture the argument was expressed symbolically by providing Sinterklaas with a black valet. It convincingly shows Dutch society as imbued with racist elements that form an integral part of the Sinterklaas tradition, which preserves the master-slave relationship of the past.
2. Zwarte Piet personifies the stereotype of the black man as created by white slaveholders to legitimize the use of blacks as slaves. He is childish, playful, simple, violent, aggressive, always up to tricks, ugly, has thick lips, and is frequently grinning and jabbering away. These characteristics are supposed to be those of the black species in general. Sinterklaas can have one or many black helpers. They do not possess an individual identity, but are interchangeable and they all display the same monkeyish behaviour. Conformable to the old adage they are genuine non-persons.
3. Through Zwarte Piet, Dutch children are spoon-fed with notions of white superiority. Racist poison oozes into their innocent souls. They learn to be afraid of black people. Before and during the Sinterklaas celebrations many black children, in the streets and at school, are called 'Zwarte Piet' without the other party realizing how badly the victims are being hurt. Moreover, the negative image is likely to stick for months.

As possible alternatives to Zwarte Piet, black activists have proposed various ways of changing the Sinterklaas ceremonial, e.g., by having a

no question of any master-servant relationship. And if, in future, some people's feelings still get hurt, the solution will be simple. We'll have white Piets then'.

black 'Saint' and white 'Piets', or, by having Piets in different colours: green, red, blue, orange etc., or by discarding Piet altogether, or even by abolishing both Sinterklaas and Zwarte Piet, and replacing them with a puppet show. When the latter solution was indeed put into practice by an organized group of black women in Rotterdam, only the Bishop's miter was symbolically present at a big 5 December children's party. Notwithstanding all precautions things still went wrong. In the puppet show-performed by Dutch players - a white king was seen punishing a black puppet for having stolen a chocolate letter (the traditional Sinterklaas gift) (Hassankhan: 1986, 12-13). The most advanced suggestion is a radical change of meaning by turning the *Sinterklaasfeest* into a feast celebrated in sympathy with the blacks in South Africa, indeed a former Dutch colony ('Apartheid' being a term of Dutch origin). On December 5th, all the people in the Netherlands should surprise each other with gifts bought from Third World shops (Choenni: 1986, 6).

Although 'anti-apartheid' and 'anti-racism' are hot issues in the Netherlands, the 1986 Trouw survey showed that 95% of the Dutch population were in favour of maintaining the institution of Zwarte Piet as part of the Sinterklaas ritual. Moreover, the Dutch language still contains the phrase *Iemand de Zwarte Piet toespelen*, to give somebody the Zwarte Piet, which is used to indicate that the responsibility of some kind of failure is secretly passed on to another party. Most Dutchmen are convinced that the whole issue is no more than an insignificant cultural misunderstanding, the tenor of letters to the editors of popular daily papers being that, instead of bothering about such inoffensive details of language and popular tradition, ethnic minorities should mind their own cultural business.

Lurking behind a harmless-looking facade, the activists argue, are both white power and racial superiority, as well as discrimination against a minority on account of the colour of their skin. They complain that 'progressive' white Dutchmen and -women, even of the extreme left where anti-racism and anti-apartheid are considered of paramount importance, abandon them as soon as the issue of Zwarte Piet is raised.[8]

---

8 In 1984, anti-Zwarte Piet activists had prepared a demonstration against the official arrival of Sinterklaas on TV, with a black counter-Saint, a brass-band, and banners reading 'Sinterklaas was a Turk'. To their utter disappointment, at the very

Taking the activists' stand would make any Dutch politician definitely unpopular. Over 80% of the population (18 and older) did agree with a statement saying: 'Zwarte Piet can arouse subliminal racist sentiments in children', and an equal number disagreed with: 'Zwarte Piet symbolizes the subordinate position of non-whites' (Hofstede: 1986, 33). A black spokesman called the issue 'the Netherlands' biggest taboo'. 'White people simply do not seem to understand what's at stake' (Hielkema: 1986, 35).

A recent work on 'ethnic difference as a Dutch taboo' states that, in the experience of present-day generations, the heyday of colonialism is long past. It was put on the shelves of history long ago and no longer seems to play a role as a standard for personal or social action. Anti-racist metaphors invariably go back to a more recent past: the extermination of the Jews by the Nazis (during the Second World War, 110.000 of the 130.000 Dutch citizens considered to be Jews by the Nazi police were carried off under the very eyes of the non-Jewish majority, to die in annihilation and concentration camps). When racism is the issue in a contemporary public discussion in the Netherlands, few people refer to the sugar plantations of the East and West Indies, or to Elmina on the West coast of Africa, a former Dutch fortress and age-long centre of slave trade. People speak in terms of new Nazis, a new Hitler, new Jews, deportations, and Auschwitz (Vuijsje: 1986, 100-101). Zwarte Piet has never been associated with Nazi practices.

For centuries the Dutch had been accustomed to small numbers of blacks in their cities, a situation which never led to civil rights problems as it did in the United States of America during the 19th and 20th centuries. The sudden presence of large numbers of black immigrants, however, is new to them. It will probably take some time before the ensuing culture shock is fully digested.

---

last moment the action was called off because their white allies from the political left (PSP = Pacifist Socialist Party) thought it too provocative. It might provoke racism, instead of fighting it, because it would undoubtedly have been interpreted as an offence against a sacrosanct Dutch tradition, spoiling young children's belief and pleasure (Hielkema: 1986, 35).

Persona non grata

It is no idle wordplay, within the frame of reference of this collection of essays, to characterize Zwarte Piet as the *persona non grata*. Society itself generates personhood in assembling roles and statuses and then conferring on individuals the qualities and powers associated with them. Concepts of the person are embedded in society (Lafontaine: 1985, 132).

In terms of 'person', the status difference between St. Nicholas and his black servant remains obvious. In the Dutch tradition, Sinterklaas is by no means an anonymous giver. He is a very real person with a definite appearance, character and name (De Groot: 1965, 180). He is the *persona grata par excellence*. It is extremely clear that, originally, Sinterklaas, the white man's cherished symbol, was given the larger part of the ceremonial cake and that only a few crumbs were left to Zwarte Piet, the former slave and still the humble servant.

His low status as a person is based on a corresponding idea of a society in which white supremacy remains a cornerstone of the continuing social whole, nothwithstanding some well-intended experiments in the Dutch mass-media to enhance Zwarte Piet's prestige by more or less 'personalizing' his role in the ceremony. The black immigrant sees himself as *persona non grata*, or even as a non-person, because of what he experiences as an offensive symbol directed against him. As things go, the white majority - though believing themselves to be devoutly anti-racist- hardly share his indignation. Black political elites in the Netherlands are convinced that the discussion about Zwarte Piet, being a symbolic core issue of inequality based on the colour of a person's skin, has only just begun (Stuart: 1984, 9).

The current Dutch quandary seems to be rooted in the historical fact that, by trading in the Devil for a Negro, the ancestors of the Dutch replaced a religious evil a potential political one. After more than three centuries the transformation has become a ticklish affair in the Netherlands. The attack on Zwarte Piet as a social and cultural symbol of the 'old world' deserves to be understood in terms of the deep ideological conflict underlying our modern world: north-south, rich-poor, white skin-dark skin. It can be seen as an outpost fight in the struggle for equal rights (civil, human, divine, on different levels of transcendence) fought by new emerging peoples and nations, and driven by an ongoing process of cross-influence between religion and politics (Luckmann: 1987, 30).

Through the ages, many dyads have been the subject of a permanent ideological struggle, e.g., between parents and children, 'official' belief and folk belief, or rational and irrational forces. The present study deals with the dyad of St. Nicholas and his servant as a symbol of the master-slave relationship, which may be extended to the relation between majority and minority in societies, ultimately becoming a problem of democracy and of human rights.

The same colour prejudice anti-Zwart Piet activists often reproach 'the white race' with, was found by Victor Turner among black people in Africa, e.g., among the Ndembu of Zambia. For them, white and black are basic colours having certain basic meanings. The sense of whiteness represents prosperity, purity, health and life. Black, on the other hand, is associated with badness and evil, misfortune, disease, witchcraft and sorcery, sexual passion, darkness, and what is 'hidden', Turner (as quoted by Morris: 1987, 245-246) indicates that the colours black, red, and white frequently have ritual significance and that there is wide agreement about their symbolic connotations.

Black is associated with inferiority, evil, pollution, suspicion; red (the colour of St. Nicholas's robe and miter) with power, might, and wealth; and white (St. Nicholas's horse, beard, skin and gloves) with purity, light and joy. The Upanishads and other Hindu texts suggest a tripartite colour scheme, the individual colours being considered as deities, and each colour being associated with specific aspects of existence. Turner even suggests that the triadic colour scheme, based as it is on psychobiological experiences (the emissions of the human body: milk, blood, and excreta) represents a kind of primordial classification of reality. In his view, it was only by subsequent abstraction from these configurations that the other modes of social classifications by mankind arose.

As Morris observes, Turner's theory obscures the hierarchic and hence ideological nature of symbolism. The Dutch anti-Zwarte Piet activists will be grateful for his remark. Otherwise, even if Zwarte Piet eventually vanishes from the scene or at least stops giving trouble, the *dramatis personae* will reappear on stage as long as humanity lives on earth.

Bibliography

Bettelheim, B.
1987 *A Good Enough Parent*, London

Braam, S.
1973 *Suriname en de Surinamers als maatschappelijke vreemdelingen in Nederland*, The Hague.

Carrithers, M. - C. Collins - S. Lukes (eds.)
1985 *The Category of the Person*, Cambridge.

Cavendish, R.
1975 *The Powers of Evil in Western Religion, Magic and Folk Belief*, London.

Choenni, Gh.
1986 'Sinterklaas was een Turk', in: *Weekblad Suriname*, 14 November, The Hague.

Foucault, M.
1975 *Histoire de la Folie à l'age classique*, Paris.

Groot, A.D. de
1965 *Saint Nicholas, A psychoanalytic study of his history and myth*, The Hague/Paris.

Hall, J.
1979 *Dictionary of Subjects and Symbols in Art*, New York.

Hassankhan, R.
1986 *Sinterklaas is een racist*. Published by Beweging Surinaams Links (BSL), The Hague.

Hielkema, H.
1986 'Grootste taboe van Nederland', in: *Trouw*, 22 november, Amsterdam.

Hofstede, B.P.
1986 'Zwarte Piet mag blijven', in: *Trouw*, 22 november, Amsterdam.

Huizinga, J.
1935 *Nederlands Geestesmerk*, Leiden.

Lafontaine, J.S.
1985 'Person and individual: some anthropological reflections.', in: Carrithers et al., *The Category of the Person*, Cambridge.

Luckmann, Th.
1987 'Social Reconstruction of Transcendence'. In: *Secularization and Religion: the Persisting Tension,* Acts of the XIXth International Conference for the Sociology of Religion, Tübingen/Lausanne.

Lukes, S.
1985 'Conclusion'. In: Carrithers et al., *The Category of the Person,* Cambridge.

Marktresponse
1986 'Onderzoek Zwarte Piet', project: 710.064, oktober, in opdracht van de Perscombinatie NV, Amsterdam, Amersfoort (Unpublished internal report).

Mauss, M.
1985 'A category of the human mind: the notion of person; the notion of self'. In: Carrithers and others (eds.) *The Category of the Person,* Cambridge.

Meisen, K.
1931 *Nikolauskult und Nikolausbrauch im Abendlande,* Dusseldorf.

Menkman, W.R.
1947 *De West-Indische Compagnie,* Amsterdam.

Morris, B.
1987 *Anthropological Studies of Religion,* Cambridge.

Moyer, D.S.
1984 'Sinterklaas in Victoria: St. Nicholaas as a symbol of Dutch ethnicity', in: *Canadian Journal of Netherlands Studies,* Fall.

Preedy, S.E.
1984 *Negers in de Nederlanden 1500-1863,* Nijmegen.

Roget's International Thesaurus, 4th edition, New York 1977.

Russell, J.B.
1979 *The Devil, Perceptions of Evil from Antiquity to Primitive Christianity,* New York.

Scheepers, P.
1986 'Ethnocentrism in The Netherlands'. Paper presented at the 9th Annual Scientific Meeting of the International Society of Political Psychology, Amsterdam.

Stuart, T.
1984 'Zwarte Piet, symbool van racisme of alleen van macht', in: *NRC Handelsblad*, 5 december, Rotterdam.

Tennekes, J. - A.W. Musschenga,
1984 'Dilemma's van een pluralistische samenleving', in: *Filosofie en Praktijk* 5/3.

Vuijsje, K.
1986 *Vermoorde onschuld, Ethnisch verschil als Hollands taboe*, Amsterdam.

EXTRATERRESTRIAL PERSONS

Wim B. Drees

1. *Introduction*

The question I want to discuss in this paper is: on what condition would we apply our concepts of person to extraterrestrials? This question is concerned with an investigation into the way *we* employ our concepts rather than with an investigation of extraterrestrials.

The applicability of the criteria presented by H.G. Hubbeling in this volume will be discussed, together with a few other philosophical contributions concerned with the concept of person, both in general (J.J. Oosten in this volume) and in relation to extraterrestials (M. Tooley, R. Puccetti).

I agree with R. Planck (1968) and L.W. Beck (1971) that claims about *contacts* between humans and extraterrestrials are at present matter for psychological research. However, the mere possibility of the existence of life and intelligence elsewhere in the universe should be taken seriously. And it is taken seriously by the International Astronomical Union, which in 1982 established a Committee on the Search for Extraterrestrial Life. Evidence of the actual existence of such life has not yet been found, but the absence of evidence in this field is not evidence of absence.

2. *Would ETIs be persons?*

The philosophical question within the context of this volume is whether a concept of person can be applied to ETIs (Extraterrestrial Intelligences). The answer depends on the concept of person used.

2.1 Individuality, self-consciousness and will as criteria.

If one uses the classical definition of Boethius, discussed by Hubbeling in this volume, 'personae est naturae rationalis individua substantia', one has to concern oneself with two components: rationality and individuality.

Rationality might be ascribed to extraterrestrial beings on the basis of the signals received. Signals should neither be too regular nor too chaotic because such signals would be ascribed to ordinary physical processes. For some kind of radio signal to be able to serve as evidence for the presence of extraterrestrial intelligence, it would be best if it could be interpreted meaningfully, say, as an expression of the prime numbers or chemical elements. Such a message need not be evidence of a living being, since there are many messages which can be produced by machines (chess computers, etc.). In any case, messages come from ETIs, or from machines produced by ETIs, or from machines which could themselves be considered intelligent.

Whereas the ascription of rationality, understood as intelligence, might be defended on the basis of conceivable evidence in the form of radio signals containing information of a certain structure, individuality is more problematic. On Earth, projects like interstellar communication require organizations composed of many individuals. In bilateral communication the time between question and answer would exceed many earthly generations. But elsewhere there might, of course, be a different life span, and biological individuality need not be the same as it is on Earth. Life might be more symbiotic, as it is in the case of termites. As long as the information content of the messages has not been deciphered, nothing meaningful can be said about the structure of individuality of the transmitting being(s).

Hubbeling characterizes 'person' as possessing *self-consciousness* and *will*, bearing moral and aesthetic values, as well as having an 'I-Thou' relation to other individuals, to the collective 'thou' of the group, and to God.

As far as self-consciousness and will are concerned I can be brief. Sending messages into outer space implies that the transmitting civilization considers it possible that somewhere in the universe there might be other civilizations. This implies a certain degree of reflection upon their own civilization, and hence something like self-consciousness. Since communication does not come about by chance, one being, or more, must have decided to send messages, signals with contents. Consequently, if 'will' is taken as the criterion of personhood, the existence of messages points to the existence of persons.

The existence of messages does not give any information about the question whether ETIs have *aesthetic* values. The contents of the messages, however, could have aesthetic value, e.g., a representation of the music of J.S. Bach.

2.2 ETIs and morality

Moral criteria for personhood can much less clearly be applied to ETIs. However, there have been some discussions on this issue.

M. Tooley has discussed the question 'Would ETIs Be Persons?' in relation to the question of 'how we *ought* to interact with extraterrestrial, nonhuman intelligences' (Tooley: 1976, 129). Tooley has based himself on the distinction between three classes, namely inanimate objects, animals and adult human beings (persons). To which class would ETIs belong? According to Tooley,

> to be a person an extraterrestrial being would have to be a conscious entity with the capacity for self-consciousness plus the capacity for envisaging a future for itself and for having desires about its continued existence (Tooley: 1976, 141).

The epistemological question arises as to how one could know whether an ETI possesses these properties.

The answer depends, according to Tooley, on one's philosophy of mind. Behaviourists (mind is a matter of there being a certain type of complex behaviour) would not have any difficulty with this question, nor would it pose serious problems to identity theorists (mental states are states of the nervous system). The issue would in fact only be problematic for dualists (mind is something non-physical and private). However, dualists give different accounts of the conviction that other human minds exist (analogy, explanatory power, use of terms referring to mental states), and these accounts can also be applied to ETIs. Tooley concludes that there are conditions which would justify anybody in believing that certain ETIs possess self-consciousness, and are capable of envisaging a future and having desires about their own continued existence, and 'this means that such extraterrestrial beings would have to be regarded as persons' (Tooley: 1976, 145).

Tooley's argument in support of the idea that ETIs may be regarded as persons rests on precisely the same grounds as his justification of our calling another human being a person. Its upshot, however, is rather trivial: if some ETIs were very similar to humans - and if they were not deceptions - those ETIs would have to count as persons. The intriguing question is under what conditions ETIs are properly considered to be persons when we do not know the extent to which they are similar to us. It seems to me that Tooley underestimates the practical difficulties. The identity theorist is not able to look for corresponding states of the 'brains' of the ETIs. The explanatory power of a mind (according to Tooley, reason for a dualist to consider ETIs as persons) is not clear if we know almost nothing about the physiology of an ETI. Of Tooley's three philosophies of mind only the behaviourists' approach seems feasible.

Tooley discusses the problem of whether ETIs are persons, because he wishes to answer the moral question of how we ought to treat them. However, as will be explained in section 3, one does not need to know whether they are persons to have reasons to treat ETIs as persons.

According to R. Puccetti, in his *Persons. A study of Possible Moral Agents in the Universe*, moral relations 'are possible only between persons, and ... any entity with which one can conceive having moral relations would be a person' (Puccetti: 1968, 26). Puccetti applies the concept to artifacts, ETIs, and God. According to him, belief in the existence of ETIs conflicts with belief in God. This theological claim will be discussed below. First I want to focus on morality.

For evolutionary reasons 'the differences [between ETIs and humans] will be relatively negligible' (Pucetti: 1968, 89). Puccetti bases this on examples of convergent evolution on Earth. He points out that some scientists refer to ETIs as 'humanoids'. He sees this as an example of parochialism. A concept at a higher level, i.e., 'person', is already available, for

> although human beings are persons, not all persons need to be human. To qualify as a person an entity must, as I said, be capable of both these things: the assimilation of a conceptual scheme and the experience of sensations, emotional states, etc. Which is to say that persons are always potential 'moral agents' (Pucetti: 1968, 99).

Convergent evolution assures him that

> despite secondary biological differences they would certainly qualify for person-

> status, since they would be both capable of assimilating a conceptual scheme and the sort of entity to which one can quite reasonably ascribe feelings (Pucetti: 1968, 106).

Puccetti then goes on to discuss moral relations within a postulated community of ETIs and possible moral relations between ourselves and ETIs. The truisms of H.L.A. Hart (1961) (vulnerability, equality in strength etc.) are

> applicable to extraterrestrial communities as well. For we have seen how the principle of convergent evolution assures a considerable uniformity between ourselves and extraterrestrials ... For this reason I think that if we ever establish communications with extraterrestrial societies we shall find their moral concepts and legal structures recognizably familiar, at least in these more fundamental respects (Hart: 1961, 109f).

The question of moral relations between ourselves and ETIs is a more complex one. If we were to come into direct physical contact with ETI's, which Puccetti justly considers extremely unlikely, this might lead to colonization and either destruction (no established moral relation) or living together, especially if the planet of one of the societies has become uninhabitable. In the latter case there would be moral relations. It would be different if contact were made by radio. Even then there are some moral aspects to the relation. It is already a moral decision to send valuable information, for it is an example of supererogatory moral behaviour to promote the well-being of the receiving civilization. And both communities may arouse certain feelings in each other, for example feelings of comfort. (If one reports the occurrence of a catastrophe the reaction of the other can make a difference.)

So far R.Puccetti. I agree with most of the issues mentioned above. But I am less confident that convergence in the evolution of different species on Earth can be extrapolated to convergence between species on different planets. Though there is room for analogical reasoning here, I maintain that we should be more careful in our consideration of things that may reasonably be supposed to be quite different.

2.3 ETIs as social persons?

Hubbeling mentions relations with other individuals, with a collectivity and with God as the fourth group of criteria constituting personhood. If signals were sent out by a group of cooperating individuals, there should be at least some practical forms of cooperation; but this neither implies personal ('I-Thou') relations within that group, nor a wish on its part to enter into an I-thou relation with another culture. There could be other reasons for sending messages, like cosmic expansion or curiosity. Columbus did not embark on his journey in order to establish personal relationships with people of other cultures. Ascription of personhood in the social sense, then, is not defensible on the basis of the mere fact that messages have been received.

J.J. Oosten's contribution to this volume adopts a different approach to the concept of person by placing it squarely within a social context. He maintains that in a discussion on the meaning of the concept of person, one should not neglect the ideological function of the concept in our society. He criticizes Hubbeling's position as representing the latter's own Western philosophical tradition and thus as not being helpful in acquiring an understanding of other cultures.

Oosten's critical remarks apply to this paper as well, because it has been written within the Western, scientific tradition. I am not concerned with the question whether ETIs have a concept like 'person', but rather with the question whether our concept can be applied to ETI's, as well as with the difficulties that might arise in this connection. In Oosten's approach the only point of discussion seems to be the social function of the concept of person within a particular culture. Obviously in that sense it cannot be applied to ETIs, given the (lack of) knowledge we have of them now, as well as the (lack of) knowledge we will have of them in the near future.

2.4 ETIs and religion

In my opinion there is no way of knowing whether ETIs have relations with God. We simply cannot tell whether they are persons in the sense of the last of Hubbeling's characteristics as long as we do not have messages that are intelligible to us. In a few publications attention has been paid to the theological implications of the existence of ETIs and extraterrestrial persons in particular. These publications mainly deal with the place and worth of man in the universe, the relation between God and mankind and the uniqueness of Jesus Christ. Since it is directly related to the concept of person, I shall discuss the position taken by R. Puccetti who claims that:'a correct analysis of the person-concept combined with the not unreasonable belief in extraterrestrial natural persons actually undermines the belief in God'. (Puccetti: 1968, 143).

As a factual statement this is not true. There are some believers who do think that the uniqueness of mankind is essential, but there are others who are delighted by the idea that the universe is full of images of God, expressing His fullness and love. Puccetti, however, is referring to the fact that it undermines the belief in God if one reasons correctly. His main argument (besides the fact that ETIs are not mentioned in the Bible and the 'scandal of particularity') is related to the person of Christ. The unity of the person of Christ is incompatible with an incarnation on every inhabited planet. Puccetti (1969, 139) estimates that 'there would be in the order of 680,000,000 to 3,400,000,000 incarnations occurring simultaneously from now to the extinction of life on all such stars'.
This contradicts the oneness of the Son of God, 'for two corporeal persons are not one' (ibid, 140).

Puccetti asks a serious question concerning Christology and the doctrine of the Trinity. However, I think he claims too much in presuming that this is a question that cannot be answered within the framework of Christianity. Some forms of Christianity cannot incorporate it, but as a whole Christianity is quite flexible. Apart from changing the dogma of the Trinity or reducing Christ to the expression of God's love *for us*, one could perform the same kind of arithmetical tricks as Puccetti does. Two is not the same as one. But the second person of the Trinity is traditionally conceived of as an infinite being. And 'infinite+1' equals 'infinite+2'! If the incarnation is the expression of God in a finite being, that finite being does not exhaust the Christ. This may seem somewhat scholastic, but it shows that Puccetti's argument is not conclusive.

Puccetti's argument seems to imply that his concept of person is not applicable to God and Christ. He suggests the conclusion that they do not exist. However, it is an old idea in theology that our concepts apply only analogically to God. So if a certain concept of person does not work, why not abandon or reformulate it? E. McMullin (1980,88) perceived 'an odd, ungenerous fundamentalism at work here, a refusal to allow for the expansion of doctrine, that is after all characteristic of both science and theology'. I think that Puccetti's argument does not by implication undermine the belief in God. However, it has a psychological aspect: the belief in ETIs compensates for a belief which Puccetti has already discarded:

> But at least it could lay to rest the provincial humanist dogma that if we abandon belief in the Divine we have nothing to fall back on but Man's values. What we have to fall back on are the values, one may reasonably hold, of a potentially universal community of persons from which we are detached by the accidental dispersion of matter in the cosmos. That is a pallid comfort, yet a comfort of a kind (Pucetti: 1968, 118).

3. *When should we call them persons?*

By way of conclusion I would like to defend the thesis that in different contexts there are different reasons for ascribing personhood to ETIs.

If extraterrestrials are considered in a *moral* or *legal* discourse, I think that it is reasonable to talk about persons. In the rare cases of moral discourse related to extraterrestrials it is morally better to treat them, at least *prima facie*, the way we would like to be treated ourselves. *Reciprocity* seems in this case to be the only argument, and not whether they 'are' persons. If, as in some science-fiction, we were to find a spaceship with frozen ETIs, we would be obliged to treat them the way we are expected to treat humans.

In *religious* discourse concerning the uniqueness of humanity, God's relation to us and to other creatures, the same reciprocity holds. We should treat them as persons and we should modify our opinions, if necessary, about the relation between God and mankind so that they can incorporate these ETIs as well. One could of course deny this equality in relation to God, and classify them as animals, but I consider that to be the sin of hubris. One could also rank ETIs among the angels, but that might prove to be false if we were to become better acquainted with them.

In *scientific* or *general philosophical* discourse, which is what the main part of this paper consists of, there is no reason to take a firm stand. I expect that ETIs, if we were to learn something about them in the next millennium, would in some respects fit our concepts of person, but there is no need to go ahead of it. The question whether they are 'real persons' presumes a fixed, platonic, concept of person. Let us wait and see.

Acknowledgements

My investigations have been supported by the Foundation for Research in the Field of Theology and the Science of Religions, which is subsidized by the Netherlands Organization for Scientific Research (N.W.O.). The author would like to express his thanks to A.F. Sanders for some useful suggestions.

Bibliography

Beck, L.W.
1971 'Extraterrestrial Intelligent Life', in: *Proceedings of the American Philosophical Association,* 45, 5-21.

Hart, H.L.A.
1961 *The Concept of Law,* Oxford.

Hubbeling, H.G.
1989 'Some Remarks on the Concept of Person', in: H.G. Kippenberg and others (eds.), *Concepts of Person in Religion and Thought*, New York/Berlin, 9-23

McMullin, E.
1980 'Persons in the universe', in: *Zygon,* 15, 69-89.

Oosten, J.J.
1989 'A Few Critical Remarks on the Concept of Person', in: H.G. Kippenberg and others (eds.), *Concepts of Person in Religion and Thought*, New York/Berlin, 24-31

Planck, R.
1968 *The Emotional Significance of Imaginary Beings:* A Study of the Interaction Between Psychopathology, Literature and Reality in the Modern World, Springfield,Ill.

Puccetti, R.
1968 *Persons: A study of possible moral agents in the universe,* London.

Tooley, M.
1976 'Would ETIs Be Persons?' In: James L.Christian (ed.), *Extra-Terrestrial Intelligence: The First Encounter,* Buffalo, 129-145.

GENERAL BIBLIOGRAPHY

Assmann, J.
1982 'Persönlichkeitsbegriff und -bewusstsein'. In: *Lexicon der Ägyptologie,* IV, 963-978

Babcock, B.
1980 'Reflexivity: Definitions and Discriminations', in: *Semiotica* 30, 1-14

Beattie, J.
1980 'Representations of the Self in Traditional Africa', in: *Africa,* 50, 3, 313-320

Bellah, R. - K. Burridge - R. Robertson
1982 'Responses to Louis Dumont's 'A Modified View of our Origins'', in: *Religion,* 12, 83-88

Carrinthers, M. - S. Collins - S. Lukes (eds.)
1985 *The Category of the Person. Anthropology, Philosophy, History,* Cambridge.

Collins, S.
1982 *Selfless Persons. Imagery and thought in Theravada Buddhism,* Cambridge.

Daniélou, J.
1973 'La Notion de Personne chez les Pères Grecs'. In: Meyerson 1973, 113-121.

Danto, A.C.
1967 'Persons'. In: P. Edwards (ed.), *The Encyclopedia of Philosophy,* VI, London/New York, 110-114.

Dieterlen, M. (ed.)
1973 *La Notion de Personne en Afrique Noire,* Paris (CNRS)

Dodds, E.R.
1951 *The Greeks and the Irrational,* London.

Dumont, L.
1965 'The Modern Conception of the Individual. Notes on Its Genesis', in: *Contributions to Indian Sociology,* VIII, 13-61
1982 'Reply' [to Bellah, Burridge & Robbertson 1982], in: *Religion,* 12, 89-91

1985 'A Modified View of our Origins: The Christian Beginnings of Modern Individualism'.(1982) In: Carrinthers - Collins-Lukes: 1985, 93-122

Durkheim, E.
1975 'L'Individualisme et les Intellectuels'.(1898); Engl. transl. In: W.S.F. Pickering (ed.), *Durkheim on Religion. A Selection of Readings with Bibliographies,* London/Boston, 59-73

Elias, N.
1988 *Der Gesellschaft der Individuen,* Frankfurt.

Fuhrmann, M.
1979 'Persona, ein römischer Rollenbegriff'. In: Marquard & Stiele: 1979, 83-106.

Geertz, C.
1965 'The Impact of the Concept of Culture on the Concept of Man'. In: J.R. Platt (ed.), *New Views on the Nature of Man,* Chicago/London, 93-118.
1973a 'Religion as a Cultural System'.(1966) In: *The Interpretation of Cultures,* New York, 87-125
1973b 'Person, Time and Conduct in Bali'.(1966) In: *The Interpretation of Cultures,* New York, 342-411
1983 'From the Native's Point of View': On the Nature of Anthropological Understanding.(1974) In: *Local Knowledge. Further Essays in Interpretative Anthropology,* 55-70

Griaule, M.
1940 'La Personnalité chez les Dogon', in: *Journal de Psychologie Normale et Pathologique,* 37, 468-475

Hahn, A. - V. Kapp (Hg.)
1987 *Selbstthematisierung und Selbstzeugnis. Bekenntnis und Geständnis,* Frankfurt.

Hollis, M.
1977 *Models of Man,* Cambridge.

Hubbeling, H.G. - H.G. Kippenberg (eds.)
1986 *On Symbolic Representation of Religion. Groningen Contributions to Theories of Symbols*, Berlin.

Jacobson-Widding, A. (ed.)
1983 *Identity: Personal and Socio-Cultural,* Uppsala.

Langer, S.
1974 *Philosophy in a New Key,* Cambridge.(1942)

Lee, B. (ed.)
1982 *Psychosocial Theories of the Self,* New York.

Leenhardt, M.
1957 *Do Kamo: La Personne et le Mythe dans le Monde Mélanésien,* Paris.
1952 'La Propriété et la Personne dans les Sociétés Archaïques'. In: *Journal de Psychologie Normale et Pathologique,* 45, 3, 278-292

Marquard, O. - K. Stiele (Hg.)
1979 *Identität,* Munich.

Marsella, A.J. - G. de Vos - F.L.K. Hsu (eds.)
1985 *Culture and Self. Asian and Western Perspectives,* New York.

Mauss, M.
1985 'Une Catégorie de l'Esprit Humain: La Notion de Personne, Celle de "Moi"'.(1938) Engl. transl. In: Carrithers - Collins - Lukes: 1985, 1-25.

Mead, G.H.
1965 *On Social Psychology,* Chicago/London.(1934)

Meyerson, I. (éd.)
1973 *Problèmes de Personne.* Colloques du Centre de Recherches de Psychologie Comparative, XIII, Paris.

Michel-Jones, F.
1974 'La Notion de Personne'. In: M. Augé (ed.), *La Construction du Monde,* Paris, 33-51.

Östör, A. - L. Fruzzetti - S. Barnett (eds.)
1982 *Concepts of Person. Kinship, Caste, and Marriage in India.* Cambridge, Mass.

Rosaldo, M.Z.
1980 *Knowledge and Passion. Ilongot Notions of Self and Social Life,* Cambridge.

Ruddock, R.
1972 *Six Approaches to the Person,* London.

Shoemaker, S.
1963 *Self-knowledge and Self-identity,* Ithaca.

Schweder, R.A. - R.A. Bourne
1984 *Culture Theory. Essays on Mind, Self and Emotion*, Cambridge

Schweder, R.A. - R. A. LeVine
1984 *Culture Theory. Essays on Mind, Self, and Emotion*, Cambridge.

Smith, P.
1973 'Principes de la Personne et Catégories Sociales'. In: Dieterlen: 1973, 467-490.

Strawson, P.F.
1959 *Individuals. An Essay in Descriptive Metaphysiscs*, London.

Teichman, J.
1985 'The Definition of Person', in: *Philosophy* 60

Wiggins, D.
1980 *Sameness and Substance*, Oxford.

Wilde, A. de
1951 *De Persoon. Historisch-systematisch onderzoek naar de betekenis van het persoonssymbool*, Van Gorcum, Assen.

Williams, B.A.O.
1973 *Problems of the Self*, Cambridge.

Williams, R.
1976 *Keywords. A Vocabulary of Culture and Society*, London.

ABOUT THE AUTHORS

Hans Bakker studied Chemistry, Philosophy and Indology. He took his degree in Indian Languages and Cultures at the University of Groningen. His thesis entitled 'Ayodhya', dealing with the history of an important Indian place of pilgrimage, appeared in 1986. At present he teaches Sanskrit, Philosophy and Indian Religions at the University of Groningen. The main object of his current research is the development of sacred centres related to the history of Rama devotion in Northern India.

Ulrich Berner is Professor of History of Religions (Religionswissenschaft) at the University of Bayreuth, West Germany. His publications include: 'Origenes' (Darmstadt 1981), 'Untersuchungen zur Verwendung des Synkretismusbegriffes' (in: 'Saeculum' 37 [1986] 83-95); 'Religionswissenschaft und Theologie. Das Programm der Religionsgeschichtlichen Schule' (in: 'Religionswissenschaft. Eine Einführung', hrsg. H. Zinser, Berlin 1988, 216-238).

Lourens P. van den Bosch studied Theology, History of Religions and Indonesian Languages. He took his degree in Indian Languages and Culture at the University of Utrecht. His thesis entitled 'Atharvaveda-parisista, Chapters 21-29' appeared in 1978. Articles of his were published in 'Indo-Iranian Journal' and 'Nederlands Tijdschrift voor Theologie'. At present he lectures in the History of Islam and Indian Religions in the Faculty of Theology at the University of Groningen.

Wim B. Drees has degrees in Physics and Theology. He worked at the Department of Theology of the University of Groningen. He was a Fulbright visiting scholar at the Graduate Theological Union (Berkeley, Ca.) and the Lutheran School of Theology at Chicago (1987/1988). His thesis 'Beyond the Big Bang: Quantum Cosmologies and God' will be published in the spring of 1990.(Open Court, La Salle, Il.).

Han J.W. Drijvers is Professor of Semitic Languages and Literatures at the University of Groningen. His main field of research is Cultures and History of Syria and Mesopotamia during the first four centuries C.E., in particular the History of Early Syrian Christianity as well as Pagan Religions and Gnosticism in this area. His publications include 'Bardaisan of Edessa' (1966), 'The Religion of Palmyra' (1976), 'Cults and Beliefs at Edessa' (1981), 'East of Antioch. Studies in Early Syriac Christianity' (1984).

Norbert Elias was born in Breslau, studied Medicine, Philosophy and Psychology in Breslau, Freiburg and Heidelberg and lectured at various universities in and outside Europe. His magnum opus, 'Über den Prozess der Zivilisation. Soziogenetische und psychogenetische Untersuchungen' was first published in 1939, but was not recognized until long after World War II. Prof. Elias is the auctor intellectualis of *Figuration* Sociology. His further publications include 'The Established and the Outsiders' (with J.L. Scotson; London 1965), 'The Court Society' (Oxford 1983), 'The Loneliness of the Dying' (Oxford 1985), 'Quest for Excitement: Sport and Leisure in the Civilising Process' (with E. Duning; Oxford 1986), 'Involvement and Detachment' (Oxford 1987). Prof. Elias now lives in Amsterdam.

Armin W. Geertz is Associate Professor of the History of Religions at the University of Aarhus, Denmark; he is chairman of the Danish Association for the History of Religions, European director of the Society for the Study of Native American Religious Traditions, and associate editor of 'Temenos' (Helsinki) and 'European Review of Native American Studies' (Budapest). His main field of interest is the religions of native Americans. His publications include 'Hopi Indian Altar Iconography' (1987) and 'Children of Cottonwood' (1987).

Barend P. Hofstede teaches the Sociology of Religion and Mass Communication at the University of Groningen. His studies in the field of overseas migration (including 'Thwarted Exodus', The Hague 1964) have received international recognition. Working as a TV-producer and director he has made some 35 documentary productions for the Dutch religious broadcasting organization (IKON) on such various issues as death and dying, authority, witchcraft and AIDS.

Hubertus G. Hubbeling (1925-1986). Born in Djokjakarta, Huib Hubbeling studied Theology at the universities of Groningen and Basel. He received two doctorates from Groningen University: one in Theology on a book on Emil Brunner (1956) and one in Philosophy on 'Spinoza's Methodology' (1964). In 1967 he took the chair of Philosophy of Religion and Ethics at the University of Groningen. He wrote extensively on subjects in Philosophy of Religion, Ethics, Dogmatics, Logic, Aesthetics and Spinoza's Philosophy. Among his major publications are 'Inleiding tot het denken van Wittgenstein' (1965) 'Spinoza' (1966) 'Language, Logic and Criterion' (1971) and his posthumously published magnum opus 'Principles of the Philosophy of Religion' (1987). Numerous articles appeared in such scholarly journals as 'Mind', 'Erkenntnis', 'Algemeen Nederlands Tijdschrift voor Wijsbegeerte', and 'Neue Zeitschrift für systematische Theologie und Religionsphilosophie'. Prof. Hubbeling received an honorary doctorate from Uppsala University in 1978 for his work in the field of Philosophy of Religion. He was a fellow of the 'Koninklijke Nederlandse Academie van Wetenschappen' and chairman of the Dutch Spinoza Society.

Jeppe Sinding Jensen is Assistant Professor in the History of Religions at the University of Aarhus, Denmark. His interests include contemporary Islam, Culture Theory and the Methodology and Theory of the History of Religions, in particular concerning the Phenomenology of Religion.

Hans G. Kippenberg, born in Bremen, studied History of Religions at the Universities of Marburg, Tübingen, Göttingen and Leeds. Having worked at the University of Göttingen and the Free University of Berlin, Hans Kippenberg at present holds chairs in the Science and History of Religions at the Universities of Groningen and Bremen. His publications include: 'Garizim und Synagoge. Traditionsgeschichtliche Untersuchungen zur samaritanischen Religion der aramäischen Periode'(1971), 'Religion und Klassenbildung im antiken Judäa' (1978), 'Magie. Die sozialwissenschaftliche Kontroverse über das Verstehen fremden Denkens' (with B. Luchesi; 1978), 'Textbuch zur neutestamentlichen Zeitgeschichte' (with G. Wewers; 1979), 'Neue Ansätze in der Religionswissenschaft' (with B. Gladigow; 1983), 'J.J. Bachofen. Mutterrecht und Urreligion' (1984), Struggles of Gods (1984).

Yme B. Kuiper studied Sociology and Anthropology at the University of Groningen and at present lectures in Anthropology of Religion at the Faculty of Theology. His publications include articles on research and methodological issues in History, Sociology and Anthropology and (historical- anthropological) studies of religious movements and elite-groups.

Fred Leemhuis is Associate Professor of Arabic at Groningen University. He has published on various subjects in the field of Arabic and Islamic studies. His current research continues to be in the field of Koranic studies and early *tafsir.* He has recently completed a new Dutch translation of the Koran.

Michel Meslin, is Professor of Comparative History of Religions and Religious Anthropology in the Université de Paris-Sorbonne. Main publications: 'Les Ariens d'Occident' (1968); 'La Fête du Nouvel An dans l'Empire romain, les kalendes de janvier' (1970); 'Pour une Science des Religions' (1973); 'L'Homme romain (1978); Le Merveilleux, l'Imaginaire et les croyances en Occident' (1984); 'L'Expérience humaine du divin, Fondements d'une Anthropologie religieuse' (1988).

Jasper J. Oosten (1939) is a member of the Department of Philosophy of Groningen University. He teaches Philosophy of Social Science and is engaged in research into the commensurability of a scientific conception of the world and a religious world-view. He is the author of 'Magie en Rede' (Assen 1983).

Andy F. Sanders was born in Rotterdam and studied Theology and Philosophy of Religion at the University of Groningen, where he is lecturer in Philosophy of Religion in the Faculty of Theology. Dr. Sanders is a member of the Christian Philosophers Group, the Polanyi Society and the Groningen Interdisciplinary Working Group on Religious Symbols. He has published 'Michael Polanyi's Post-Critical Epistemology' (1988); articles of his have appeared in 'Wijsgerig Perspectief', 'Neues Zeitschrift für systematische Theologie und Religionsphilosophie', and 'Tradition and Discovery'.

Herman te Velde studied Theology, Comparative Religion and Egyptology in Groningen and Marburg an der Lahn. His publications include the dissertation 'Seth, God of Confusion' (Brill, Leiden, 2nd ed. 1977) and several articles. He has visited Egypt many times, e.g., as research associate of the Brooklyn Museum Archeological Expedition to Egypt. He is Professor in Egyptology and especially Ancient Egyptian Religion at the University of Groningen.

Hans A. Witte has worked as curator of the Afrika Museum in Berg en Dal; since 1981 he has been senior lecturer in West African religions and iconography at the University of Groningen. Hans Witte is specialized in Yoruba culture. His recent publications include 'Earth and the Ancestors: Ogboni Iconography', Gallery Bololu, Amsterdam 1988; 'Les religions de l'Afrique occidentale', in: 'Histoire des Croyances et des idées religieuses', vol.4, ed. Mircea Eliade (in press).

INDEX